DATE DUE

OCT 4 2005			
GAYLORD			PRINTED IN U.S.A.

Mind Matters

By James P. Hogan

* Published by The Ballantine Publishing Group

MIND MATTERS

exploring

the

world of

artificial

intelligence

James P. Hogan

THE BALLANTINE PUBLISHING GROUP
NEW YORK

A Del Rey® Book
Published by The Ballantine Publishing Group

Copyright © 1997 by James Patrick Hogan

http://www.randomhouse.com/delrey/

Library of Congress Cataloging-in-Publication Data
Hogan, James P.
    Mind matters : exploring the world of artificial intelligence / James P. Hogan.—1st ed.
        p.   cm.
    "A Del Rey book"—T.p. verso.
    Includes bibliographical references and index.
    ISBN 0-345-41240-0
    1. Artificial intelligence.   2. Philosophy of mind.   I. Title.
    Q335.H634   1997
    006.3'01—dc21   97-17127
                                                                                      CIP

Manufactured in the United States of America

First Edition: March 1998

10   9   8   7   6   5   4   3   2   1

There comes a time in life
when dedications to grandchildren
start taking over from the
earlier ones to children.
This is for the latest two,

LEANNE and PETER

Contents

Acknowledgments

The help and advice of the following people is gratefully appreciated.

Science-fiction writers, editors, and readers for explaining some of their own work in areas relating to machine intelligence and robots and for referring me to some fascinating works by others: Poul and Karen Anderson, Greg Benford, Charles Brown, David Gerrold, Ashley Grayson, Louis James, Stanley Schmidt, Charles Sheffield, Vernor Vinge, and Margaret Withrow.

Professionals from the artificial intelligence and related fields for their time and patience, materials too voluminous to detail, and for much informative and enjoyable conversation: Boston College, Boston, Massachusetts: Peter Kugel, Department of Computer Science. California Institute of Technology, Pasadena, California: Paul Stolorz, Jet Propulsion Laboratory. Carnegie Mellon University, Pittsburgh, Pennsylvania: Herbert Simon and Janet Hew Hilf of the School of Computer Science; also Joseph Bates, Hans Berliner, Scott Fahlman, Andrew Moore, Raj Reddy, Reid Simmons, Tom Mitchell; Jill Fain Lehman and Paul Rosenbloom of the Soar project; Hans Moravec, Kevin Dowling, and Mike Blackwell of the Robotics Institute; David Touretzky of the Center for the Neural Basis of Cognition. Cycorp Corporation, Houston, Texas: Douglas Lenat, Tony Davis, Bill Jarrold, Fritz Lehmann. IBM Research, Thomas J. Watson Research Center, Yorktown Heights, New York: Murray Campbell, Marcy Holle. Indiana University, Bloomington, Indiana: Douglas Hofstadter, Department of Computer Science. Lockheed Research, Palo Alto, California: Rodger Cliff. Method Software Inc., Brookline, Massachusetts: Steve Strassman. Microsoft Corporation, Redding, Washington: Usama Fayyad. MIT, Cambridge, Massachusetts: Rodney Books, Patrick Winston of the AI Laboratory; Gerald Sussman, Eric Grimson, Computer Science; Marvin

Minsky, Betty McClanahan, and Pushpinder Singh of the Media Laboratory. NASA, Goddard SFC, Maryland: Brent Warner. NYNEX Science & Technology, White Plains, New York: Tom Fawcett and Foster Provost. Pensacola Junior College, Pensacola, Florida: Sandra Lockney-Davis and Charlotte Sweeney of the Learning Resource Center. Rochester Institute of Technology, Rochester, New York: John T. Sanders, Department of Philosophy, and Victoria Varga. Stanford University, Palo Alto, California: John McCarthy and Terry Rodriguez, Department of Computer Science; Tom Binford and Steven Lavalle of the Robotics Laboratory; Patrick Suppes, Department of Philosophy. Tulane University, New Orleans, Louisiana: Frank Tipler, Department of Mathematics. University of California, Los Angeles, California: Haywood Alker, Department of Political Science. University of Michigan, Ann Arbor, Michigan: John E. Laird, Department of Computer Science. University of West Florida, Pensacola, Florida: Ken Ford and Patrick Hayes, Institute for the Interdisciplinary Study of Human & Machine Cognition.

For invaluable help in providing additional materials and putting it all together: Sheila Phelan and Owen Lock of Ballantine Books. Eleanor Wood, my agent. Jim Baen and Toni Weisskopf of Baen Books for being understanding when this project interrupted one that I was already in the middle of for them. Karen Reedstrom and William R. Minto for the illustrations. Jackie Hogan for E-mailing, phoning, faxing, and all the general coordinating and secretarial effort that never shows in the final product. And last but by no means least, Alex Hogan, Michael Hogan, and Joe Hogan for plotting graphs, converting chess game notation, photocopying, and other chores that adults turn to young people for to get them out of trouble when they've left too much till the last moment.

Mind Matters

Futuristic Visions

INTELLIGENT MACHINES IN FICTION

"Prediction is very difficult, especially about the future."
—Niels Bohr (attrib.)

"The Future . . . something which everyone reaches at the rate of sixty minutes an hour, whatever he does, whoever he is."   —C. S. Lewis, *The Screwtape Letters*

You're feeling refreshed and looking forward to dinner with your friends by the time you arrive at the restaurant. The car's built-in chauffeur brought you to the door using its onboard database, checking along the way with the city traffic net for changing conditions. It's a smooth and relaxed driver, easy on passengers' nerves. Constantly communicating with the other vehicles around it, it never has to hit the brakes for a short stop or sudden lane-jumper, won't misread the speed of oncoming traffic at an intersection, and doesn't get walled off from turn lanes or exit ramps. It ferries the children where they need to go, talks to satellites if it needs directions, and takes itself to the shop when service is due. When it drops you off, you tell it to go and find a parking spot and come back at nine. It reminds you that you have a package to be collected from a store just a mile away and asks if you'd like it picked up while the car has some free time.

The vice president in charge of legal affairs at Trans Global Airlines is puzzled. At the last operational management meeting, a report concerning an outbreak of a strange form of neck rash among some of the company's flight attendants was flagged for priority action, but the preliminary checks run by the medical people have thrown up nothing. The rash takes a distinctive bright-red form with mild soreness and itching, yet none of the standard records describe anything resembling it. The curious thing is that the victims are all New York–, Washington–, San Francisco–, or Los Angeles–based, which at first suggested something infectious being carried around the country, originating at one of those locations. This now seems unlikely since a general spread would be predicted, but nothing has been observed at any of the intermediate hubs. Dietary contamination seems unlikely since only flight-crew members are affected, while the absence of anything comparable among passengers or other members of the general public seems to rule out local geographical or environmental factors.

Baffled, the VP and the medical director consult once more with the corporation's Integrated Information Manager (I²M) via a terminal in the legal department's offices. The only fact that the system finds to remark upon that didn't seem worth mentioning before is that the rashes all occurred on the left side of the neck. Is there any reason why that might be significant? Neither of the executives can think of one. I²M ruminates some more and then comes across an obscure item in FAA regulations that shows a correlation: an extra set of safety rules applied to all the flight numbers that the affected cabin crew members were working on. Could that be significant? The medical director shakes his head and seems a trifle impatient. Rashes don't have anything to do with safety rules. The VP, however, is curious and asks what was different about those flights. The machine thinks about it, studies the destinations, and notes among other things that the routes, to some degree at least, all lay over water. And the mystery is soon solved. For flights over extended stretches of water, the safety demonstration included putting on inflatable life jackets. The life-jacket manufacturer had recently changed to a new type of red ink for the stenciled markers, and the ink was failing to cure properly. The itching and soreness the victims experienced were from the scratching induced in response to the tacky ink.

To the robot spacecraft approaching from space, the asteroid—one of the countless minor planets circling the sun in a belt between the orbits of Mars and Jupiter—looks somewhat like an elongated, lumpy potato. Seventy miles long and thirty or so across the middle, it's of a type known as "carbonaceous chrondrites," which means that in addition to rocky minerals and metals it also contains ice and about 5 percent of a tarry hydrocarbon substance called kerogen. Kerogen, sometimes described as "condensed primeval soup," is formed from elements such as carbon that places like the moon lack, and forms the basis of organic compounds. Five percent may not sound like a lot, but it still works out at a cool 50 billion tons, or somewhere around three hundred times the annual production of organic chemicals in the United States.

The craft lands and disembarks a crew of tracked, legged, and wheeled surveyor and mining robots that spread out across the surface and commence delivering ores and other materials back to the central site, where other machines have begun the construction of a nuclear-fusion-powered materials extraction and processing plant. A parts-making facility is added next, followed by a parts-assembly facility, and stage by stage the plant grows itself into a fully equipped general-purpose factory complete with its own control computers carrying programs copied from the ship. The factory then starts making more robots. When a critical size is reached, a mixed robot workforce detaches itself from the main center of activity and migrates a short distance across the surface to build a second factory, a replica of the first. Third- and fourth-generation factories soon follow. When each has spawned its assigned number of descendant factories, it stops reproducing and switches to a production mode, producing and stockpiling materials and products for eventual shipment to Earth or other parts of the solar system. In time, this self-replicating pattern will spread to transform the entire asteroid surface—about equal in size to the state of Massachusetts—into a totally automated manufacturing complex dedicated to supplying humanity's expanding civilization from local resources. In a sense, the asteroid could be thought of as being consumed by mechanical, remote-directed digestive enzymes sent out from three-hundred-million-mile-distant Earth.

All very positive and reassuring. And there's nothing especially bad about that. But tension and things going wrong are the stuff of fiction, and when artificially created intelligences become central to the theme as opposed to background scenery in a futuristic setting, the depictions are rarely as sanguine as the foregoing. A favorite reason for departures between actuality and what was expected, as anyone who has ever written a computer program will readily appreciate, stems from the irritating tendency of machines to do what they're told instead of what they're supposed to know was meant. The kind of trouble this can get you into is amply exemplified in Ambrose Bierce's story "Moxon's Master," in which the inventor's creation murders him in the process of following directions not to allow itself to be beaten in a game of chess. Well, nobody told it that you weren't supposed to do that, you see, and nothing in the official rules of chess expressly forbids it.

Sometimes, unexpected consequences arise from a machine's genuine desire to please, when it thinks it's discovered a better way to deliver what's wanted but doesn't fully understand the situation. In James P. Hogan's *Two Faces of Tomorrow*, when a system in charge of lunar engineering operations is instructed to remove a ridge that's obstructing a proposed construction site, it does so by redirecting several loads of moon rocks being catapulted off the surface for orbital construction and using them as improvised high-kinetic-energy demolition bombs. Very efficient from the point of view of machine logic, and a lot faster than shipping in heavy earthmovers as the humans had anticipated; the only trouble is, it almost wipes out a survey team in the process.

The ultimate form of things not working out exactly as hoped has to be the machine going out of control completely, and even taking over. Most of us are familiar with HAL (although how many spotted that the letters are one removed from spelling out IBM?), the electronic intelligence that ran the spaceship in the movie *2001: A Space Odyssey*. The precise nature of its problem was never spelled out—which would have been difficult to do since the human protagonist never found out—but it seemed to revolve around insecurity over the realization that it could be turned off, coupled with worry about how to comply with the directive of protecting the human crew if it ever was. It resolved the issue by eliminating them itself, which I suppose at least had the merit of putting it out of its anguish of uncertainty. In Robert Heinlein's novel *The Moon Is a Harsh Mistress*, "Mike," the system that runs everything in a lunar penal colony, sides with the rebels against its terrestrial creators and masterminds the military strategy that eventually wins them independence. It then goes incommunicado, which is never really explained but has led some to speculate that its real motive in helping the humans was to manufacture an escape from its chores and retreat into some higher, arcane realm of electronic navel-contemplating.

The idea of this kind of thing eventually leading to all-out war between humans and their creations goes back, of course, to long before the *Terminator* movies. In a sense, Samuel Butler anticipated it in *Erewhon*, his novel on the mythical land of Erewhon (which for those who missed the cryptic HAL connection is an anagram of "Nowhere"), where the "antimachinists" clash with the "machinists" and succeed in eliminating mechanization from their lives. In fact, the whole thing was an ironic commentary on the institutions of Victorian England. Crime in Erewhon was considered a disease and disease a crime; religion was a banking system to which all paid lip service, but their real deity was social propriety. Although captivated by Darwin's theory of evolution, Butler deplored its emphasis as a mechanistic process, which he considered an affront to human intelligence. Voicing a thought that has occurred to many since, he speculated that the time might come when "man shall become to the machines what the horse and dog are to us."

Poul Anderson takes a more constructive view in *Harvest of Stars* and *The Stars Are Also Fire*, in which mankind's affairs have become so complex that a global network known as the "Teramind" is necessary to comprehend and manage them, which it does in an advisory capacity to the humans, who still make the laws, although this could turn out to be a temporary state of affairs as the Teramind begins developing ambitions of cosmic immortality. Such giant networks have become a staple of today's speculative fiction. Dan Simmons, however, in his two-part *Hyperion* and *Fall of Hyperion*, takes a different tack with myriad of constantly evolving intelligences, some benign, others hating the humans, while most have concerns of their own and simply don't care about us all that much. Considering the degree to which diversity seems to be the name of the evolution game, maybe this makes a lot of sense.

Mike Swanwick, in "Vacuum Flowers," raises the interesting concept of a hybrid consciousness emerging from the association of a planet-wide network and the collective human intelligence interacting with it. This can be viewed either progressively, as an evolutionary step toward a superior composite being, or with alarm, as the mental equivalent of advancing, all-dissolving green slime. It all depends on whether one is on the inside and adapted, or fleeing at close-to-light speed before the expanding periphery.

As far as Greg Benford is concerned in his "Galactic Center" series, which began twenty years ago with *Ocean of Night*, included *Great Sky River*, and reached its sixth volume with *Sailing Bright Eternity*, it's all over—at least for the aliens who have been superseded by their machine creations, which are continuing to evolve and spreading out across the galaxy. Now the machines have found us, and it's our turn. Here, the humans are forced to develop their own artificial intelligences not as servants or curiosities but as crucial allies in a survival contest that they haven't a hope of winning unaided. One wonders if we'll end up becoming the next race of organic progenitors to be discarded, when judged appropriate, along the way.

If something as pivotal as bringing into existence our own evolutionary successors could be the outcome, what prompts the rush into producing such entities in the first place? One answer is that we don't always realize that we're doing it. Sometimes, a giant system spontaneously "wakes up" on reaching a critical level of processing ability and complexity. In David Gerrold's *When Harlie Was One*, experiments with a deliberately designed high-level cognitive system achieve more than was planned and result in a fully sentient being, to be guided into a journey of self-discovery. "True Names," by Vernor Vinge, has surrogate characters in a multiuser adventure game acquiring awareness as the learning programs that support them turn out to be a lot better than anyone thought.

As for evolutionary successors, Vinge, in *Fire Upon the Deep* and various nonfictional writings,[1] gives perhaps the most direct treatment in asserting bluntly that it's going to happen; we can't stop it, so we might as well lay back and enjoy what we can. If we can create human-level intelligence, then we—or it—can create superhuman-level counterparts too. "Shortly after," Vinge maintains cheerfully, "the human era will be ended." When asked to be more specific, he replies, "I'd be surprised if this event occurs before 2005 or after 2030." Solemnly passing laws in attempts to stop it (the mission of the "Turing Police" in William Gibson's *Neuromancer*) won't do any good. The world's competitive pressures being the way they are, the only thing such measures are likely to achieve is ensuring that some other country or corporation will do it sooner. And what happens after that? Nobody knows. All the processes that define the rates of technological change and evolution, and the laws that describe the processes, take off into exponential growth, and everything becomes unpredictable. Vinge refers to this event as the "Technological Singularity," from its analogous role to the mathematical "singularities" believed to mark the centers of black holes and the zero-point of the big bang, beyond which such concepts as space, time, and physics cease to have any meaning. Perhaps Frederick Brown got it right in his short story "Answer," in which the ultimate machine, on being asked the ultimate question, "Is there a God?" responded, "There is now."

Hephaestus, the blacksmith god of the Greeks who built the Olympian palaces, forged the armor of Achilles, and bound Prometheus to the rock, constructed the bronze giant Talos, who was given to King Minos as a guardian and patrolled the shores of Crete. Another myth tells how Rabbi Löw of Prague, in the sixteenth century, invoked God's help to fashion the Golem, an animated clay giant who became the protector of the Jews faced by threat of a pogrom. Goethe's *Faust* imaginatively evokes the medieval legends of "homunculi," miniature humanoids chemically synthesized in alchemists' glass retorts. Baron Frankenstein, courtesy of Mary Shelley, added the first hint of ingredients drawn from modern science. Generations of fiction and fable have depicted artificial beings as slaves, slavemasters, rivals and saviors, children's teachers and companions—even as pets and personality-endowed imitation animals that don't bring in fleas or need cleaning up after. To comprehend our own nature and mimic its abilities has remained one of the most intriguing questions that has challenged discoverers and thinkers through the ages. In the last couple of centuries, with better understanding of biology and chemistry eliminating much of the mystery previously attributed to "life," attention has shifted to focus upon that aspect of it that we term "mind." Early models tried to capture the brain's operations in terms of clockwork, when chronometers and mechanisms represented the highest of the precision arts; in the late 1800s it became a hydraulic system, by the 1930s an elaborate telephone exchange, and after World War II an amassment of feedback-driven servocontrol loops. All of them to a degree amusingly, perhaps inevitably—and probably informatively, if we pause to reflect—faithfully reflected whatever happened to be the latest technology of the times. Nowadays, of course, it has to be a computer.

But before getting embroiled in the current situation, let's set the scene by taking a quick look at the history that led up to it—from the first serious attempts by modern science to understand what goes on in the parts of us that think they're different, somehow, from the parts that don't think anything at all. Lumped together with the latter, of course, is the rest of the natural world.

1. Vinge (1993a), (1993b).

Medieval Mind

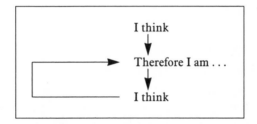

The Mind's Virtual-Reality Show

Most people don't spend a lot of time thinking about the processes going on inside their heads that enable them to think about the world and themselves, the relation between the two, and about the processes going on inside their heads. Their intuitive notion would probably be one of existing "here" on the inside, observing the outside somewhat in the way they might sit in an apartment and look out at life going by in the street. If pressed to elaborate further and be more precise, however, they would likely recall accounts from school and college years of such things as retinal images being transmitted as nerve impulses and the body's networks of touch, pain, and heat sensors, and concede that the impression of direct experience is really an illusion. While it doesn't make a lot of difference to the way we go about our affairs, what we actually deal with are internal representations that we manufacture in the brain. Instead of gazing out directly at the world from its apartment, the mind is more like the audience in a movie theater, watching re-creations on a screen of what cameras and microphones capture on the sidewalk outside.

Disputes sometimes arise—among the professionals and enthusiasts who concern themselves with such things, not among sane, ordinary people going about their day-to-day business—over whether we encode the world as "words," "concepts," "propositions," or whatever. The important thing for the purpose of this chapter, however, is the underlying general acceptance of "thinking" as a process of manipulating representations in some form, distinct from the realities they represent. It is this shared assumption that makes the idea of machines being capable of thought even intelligible. For if "thinking" consists of manipulating encoded representations in some form, why, then, should different machine states not be equally capable of "standing for" the same things, and thought processes be duplicated by suitable transformations between them? Without the concept of indirect representation, the notion that thought might go on inside a machine—and hence, the whole idea of "artificial intelligence" in its modern sense—becomes literally inconceivable. This fundamental condition was not realized before the great revolution in Western thought that took place in the seventeenth century and marked the rise of the present scientific outlook.[1]

Aristotle's Legacy

SCHOLASTICISM AND THE
DIRECT APPREHENSION OF KNOWLEDGE

Before the Scientific Revolution, such things were viewed very differently. It's difficult, and perhaps not really possible with the legacy of attitudes built deep into the foundations of our own worldview, to have a clear grasp of the pre-Modern conception of thought. In fact, while the earlier view does recognize such specific acts as "seeing," "remembering," "calculating," "dreaming," and the like, there is nothing in it that corresponds to our notion of thinking as a generalized faculty. The revolution thus entailed such a thorough reformulation of concepts and ways of looking at the world that it requires a struggle today to find words in which to discuss it. "Seeing," however, is something that we can reasonably suppose people then to have experienced pretty much the way we do, and their way of accounting for it probably reveals much about how they saw other things too.

"Scholasticism" is the name given to the general philosophical and intellectual tradition that guided European thought through the Middle Ages, before the scientific upheaval. Its main thrust lay in championing the doctrines of the medieval Church and preserving stability in a politically and economically restless age. The scholars of those times have been criticized for apparently being unable to come up with the method of resolving issues by experiment that seems so obvious to us today and are often ridiculed for recourses into interminable logical debates that sometimes went on for centuries. Before being too hasty in judgment, though, remember that the purpose of learning as it was then seen was not to discover new knowledge but to understand and defend the existing system. Knowledge wasn't out there to be discovered like paths through a wood. Truths that mattered were revealed through signs and divine inspiration, not uncovered by poking around in ponds or watching how weights fall and pendulums swing. Hence, scholarship lay in developing powers of argument and knowing the constructions of standard proofs. Measurement and numerics were technicalities of the artisan's and astrologer's trades, of little use or interest to the philosopher. The concept of knowledge, external or divinely revealed, imparting itself directly in the mind of the knower follows almost inevitably as part of the natural scheme of things in this kind of setting.

For the medieval scholastic Thomas Aquinas, to "see" something meant grasping its "form." The notion of a thing's form goes back to Aristotle and isn't something we pay a great deal of attention to today (although, as we shall see later, something very close to it is beginning to be recognized in efforts to get computers to make associations in ways that exhibit what we would call common sense). Aristotle's concern was in trying to fathom what it is about something that makes it the kind of thing it is. Clearly, more is involved than simply a list of the materials from which it's made—a home, for example, presents a very different prospect from the pile of rubble left after an earthquake or the same materials in a contractor's yard before the house is built. Shelves of volumes were devoted to the theory of this kind of thing, but one of the central ideas that emerged from it all was that of the *form of organization* of constituents into a whole and the nature of the relationships between them.

Even without taking matters further, this way of looking at things had two important consequences. The first was that it gave things a nonmaterial dimension of existence—an intangible quality extending beyond their physical components. Second, form identifies the generality that establishes a thing's essence—the quality of "houseness," for example, that is common to all houses irrespective of their differences in design and appearance. It was a view that looked beyond immediate instances to seek out the significant commonality that individual cases implied—to see *roundness*, not just round coins and wheels on wagons; *virtue* as a concept, not just people who were good in various ways. Plato went as far as to envisage a separate realm of existence populated by pure Form, which he felt had to exist apart in order for us to be able to apprehend it. About the only relics that remain in today's world are words like in-*form*-ation and con-*form*-ing to type.

"Seeing," then, according to Aquinas, consists of first rendering "intelligible" the form of the object seen and then "grasping" and retaining that form. From consideration of such words in context, it's evident that form is thought of as in some way separate from the thing whose form was abstracted. What makes this obscure to anyone with a Modern perspective is that it appears to require no establishing of contact across distance—as our interpretation is achieved by light rays. If any gap is to be bridged, it's more the problem of how objects, which are material, interact with the intellect, which is not. And this is where the Aristotelian idea of form has it relevance: In endowing perceptions with an aspect that went beyond the immediately sensible, it provided a common framework in which immaterial intellect and otherwise material objects could meet. The world, then, made itself known to mind in the sense of being "understood" (again, used not in the sense that we use the word but more akin to "absorbed" or "shared")—much in the way that revelations and other forms of knowledge became understood. Since the direct role of mind was integral and essential to the process, the suggestion that such "understanding"— the nearest to what we mean by "thinking"—could be imparted to a machine would have been not just far-fetched but meaningless. Until the conceptual shift occurred to that of mind as a processor of representations, the idea of an artificial intelligence was literally unthinkable.

A residue of the old view persists today. Many people consider emotional awareness as different from more intellectual activity because of the impression it gives of direct immersion in reality—and perhaps because we don't always handle it with as much control and judgment as we would wish. That probably has a lot to do with the oft-heard assertion that machines could never "really" be "like us." It's not easy to imagine an "emotion processor," working on feelings or whatever components go to make up feelings in the kind of way a word processor operates on character strings and sentences, caring and getting involved. More on this later.

The Scientific Revolution

KNOWLEDGE AS SOMETHING TO BE DISCOVERED

The assault on the traditional school began in earnest with people like Francis Bacon, who maintained that improving the quality of life on Earth was not at odds with any of Man's higher beliefs and could be accomplished by extending our knowledge of the world. How this was to be undertaken on the basis of graspabilities of forms was not readily apparent, and a new breed of experimentalists typified by Robert Boyle and Isaac Newton embarked instead on the more direct route of studying what would today be called the properties of things and substances while the scholars debated. John Locke lay the philosophical grounds for bringing together what had been regarded as a variety of more or less unrelated activities into a general scheme of essentially similar representations being processed in essentially similar ways. But it was Descartes who set the lead in erecting screens around the observer of the world, turning him into a cinema patron for whom projections replaced the direct interaction with reality that had previously been assumed.

DESCARTES'S MECHANICAL UNIVERSE

René Descartes (1596–1650) was a French philosopher, mathematician, and scientist, perhaps the single most influential contributor to developing the ideas and methods that ended the medieval era. Like Aquinas, he was a generalist who sought to synthesize all knowledge into a unified whole; his writings were clear, graceful, and livened with human interest in a way not seen in Europe since Plato's *Dialogues*, and they were rivaled in popularity only by Galileo's (they were contemporaries) *Message from the Stars*.

The scientific system that Descartes constructed was in conflict with Aristotelian principles on just about every point. It rejected the assumption that heavenly bodies were made of different stuff and subject to different laws; that "natural" motion was directed toward an end, and hence, purposive, which set it apart from "unnatural" motion; and it discarded the notion of the four elements in favor of a theory of mechanical adjustment of fundamental particles as the basis of chemical changes. Motion was a key feature of the Cartesian universe, accounting not only for light, heat, and sound, but also for such qualities as color, flavor, and odor that introduced superficial differences into otherwise similar objects. Such focusing on mechanical analogies followed Galileo's precedent and led to the revolutionary proposal of a mechanistic universe, carrying with it the implication of the Deity as an ingenious machine designer or Divine Engineer. The revolutionary became the heretical and, also like Galileo, got Descartes into trouble with the Church when he considered extending Galileo's mechanical principles to encompass human behavior as well, making Man just a part of the mechanistic creation. That went against the teaching of the institutions that proclaimed human action to lie outside natural law and saw experimental science as a threat, which was what got Galileo silenced and placed under house arrest for life. (But force and suppression never work in the long run. Today, everybody remembers Galileo. How many can name the bishops and professors who refused to look through his telescope?)

REFLEXIVE MIND?

The line of thought that led Descartes to ask if humans were just complicated mechanisms along with everything else resulted partly from his investigations of reflexes. The French Royal Gardens at the time of Louis XIV were a seventeenth-century Disneyland with their own miniature society of hydraulically controlled robots, activated by visitors stepping on tiles as they walked along the paths, that moved and enacted rituals, made sounds, and even played musical instruments. If visitors approached the figure of bathing Diana, she hid in the rosebushes; when they tried to follow, Neptune advanced, threatening them with a trident. Descartes made several such devices himself. In 1649 he built one that he called "daughter Francine." On one of his voyages, the case holding Francine was opened by a superstitious ship's captain, who, frightened by the automaton's lifelike movements, had container and "daughter" thrown overboard.

The automata in the Royal Gardens acted like humans and appeared to display rational motives and choice, but they were mere machines reacting to utterly thoughtless external forces. Descartes believed there was a precise analogy between their internal workings and the structure of the human body. The tubes carrying the water that directed the automata, for example, corresponded to nerves. The springs and motors that controlled movement played the parts of muscles and tendons. The water itself, carrying "commands" from place to place, was like blood, with its vaporous particles communicating "animal spirits"—the true function of blood was not yet understood. And, indeed, the action of certain human responses, such as knee jerks and the contraction of the pupil in the eye when light is shone on it, seemed to be just as mechanical as those of the dolls in the park. Expressed in the concepts that Descartes held, an external stimulus activated the nerve fibers, causing the threads of the nerve marrow to be pulled; this opened an orifice in the brain, allowing vaporous spirits to flow through nerves leading to the muscles and tendons, causing them to move through inflation—an explanation that, with electrochemical processes substituted for the animal spirits, is remarkably close to the contemporary one.

The significant thing was that the terminal response triggered at the end of it all was automatic, determined solely by the stimulus and the pattern of nerve connections. Barring failures, it was impossible for the system to do other than what it did. Terminal responses could be internal or external, conceivably giving rise to cognitive and emotional reactions as well as motor movement. Hence, even the impression of voluntarily evoking a thought or initiating an action could be a response, completely determined by the particular configuration of stimuli impinging on us at the time. Descartes could see no theoretical limit to the behavioral potential of a sufficiently complex combination of such reflexes. It thus became logically possible that everything that humans did and thought—or thought they thought—was no more than the outcome of exotically complicated systems of reflexes.

MIND-BODY DUALISM

Although he considered the question, Descartes's answer when he emerged from his philosophical meditations on the matter was an unequivocal "no." There remained, he concluded, a fundamental difference between voluntary and involuntary actions that couldn't be explained away. Let's take a jerking knee as an example. There are, said Descartes, two entirely different reasons why the knee might move: (1) it gets tapped in the right spot and moves via the reflex, or (2) the owner of the knee decides to move it. Asking *why* in the first case leads to a potentially endless chain of further mechanical causes and generates deeper levels of explanation without limit. Thus, asking why the reflex works produces the answer that (using today's concepts) it was sufficiently advantageous to have been selected in the course of evolution; why does evolution work? Because . . . and you can chain explanations all the way back to the big bang. Again, asking why a stimulus had such and such a strength is explained by the force of the impact, which is explained by the momentum of the object imparting it, which is explained by. . . . But in the second case, the questions come to an abrupt end with "because he felt like it"—and that's about all that can be said of the matter. (True, we could go off into speculative realms about why he felt like it, but the point is that the explanations cease being scientific in the sense of being expressible in cause-and-effect terms. They resist further reductional analysis.)

Note at this point that the rejection of reflex as an explanation of human behavior was not in itself sufficient to rule out the possibility that behavior was nevertheless mechanical. After all, showing that a radio isn't driven by clockwork doesn't prove it to be supernatural. Modern materialists would certainly pick up this point on the grounds that even today's accounts of mind and volition are woefully incomplete, and contend that knowledge of all the pertinent facts would show behavior to be every bit as mechanical as Descartes speculated it might be. They may be right too, but deciding the issue isn't our purpose here.

What led Descartes eventually to reject a materialistic account of mind was at root the intuitive conviction that mind alone stood apart from everything embraced by the entire realm of experience in being the one thing whose certainty was assured. Descartes has been called the "father of skepticism." In seeking a solid foundation upon which to base his belief system, he begins by ruling out everything that we can't be absolutely sure about. To paraphrase Sherlock Holmes: When you've eliminated the dubitable, then what's left must be indubitable. (I've always found Holmes's dictum about the impossible and the truth pretty flaky and wondered why it gets quoted so much. When you've eliminated the impossible, what's left isn't the truth; what's left is the possible, which *includes*—somewhere—the truth. The world we live in is rarely so obliging as to leave one plausible answer after all the impossible and absurd ones have been weeded out. Real science and police work begin where Conan Doyle leaves off.)

Thus, we can't be certain of what our sense experiences tell us, for we know we sometimes have illusions and hallucinations. Logic can't give us certainty because we can make mistakes; besides, logic only shows what conclusions follow from the premises we assume, and the whole object is to find sure premises. Even the existence of a material body can be doubted, and so on, until Descartes arrives at the one fact that he feels he can be absolutely certain of: the famous *"Cogito ergo sum."* He cannot doubt that he exists as a thinking being. Even the act of doubting all the other things that he has considered affirms that he exists and is thinking it.

He does not, however, as might be expected, go on to establish this as the major premise of deductions leading to new conclusions; rather, he concludes that since we have become certain of one fact that we did not learn through the senses or by deduction from other beliefs, there must be some unique, fundamental difference about the mind that has learned this and a process by which it has done so. Hence, the mind emerges as an agent capable of performing a kind of psychokinesis in deploying immaterial powers to move the material body, and Descartes arrived at his philosophy of dualism—mind and body existing as completely different kinds of things, res cogitans and res extensa, one governed and constrained by the laws of physics, the other free to exercise will as it chooses.[2]

At first glance, Descartes's proposal of an incorporeal mind not subject to mechanical laws makes it difficult to understand why the Church should have been upset, especially since his writings also included two proofs of the existence of God and arguments for the immortality of the soul. Even his implied conclusion that no materialistic explanation could succeed in principle fails to draw any enthusiasm. The point is that in seriously taking up the question he had dared to think the unthinkable, and that, to every form of totalitarianism, is the ultimate crime.

So even to Descartes, often viewed as synonymous with materialism, "mind" remained essentially supernatural, endowed with medieval mystery.[3] But the rest of the universe—including animals, by a not very convincing argument—was reduced to a mechanism. The objects that the mind perceived, now stripped of any "form" that could pervade the mind like an odor and influence it directly, were totally contained in the world outside. It thus followed that what was experienced and manipulated inside had to be representations of them. Perhaps, then, other representations of the world could be manipulated in other ways. Even if part of what we call "human" would forever be permanently beyond reach, the notion that some cognitive processes might be artificially imitated became at least conceivable. The stage for the mechanization of thought had been set.

1. See Pratt for a more thorough discussion of this and much of the subject matter in this chapter.
2. The account I have given draws heavily from Flanagan.
3. For a recent defense of dualism, see Popper and Eccles.

3

Mechanical Mind

"When a man reasoneth, he does nothing else but conceive a sum total, from addition of parcels; or conceive of a remainder, from subtraction of one sum from another."
—Thomas Hobbes, *Leviathan*

The fundamental shifts in outlook of philosophy and science at the end of the medieval era permitted a view of thinking that made the idea of mechanizing thought conceivable. Internally, the mind operated not with reality directly but with representations that stood for or symbolized it; therefore, analogous operations performed on appropriate symbols of the same things ought to be capable of reproducing something comparable to what the mind did. But for the conjecture to become actuality, a suitable system of symbols and rules for their manipulation first had to exist. The rise of modern mathematics that occurred as part of the same Scientific Revolution provided models of formal representation and procedure to which methods of mechanization might conveniently be applied.[1]

The Rise of Mathematics

EARLY NUMEROPHOBIA

Through most of the Middle Ages, calculation was not popular. Numbers tended to be ignored altogether if at all possible and kept small when they couldn't be avoided. The prime reason was the continuing use through most of this period of Roman numerals, with their cumbersome form and lack of any system for denoting the relationship between various multiples of ten. Although "XX," for example, expressed the number that is twice that represented by "X," there was no way of relating "C" and "M" to it in the kind of way in which we can see immediately that "100" and "1,000" are ten and a hundred times bigger, respectively, than "10." Since position had no meaning comparable to denoting successive powers of ten as in our notation, addition could only be accomplished, as far as I can see, by introducing one new numeral at a time and transferring appropriate substitutions through the accumulating total (replacing an existing "V" by an "X" if the newcomer is a "V"; then, if four "X"s were there already, replacing the five now present with an "L," and so on).[2] I have no idea what the rule for multiplication would be—possibly one can't do better than repeated addition. Gerbert of Aurillac (later Pope Sylvester II), in the tenth century, recorded how a four-page booklet on reckoning cost him "almost impossible toil" to produce.[3] And this from an accomplished logician!

Positional notation as we use it today was the key innovation that did away with all the ungainliness that had retarded mathematics. Introduced first in the form of the abacus, and later with the adoption of the Indo-Arabic numeral system, it enabled quick and accurate calculation over a greatly enlarged range of applications. What makes the positional system possible is its use of a numeral to denote zero, which nobody (in Europe, anyway) had thought of before.

STAKING OUT EMPIRES—THE DEMANDS OF NAVIGATION

The fifteenth and sixteenth centuries were a time not only of scientific upheaval but of tremendous geographic expansion as well. This was when the new empires of Holland, Spain, France, and England flung themselves around the world. Enormous wealth stood to be made from the expanding commercial opportunities; navies able to operate over vast distances were needed to protect the trade routes and acquired territories. The need for accurate navigation across the Earth's surface, probably more than any other factor, drove the developments in mathematics that propelled the new sciences.

Navigating requires fixing your location relative to other places, which means knowing how far north or south or east or west of them you are. Measuring the elevation of astronomical objects such as the polestar or the sun above the horizon will give you your distance north or south of the equator (latitude). This requires instruments, and, therefore, precise techniques for designing and making them, and tables and charts to interpret the readings, which in turn call for extensive recording of observations to construct the tables and charts. Since the sun and everything else crosses the sky every day, measuring its position can't tell you your longitude or how far east or west of anywhere you are. What it can tell you is knowing how far the sun's progression differs from that seen right now from some reference point whose location you know. To work this out, you need accurate clocks. Fixing longitude to within half a degree after a voyage of six weeks requires that the timekeeping error be not greater than three seconds per day. And then, having figured out where you are, planning a course to get to where you want to be involves consulting more charts and tables of winds, currents, tides, and so forth, all of which have to be organized and compiled. And then there are the maps themselves, which involve projecting information from the surface of a world that's round into a representation of one that isn't, and in such a way that it is still usable—for example, by preserving compass directions correctly.

From Clocks to Calculators

Better and more precisely fashioned mechanisms were appearing, while at the same time demand was soaring for bigger and always more accurate mountains of calculation. As was only to be expected in such a situation, it wasn't long before the clock makers and the calculators got together and began coming up with ideas for mechanizing the mathematics. And mathematics above anything provided a clear demonstration of one area, at least, of "thinking" that was representational. Faced with concrete problems of finding the accrued interest on an investment, the angle for artillery fire, or the length of a bridging span, the mathematician would let symbols stand for the essential elements, perform the appropriate manipulations, and deliver the result back in real-world terms as a solution. And if the procedures for manipulating these kinds of symbols could be mechanized, why shouldn't the same be done with symbols that represented other things too? The best known of the early names to conceive of such a functional extension was probably Leibniz.

THE MATHEMATICS OF CHANGE:
LEIBNIZ, NEWTON, AND THE CALCULUS

Gottfried Wilhelm von Leibniz (1646–1716) was a German philosopher and mathematician best known for developing the methods of calculus contemporaneously with Isaac Newton in England. He became involved in a dispute with friends of Newton over who thought of it first, and there are some today who believe that Newton stole it. In fact, many mathematicians around that time were working on problems related to the summation of infinitesimal quantities, and as is often the case with scientific ideas, there was nothing unlikely about something like the calculus being formulated more or less simultaneously in different places. Whereas the operations of standard arithmetic—addition, multiplication, and so on—apply to static situations, the calculus makes it possible to deal with rates at which quantities *change* with respect to each other or with respect to time. The alteration of an object's position over time, for example, describes its movement through space—a cannonball, a machine part, a planet; the way the orientation of a surface varies from point to point measures its curvature. The relationships between such quantities are expressed in what are known as differential equations. It has been said that physics is the science of differential equations. One of the most basic examples of their use is relating the forces exerted on a moving body to the changes in its speed and direction—the ones that throw you back in the seat of your car when it accelerates or sideways when it corners. An aircraft's or missile's "inertial" navigation computer can keep track of where it is on the Earth's surface by summing all the tiny pushes and jolts that occur on a precisely made reference mass every time a course change occurs.

Leibniz's calculating machine, still preserved today in the Hanover State Library in Germany, was an improvement on several that had gone before, which followed naturally from the design of clocks—one, for example, made by Blaise Pascal (1623–1662), another noted mathematician. A clock is essentially a generator of regular pulses that the rest of the mechanism counts. What amounted to gear-train counters were therefore well developed and understood by the end of the seventeenth century, and it was a straightforward matter to adapt them to adding impulses that represented numbers instead of clock ticks, and that was what the earliest calculators did.[4] Leibniz's machine included some ingenious innovations that enabled it to handle multiplication, root extraction, and other operations as well. One of his ideas was to use pulleys between different-size wheels to vary the number of times that one shaft would turn another. A variation was the "Leibniz Wheel," in reality a cylinder with ten teeth, each extending progressively farther along the cylinder so that only one covered the full length; thus, it effectively provided a variable-tooth wheel, depending on which point along its axis the wheel engaging it was positioned.

LEIBNIZ'S VISION OF MECHANIZING THOUGHT

By the standards of the day, Leibniz's machine worked well, and in 1643 he went to London to demonstrate it before the Royal Society, of which Newton was president. (Newton was said not to suffer fools gladly, and rivals not at all, which is perhaps where the acrimony between him and Leibniz began.) Leibniz, excited by the further prospects, went on in subsequent years to develop the proposition that the whole process of reasoning might be mechanized. To this end he conceived the formulation of an ideal language to overcome the shortcomings of ordinary language that caused no end of trouble in human affairs through muddled communications and misunderstandings. The language would encode not only descriptions of things but also knowledge about the relationships between various classes of things—for example, the facts that all animals are living things and some living things are people, which the individual terms used in ordinary language fail to convey. The mechanization of such language would thus make automatic and error-free the entire system of syllogistic reasoning that was still generally held as capable of expressing all practical knowledge. (A syllogism is a three-part statement in which assertion of two premises as true leads to a necessary conclusion. For example, *if* all scientists are pianists, *and* this person isn't a pianist, *then* this person isn't a scientist. Syllogisms can get more involved than this, of course.)

And so, Leibniz thought, the misreading of intentions and confusions of meaning that led to strife and tragedy could be eradicated from human affairs. Now, when disputants found themselves locked in controversy, all they would need to do to resolve things would be to take out their machines and calculate; disagreement didn't arise about facts, which were self-evident, but over the conclusions that followed from them. Visions of this kind were probably inspired by Leibniz's early experience in the service of the bishop of Mainz, who was concerned over preserving peace within the Holy Roman Empire and sent Leibniz on a diplomatic mission to Louis XIV of France, who was considered the greatest threat to European stability at the time. Leibniz urged him to go and conquer Egypt instead, which would have been a much more grandiose and fitting undertaking for a Christian monarch than worrying about the insignificant countries of Europe. Louis didn't buy the idea, but it was well thought out and may have had something to do with Napoleon's embarking on a virtually identical campaign almost a century later. Presumably, Napoleon didn't take along a calculator. He barely escaped through Syria and was forced to leave the army stranded after Nelson wiped out his fleet in the Battle of the Nile.

As we know, things didn't work out the way Leibniz imagined. His faith in the adequacy of deductive logic to yield all human knowledge was misplaced. And the picture of an "alphabet of thought" out of which all the complexities covered by language could be built was an impossible task then. The specialists attempting to construct representational languages as part of today's AI research are still far from realizing anything close to it with the far more sophisticated methods at their disposal now.

Number Factories

HOSTS DE TABLES
So, for a while, the vision of automating thought foundered. But following the Scientific Revolution, the expansion of engineering, manufacturing, and commerce that we call the Industrial Revolution led to colossal demands for more comprehensive and more accurate numerical tables of every description. This not only entailed enormous effort, but the sheer volumes of calculation posed an insoluble problem of protecting against errors. Generally, the procedures followed were serial in nature (operating on the last entry in a table to generate the next and so forth), which meant that a single error, once committed, could propagate through from there and render the remainder of the work worthless. As an illustration, near the end of the eighteenth century the new French Republic determined to have a new set of logarithmic and trigonometrical tables drawn up with such accuracy as to become a monument to the Revolution; it was at that time the most imposing exercise of its kind ever executed. A half-dozen eminent mathematicians headed the enterprise, another eight to ten

qualified mathematicians acted as supervisors, while one hundred "computers" (the name given to human calculating specialists—essentially adders—before the modern use of the term) conducted the work. Every result was calculated independently by two different operatives, and a third party checked to see that their results agreed. Nevertheless, it is possible for two people to get the same answer and still be wrong, and in a project of this magnitude it was bound to happen repeatedly.[5] The manuscripts took up seventeen volumes but were never put to use since publication was abandoned.

Strange as it may seem, the further improvement of mechanical calculators as the obvious response to this challenge was not pursued extensively. The reasons seem to be that reference to tables was found more convenient for the more usual small-scale undertakings, while inability to manufacture parts with the requisite precision made impracticable the larger projects that mechanization might usefully have benefited. Where accuracy was of less concern than the convenience of making quick, on-the-spot approximations, e.g., with engineers, builders, and surveyors, such devices as slide rules were preferred.

CHARLES BABBAGE—
THE VON NEUMANN OF THE MECHANICAL AGE

It was not until well into the nineteenth century that Charles Babbage (1792–1871) resurrected Leibniz's theme by conceiving a calculating machine of power to take in the whole of arithmetic. But beyond that, it would implement a logical algebra capable of representing the complete process of reasoning. This was his famous "Analytical Engine," heroic in concept, a hundred years ahead of its time, and never built. Before that, however, he initiated a preparatory project in the form of his "Difference Engine," which *was* brought to completion and did useful work, though not by Babbage himself. His own venture, only partly completed, is displayed at the Kensington Science Museum in London.[6]

Babbage was an English mathematician and technician, celebrated for developing the principles that virtually all of today's computers embody, though long before they could be put to practical use—a kind of von Neumann of the mechanical age. He became a Lucasian Professor of Mathematics at Cambridge in 1828 but resigned the position in 1839 to devote himself to designing mathematical machines.

There had been a few unexceptional experiments in building mechanical calculators in the hundred-plus years since Leibniz's time, but none really went beyond elaborating on techniques that Leibniz had used, or even Pascal before him. Babbage decided it was time to put an end to all that by doing what should have been done years before: using the power of machines to generate, once and for all, accurate and reliable mathematical tables. To attract financial backing, he completed a working model of the calculating part of his proposed device and on the strength of it circulated widely an open letter nominally addressed to the president of the Royal Society, securing eventually the support of the British government.

A MATHEMATICAL WORKHORSE:
THE DIFFERENCE ENGINE

The term "Difference Engine" follows from a method that had been established for generating mathematical tables in a way that required addition only—in fact, the same method that had been used in the ill-fated monumental French project, enabling the bulk of the work to be tackled by operators with limited mathematical abilities. To see how it works, let's take an easy example by supposing we want to create a table giving the values of the function x^2 for successive whole-number values of x. So let's make a table and begin by writing the values of x down the first column and the corresponding values for x^2 in the second—see Table 3.1, where the process is continued as far as $x = 10$.

Now, for the third column, enter the differences between the numbers appearing in the second column. That is, subtract the square of 1 (1) from the the square of 2 (4) to give 3; the square of 2 (4) from the square of 3 (9) to give 5, and so on. This gives the column of First Differences. (The symbology at the top of the column is just a general way of saying that D1 for any line n is given by the nth entry for x^2 minus the $(n-1)$th entry for x^2, i.e., from the line above.) Now follow the same procedure again to give column four of Second Differences by subtracting each First Difference in column three from the one below. (Again, in general, the nth entry for D2 is given by the nth value of D1 minus the $(n-1)$th value.) It quickly becomes apparent that all the Second Differences are the same.

And this gives us a method for calculating as many more squares as we like

Number	Square	First Differences D1	Second Differences D2
x	x^2	$x^2 - (x-1)^2$	$D1_x - D1_{(x-1)}$
1	1	-	-
2	4	3	-
3	9	5	2
4	16	7	2
5	25	9	2
6	36	11	2
7	49	13	2
8	64	15	2
9	81	17	2
10	100	19	2

Table 3.1 Difference Table for Squares

by using nothing but addition on the previous result generated. For example, if we've gotten as far as $x = 456$ in the table and obtained its square, which is 207,936, and if we also have 911 as the First Difference for the 456 line, this being the difference between 456^2 and 455^2, then the First Difference for the 457 line must be 913. And this, added to the 207,936 that we already have for the square of 456, will give us 208,849 as the square of the next value for x, i.e., 457. And so on.

A more important realization is that the same "method of differences" can be applied to tabulating any expression that can be expressed as a "polynomial," i.e., in a form of the general pattern:

$$f(x) = a + bx + cx^2 + dx^3 + \ldots zx^n,$$

where $f(x)$ means whatever "function" of x we're interested in (in the above example, its square), a, b, c, etc., are some set of constants, x again represents the successive values to be used for generating the table, and n can be any whole number.[7] In the example we've used, $c = 1$ and all the other constants are zero.

For more complicated polynomials—ones where higher powers of x appear—more columns will be needed before one showing an unchanging difference value is reached (in fact, the number of "difference columns" will equal the highest power of x that appears in the expression, in our case, 2). But such a column *will* be reached eventually. It turns out that most of the expressions encountered in engineering, physics, and mathematics can be put into the form of a polynomial. A general-purpose difference-processing machine therefore promised a fast, accurate, and reliable means of generating tables for use in fields of every kind. Babbage even included in the design a provision for the results to be impressed directly into a copper plate for printing, thereby eliminating the risk of errors creeping in through clerical copying.

LEIBNIZ RESURRECTED: THE ANALYTICAL ENGINE

It is sometimes suggested that Babbage's ideas were too far ahead of the technical capabilities of the time, but this doesn't seem so of the Difference Engine. He scoured the country to take advantage of the most precise machining methods available—indeed, some special tools were designed for the project— and by the end of 1832 the central part of the hand-cranked machine was a reality to the extent that Babbage was able to entertain his dinner-party guests with it. It worked perfectly, as it still does today. But Babbage's affairs gradually degenerated into a tangle of frustrations; an unstable political background led to funding being discontinued, and the project came to a halt. However, a Swedish printer by the name of George Scheutz had become sufficiently attracted to the concept to attempt building a revised design with the help of his son, Edward, which they completed and brought to the London Exhibition of 1854. Their experience was somewhat different from Leibniz's a century and a half before. Babbage, to his credit, received their achievement not with envy as might perhaps have been anticipated but with congratulations and admiration. Eventually, the Scheutz machine was bought by the Dudley Observatory at Albany, New York, and used for producing astronomical tables. Today it survives in the Smithsonian. Ironically, the same British government that had withdrawn its support from Babbage's work had a copy made of the Scheutz machine, which was used by the registrar-general's office in Somerset House, London, to generate life-expectancy tables. The copy is also in the London Science Museum, along with the incomplete version of Babbage's.

Another major factor, perhaps the greatest, that was material toward the demise of Babbage's project was the turning of his attention toward more imaginative realms. What he glimpsed were the possibilities implied by a machine that, instead of being confined to accepting as inputs the first entries for some particular table, would be capable of using its own results as input for further calculations—and not only that, but also of having its instruction sequence altered to specify different kinds of calculation to be performed. This was the Analytical Engine that Babbage is best remembered for, utterly innovative, too advanced for the government of the day to comprehend, let alone think seriously about funding, anticipating concepts that wouldn't be realizable for a hundred years. Although never built, the Analytical Engine was what earned Babbage the title "father of the computer." The engine was as ahead of its time then as it would be now, and we'll come back to it in the next chapter.

End of a Lineage:
The Giant Calculators

From the middle of the nineteenth century on, mechanical desktop calculators finally began to appear on a more widespread basis as aids to the more mundane, day-to-day chores that Leibniz's pioneering effort should have been applied to easing but hadn't been. What finally brought about the move was more the demands of business than science. The growth of commercial and manufacturing organizations stimulated development of these devices into various forms of office machinery with automatic reading of data for tallying and sorting. And then there was the huge emerging bureaucracy of the state itself. Estimates for the U.S. Census for 1890 indicated that trying to conduct it by the same methods as had been used for the previous census would require the repeated handling of five hundred miles of paper or, alternatively, a stack of cards over ten miles high.[8]

Herman Hollerith's proposal for new equipment to handle the load made use of electricity for the first time by sensing contact through the punched holes instead of probing mechanically with needles. By the 1930s, clusters of specialized machines were being linked together by electrical switching systems to perform elaborate operations in statistics and accounting. At the same time, other approaches were experimenting with using electrical components not just for switching between subsystems but also for performing the computations. A system developed by George Stubitz and installed at Bell Laboratories in 1939 used several thousand relays as binary elements in a solver of the "complex number" equations that are extensively used in electrical work—an extension of the use of switching relays perhaps to be expected in a telephone company. But these were still giant, single-purpose calculators—direct descendants in the conceptual sense of Leibniz's cog-driven adder, not of his flight into the fancy of automating thought. The line can probably be traced through to the cabinets of specialized, hard-wired switching circuits that were still controlling things like machine tools and typesetting machines in the 1960s, but it effectively came to a dinosaur end with the advent of low-cost programmable computers.

The Harvard Mark I machine, or ASCC, standing for Automatic Sequence Controlled Calculator, first proposed in 1937 as a research calculator for helping solve problems connected with electrical engineering and completed in 1944, probably represented the *Queen Mary* of its kind. It stood fifty-two feet long by eight feet high against the wall, had twelve full-height panels of plug boards, four paper tape feeds, two card readers, a card punch, and two electric typewriters. Internally, a rotating shaft running the length of the machine used electrically operated clutches to transfer number representations between subsystems containing seventy-two addition registers and sixty twenty-three-digit-capacity storage registers.

It's probably no exaggeration to say that the computer that I carry with me on an airplane has over a billion times its power.

1. Covered fully in Pratt.
2. Hayes describes a lexical scanner for Roman numerals, giving an idea of the cumbersome manipulations involved.
3. See Murray, chaps. 6 and 7, for an account of the innumeracy woes of the period.
4. For more on medieval calculating clocks, see Pratt, chap. 3.
5. To take a different example, in the navigation tables published for the British Board of Longitude in 1767, more than a thousand mistakes were identified by one user. Pratt, p. 82.
6. For general treatments of Babbage's work, see Dubbey; Hyman; and Morrison and Morrison.
7. In fact, n can even be infinite, which sounds as if the computation will never end. Such expressions, however, can usually be manipulated into a form where the higher terms quickly get too small to make any difference worth worrying about, and the computation need only be taken as far as is necessary to obtain whatever accuracy is required.
8. Randell, p. 129.

4

Logical Mind

"The world does not encourage a perfectly rational lover, simply because a perfectly rational lover would never get married. The world does not encourage a perfectly rational army, because a perfectly rational army would run away."
—G. K. Chesterton, *Father Brown* series

The end of the 1930s brought the giant calculators—assembly lines for producing results out of numerical components—which had never been conceived of as anything else. As far as mechanizing human reasoning goes, we left Leibniz in the early eighteenth century, pondering over a better language for representing the reasoning process. At that time this meant the valid construction of syllogisms and their organization into logical arguments, which was the system that had been studied exhaustively since the time of Aristotle. Since a large part of "intelligence" is generally thought of as an ability to think logically, this might be a good place to make sure we have a clear idea of what this means before going on to consider how it might be achieved artificially.

Searching for Truth

REASONING

Reasoning is a process for arriving at a conclusion as to whether or not a given "proposition" is true. A proposition is a statement that can be affirmed or denied, i.e., judged to be true or false (unlike a question, a command, or an exclamation). The proposition "Gottfried is a scientist" might be true or it might not. The same cannot be said of "What does Gottfried do?" or "My word, a scientist!" Logic is the art of manipulating propositions.

To reach a conclusion, one or more propositions are accepted or assumed as the starting point, perhaps from being agreed on as self-evident (straight lines cross at only one point) or, literally, "For the sake of argument, let's assume that . . ." From these, the truth or otherwise of further propositions are claimed to follow until a final proposition can be evaluated, for which the others—the "premises"—are said to provide the proof. The collection of propositions leading to a conclusion is called an argument. A particular proposition can at the same time be the conclusion of one argument and a premise in another, just as a man can be son to one person and father to another. Thus:

If, *(Premise)*,
 "It's nine o'clock already" is true,
Then, *(Conclusion)*,
 "I've got half an hour to make the nine-thirty flight," is true.
Also:
If, *(Premise)*,
 "I've got half an hour to make the nine-thirty flight," is true.
And, *(Premise)*,
 "I need forty minutes," is true,
Then, *(Conclusion)*,
 "I've missed it," is true.

Arguments come in two categories: *deductive* and *inductive*. A deductive argument claims (validly or invalidly) to show that the conclusion follows necessarily from the premises, that it is absolutely impossible for the premises to be true without the conclusion being true also. An example would be that if all parrots are birds, and Polly is a parrot, then Polly is a bird. An inductive argument claims to show *some* evidence for the truth of its conclusion but not enough to make it certain, such as inferring a general truth from a number of instances. An example would be guessing that since every bird seen has a beak, all birds have beaks. Inductive arguments are evaluated not as valid or invalid but as being more or less *probable*. Someone who had been living among birds for fifty years would have a lot more confidence in such a conclusion than an alien who landed yesterday and had seen only ten local ones. Induction forms the substance of science and most of what we refer to generally as "common sense" reasoning. We shall have more to say about this in chapter sixteen.

IT STARTED WITH THE GREEKS: CLASSICAL LOGIC

The term "mechanical" is virtually synonymous with "predictable." What defines a machine is that when it is set in motion, a definite series of actions follows (some computer users and car owners I know might disagree). What Leibniz had in mind when he talked about mechanizing thought was mechanizing the system of deductive logic.

We mentioned earlier that deductive arguments are traditionally built from structures called syllogisms, which consist of three propositions. The classical study of logic focused on a type of proposition known as *categorical propositions*, which make statements about "categories," or classes of things, affirming or denying that one class is included in another, in whole or in part. The class of all parrots, for example, is included in the class of all birds. The class of birds, however, is only partly included in the class of animals with green coloring (since some, in fact, most, birds fall outside it).

Categorical propositions are usually expressed as a statement of the degree to which a "Subject" class of things—let's call it "S"—is contained in a "Predicate" class of things—no guesses, "P." There are four standard forms, conventionally denoted in a conveniently memorizable way by the first four vowels of the alphabet, A, E, I, and O. Using our piano-playing scientists from the previous chapter once more as the example:

A *The Universal Affirmative:* "All scientists are pianists."
Affirms that the class of scientists is universally, or completely, contained in the class of all pianists. All members of S are included in P.

E *The Universal Negative:* "No scientists are pianists."
Denies that the class of scientists is included in the class of pianists to any degree. S and P contain no members in common.

I *The Particular Affirmative:* "Some scientists are pianists."
Affirms that the class of scientists is partially included in the class of pianists. S and P contain some common members.

O *The Particular Negative:* "Some scientists are not pianists."
Denies that the class of scientists is completely included in the class of pianists. Members of S exist who are not members of P.

AN AID TO CLARIFICATION:
JOHN VENN'S DIAGRAMS

Already we may find that we have to pause for a moment to visualize clearly just what a proposition is saying. An aid often used for this is the so-called Venn Diagram of intersecting circles—see Figure 4.1.

The left-hand circle, S, represents the class represented by the subject (scientists); the right-hand circle, P, that class represented by the predicate (pianists). Since each circle represents a class of things, the area of overlap represents all things that are common to both S and P—which defines another class. The remaining portion of the left-hand circle represents all things that are members of S but not of P (scientists who are not pianists); similarly, the remainder of the right-hand circle represents all things that are members of P but not S (pianists who are not scientists).

Depending on what is affirmed or denied by the propositions of a particular argument, each of these classes may or may not contain members. A

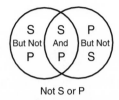

Not S or P

Figure 4.1 Venn Diagram Showing Two Classes

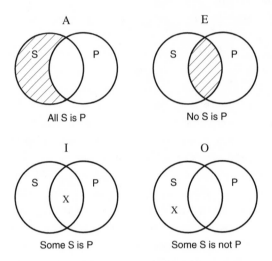

Figure 4.2 Venn Diagrams
Illustrating the Four Standard Categorical Propositions

class that contains no members is one that doesn't exist. This is indicated by shading out the corresponding section of the diagram. The four standard categorical propositions are shown in Figure 4.2.

A states that "All S is P," i.e., all of S that exists does so as part of P. No S exists that is not part of P. Hence, the part of S shown as lying outside P doesn't exist and is shaded out.

Similarly, E states that "No S is P," i.e., all of S that exists does so outside P. Hence, the part of S shown as lying inside P doesn't exist and is shaded out.

I states that "Some S is P." This means that at least one member of S exists that is also a member of P. We indicate it with an "X."

And finally, O states that "Some S is not P," i.e., at least one member of S exists that is not a member of P, and again it is indicated by the X.

I'm dwelling on this a little to give a feel for the kind of intricacies that this can lead into—and because I think it will probably be of interest to most people reading a book like this. Is it obvious, for example, that if it is true that some scientists are not pianists, then it may or may not be true that no scientists are pianists? But if it is false that some scientists are not pianists, then must the proposition "No scientists are pianists" also be false?

There are various ways in which propositions logically relate to each other, which is what building logical arguments is all about. Two propositions are *contraries* if they cannot both be true—a scientist can't be a pianist (A proposition) and a nonpianist (E proposition) at the same time; in other words, there is no class S. But both could be false—if only some scientists are pianists, then both A and E are false.

Two propositions are *subcontraries* if they can both be true but not false, for example, I and O.

Two propositions are *contradictories* if both cannot be true but one must be, for example E and I.

And finally, one proposition *implies* another if the first cannot be true unless the second is also, for example, A implies I. These relationships are summarized in a diagram called the Square of Opposition—see Figure 4.3.

But this is only the beginning. More relationships spring from such operations as interchanging subjects and predicates ("All pianists are scientists," etc.); taking the *complements*—all things other than those specified by the given terms—("All nonscientists are nonpianists" . . .) and replacing the subject with the complement of the predicate and the predicate by the complement of the subject ("All nonpianists are nonscientists" . . .). Frequently, some of these

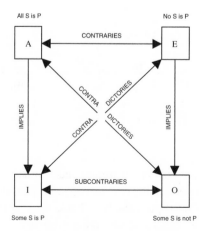

Figure 4.3 The Square of Opposition

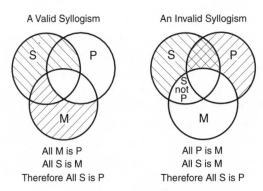

A Valid Syllogism

All M is P
All S is M
Therefore All S is P

An Invalid Syllogism

All P is M
All S is M
Therefore All S is P

**Figure 4.4 Venn Diagrams
for a Valid and an Invalid Syllogism**

propositions *seem* to be saying the same thing but turn out, on closer analysis, not to be.

And this is all just to express the relationship between two propositions—to state succinctly what both of them taken together mean. We haven't gotten into syllogism yet, which involve three propositions. Just to round it off, a *categorical syllogism* is one made up of three categorical propositions and involves three classes of things. A corresponding Venn Diagram has a third circle to represent the additional term, intersecting the other two so that an area exists for each possible class that might exist. The conditions stated by the two premises are marked as before, and the result is inspected to see if it conforms to the conclusion. If it does, then the syllogism is valid. In Figure 4.4, a further class, M, all Married people, is added. The diagrams show an example of a syllogism that is valid, and one that is not.

In the first case:

All married people are pianists (shade out nonexistent married non-pianists).

All scientists are married (shade out nonexistent unmarried scientists).

Therefore, all scientists are pianists, which is confirmed from the diagram by noting that the existing scientist class that's left (unshaded part of S) is completely included in pianists, P.

In the second case:

All pianists are married (shade out unmarried pianists).

All scientists are married (shade out unmarried scientists).

Therefore all scientists are pianists. But that is not confirmed from the diagram, which shows a class (S not P) remaining that consists of members who are scientists but not pianists. Hence, the conclusion stated does not follow from the premises given.

Venn Diagrams weren't introduced until late in the nineteenth century (by the English logician John Venn). No wonder the bickering over which meant what lasted through centuries of the Middle Ages, when it was all argued through in interminable, tortuous language. This was what Leibniz was trying to extricate things from in his search for a language to represent reasoning. Since Leibniz was a mathematician, it is likely that he had in mind something more symbolic and suitable for manipulation than the forms of everyday use, but a system based on formal rules comparable to those of numerical mathematics eluded him. This had to await the appearance of another Victorian logician, a contemporary of Babbage's, George Boole.

Symbolizing Logic

BOOLEAN ALGEBRA:
GEORGE BOOLE'S LAWS OF THOUGHT

George Boole (1815–1864) was an English mathematician who established a successful private school in Lincoln and went on to become professor of mathematics at Queen's College, Cork, in Ireland. Boole's contribution was the development of a symbolic system, still used extensively today, for example, in the design of switching networks and electronic logic circuits. It was originally intended to clarify relationships between "sets."[1]

A mathematical set, very close to the classical concept of a category, is a collection of objects having some property that defines them as members of that set, for example, the set of all cats. What extends the idea beyond categories is the introduction of the "universal set," which contains everything, and the "null set," which contains nothing. These make possible a practical system of rules for manipulating sets as symbols in a way comparable to ordinary arithmetic, in which the universal and null set play roles analogous to "1" and "0" and are denoted accordingly.

In place of the familiar operations of addition and multiplication, we have:

The "union," C+P, of two sets C and P, defined as the set of all objects that are members of C, P, or both. Thus "Cats+Pets" consists of wild cats, other pets, and pet cats.

The "intersection," C.P, is the set of all objects that are members of C and of P. "Pets.Cats" consists of objects that are cats and pets.

C → A means C is a "subset" of A, or C "implies" A, when all the members of C are included in A. Thus, all cats are animals.

Finally, *C means the "complement" of C, the set of everything not included in C. *Cats consists of everything that's not a cat.

The rules for relating these basic identities don't look the same as those of familiar arithmetic. For example:

C+C = C   (the union of a set and itself is itself)
C.C = C   (the intersection of a set and itself is itself)
C+1 = 1   (the union of a set with everything is everything)
C+*C = 1 (everything is either a cat or not a cat)
C.*C = 0 (nothing can be a cat and not a cat)

A further basic identity is that when it is true for sets C and A that
C.*A = 0, then C → A. (In other words, if nothing exists that is a cat and
not an animal, then if it's a cat, it's an animal. Try it on a Venn Diagram
and see.)[2]

From these beginnings, a whole algebra builds up that has the power
to untangle complex logical implications in the kind of way that regular
algebra makes it easier to keep track of relationships between numeric
variables. Here's an example, taken from Lewis Carroll, who was a logician as well as a writer of children's stories.[3] Consider the following group of
propositions:

1. No cat that loves fish is unteachable.
2. No cat without a tail will play with a gorilla.
3. Cats with whiskers always love fish.
4. No teachable cat has green eyes.
5. No cats have tails unless they have whiskers.

What can be made of this?

Well, let's divide the universe of all cats, "1," into the following sets:

F Fish-loving cats
T Teachable cats
L cats with taiLs
G cats that play with Gorillas
W cats with Whiskers
Y green-eYed cats

The first proposition states that the set of Fish-loving cats *and* (i.e., intersection with) the complement of the set of Teachable cats has no members.

1. F.*T = 0

Similarly, for the other four propositions:

2. *L.G = 0
3. W → F

4. T.Y = 0
5. L → W

From what we said earlier, rules, 1, 2, and 4 can be transformed into:

1. F → T (cats that love fish are teachable)
2. G → L (cats that will play with gorillas have tails)
4. T → *Y (teachable cats do not have green eyes)

All the propositions are now expressed in the form of subsets, which means one set contained within another. Arranging them in the order 2, 5, 3, 1, 4 yields a succession of subsets contained within progressively larger sets:

$$G \to L \quad L \to W \quad W \to F \quad F \to T \quad T \to *Y$$

Obviously, the smallest, at the left-most end, must be contained in the largest, at the right-most. Hence, G → *Y, or in words, "No green-eyed cat will play with a gorilla," an inference hardly obvious (to me, anyway) from the five propositions in their original verbal form.

Mechanizing Logic

BABBAGE'S VISION: THE ANALYTICAL ENGINE

This gives an idea of the kind of thing Charles Babbage had in mind for his Analytical Engine when he talked about manipulations of symbols standing for more than just the operations of regular algebra and arithmetic. Unlike the Difference Engine, which was brought to a successful completion—though not by Babbage himself, as we have seen—the Analytical Engine was never built. (In 1889, Babbage's son did put together a cut-down version of the central "mill" from drawings his father left. It worked, though somewhat stickily, and still exists in London's Science Museum.) It was remarkable, nevertheless, for anticipating in every vital concept the general-purpose computer as we know it today.

Designed to be driven by steam power, it would have stood ten feet high by ten wide and five feet deep. The mill corresponded to a central processor of numbers (or more general symbols) brought from a store to which results would also be returned—columns of wheels standing forty-one wheels high. The system was programmable. Touring Europe in search of innovations that might be relevant, Babbage discovered and applied the method of sequence control using punched cards that the French engineer Joseph Jacquard (1752–1834) had perfected for specifying the patterns to be woven on a mechanical loom. Babbage's implementation used two sequences of cards, one to tell the engine what operation to perform next, the other giving the storage columns of the numbers to be operated on and where the result was to be put back, exactly the functions of the instruction register and address registers of a modern computer. And finally, the Analytical Engine had what we would call "conditional branching," the ability to choose an alternative continuation from a key point in a sequence, depending on the outcome of what went before. This originated with the provision of a "sign" wheel at the top of each storage column, the function of which was to keep track of whether the number stored was positive or negative (just like the sign bit in a computer data word). A lever activated by the sign wheel could signal when a number changed through zero, for example, marking the end of a countdown sequence. This in itself was enough to cause astonishment among contemporaries. But its significance went further. For it introduced into the machine the ability to manipulate a symbol representing something other than a number, which could initiate any pattern of rules that might be associated with it. It could manipulate, for instance, symbols representing the logical operations that George Boole was formulating at that very time.

There were others upon whom the significance of the Analytical Engine's general potential was not lost. One of the most often cited is Ada, Lady Lovelace,[4] who envisaged it processing a symbolic language able to implement laws governing change of any relationships, for example, musical composition. But Babbage became embroiled in a constant process of revision of various submechanisms, testing, and redesign, and the project never emerged as a coordinated whole. Here, he was genuinely up against the state of the art at the time, and this was doubtless a source of much of his frustration. He died somewhat embittered, better known in his day for his vociferous campaigns against the noise of street musicians than for the inspirations that have become appreciated only in more recent years. In 1879 the British Association for the Advancement of Science commissioned a study of the feasibility of completing the project from the drawing that he left, but came to the conclusion that such a machine could not be built.

BEYOND PROPOSITIONS:
GOTTLOB FREGE AND THE PREDICATE CALCULUS

Aside from the limits of current engineering techniques, another factor that may have contributed to Babbage's ongoing conceptual revisions and changes of plans was the extension of logical science itself that was taking place during this period, presenting such an enterprise with a foundation that was constantly shifting.

It had become recognized that much of everyday reasoning and observation can't be expressed in the traditional forms of propositional logic—the kinds we have looked briefly at. Simply, the real world that we have to deal with involves more than just classifying things into categories that do or do not have a particular property. Real-world things, for example, differ from one another by having a property to a greater or lesser degree, or in a higher or lower number of instances. Propositional logic was able to handle this kind of thing to some extent by asserting relationships between classes of things defined according to their degrees of generality, such as: "Some cats are wild. All wild animals are health hazards. Therefore some cats are health hazards."

But many arguments in which degree of generality is crucial depend on relationships that exist not between propositions but within the propositions themselves. Thus, the statement "Every cat has an owner" includes a relationship, "being owned by," between cats and owners, the generality of which determines the truth or falsity of the proposition. But propositional logic handles the whole proposition as an impenetrable atom, unable to say anything about its internal relationships.

Needed, then, was a way of defining basic elements (such as cats and owners) that are not propositions in themselves and that combine statements about their relationships into expressions that could be true or false. This was provided in 1879 by Gottlob Frege, a German mathematics professor at the University of Jena, in the form of what today is called the *predicate calculus*. Here, "predicate" (not to be confused with the sense in which the same word appeared earlier—when did logicians ever make life easy for others?) is a logical entity with a true or false value but one containing "arguments" (again used in a sense different from before—this time taken from the mathematicians' use of the word) that are not logical variables. Thus, a predicate OWNEDBY (P,C) could be constructed that stood for relatedness of a particular cat C to a person P by virtue of being owned, which may or may not be true depending on whether the condition is satisfied. In conjunction with "quantifiers" denoting degree of generality, predicates can be used to construct statements in the form of "For all C there exists a P such that OWNEDBY (P,C)," which to the rest of us means, "All cats have owners."

FORMALIZING MATHEMATICS: RUSSELL'S PARADOX

What Frege did, in effect, was treat propositions in the manner of a mathematical function. This had great applicability to mathematics itself and suggested for the first time the possibility of deriving all of arithmetic and mathematics systematically from a single set of logical axioms. The question such an endeavor sought to address can be summed up as "Is there a consistent set of axioms from which all true theorems of mathematics can be proved?" ("Consistent" means incapable of generating contradictions, for otherwise how would we know which of its proofs were true?) This goal was also pursued by such noted names as Georg Cantor and Giuseppe Peano in the final decades of the nineteenth century, and by 1902, Frege believed he had accomplished it. Then Bertrand Russell, the English philosopher and mathematician, wrote him a letter showing that one of the axioms in his system was guilty of generating a contradiction: Frege's Axiom (v) yielded the theorem that if a set were a member of itself, then it was not a member of itself. This is the famous "Russell's Paradox."

It's typically quoted in the form "If the barber shaves everyone in the

village who doesn't shave himself, does the barber shave himself or not?"
(Smart answers like "no because the barber's a 'she'" aren't allowed.)
Whichever way you try and answer, you arrive at the opposite of the assumption you begin with.

An alternative illustration I rather like is to suppose that all the adjectives of the English language are divided into two sets: those that describe themselves and those that do not. For example, "polysyllabic" is polysyllabic, whereas "monosyllabic" is not monosyllabic; "English" is English, but "French" isn't French, and so on. Let's call all the adjectives that describe themselves *autodescriptive* and all the ones that are not *heterodescriptive*. We could use these as headings of two columns in which to list all adjectives on one side or the other according to which type they fall under. Now, "heterodescriptive" is an adjective, yes?—and since we said our list was to cover all adjectives, it ought to be included somewhere. So which column do we put it in? Well, let's suppose that "heterodescriptive" is heterodescriptive. But that would mean it describes itself, which would make it autodescriptive. Okay, let's put it under "autodescriptive" then. But that means adjectives that describe themselves, and by definition "heterodescriptive" doesn't describe itself, so it will have to go under "heterodescriptive" . . . And so you go round and around.

KURT GÖDEL: SOME QUESTIONS
WILL ALWAYS BE UNDECIDABLE

Despite this torpedoing of Frege's formulation, further attempts to establish a complete axiomatizing of mathematics continued. From 1910 to 1913, Russell and Alfred North Whitehead published their celebrated three-volume *Principia Mathematica*, which avoided Frege's fate by effectively outlawing self-referencing. But hopes of a complete formal foundation for all of mathematics were finally run aground in 1931 by Kurt Gödel (1906–1978), an unknown twenty-five-year-old Austrian mathematician, with his famous proof[5] that no consistent formal system that is at least rich enough to express arithmetic can prove every true statement. In other words, at least one true statement will always exist that can't be proved one way or the other within the rules of the system. (Argument continues to this day as to whether or not this theorem says anything about a machine's ability, even in principle, to "think.")

What Gödel did was show that in any sufficiently powerful and consistent symbolic system, a statement can always be encoded in the language of the system that says, in effect, "This statement cannot be proved using the rules of this system." The intriguing result is that it has to be true. But let's suppose that it's false. Since it says it can't be proved, that means it can be proved. But then the system would have proved a false statement, which means the system is inconsistent. So the original statement must be true, which means that a true statement exists that no amount of manipulation of the symbols of the system will ever prove.

Had such a system existed, the implication would have been that all of mathematics, in all its branches and elaborations, could be deduced from a tiny set of axioms, a process that something like the Analytical Engine could accomplish automatically. But we see that long after Babbage's time, the situation was far from settled with regard to knowing if such a system could even exist, let alone how to formulate it. It's hardly surprising, therefore, against this background, that thoughts of mimicking human cognition went into abeyance and the technical advances of this period concentrated more on the engineering, commercial, and administrative needs that resulted in the giant calculators. When the question of imitating human thinking again came to receive serious attention, the model used wasn't drawn from calculating machines or data tabulators at all but from work more directly involved with the workings of the brain itself.

1. Boole (1847), (1854).
2. Of course, there are scores of books that one might cite as references on symbolic logic. One that I found less daunting than most was Suppes.
3. For an entertaining treatment of the subject, I can't resist adding Bartley.
4. For example, Menabrea.
5. Gödel.

5

Cybernetic Mind

"He who studies the nervous system cannot forget mind, and he who studies mind cannot forget the nervous system." —Norbert Wiener, *Cybernetics*

A Control-Theory View of Mind

Descartes wondered if the mind was no more than an elaborate bundle of reflexes. Freud was so taken by the complexity of the Viennese sewer system that he speculated about the brain in terms of an intricately connected hydraulic network directing flows of biological energies. By the early decades of the twentieth century, the brain had become a telephone exchange busily routing incoming sensory callers through to local switchboards in the motor system. The 1940s saw a movement toward viewing mind from the perspective of "control theory." General control theory had been advancing rapidly as a result of work in two particular fields: the study of how biological systems manage to keep vital functions constant within narrow limits and the concentration on developments in control systems engineering that took place during World War II.

FEEDBACK

The most fundamental level of control is "regulation," which means keeping some quantity at, or close to, some desired value, even when it tends to drift or other influences try to change it. The best-known example from everyday life is the ordinary room thermostat. In order to decide whether to turn the furnace on or off, the system has to "know" if the temperature that its output commands

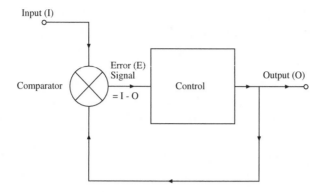

Figure 5.1 Basic Feedback Control System

are supposed to regulate is above or below the setting that it's been given, which is its input. Hence, it needs to compare the output with the input, and if a difference exists between them, it uses this to produce an "error signal" to instruct the regulator which way to alter the output. In effect, the system responds in such a way as to make the error zero. Figure 5.1 shows a general schematic form of the arrangement.

The output is fed back to be compared with the input, hence the term "feedback." In the thermostat example, the signals are all of the simple "on/off" variety (temperature below setting or not; turn the furnace on or don't). More sophisticated systems feed back an actual measure of the output value to produce a varying error signal that will drive the system hard when the error is large but slacken off smoothly as the error gets closer to zero—an automobile cruise control, for example. The principle should not be thought of as essentially new. James Watt used it in his design for an improved steam engine in 1781, in which a pair of weights spinning with the driveshaft were thrown outward against a spring under centrifugal force, opening or closing the steam supply valve through a linkage as the shaft revolved slower or faster.

It gets more interesting when the input, instead of having a fixed value like a temperature or speed setting, is also a variable; in other words, instead of just keeping the output at a constant level, we're tracking an input quantity that's changing. One of the earlier examples of this is a ship's "steering engine," which turns the rudder, possibly weighing tens of tons, to follow the movements of the wheel up on the bridge. In a more modern setting, the input might be the position of an attacking aircraft reported by radar and the output the commands to an automatically controlled antiaircraft gun trying to predict its path.

The path from output to comparator and through the control system forms a closed loop in which the current condition at the output is sensed and used to generate a result that eventually makes itself felt back at the output. Nothing in the real world happens instantaneously, and so it takes time for the effects of a signal to propagate around the loop. When the delays get too long, undesirable things start to happen. Imagine, for example, the result of adding a two-second delay into the loop formed by your visual system (comparator of where the car is in relation to the center of the lane, where it ought to be) and the steering response of your car. What would happen is a rapidly growing series of over-compensations until you either go off the road or into oncoming traffic. Such a system is said to be "unstable." The effects become particularly dramatic when the oscillations induced resonate with natural mechanical or electrical frequencies of the physical system and can result, for example, in a structure literally shaking itself to pieces.

BIOLOGICAL FEEDBACK

Feedback had been shown early in the century also to be the key to the way biological systems—with little tolerance for extremes of physical conditions—manage to stabilize things like body heat and metabolic chemical concentrations in a world full of fluctuations and disturbances, a phenomenon known as *homeostasis*. A variation of a half a degree centigrade is generally a sign of illness. But it turned out that feedback was also crucial to the correct operation of the nervous system—now known to consist not of simple connecting fibers but astonishingly complex chains of interconnected branching cells—in coordinating voluntary motor movements. A patient with impaired feedback might, for example, walk with a peculiar kicking gait that requires constant visual fixation upon the feet because internal sensations that normally report the conditions of the muscles and joints are lacking; another might make wild swings in the air forward and backward past an object when trying to grasp it, unable to "home in."

Homeostatic functions are different from voluntary ones in that they involve much slower rates of change; hence, they should be able to get by with lower propagation speeds of signals. And this turns out to be the case. The nerve fibers reserved for regulating homeostatic processes—the sympathetic and parasympathetic systems—typically lack the outer layer of myelin that enables fibers serving the voluntary system to transmit impulses faster. The smooth muscles and glands that constitute homeostatic actuators are slow in their action compared to the striped muscles responsible for regular movement.

The Brain as
an Information Processor

What brings engineering control theory and biological feedback together is the common notion that emerges of them as processing and routing flows of *information*. Information theory itself was a new field of specialization that was emerging as a science of its own with the rapid prewar growth of telephone and radio communications. Claude Shannon, who would publish a full mathematical treatment of information theory in 1948,[1] was applying Boolean algebra to the design of the switching circuits for the Bell Telephone Laboratories electrical-relay calculator mentioned in chapter three and made it the subject of his master's thesis at MIT.[2] Seen now as an information processor, the brain became freed from the role of conductor of some kind of biological energy that Freud, for example, had cast it in, becoming available for consideration, later, as what would come to be called a computer.

NORBERT WIENER AND "CYBERNETICS"

The system that sought to unify elements of these fields into a single discipline for exploring their common grounds was Norbert Wiener's *Cybernetics*,[3] which he defined as "the science of communications and control both in machines and living organisms." Wiener began as a mathematician at Harvard but developed into more of an all-rounder, dabbling along what he called "frontier areas," studying logic and statistical mechanics under Bertrand Russell in England, physiology and neurophysiology with Dr. Arturo Rosenblueth of Harvard Medical School (the term "homeostasis" was coined by Walter Cannon, a colleague of Rosenblueth's), and servocontrol systems at MIT with Dr. Yuk Wing Lee during World War II—in fact, in connection with the control of anti-aircraft guns.

Another characteristic common to biological and engineering control systems was that even subsystems that are stable in themselves can interact in peculiar ways when connected together and cause the system as a whole to go into unpredicted modes of behavior. The motion of a hand or a finger, for example, involves a system with a number of joints whose final output is given as a complex resultant of all the individual actions, which cannot be stabilized by a single feedback. Although overall final coordination is obviously necessary, the coordination was found in such situations to be built up from local coordination of subsystems and subsubsystems organized hierarchically rather than in response to central step-by-step direction. This required not only communication between the individual processes but also between levels of coordination. Studies by Wiener and Rosenblueth in the mid-1940s of the control of heartbeat and the leg-muscle contraction of the cat[4] and analysis of neural operations by Warren McCulloch and Walter Pitts at the Medical School of the University of Illinois[5] contributed to a growing understanding of neurons not just as complex interconnection channels for information but as logical switching elements in their own right.

By 1943, McCulloch and Pitts were mimicking neural connections with artificial cells, which some years later led to their incorporation into techniques for enabling the blind to read printed material by ear. The notion, involving the use of photocells to produce a distinctive tone for each letter, was not especially new in itself, and a number of methods had been tried with reasonable success. The difficult part was to keep the sound constant irrespective of the size of type being scanned. McCulloch and Pitts's approach involved scanning the letter at a series of different magnifications and comparing the results with standard templates of a fixed size. The selective reading was done by cells arranged in several layers incorporating feedback loops in much the way that neural arrays are, in fact, frequently connected; indeed, on being shown a schematic of the system in 1947, one neurophysiologist asked, "Is this a diagram of the fourth layer of the visual cortex of the brain?"[6]

THE BRAIN AS A SWITCHING NETWORK

The analogy between the all-or-nothing firing of neural cells (as they were understood then) and the on-off characteristics of, first, relays, and, by the postwar period, the vacuum tubes used in machines whose construction the war had stimulated and from which the general computer would emerge, was unavoidable. Could the biological networks that resulted in mental logic be imitated by artificial networks of switching logic? Various speculations followed, casting various functions of the brain in roles modeled on the emerging technology: memory, for example, perhaps operated through the reactivation of characteristic patterns flowing around circuits analogous to feedback loops. Since there would be no trace of when the first activation took place, it was conjectured that this might explain the peculiar vagueness of memory with regard to time—in general, unless there is some strong association to pin it to, we can recall the nature of an event fairly accurately but tend to be unsure when it took place. Suggestions for emulating thinking with artificial nets were received enthusiastically, and it was claimed that such systems would be equivalent to the general digital computers then being conceived. The claim turned out to be exaggerated, however, or, at least, premature.

Wiener himself, in the summer of 1940, had sent a memorandum[7] to Vannevar Bush, who had built several mechanical "analyzers" at MIT for solving differential equations, with recommendations for a more advanced machine using the techniques then coming into use or being considered. Basically, they were that a future machine should:

1. Use numerical representations, not rely on measurement of mechanical quantities like shaft rotation, as in the present analyzers (what we would call "digital" as opposed to "analog").
2. Use vacuum tubes for speed, not gears or relays.
3. Employ binary, not decimal, arithmetic.
4. Apart from data input and output, operate entirely under the direction of internally stored programs.
5. Include a fast-access internal store.

Apart from its specification of binary arithmetic, this list could be read virtually as an updating of Babbage's concept of three quarters of a century previous and an accurate prediction of the von Neumann architecture that emerged within a decade and remains standard to this day. In fact, John von Neumann was a close acquaintance of Wiener's and attended many of the cyberneticists' meetings.

In this period, it's probably true to say that it was the cyberneticists more than anyone else who both understood the computer conceptually and, with their involvement in biological and neural systems, glimpsed its potential for modeling the mind. The pure mathematicians understood the machines' capabilities, of course, but in the main their interest was focused on their applicability in advancing mathematics. Also, there were engineers and administrative users who were gaining experience with the new machines, but, again, experience was confined within the applications that had produced the giant calculators. Just as Wiener had claimed to be his own field of calling, it was in the boundary area unexplored by established disciplines that his science found its element.

What drew the interest of the cyberneticists to computers initially was the prospect of using them as programmable simulators for modeling nerve-net configurations. But it soon occurred to some that this might be a roundabout way of going about things. If neural systems were just nature's biological hardware for handling the abstract representations of the world that we call thinking, why use a computer to model the biology, which is incidental? Why not use it instead to manipulate its own representations directly?

The question followed from a growing appreciation in the postwar years of a potential that set the computer apart from any machine that had ever been built before. Before carrying on with the story of AI, the next chapter examines this more closely.

1. Shannon (1948).
2. A paper in the AIEE Transactions, Shannon (1938), was based on the thesis, which has been described as "one of the most influential master's theses ever" (Pratt, p. 197).
3. Wiener.
4. Rosenblueth, A., N. Wiener, and J. Bigelow (1943).
5. McCulloch and Pitts.
6. Wiener, p. 22.
7. Ibid., p. 3.

6

Calculator to Computer

ALAN TURING'S UNIVERSAL MACHINE

"Where a calculator on the ENIAC is equipped with 18,000 vacuum tubes and weighs 30 tons, computers in the future may have only 1,000 vacuum tubes and perhaps weigh only 1.5 tons." —*Popular Mechanics*, March 1949

"I think there is a world market for maybe five computers."
—Thomas Watson, chairman of IBM, 1943

Back in the 1960s in London, I worked for Honeywell as a computer sales engineer specializing in real-time scientific and industrial applications. (A "real-time" application is one in which the flow of time in the real world sets a maximum limit on how long a computation can be allowed to take. In areas that involve rapidly changing situations, such as missile guidance or industrial process control, a result is obviously worthless if it takes so long to produce that the circumstances it was supposed to address no longer exist—it's no good aiming at where the target was two seconds ago. Real time therefore usually means on-line: sensors and actuators wired directly into the processing system.) One of our customers at that time—actually a subsidiary of a U.S. corporation—was a leading manufacturer of typesetting equipment that it sold throughout Europe. A typical machine came as two huge cabinets, one of which performed the actual typesetting function, while the other contained the electronic logic to direct it. I was earning the British-pound equivalent of somewhere between $5,000 and $7,500 per year, which was considered a pretty good salary at the time. The electronic controller cost about $120,000. Its logic circuits were hard-wired, which meant that modifications and updates involved messy engineering changes and costly labor overheads, and incorporating extras or variations to suit different user needs was virtually out of the question. We replaced the controller with a sixteen-bit general-purpose computer that cost $10,000 and fitted into the typesetter, thus making a separate control cabinet unnecessary. And it could readily be reprogrammed to incorporate modifications or special customer requests. In fact, one of the big selling points of the system became the attraction of acquiring a general-purpose computer to play with as part of the deal, not just as a typesetting system. (This was thirty years ago, after all; everybody didn't have one sitting in his office, and probably at home too, in those days.)

Special Purpose
and General Purpose

I mention this because it illustrates something of what distinguishes a general-purpose computer from special-purpose machines able to do just one job. We're not talking about price and size here. The difference that matters has to do with a limitation on capability in one case that is inherent in the fundamental class of devices that it belongs to, in contrast to an absence of any such limitation in the other. This can be best understood by stripping away the irrelevancies and simplifying each class down to its minimal theoretical bones. But before doing that, let's prepare the conceptual ground by looking at the simplest class of all, which is known as "finite-state" machines or "finite-state automata."

FINITE-STATE AUTOMATA

A good example that I've come across[1] that illustrates the principle is the older-style turnstile that can still be seen at some stations on the New York subway system. This is an extremely finite-state system. In fact, it has two states: locked, when the turnstile won't turn, and unlocked. There are two input functions that can be applied to the system: (1) inserting a token and (2) pushing against the bar. Putting a token into a slot alters the locked condition to the unlocked state. Rotation of the bar through ninety degrees to allow a person through causes a transition back to the locked state, denying further admission without another token. Nothing else—threats, promises, the fact that you're a celebrity or a doctor with an emergency to get to—means anything in the internal mechanism's limited conceptual universe.

How the machine responds to an input depends on what the input is and which state the machine is in when the input is applied. Pushing against the bar while the machine is locked doesn't do anything. Inserting a second token in the unlocked state results only in an unnecessary alteration to the contents of your pocket, not any further transition within the machine. (Although if the authorities had been really mean, I suppose they could have arranged for this to

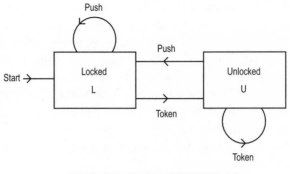

**Figure 6.1 Functional Diagram
and State Transition Table for a Subway Turnstile**

take it back to the locked state again, thereby charging you two tokens to get back to where you started.) This is summed up in Figure 6.1, which is a more compact way of saying the same thing.

So why can't a party of us save time and hassle by putting all our tokens in at once and filing through? The reason is that the mechanism can't count how many tokens it has received. It has no memory apart from the rudimentary one of having two different states that tell it whether its last input was a token or a push. No record exists of anything that happened before that.

This isn't true of all coin-operated devices. Vending machines involve more states than two and reject extra coins after entering the state where the correct sum of money has been accepted. A set of traffic lights is a finite-state machine; a typewriter is another, where every keystroke advances the cycle through a series of carriage and roller positions. A digital clock showing the month, date, and time down to seconds has 31 million states, each of which it visits precisely once a year. What they all have in common are:

a number of states that are discrete, or clearly distinguishable
a finite number of them
inputs and outputs that can occur with any state
effectively instantaneous transitions between states, i.e., short compared to
    the duration of a state
and the key defining feature, no memory external to the system

Many biological processes can be represented as finite-state machines—for instance, the transcription of DNA code into proteins via cellular enzymes. The restrictions of permissible energy transitions that quantum mechanics imposes make the atom a finite-state machine. This is an example of a particular type, perfectly permissible, in which the output (emission of a photon) depends on the transition, not on the initial state; also, a transition can take place without application of an input (spontaneous emission).

Locking and unlocking subway turnstiles, transcribing three-letter genetic codes into the next amino acid of a protein sequence, or emitting one of a limited repertoire of photons doesn't equate to a capacity for very colorful varieties of behavior. And this is the point. What turns such a device into something that justifies being put in a class apart is adding the capability that the finite-state machine lacks: unlimited external memory. In fact, astonishing as it may seem, a machine thus equipped is capable of computing anything that can be computed. To see the relevance of this, we need to go back to where we left things in the world of mathematics at the end of chapter four.

HILBERT'S CHALLENGE AND TURING'S MACHINES

Kurt Gödel, in 1931, had toppled any further hope of deriving all mathematical theorems from one consistent set of axioms. In other words, not all theorems that were true were provable. That would have been nice because mathematicians could then have set about the task of mechanizing a process to generate a list of all of them. Then, to see if a particular theorem was true, it would only have been necessary to check the list to see if it appeared there. Very well, if that wasn't possible, was there a way to tell which theorems were provable? Given a conjectured theorem and the set of axioms, was there a way to decide whether or not the theorem derived from the axioms, even without certainty of its being true? This was included as one—the "decision problem"—of a list of unsolved problems that mathematician David Hilbert presented as a challenge before the International Congress of Mathematics held in Paris in 1900. After Gödel showed that there was no hope of formally deriving every true theorem, this became one of the crucial issues of mathematics. Among the people who took up pursuit of the question, and the one who finally settled it, was Alan Turing.

Alan Mathison Turing (1912–1954) was a British mathematician remembered, like Babbage before him, for his early insights into the principles of general computing and whose name is associated with machines. Unlike Babbage's, the machines that Turing conceived were never intended as more than thought experiments to clarify the methods of mathematical proof by reducing them to mechanical, step-by-step operations—or, as we would say today, analyzing them in terms of computational algorithms. Any computation, it turned out, could be broken down into steps that could be performed by a minimal finite-state machine with a large enough memory.

In 1936, when he was a fellow of mathematics at King's College, Cambridge, Turing published a paper proving that the answer to Hilbert's question was "no."[2] By an argument that referred to one of his abstract machines, Turing was able to show that no formal procedure could decide whether a given proposition was derivable from a stated set of axioms. The result went far beyond the immediate problem, for in answering it, Turing had shown that a class of problems existed that no amount of computing could resolve.

Although in fact no more than a logical construct, a so-called Turing Machine is usually depicted as a device embodying a finite number of physically unspecified states and a movable head with the abilities to read, write, or erase a symbol of whatever coding scheme is to be used (customarily shown as 0 and 1, but it doesn't have to be, as long as the alphabet of symbols is finite in length). The head steps along a tape that can be any length, divided into fixed-position frames for storing symbols. Operation of the machine consists entirely of discrete steps. At the beginning of each step, the machine has two inputs that determine its action: the state that it is presently in and the symbol appearing in the tape frame currently being read. Its response is specified by an instruction table—the equivalent of the state transition table for the turnstile—which for every possible input combination supplies three things: the symbol to write into the current frame of the tape, the internal state to assume next, and the direction to move, left or right, for the next frame.

To give the general idea, let's consider a Turing Machine for adding two "unary" numbers together, M and N, represented by strings of 1s on the tape and separated by a 0. What we want the machine to do is produce a string of $(M+N)$ 1s and then stop (its final state). What would accomplish this would be shifting the left-hand string one position to the right and simply eliminating the 0. A Turing Machine can't shift multiple 1s together, however, since it can only move one frame at a time, so it would have to break the operation down into simpler steps. One way the machine could do this would be to scan the tape from left to right, doing nothing but step and inspect the next frame, until it encounters the first 1. It changes that 1 to a 0 and enters a new state, which means "First 1 found. Looking for 0." It then continues moving to the right, altering neither its state nor the succession of 1s that follows. When it finally encounters the 0 separating the two strings, it changes the 0 to a 1 and proudly assumes its "done" state.

Most small Turing Machines, namely, ones with only a few possible states, do not carry out any useful or even sensible task but typically get hung up in endless cycles of shuttling back and forth along the tape. Yet by combining a few well-chosen routines, the power of the Turing Machine increases explosively. Turing was able to prove that a routine, or a combination of routines, could, given a possibly large but nevertheless finite amount of time, compute the solution to any problem for which a computable solution existed. Any polynomial expression, for example, can be evaluated by combining routines for adding, copying, and multiplying. But no machine of that nature could be devised that would solve Hilbert's problem. Thus, the problem was insoluble.[3]

THE UNIVERSAL TURING MACHINE

This, in Gödelian fashion, dealt a second body blow to the visionaries who had sought a mathematical Eden permanently cleansed of the risk of getting sullied due to human frailty. But it also had further implications that concerned the entire theoretical future of computing. Every Turing Machine is uniquely defined by its table of instructions, and the table must be of finite size since the number of machine states is finite and so is the alphabet of tape symbols it uses. Hence, *any* Turing Machine, TM, can itself be encoded on a tape, say, as a sequence of 0s and 1s. So it isn't necessary to build lots of different machines to perform various specialized computational tasks in the kind of way the monstrous Mark I at Harvard linked together data-handling subsystems. The specialized TMs can all be simulated by the operation of a "Universal Machine." Such a UM would take the symbol sequence that a particular TM would encounter in the process of tackling a given problem, consult the encoded version of that TM on the tape to determine what the TM's action would be, and take the same action itself, identically. In a way, it could be thought of as redefining its parts to suit the requirements of the moment as it proceeds, instead of having to possess all kinds of different specialized parts, most of them for most of the time doing nothing. Or, another way to think about it might be to say that a UM can use a relatively small number of states—a number realizable in practice—to perform a virtually limitless variety of operations that would otherwise require impossibly huge numbers of states.

The Modern Computer Emerges

ONE SIZE FITS ALL: PROGRAMMABILITY

This flexibility, as we have said, stemmed from giving the machine access to unlimited external storage. The store doesn't have to be a tape light-years long. The bulk of it might comprise, for example, a library remote from the machine, of applications that we aren't interested in today. But for practical application— where results would be preferred sometime between now and the next ice age—the part we are using should be organized into sections so that the instruction tables and scratch pad recording what's currently going on can be available in some rapidly accessible form. This is another way of describing a machine that is *programmable*, with at least a working area of reasonably fast storage. This is the crucial concept that defines the modern computer—

possibly so taken for granted today that we tend to lose sight of what makes it so different from anything that has gone before.

Although it isn't an essential feature of the theoretical Universal Machine, we're almost certainly also talking about a practical machine's being electrical. The cumulative error that creeps into mechanical linkages attempting to communicate numbers from one part of a machine to another was what defeated Babbage's engineers. Electrical signals, especially with the adoption of binary representation as exemplified by Claude Shannon's relay systems, can be routed through wires anywhere, with high immunity to distortion. Relay systems like the Bell calculator were a lot faster than cogs and levers, and general-purpose versions, though thousands of times slower and bulkier than what we have become accustomed to today, would probably have been feasible. In fact, in 1939 in Germany, an engineer by the name of Konrad Zuse proposed a design for a relay-based machine that recapitulated Babbage's concepts of punched data and program instructions (on paper tape), a central processor served by an addressable store but one that lacked conditional branching.[4]

MACHINES WITH THE SPEED OF LIGHT:
ELECTRONIC SWITCHING

The key, however, to handling complex computations efficiently, the forerunner of silicon-crystal transistors and hence the integrated circuit chips of today, was the electronic vacuum tube, adapted to the role of logic switching with the systems that appeared during World War II. The simplest kind of vacuum tube, the diode, had been invented by J. J. Fleming in 1904 as an electrical "valve" (the term still used in England) to allow electrical current to flow only one way. It works rather like a diving board, where you can leap off but not back again, with electrons playing the part of divers and being propelled by an electric field instead of gravity. In 1906, Lee de Forest added a mesh "grid" into the path, which allowed a small applied signal to produce large changes in the current of hurtling electrons, enabling the tube to be used as an amplifier in the kind of way that power steering makes it possible for alterations of finger pressure to guide a truck. Turning such a tube either full-on or full-off makes it a two-state device like a switch, capable of representing the variables of two-state Boolean algebra. Therefore, it can be built into logical and computational switching networks like relays but operating millions of times faster. One of the early experimenters in this was John V. Atanasoff, an applied mathematician at Iowa State College, who in the 1930s used electronic switching as the arithmetic unit of a device for solving large systems of algebraic equations, with the numbers to be operated on held in banks of capacitors.[5]

In Britain the prime application to make use of this capability was the deciphering of military and diplomatic communications codes, which the British, through the agency of the Admiralty's "Room 40," had pioneered and excelled at in World War I. One of Room 40's more spectacular triumphs was decrypting the famous "Zimmermann telegram" in February 1917, in which Germany sounded out Mexico as a potential ally in the event of German hostilities with the United States, offering the return of Texas, New Mexico, and Arizona as an inducement. The information was released to the press following its disclosure to the Wilson administration and guaranteed—or at least served as adequate justification—for the U.S. entry into the war soon afterward. The fiction of a master spy who had purloined a copy of the telegram in Mexico was invented to conceal the true source. The Germans continued to use the channel, and the exchange of furious accusations of security lapses and indignant denials that followed between the Foreign Office in Berlin and the German embassy in Mexico were read with amusement by the denizens of Room 40 in London.[6]

By the time of the Second World War, the mechanized encryption techniques that the Germans had introduced (the Enigma system)[7] demanded higher-horsepower methods to crack than could be brought to bear by a room of tweedy intellectuals, however brilliant, armed with calculators and statistical tables. The center of the British effort was at Bletchley Park in Buckinghamshire, where Turing designed a series of machines known as "bombes," after the Polish *bomba*, prototype devices built by the Poles in the course of some effective prewar intelligence work on German encoding systems. One of the more sophisticated designs was the COLOSSUS series, which employed around two thousand vacuum tubes and operated from 1943 onward.

ENIAC—ELECTRONIC LEIBNIZ WHEELS

At about the same time, Helmut Schreyer, who had collaborated with Zuse in Germany on the relay calculator, built an electronic version but failed to get government backing. In the United States, John Mauchly at the Moore School of Engineering in Pennsylvania was looking for something to replace the mechanical differential analyzer being used to produce artillery tables. A big limitation of analog calculators, which represent numbers by the magnitude of some physical quantity like the amount of rotation of a disk, is that to work to one more decimal place of accuracy means machining and measuring to ten times the precision, which can easily mean ten times the cost—and that's only when the goal sought is technologically practicable anyway. With a digital system you use the same circuits to add on as many places as you want. (Whether or not you have data pertaining to the real world that makes the extra precision meaningful is a separate issue. An egg timer that counted to milliseconds wouldn't make much sense.)

Again, the solution was to turn to electronics. This was provided by ENIAC, financed by the Ordnance Department and eventually completed in 1946, which used 18,000 vacuum tubes. Instead of switching binary digits, however, the circuits were connected as ten-state "ring counters," in which ten successive pulses shifted each stage through a cycle (finite-state system again) then sent a "carry" pulse to the next stage—"electronic cog wheels."[8]

JOHN VON NEUMANN AND THE FINAL COMPONENT: INTERNAL STORED PROGRAM

Although ENIAC worked, it wasn't a Babbage Machine with a central "mill" but instead consisted of specialized subsystems linked together, more in the manner of the Harvard Mark I. Its main shortcoming, as with all these early ventures into electronics, was the complexity involved in setting it up for a particular calculation. Although the use of punched cards or paper tape enabled different sequences of instructions to be specified, the card and tape readers couldn't hope to keep up with the internal electronics, which sat idle for most of the time, waiting for something in the outside world to happen. The answer to this was to put the currently executing portion of the instruction sequence into electronic form too, along with the numbers being operated on. (It would have been nice to have the whole instruction sequence in electronic form, of course, but the equipment for 18,000 tubes needed a small power station and there was enough to fill a ballroom as things were.) Thus came the proposal in 1945 for a new machine with a "stored program," the final element of the computer as we know it. This was the contribution of von Neumann, who had become a consultant to the Moore School project a year previously.

John von Neumann (1903–1957), a Hungarian, has been described as one of the most brilliant mathematicians of the twentieth century. Also very much involved in Hilbert's earlier school to develop an axiomatic foundation for mathematics, he turned his attention away after Gödel's demonstration that the program could not be carried through and became the first person to formulate the probabilistic interpretation of quantum mechanics. In 1933 he moved to the United States to become a professor of research mathematics at the newly founded Institute for Advanced Study at Princeton. One of the stories told about von Neumann concerns the problem—familiar to most people these days—of the fly buzzing back and forth between two approaching trains. Usually it goes something like, "Two trains, A and B, start out 140 miles apart, heading toward each other, A at forty miles per hour and B at thirty miles per hour. At the same time, a fly that travels at sixty-five miles per hour leaves A, flies to B, returns to A again, and continues crossing the diminishing distance between them in that fashion. How far will the fly have flown by the time they pass?" The trick is to convert the problem from the distance domain to the time domain and spot that at the combined closing speed of seventy miles per hour, the 140 miles will be eaten up in precisely two hours. It then follows easily that in that time the fly will cover 130 miles. As the story goes, von Neumann, on being given the problem by a colleague, went quiet, thought for a while, and returned the correct answer. The colleague laughed and said, "Oh, you saw through it. Most people try to work out a series of decreasing terms and compute the sum." Looking puzzled, von Neumann replied, "But that's what I did."

The machine that von Neumann's proposal engendered was the EDVAC, installed in the Moore School as ENIAC's successor after the war. Von Neumann himself went on to develop the IAS Machine at Princeton, which became operational in 1952, employing all the concepts that characterize the "von Neumann architecture," still the standard today.[9] There was close communication among the community that had produced both the British and American wartime systems, however, and the first electronic machine to use an internally stored program was probably the MADM at the University of Manchester in England, first run in 1948 by a team under M.H.A. Newman, several members of which had contact with the Moore School. Alan Turing himself was also building a machine called ACE at the National Physical Laboratory in Teddington, which he described in a lecture to the London Mathematical Society in February 1946.[10]

One thing that these machines and others being conceived or taking shape at around this time sought were alternative methods of internal storage. Electronic tubes with their speed were indispensable for the central processing registers that were in use all the time, but Times Square–like arrays of them guzzling megawatts of power were hideously expensive and placed serious restrictions on executable program size and the amount of data that could be kept immediately available. The possibilities explored included dots of charge stored on cathode-ray screens, magnetic wire, and acoustic pulses recirculating through delay lines. The massive WHIRLWIND project at MIT used magnetic core storage for the first time, introducing what would remain the principal main-memory storage device until the advent of cheap semiconductor RAM (*R*andom *A*ccess *M*emory) in the seventies.

Reprogramming and set-up was still a horrendously complicated task that involved patching plug boards, rerouting cables, and managing libraries of card stacks and reels of paper tape. But these were the beginnings of the global industry we see today of harnessing electronic speeds and total recall to do the things that computers do best, from the information-shifting earthmovers that support Wall Street, weather-system simulators, and galaxy-colliders to supermarket checkouts and the home PC. All are working demonstrations that we take for granted today but which, early on, few people appreciated because they did not know what the cumbersome contrivances meant and what they portended—the first-ever possibility of realizing the Universal Machine that Alan Turing had envisaged in 1936—a machine that could compute anything.

---

1. Hayes, who also shows finite-state machines for translating the generic code into protein and modeling the theology of Thomas Aquinas.
2. Turing (1936).

3. See Hopcroft for more on Hilbert's problem and Turing's paper. For a general biography of Alan Turing, see Hodges.

4. See Pratt, p. 155. Also, Zuse's paper "Some Remarks on the History of Computing in Germany," included in Metropolis, Howlett, and Rota.

5. Pratt, p. 136.

6. For more on World War I decryption shenanigans: Ewing; Friedman (1976), (1977); Tuchman; and West.

7. And on World War II Enigma code breaking: Beesley, Calvocoressi, Cave Brown, Jones, and Winterbotham.

8. A full account of ENIAC's workings is given by H. H. Goldstine and A. Goldstine, "The ENIAC," in Randell.

9. The IAS Machine is referred to in some places as the JOHNNIAC (after von Neumann), which can be confusing since a machine built by the Rand Corporation in California at around the same time is also generally known by the same name. We'll talk more about the Rand JOHN-NIAC later.

10. "A. M. Turing's ACE Report of 1946," Charles Babbage Institute Reprint Series, vol. 10.

7

Computational Mind

". . . although there are limitations to the powers of any particular machine, it has often been stated, without any sort of proof, that no such limitations apply to human intellect."
—Alan Turing,
Computing Machinery and Intelligence (1950)

The First-Ever Versatile Machine

Leibniz had conceived the idea of mechanized reasoning as an extension of mechanized calculating, but he had been stuck for a suitable language of representation. Babbage had available the logical algebra that Boole was developing, but not the technology for a practicable machine. The electronic, stored-program computer offered in a single package the potential to do anything that any calculator could do, anything that any office system could do—and more.

If the human mind specializes in anything, surely that thing is versatility. We don't need different heads for calculating, speaking, reading, dreaming, and so on that we have to change all the time like the attachments for a vacuum cleaner. The generality of the new machines provided an analogy with minds in a way that nothing previous had even come close to suggesting. If they could be programmed to do anything that was possible with numbers and manipulate the logical symbols of propositional and predicate calculus, then what about the rest of the things that the mind can do as well? Norbert Wiener wrote in *Cybernetics*, "The mechanical brain does not secrete thought 'as the liver does bile,' as the earlier materialists claimed, nor does it put it out in the form of energy, as the muscle puts out its activity. Information is information, not matter or energy." And information was the stuff that computers worked with. Computers seemed to be saying something very important about mind and its nature, although it was not clear exactly what.

Turing's 1950 Paper

THINKING MACHINES?

In October 1950, Alan Turing published a celebrated paper entitled "Computing Machinery and Intelligence,"[1] the opening sentence of which reads: "I propose to consider the question, 'Can machines think?' " Well, you couldn't put it more directly or succinctly than that. Not much that's useful can be given by way of an answer until we're clear on what's meant by "machine" and "think." Turing makes it plain that what he means in the first case is a digital computer, and he devotes some space to acquainting his readers with what a digital computer is. In the second half of the 1990s, and especially after the last chapter of this book, let's hope we don't need to go into that. More worth stopping to take a look at would be what he had in mind when he said "think."

THE TURING TEST

Turing seems to have been a person who defined things not abstractly but in terms of concrete procedures necessary to demonstrate them. To attack Hilbert's problem, which was essentially one of logic, he expressed it as computations that could be performed by imaginary machines. His proposal for establishing what constitutes thinking was presented in similarly operational terms. Let's not, Turing says in effect, get bogged down in the kind of philosophical and semantic quagmires that result from speculating about unobservables that go on inside people's heads, and talk instead about how we would expect to know a thinking entity when we meet one. What kinds of things would it be able to do that entities we don't consider capable of thinking—rocks, potatoes, all the programs run on digital computers by that time and since—can't? This is the "Turing Test," which is alluded to a lot, though usually in a somewhat simplified form.

The way that Turing proposed the test was that two subjects, one a man, A, the other a woman, B, answer the questions of an interrogator (man or woman) who is in contact via a terminal (in his day, a teleprinter) with each of them and no one else. The interrogator can pose questions of any kind. The object is to determine which of the subjects is which, when A's aim is to mislead the interrogator and B wants to be identified correctly. Turing's guess is that B's best strategy would be simply to answer truthfully. Injecting appeals like "I'm the woman, don't listen to him!" achieve nothing because A can just as easily say the same thing. The crucial question then becomes, If a machine takes the place of A in the game, will the interrogator be wrong as often as in the first case? When the interrogator is evidently unable to discern a difference, the machine will have become as artful as a human in displaying the skills needed to deceive another human successfully—with all the implied capacity for thought that entails. (The version usually cited today is that the interrogator communicates with a human and a machine trying to come across as a human. The snag here, it seems to me, is that a successful test could mean a smart machine or a not-very-smart interrogator. Perhaps the answer would be to let the machine being tested play the interrogator.)

In characteristic Turing fashion, this test refuses to be drawn into unresolvable arguments about subjective sensations like awareness and feelings. What Turing had in mind to probe by this kind of approach becomes clear from the questions he used to illustrate a sample dialogue:

Q: Will X please tell me the length of his or her hair?
A: My hair is shingled, and the longest strands are about nine inches long.
Q: Please write me a sonnet on the subject of the Forth Bridge.
A: Count me out on this one. I never could write poetry.
Q: Add 34957 to 70764.
A: (After about thirty seconds) 105721.
Q: Do you play chess?
A: Yes.
Q: I have K at my K1 and no other pieces. You have only K at K6 and R at R1. It is your move. What do you play?
A: (After a pause of fifteen seconds) R-R8 mate.

Nothing particularly onerous or demanding—*in its respective field*. But consider the diversity of human knowledge and experience that is represented by even just these few questions. *Versatility*, in a word, was what Turing was looking for. It would have been pretty clear that before very much longer there would be programs able to play games, look up information, handle office routines, interpret scientific data—and even advise on hairstyles and write sonnets; but when it could turn its hand to *any* of them with the same alacrity that justifies our claim to be "thinking"—and converse about them at the same time in a natural language—then by what distinction would it not qualify for being described as a thinking entity too? Turing concedes readily that it might well be a different "kind of" thinking—and then goes on to ask why that should trouble us.

Turing identified the critical requirements as enough memory, adequate speed, and appropriate programming. He believed that after fifty years they would be well enough met to give the average interrogator a not-better-than 70 percent chance of getting the right answer after five minutes of questioning. As would any good scientist, he listed and responded to a lengthy list of opinions opposed to his own. Some were making a big thing out of Gödel's proof that, for every machine, questions could be asked that it was incapable of answering.

Turing didn't attach much importance to this as saying anything about limits on thinking—there are plenty of questions that people can't answer either. With regard to Lady Lovelace's observation regarding the Analytical Engine, that it could only do "whatever we order it to perform," usually expressed as "machines can never take us by surprise," Turing responded that on the contrary, "Machines take me by surprise with great frequency."

For the most part, the objections have a feel about them of rationalizations cloaking a deeper rejection on principle of any notion that thought could emerge from mechanical matter. In a way, this recapitulated the position of the vitalists of the previous century, who insisted that the phenomenon of life couldn't arise from chemistry and that animate matter had to contain a mysterious "something extra" to explain it. Drawing such an analogy doesn't prove that those disagreeing with Turing were wrong, of course—indeed, nothing that has happened to this day proves them wrong. But as Turing observed in his paper, the thousands of machines that everybody encountered in a lifetime all added to the conclusion that machines are ugly, highly restricted in their variability of behavior, useless for any purpose other than that for which they were designed, and so forth. All the machines built before the advent of the digital computer were limited in the number of states they were capable of assuming—closer to the New York City subway turnstile than the brain of even an insect. With simply no experience of truly vast machines, it was understandable that people should hold such views on the nature and limitations of what a machine is.

By contrast, he estimated the number of possible states that could be assumed by the MADM Machine, then being built at the University of Manchester, as $10^{50,000}$, a number so inconceivably huge that no metaphor can suffice to give a sense of it. And this was based on its memory capacity of 165,000 bits, which is laughably small by the standards of the machines that children today play games on, in comparison to which the "state space" of the MADM shrinks into insignificance. And the human brain, in turn, is still vaster than those by many orders of magnitude. (When I visited mathematical physicist Frank Tipler of Tulane University in New Orleans, he said that the theoretical limit is given by the number of discrete quantum states that can exist in a volume of space the size of the human brain at a given energy density—a number known as the "Beckenstein Bound." I told Tipler I'd always thought that was a dance step.)

A Huge Finite-State Machine

THE BRAIN'S MECHANICAL BASEMENT

So are we saying that the brain is a huge, finite-state machine, immense beyond imagination in the number of different states it can be in but finite nevertheless? This is the hypothesis that Turing was proposing, with its corollary that whatever the brain can do, a general-purpose computer ought to be able to do also. And that remains the core of AI thinking today. Lady Lovelace's objection is often repeated in the form "A machine [or computer] always responds in the same way to the same inputs." This is true in a sense but not in the way intended. As we saw with the turnstile, a machine that's *in the same internal state* will respond in the same way—specified in its transition table—to a given input or combination of inputs. When the number of possible internal states becomes huge, it's improbable that the same one will ever precisely repeat twice. Indeed, even if everything else were identical, the memory of the situation as having occurred before would still create a different internal state from the previous occasion, in general giving rise to different behavior as a consequence.

Yes, some would say, but that still isn't convincing. Thinking is unpredictable and original, whereas computers operate purely mechanically and can only carry out what they're directed to. And certainly it is true that at its elementary level a computer is constructed from components that function predictably and repetitively. But then, the same could also be said about us. The molecules of DNA, proteins, and other constituents of the cells making up our bodies function in ways that are totally mechanical and repetitive. The brain's basic neural hardware consists of bewildering interconnections of an enormous number of neurons, each of which behaves predictably. If the excitory and inhibitory inputs that reach a neuron add up to a value that exceeds its activation threshold, it will fire; if they don't, it won't. The neuron doesn't go through agonies of indecision trying to make its mind up what to do. At its level there isn't any property of "mind" to make up. The decision is made according to fixed rules, just like the decision of a logic circuit to generate an output.

TRANSCENDING THE PARTS:
EMERGENT PROPERTIES

On a larger scale, the Earth's atmosphere consists of a vast number of interacting molecules. Each in itself is a simple entity, responding at the microscopic level to the jostlings of other nearby molecules in ways that are mechanical and predictable. But at the macroscopic level, totally new *emergent properties* manifest themselves as storm centers, cloud banks, and so on that can only be expressed in such macroscopically meaningful terms as temperatures, pressures, humidities, and so forth, which help make up the world of our experience.

There is effectively no limit to the number of different books that have been written or could, one day, be written. We might describe our impression of one we've read as "inspiring," "passionate," "entertaining and witty," and so on. These seem to be real properties that evoke real feelings. So where, in these creations, do such properties exist? At its elementary level, every book consists of letters drawn from the same, very limited alphabet of characters and punctuation marks. Clearly, it would be ridiculous to look for traces of inspiration or passion at that level. A letter of the English alphabet can be one of only twenty-six possibilities, so the amount of information it can convey is very limited. But just the act of stringing letters together to form words can convey enough concepts to fill all the dictionaries of all the world's languages, plus form all the other strings of letters that might have been words but which, as it so happens, aren't. Just this simple raising to a higher level of organization brings about an increase in richness and a possible variety of expression that is staggering. And, beyond that, words can be arranged into sentences, sentences into paragraphs, until at higher levels it becomes possible to express everything from nursery rhymes to encyclopedias.

Language is organized as a hierarchy of increasing complexity. New orders of meaning and relationship come into existence that cannot be expressed as properties of the elements that form the lower levels, but they arise from the ways in which these elements are put together. In the same kind of way, every musical composition is built from the same scales of notes, and every material substance from the same set of atoms, which, in turn, arise from the same three subatomic particles. Perhaps the most striking illustration is the way in which the chemical computers inside every living cell read three-letter words from the same four-letter alphabet and, operating through programs involving layer upon layer of complex feedback and control, assemble the same constructor kit of amino-acid parts into the different proteins that make up every plant and animal. Thus, a single amino-acid molecule does not possess an attribute of "elephantness"; a sufficiently large number of them, however, put together in the right way, do.

PREDICTABILITY SUBMERGING:
THE WHIMSICAL MACHINE

As the capacity for the expression of wider realms increases at successively higher levels, the precision and predictability that characterizes lower-level activity is lost. Behavior takes on a progressively greater degree of uncertainty and "whimsy," requiring qualitatively new terms and concepts to describe it. Weather patterns cannot be predicted from equations of molecular physics; protein assembly codes don't describe the moods and behavior of elephants; a novel's emotional impact isn't contained in its rules of syntax. The concepts that take on meaning at the higher levels of such hierarchies grow more abstract—farther removed from the low-level world of immediate physical reality—and are communicated in different languages. Above the level of molecular machinery operating via electrical forces, the various cells and organs of the body exchange messages written in chemical messages and patterns of nerve impulses.

The question such considerations prompted, then, was, Are "minds" that think and communicate in terms of persons, places, ideas, and things emergent phenomena that arise from the brain's manipulations of higher, more abstract representations still? The symbolic information-processing view of mind said yes, they are. The fallacy with the machines-are-just-mechanical objection lay in comparing the functions of the brain's highest, most abstract level of operation with the computer's lowest, most physical. It was a bit like saying that DNA and transcription enzymes could never equate to an elephant because all they do all day is mechanically build amino acids into proteins, while elephants can do things that are variable and more interesting.

THE COMPUTER AS A HIERARCHY

And the general-purpose computer too was a hierarchical system of organization in which the units of information being handled took on progressively more abstract meanings with ascending levels. At the lowest level of all, the physical circuits lead a somewhat monotonous life comparable to that of a neuron, shuffling binary digits through registers and combining them according to purely mechanical rules. At the lowest level of software activity that this hardware traffic supports, the bits combine into codes that represent numbers, characters, and instructions in order to convey meaning in the more symbolic terms in which programmers, rather than hardware engineers, think. And at higher levels still, these codes are subsumed into representational languages whose functions quickly lose all connection with electronics and program codes but relate instead to the real world of geometric shapes, objects, images, and logical constructs. Given the right program—and this is perhaps where Turing underestimated the task—could not "mind" emerge from such a hierarchy of progressively more complex and abstract representations of concepts and perceptions in the same way that it does in the biological counterpart? Admittedly, it had taken the program that puts biological brains together a long time to reach its present form. But, then, on the other hand, that had started with blobs of jelly floating around at the edges of the oceans. Shouldn't a few Ph.D.'s of computer science, equipped with the same head start that had already enabled humans to rival or surpass nature with traveling machines, flying machines, communication machines, and hardworking machines, be capable of doing at least as well too when it came to thinking machines? Some said yes, others said no, and the matter is still far from settled.

Representations Beyond Numbers

THE COMPUTER AS A GENERAL SYMBOL-MANIPULATOR

While these debates went on among the theorists, others had begun exploring what was possible beyond the representational realm of just numbers. Arthur Samuel at IBM—formed from the merging of Hollerith's original tabulating company and other interests—was looking into the potential for machine learning by teaching computers to play checkers.[2] Claude Shannon was sketching ideas for chess-playing programs.[3] Progress was slow, partly because computers were laborious to program and the available programming codes rudimentary; also, the few machines that existed were mainly dedicated to defense work. In fact, the first systematic investigation into using human problem-solving strategies as a guide for constructing better programs originated in such a context. This was the work begun by Newell and Simon in the early fifties.

NEWELL AND SIMON—
OBSERVING THE WAY WE *REALLY* DO THINGS

Herbert Simon's background was very different from that of the other people we've talked about so far. A political scientist and administrator, he had been involved in the Marshall Plan, which rebuilt Western Europe after the war. His special field of interest was the way in which management and administrative organizations went about the business of making decisions. In 1947 he had written a book called *Administrative Behavior*,[4] which became a standard reference on the subject and was cited by the Swedish Academy of Sciences in 1978, when Simon received the Nobel Prize for economics. In 1949, he helped found the Graduate School of Industrial Administration at the Carnegie Institute of Technology, Pittsburgh—now Carnegie Mellon University.

Simon was one of those rare people with the ability to see the world as it is, not as everyone else imagines it is. His observations told him that human organizations don't make optimal choices by rationally considering all the alternatives in the kinds of ways that textbooks—then, and still to a degree today—describe (usually before going on to derive equally unrealistic theories from that imagined behavior). The assumption that a corporation directs all its efforts on maximizing some easily measured quantity such as profit, or minimizing costs, simplifies the mathematics for producing tidy charts and diagrams but reflects little of what managers spend most of their time actually doing. The real world, with its time pressures, personal issues, and all the other factors that necessitate compromises, doesn't admit to perfection. As the British World War II general Bernard Montgomery observed, waiting until all the information is available will guarantee merely that a decision will be too late. Instead, human decision makers make decisions that are "good enough," judged, more often than not, by predetermined criteria based on experience of what worked before rather than exhaustive analysis of the situation at hand. In other words, human organizations act pretty much the way humans do. A shopper, for example, doesn't usually tour every store in town methodically listing product details and prices before making a purchase. Beyond a certain point, the saving simply isn't worth the time and effort. What we do instead is make a choice that's satisfactory, based perhaps on a few sample visits to get a feel for the going norms relating price and quality. The process of searching for a solution has an associated cost of its own that has to be taken into account, although this is seldom formally acknowledged.

The other significant thing that Simon had noticed was that in their regular day-to-day functions, the individuals and departments of an organization don't relate to the remote, overall purpose of the organization as a whole but to their own immediate aims and objectives. The Sales Department concentrates on improving sales, even if Manufacturing is behind on producing the goods. The Medical Department is concerned with acquiring new equipment. Personnel people interview, hire, and organize clubs and outings. Few of the individuals involved plan their working day in terms of the longer-term survival and profitability of the corporation. It was the same kind of hierarchical coordination that the cyberneticists had identified in engineering and biological systems. The smaller units focused on and were motivated by the achievement of their own subgoals; the prime role of management was coordinating the subgoals to the eventual attainment of the higher goals. By the early fifties, Simon had reached the conclusion that conventional mathematics did not really lend itself to expressing and modeling such concepts and was on the lookout for some alternative means of representation.

THE RAND STUDY—
THE BEGINNINGS OF A FORTY-YEAR PARTNERSHIP

In 1952, Simon arrived from G.S.I.A. as a consultant to the Rand Corporation in Santa Monica, California, for a study the company was doing for the air force on procedures followed in the regional air defense control centers for scrambling interceptor fighters. What fascinated Simon more than the study itself, however, was the technique that the Rand people had developed for modeling the entire air defense sector by means of a computer simulation. Especially intriguing was their use of an old card-programmed calculator to generate the simulated radar maps. Here was a computer being used not just to process numbers but to create points and graphics on a chart. The notion of computers manipulating symbols in general to represent procedures other than calculation might have been familiar to writers of papers like Turing's and the audience that typically read them, but to most people from Simon's world it was completely new. Here, perhaps, was a medium capable of modeling behavioral concepts in the dynamic kind of way he'd been looking for.

This project saw the beginning of a partnership that would last forty years. Allen Newell had graduated in physics at Stanford and then gone on to study mathematics for a year at Princeton before deciding that he wasn't a mathematician at heart. Seeking more involvement with tangible problems from the real world, he joined Rand in Santa Monica in 1950 and was assigned to the air defense project, which was where he met Simon. Newell had been struck by the degree to which organizational changes at the air control center could affect the performance of personnel. He had also noticed similarities between the ways people there communicated and made decisions and the ways computers handled information. This common view that he shared with Simon, of the mind as a pragmatic problem solver using rule-of-thumb methods worked out in the course of experience, sparked vigorous discussions between them virtually from their first meeting. The notion of using a computer to model some of the mind's more readily identifiable processes didn't take shape fully until 1954, however—after Simon had returned to Carnegie Tech in Pittsburgh. Oliver Selfridge from MIT's Lincoln Labs—a former assistant to Norbert Wiener—visited Rand to give a talk about a pattern-recognition program that he was working on with the aim of enabling computers to accept typescript directly as input.[5] This involved identifying the same essential features in slightly different versions of the same pattern—in other words, performing the kind of abstraction that humans do. Selfridge's program could also learn to improve its performance from experience. This in itself was groundbreaking for its time, although, as it turned out, the particular approach being followed didn't have a big future as far as AI was concerned.

But what really seized Newell's imagination was the way in which highly complex behavior could result from a collection of simple subprocesses organized and interacting in the right way. This was precisely the kind of thing that he and Simon had concluded formed the basis of human and organizational behavior. The following year, 1955, Newell left Rand and joined Carnegie Tech to work with Simon on developing a computer program that would exhibit intelligence. Naturally, they didn't expect to produce anything comparable to human capabilities to begin with, or anytime soon. But everything has to begin somewhere.

As Alan Turing said in concluding his 1950 paper, "We can see only a short distance ahead, but we can see plenty there that needs to be done."

1. Turing (1950).
2. Covered in chapter ten of this book.
3. Shannon (1950a), (1950b).
4. Simon.
5. Selfridge.

8

Computer to Symbol Processor

EARLY VISIONARIES AND THE FOUNDING OF AI

"There is no security against the ultimate development of mechanical consciousness in the fact of machines possessing little consciousness now." —Samuel Butler, *Erewhon*

Dealing with Everyday Life

THIS THING CALLED COMMON SENSE

If I need to mail a package and there's only one post office, P, in town, planning the trip doesn't involve an agonizing amount of effort. If I decide to visit the bank, B, as well, while I'm out, I can go to P first and then B, or to B first and then P, and it doesn't much matter which since the round-trip in either case is the same. Suppose now that I add the supermarket, S, to the list. The number of ways I might arrange the trip jumps to 6:

—P first, followed by B then S, or S then B
—B first, followed by P then S, or S then P
—S first, followed by B then P, or P then B

There are three possible choices for the first visit after leaving home. For each of the three, there are two possibilities for the second place to visit. And each second choice leaves a single option remaining for the place to visit last. So the number of different ways in which the trip might be organized is given by $3 \times 2 \times 1 = 6$ possibilities, usually written as 3!, or "three factorial" (all the numbers up to three multiplied together as factors). Similarly, if we add

The alternatives could be represented as follows:

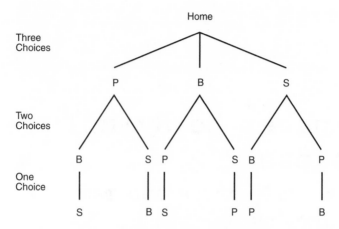

Figure 8.1 Decision Tree for Three Variables

a fourth stop, say because we realize we need to fill the car up with gas, the number of possible routes would be given by 4!, which equals 24. This is already more choices than anybody would consider when contemplating going out to perform a few simple chores. Very well, since it looks like a fine day, let's check out three appliance stores for prices on the replacement dryer we've been meaning to get and two toy stores for something for Tommy's birthday—and somewhere along the way we'll probably want to stop for lunch, which gives us ten stops total. Not unreasonable. The number of different ways we could plan the route has become 10! = 3,628,800. Just adding one more stop would raise it to almost 40 million.

It's not just that the number of choices gets bigger as the number of stops increases; it gets bigger at an ever faster rate. This is the phenomenon known as "exponential growth."

ELIMINATING THE NONSENSICAL
Humans don't spend days planning every shopping trip with calculators and maps or half their lives driving around the locality like lunatics (although parents with young children in constant need of being ferried around might be unconvinced). We arrive at decisions by processes other than considering all the alternatives and rationally finding an optimum in the kinds of ways that textbooks idealize. Rather, we use rules of thumb based on our experience to reduce the problem to something that is manageable and capable of yielding a result that we're willing to settle for. One of the first simplifications is to eliminate the usually enormous numbers of choices available for most everyday decisions, which, while theoretically possible, are so self-evidently preposterous or

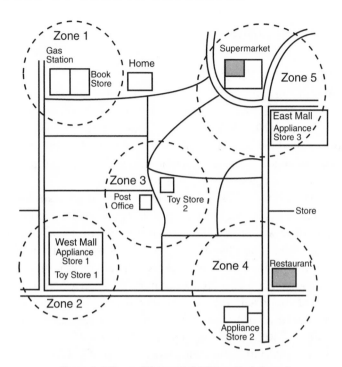

Figure 8.2 How to Reduce 3.6 Million Choices to 3

inferior that we don't even consider them. In the above example, that would cover all routes involving wild zigzags or pointless doubling back. If the situation were as shown in Figure 8.2, nobody in his or her right mind would go from Appliance Store 1 in the West Mall to look at the dryers in Appliance Stores 2 and 3 and then come back to Toy Store 1.

We'd probably not want lunch before half the chores, say, are done, which further rules out all the routes that include lunch in the first five stops. We'd look for clusterings that break the problem down into natural subunits, and, where choice permits, we'd keep within the clustering by noting things like "There's a gas station next to the bank" and "That new restaurant near the second appliance store would be good for lunch," which transforms the problem into one of making just five stops. The only sensible order to tour them in would be as close to circularly as we can manage, leaving as the only real decision whether to make it 1-2-3-4-5, 1-3-2-4-5, or 1-2-4-3-5—and, in all probability, whichever we choose won't make any difference that's worth worrying over.

The First AI Program

THE BIRTH OF "LOGIC THEORIST"

Applying rules drawn from practical experience and breaking a problem down into goals and subgoals—these were the key elements of human problem-solving behavior that Newell and Simon identified in their observations of organizations and administrators. The next step toward seeing if a computer could be programmed to work in a comparable fashion was to select a suitable subject for study. Their first thought was for a chess-playing program. Games offer a natural subject for this kind of study by providing a restricted problem domain in which the rules are clearly defined; furthermore, success is easy to measure—you either win or you lose, and improvement, or lack thereof, over time can be followed. But Shannon and others were already involved with chess, and Samuel was looking into checkers. The next possibility that Newell and Simon considered was geometry theorem proving, where there seemed more likelihood of progress. In the end, however, they settled on logic theorems—for no better reason, according to Simon, than that he happened to have a couple of volumes of Russell and Whitehead's *Principia Mathematica* at home.[1] For the actual programming, they enlisted the help of J. Clifford Shaw, who was working on the newly installed JOHNNIAC computer at Rand, named affectionately in recognition of John von Neumann.

PROVING LOGIC

Proving a logic theorem is a fairly straightforward process in principle, similar to deriving theorems in geometry. A set of premises, or "axioms," that are considered self-evident or incapable of reduction to simpler concepts is proposed. An example from geometry would be, "Two straight lines have only one point in common." The basic axioms are then operated on by a number of "rules of inference" to produce further statements, known as "theorems," that must follow and are thereby proved valid within the axioms-rules system. The inference rules may then be applied to the resulting theorems and the axioms to generate more theorems, and so on indefinitely.

The task selected by Newell and Simon was to prove theorems of the "sentential calculus," where the variables $p, q, r, \ldots$ A, B, C, $\ldots$ stand for propositional sentences, which along with their negations $\star p$, $\star$A, etc. (recall chapter four) may be combined via the *connectives* "or" and "implies" into expressions that are also propositions, i.e., capable of being true or false.

The five axioms given by Russell and Whitehead were:

1. (p or p) implies p
2. p implies (q or p)

In other words, if p is true, then the broader statement that q is true or p is true (or both) is also true. Pretty basic, really. But the whole idea of axioms is that you can't get any simpler:

3. (p or q) implies (q or p)
4. [p or (q or r)] implies [q or (p or r)]
   This is analogous to saying in ordinary arithmetic that $X+(Y+Z) = Y+(X+Z)$. Again, nothing exactly earth-shattering.
5. (p implies q) implies [(r or p) implies (r or q)]
   If it's true that "this is a pig" implies that "This is a quadruped," it will also be true that "this is a robin or pig" implies that "this is a robin or quadruped."

The rules of inference were:

RULE OF SUBSTITUTION
Any expression may be substituted for any variable in any theorem as long as the same substitution is made everywhere the variable appears. Hence, substituting "p or q" for p in axiom 2 gives: (p or q) implies [q or (p or q)]

RULE OF REPLACEMENT
Connectives can be replaced by their definitions and vice versa. It's supposed to be obvious that the connective

$$p \text{ implies } q$$

is the same thing as

$$\star p \text{ or } q$$

It wasn't immediately so to me, so let's look more closely at it. "This animal is a pig" implies "This animal is a quadruped." What we're saying is that if p is true, q must be true; but if p is false, q may be either true or false. Knowing only that this isn't a pig leaves open the possibilities that it could be a horse or a dolphin.

Now consider the second expression. "This animal is other than a pig, or it's a quadruped." When the animal really is a pig, the first part of the statement is false; however, the second part is true and makes the statement as a whole true. But when the animal is not a pig, the first part alone is sufficient to ensure that the statement is true, and whether or not q is too makes no difference. Hence, the two are indeed identical.

So, for example, we can obtain [$\star p$ or (q or p)] from axiom 2.

RULE OF DETACHMENT
If "A" is a theorem, and "A implies B" is a theorem, then
   "B" is a theorem.
   And that's about it.

ALGORITHMS

A proof is like showing that "you can get there from here" by connecting a starting point to a destination on a map, where the starting point is either an axiom that we've assumed to be true or a theorem that we have already proved to be true by deriving it from the axioms, and the destination is some "target" theorem that we want to prove. The intermediate theorems represent stops along the way, which we move through by applying the appropriate inference rules. And a computer is ideal for rapidly applying the same set of rules over and over again. So what we do is set it up first to apply all the permissible rules to all the axioms, thereby generating all the theorems that can be proved in a single step; then we do the same thing to all the one-step proofs to produce a next generation of two-step proofs, and so on. Once in a while we check the list of accumulating proofs to see if the target has appeared yet, perhaps by specifying a format that will enable theorems to be listed alphabetically in the symbol language employed. Sooner or later, if a proof (a path to the required destination) exists, the program will have to come up with it.

And that's true. Such a procedure, which systematically follows rules guaranteed to find a solution if there is one, is termed an "algorithm." The routine we learned at school for multiplying two numbers together is another example. Turing's proof in response to Hilbert's question was to show that no algorithm of the kind desired to meet Hilbert's challenge existed. But the rub comes, as far as the logic proofs go, in the "sooner or later" part that in our excitement we skated so lightly over. Trying every possibility in turn on the combination lock of a safe is an algorithm guaranteed eventually to open the safe. The lock is effective nevertheless because the cost in terms of the time needed to apply the algorithm is simply too high.

Newell and Simon dubbed the procedure for blindly trying every logic proof the "British Museum Algorithm," after the legendary monkeys at the museum who randomly tap at typewriters and, given enough time, will at some point produce all the works of Shakespeare. To find all of the sixty-odd theorems contained in chapter two of *Principia*, the number of proofs that such an unguided algorithm would need to generate, according to Newell and Simon's estimate, would be in the order of a number the size of one followed by two hundred zeros.[2] But Russell and Whitehead did it—and without using a computer at all.

The trick is to know—or be able to make a good guess at—which rules to apply and in what order. But *how do* humans know—or guess? The object of "Logic Theorist," or LT, as Newell and Simon called their program, was not to prove theorems, of which there were already more than enough to keep logicians occupied. It was to try and find out what kinds of rules of experience people use to pick which way to go next when they talk about "hunches," "intuition," things just "feeling right," and so on. By using richer systems of axioms, it would have been quite feasible to devise powerful algorithmic programs capable of outperforming humans, which shouldn't be too surprising in a field like this. In fact, within a couple of years of LT, a program was published that proved in one fourth of a second a theorem that Newell and Simon estimated would take LT "tens of thousands of years."[3] And important advances in theorem-proving programs that exploit the kind of reasoning that computers are powerful at have continued to this day. In fact, while this book was being written, there was a major news item that researchers at the Argonne National Laboratory in Illinois have finally produced a computer proof of a conjecture that logicians have been wrestling with since it was first proposed in the thirties.[4] But the purpose of LT was to explore how *humans* reason.

Human Problem Solving

DECISIONS, DECISIONS . . .
THE COMBINATORIAL EXPLOSION

Claude Shannon calculated that there are 10^{120} possible moves in a game of chess. That's a 1 followed by 120 zeros. A billion—the number of seconds in thirty-two years—is 9 zeros. A billion times a billion is the number of nanoseconds (the time that light, covering 186,000 miles in a second, takes to travel one foot); in thirty-two years yet that's still only eighteen zeros. There is no way to illustrate or grasp a number as vast as 10^{120}. The number of nanoseconds since the big bang and the number of atoms in the universe don't even come close.

If anything, surely it's the ability to deal with this problem of insanely multiplying possibilities, known as the "combinatorial explosion," that more than anything lies at the heart of distinguishing any behavior deserving to be called "intelligent" from the mindlessly mechanical. And it's not just in fields like logic or chess, or even business, science, and engineering, but everywhere in our everyday lives as we saw in the case of the shopping expedition. The number of ways to arrange furniture in a room, books on a shelf, or tools in a workshop soars astronomically as the number of items increases. But faced with countless complex tasks every day, most of the time we manage to come up with solutions that are good enough for the purpose. The object of LT was to see if some of these tricks could be identified and programmed into a computer.

HEURISTICS:
COMPUTERS ARE QUICKER BUT PEOPLE ARE SLICKER

In the logic-proving procedure we looked at above, every proof begins at some initial proposition, either an axiom or an already-proved theorem, from which possible continuations branch to further theorems, each of which leads to more theorems in the pattern of a rapidly spreading tree. Proof consists of searching the tree for the particular sequence of branchings that leads (if such a proof exists) to the target proposition. LT's aim was to find ways of pruning the search tree down and concentrating on paths more likely to contain the proof it sought. At each decision point, the program applied rules of thumb designed to identify promising candidates. It might, for example, have tried substitution, replacing one symbol with another as allowed under the axioms, or perhaps with an entire logical expression, to see if it had the target already but wrapped in a different guise. Or it might have tried working backward from the target and looking for an intermediate result whose proof would be simpler, in effect identifying subgoals. Another technique was to screen candidate branches by looking for similarities in the target's structure and the current options and using them as a guide for which substitutions to try, or else abandoning that line if the degree of matching seemed unpromising.

Newell and Simon called these rules "heuristics," a word coined by mathematician George Polya, who had been Newell's tutor at Stanford.[5] A heuristic approach may find a solution but can't guarantee it since it's always possible that, despite the designers' best efforts, the solution might lie in the parts of the tree that the heuristics fail to explore. The point, of course, is that using well-chosen heuristics makes a solution likely in a humanly reasonable timescale. Although the method does open up a possibility of failure, to a far greater degree it increases the chances of actually experiencing success.

LT'S PERFORMANCE

The result was that of the fifty-two theorems from chapter two of *Principia Mathematica* that were put to it, Logic Theorist produced proofs for all but fourteen. The departure from standard algorithmic methods of programming represented a profound step in the use of computers. Here was a machine using its knowledge of the world to grope its way selectively toward where it hoped the solution to a problem lay, possibly going the wrong way but giving up certainty in exchange for a better chance of succeeding sooner—much more like the way humans go about things. Admittedly, the knowledge had been implanted and the world was a very restricted one, but everything has to start somewhere. It's interesting to note also that even something as primitive as LT, which has been called the world's "first AI program," managed to achieve a trace of originality. The proof that it discovered for theorem 2.85 in *Principia*—which, incidentally, LT hadn't been specifically given as a problem to solve but stumbled on anyway—turned out to be shorter and more elegant than the one given by Russell and Whitehead. Newell and Simon submitted it to the *Journal of Symbolic Logic*, listing the machine as coauthor. The editors, however, missed the implication and declined to publish it on the grounds that proving something from the half-century-old *Principia* was really no big deal.

Dartmouth 1956: The Founding Fathers

JOHN MCCARTHY NAMES THE NEW FIELD

In June 1956, Newell and Simon were able to exhibit preliminary runs of Logic Theorist at the Dartmouth College conference at Hanover, New Hampshire, often cited as the official birthplace of AI. As the only team present with an actual working AI program, they made a considerable impression, not always endearing. As Herbert Simon later conceded, "We were probably fairly arrogant about it all."[6] In September they presented their first formal report to the Symposium on Information Theory held by the Institute of Radio Engineers at MIT.[7] Here, they claimed, beyond any argument, was proof that behavior that would normally be considered to require intelligence—theorem proving— could arise from comprehensible mechanical processes.

The Dartmouth conference was organized by John McCarthy, who was an assistant professor of mathematics there, having obtained his bachelor's degree at Cal Tech in 1948 and graduated from Princeton in 1951. He became interested in von Neumann's work on finite automata and spent some time with Claude Shannon investigating Turing Machines as possible agents of intelligence. While useful in some ways for modeling theories in the abstract, however, they did not offer a suitable tool for actually carrying out concrete experiments. A summer spent working at IBM in 1955 led McCarthy to the same conclusion that Newell and Simon had already reached and that others from the cybernetics movement and information-processing disciplines were also reaching: the digital computer was the way to go. So in 1956, McCarthy became the prime mover in persuading the Rockefeller Foundation to sponsor a two-month summer workshop with the aim of bringing together people from diverse fields with a common interest in thinking machines and forming some sort of a consensus on the nature of this emerging new field of study, and where it might be heading. "Artificial intelligence" was the term introduced by McCarthy to describe it then, and it persists to this day.[8]

MARVIN MINSKY AND
THE TRAINING OF THE "SNARC"

Another name present at the conference, which, along with McCarthy's, has come to form a second duo as well known in AI circles as Newell's and Simon's, was Marvin Minsky. Minsky had spent a somewhat itinerant undergraduateship at Harvard in the late 1940s, nominally a physics student working on optics but also running a project involving crayfish neurophysiology in the zoology department and designing equipment for behaviorist B. F. Skinner in psychology. As if this didn't offer enough diversity, he worked on developing mathematical models of the mind with psychologist George Miller and switched to the mathematics department to write an undergraduate thesis on topology and the distribution of the Earth's surface temperature. And in September 1956, at the same MIT symposium where Newell and Simon formally announced Logic Theorist, Miller would deliver a famous paper claiming that human short-term memory is unable to hold more than seven items at a time.[9] The paper's style convinced Minsky's tutor, Andrew Gleason, that Minsky was a natural mathematician, and, following Gleason's advice, Minsky registered for his Ph.D. with the mathematics department at Princeton.

Minsky had been influenced by the artificial neural-net approach of McCulloch and Pitts to modeling cognition and had attended Norbert Wiener's cybernetics meetings. In collaboration with another graduate student, Dean Edmonds, whose field was electronics, he decided it was time to put all the theories about reward, reinforcement, and learning behavior to a practical test and try building something that worked on the same principles. Returning to Harvard in 1951, Minsky and Edmonds raised a grant with George Miller's help from the Office of Naval Research and assembled a neural-net machine from three hundred vacuum tubes and an autopilot from a B–24 bomber. Called the "Snarc," it simulated a network of forty neurons of a rat learning to negotiate a maze. The reward system consisted of mechanically turning potentiometers associated with each neuron that had fired recently, and it was accomplished by linking them via magnetic clutches to a bicycle chain driven by a motor. The idea was that when the "rat" made a correct series of decisions to get itself out of the maze, the connections to the neurons involved with the choices along the way would be strengthened, resulting in a learning of the successful strategy. It soon became clear, however, that techniques such as this, which were based on Skinnerian behavioral conditioning, were not the answer. They allowed no way for the system to reason about what it was doing and hence exhibit the kind of planning that seemed an essential ingredient of intelligence. In a way, then, they had recapitulated with the aid of electronics the conclusion that Descartes had arrived at three centuries before.[10]

(As an interesting side note, the Snarc possessed neurons corresponding to definite points in the maze, so that when they fired, the hypothetical rat knew where it was. In 1996, when I was collecting material for this book, Dave Touretzky of the Center for the Neural Basis of Cognition, just opened by Carnegie Mellon University and the University of Pittsburgh, told me over dinner about a recent discovery of "place cells" in the brains of rats. The cells become associated with distinct physical locations in the environment and fire only when the rat is at the corresponding place. For instance, in an experimental setup, they could mark fixed points around a circular "arena." Through some ingenious experiments it was shown that the cells "know" where they are even in darkness and deprivation of other sensory data by integrating the path that the rat has followed from a known reference point such as its nest—like the aircraft "inertial" navigation system mentioned in chapter three, but in this case keeping track of ground movements instead of accelerational forces exerted on a mass. If the rat is surreptitiously moved while at the far point of a task involving an excursion from the nest—say, by slowly displacing through a distance of one foot a box that it has entered—then, sure enough, it ends up a foot out in the same direction on returning to the nest. The discovery was causing considerable excitement and controversy within the neurophysiological community; yet Snarc, with its vacuum tubes and bicycle chain, had anticipated it by forty-five years.)

THE DIGITAL COMPUTER PARADIGM:
AN INFORMATION-PROCESSING MODEL OF THE MIND

Minsky obtained his doctorate in 1954, convinced by that time that trying to coax initially random patterns of neurons to organize into systems capable of complex behavior was a dead end. It had taken nature somewhere in the order of 3 billion years to achieve, he reasoned; for someone on a more limited schedule, a better strategy might be to take advantage of already-existing intelligence by designing in as much learning capability as possible at the beginning. This would mean doing the work of thousands or even millions of neurons, and clearly he wasn't talking about an acres-wide extension of the Snarc. What it needed was a fast, compact system that could model what brains did without necessarily being built to do it in the same kind of way. And that was exactly what digital computers offered. In the 1955–1956 academic year, Minsky formed a close association with McCarthy, who was equally fascinated by the same prospects, at nearby Dartmouth and worked with him in recruiting backing for the conference.

Other notable attendees at Dartmouth, in addition to Newell and Simon and Minsky and McCarthy, were Nathaniel Rochester of IBM, who had designed the world's first production computer, the IBM 701, and who was using the newer 704 to solve numerical equations describing neural networks; Claude Shannon, whom Minsky and McCarthy both knew from work they had done in 1953 at Bell Labs; Ray Solomonoff from MIT, who had converted Minsky to the symbol-processing model; Oliver Selfridge from MIT's Lincoln Lab, the same man who had brought about Allen Newell's conversion with his talk on image recognition at Rand in California; Arthur Samuel from IBM, the experimenter with checkers-playing programs; and Trenchard More, a Princeton student who was also looking into deductive theorem proving.

Although the conference did serve the function of performing introductions and familiarizing the participants with the kinds of things that were going on, the result was not as conclusive as had been hoped. Although the groups that were represented continued to test out ideas on each other and maintained an informal contact, by and large they stuck to their own approaches without reaching any real consensus on which way the future lay. Not all were able to attend for the full two-month period. And Simon describes a coolness displayed toward the first working AI program that he found surprising, although he readily admitted that none of the others had much to offer that he particularly wanted to hear about either.

There were differences of opinion between those who viewed the newly introduced term "artificial intelligence" to mean getting machines to:

1. display general, all-round, human-level intelligence with all its subtleties and ramifications.

or

2. perform specific, environment-oriented tasks efficiently, i.e., do things that would be considered intelligent if done by humans.

This, however, was largely academic. Since not enough was understood about how minds worked (or is today, for that matter), and there was not adequate technology available for realistically pursuing the first goal, the enterprise was destined to take the form of a collection of separate projects devoted to some aspects of the second goal anyway.

The gathering set the paradigm of AI thinking that was to remain dominant in the field for decades. The opening statement, intended to set the conference's theme, proposed that "Every aspect of learning or any other feature of intelligence can in principle be so precisely described that a machine can be made to simulate it."[11] This was where the hypothesis of the mind as a symbol-processing system was in effect agreed on as the guiding assumption of AI research. The symbol structures representing the world and the manipulations performed on them are what matter, not the physical system supporting them. They can exist equally as patterns of circuit paths in an electronic system or neural connections in a biological brain. This effectively defined what became AI's dominating principle: the theory that through analysis and understanding, the processes that constitute "thought" can be specified with sufficient precision to be encoded into formal symbolic systems. Although it has been questioned and alternative philosophies have been proposed in the years that have gone by since, the formal symbolic method continues to be one of AI's mainstream philosophies today. John McCarthy, now at Stanford, has remained undeviatingly among its staunchest proponents, his sights set firmly on goal one—the attainment of general, humanlike performance.

Dartmouth thus supplied the paradigm and defined what would become the AI establishment subscribing to it. Nearly all of the significant advances in the field for the rest of the fifties and well into the sixties were made by members of that original group or by their students in a climate that was buoyantly optimistic. Carnegie Mellon and MIT grew to become major centers of AI research and were soon followed by Stanford University in California.

As for the emerging computer industry itself, commercial data processing and the perceived need to maintain technical leadership in the Cold War remained the primary driving forces of research and development effort. For the most part, this resulted in a view of computers as a means of improvement rather than radical innovation, i.e., of doing known things more efficiently and faster rather than attempting novel things. There were, however, a few pioneering minds here too, curious to discover what the new machines were capable of beyond conventional calculating, sorting, and tabulating.

1. Crevier, p. 44.
2. The original paper, Newell, Shaw, and Simon (1956), p. 108, estimates as 10^{235} the number of symbol strings not greater than twenty in length (taken as a practicable limit for a usable theorem) that a BMA algorithm would generate. In the reprint in Feigenbaum and Feldman, the number appears as a thousand, but when I queried the difference with Herb Simon, he agreed that this figure is probably too high.
3. Wang.
4. Kolata.
5. See Polya, an influential little book, still much cited.
6. Crevier, p. 48.
7. Newell, Shaw, and Simon (1956).
8. See McCorduck for more on the Dartmouth conference.
9. G. A. Miller.
10. Marvin tells me that the Snarc mysteriously disappeared and its whereabouts today is unknown. So watch out for any unlikely-looking contraption in a yard sale. It might be a priceless technological relic.
11. Crevier, p. 48.

9

Charting New Territory

THE COMPUTER AS PROBLEM SOLVER

"I have traveled the length and breadth of this country and talked with the best people, and I can assure you that data processing is a fad that won't last out the year."
—Editor in charge of business books for Prentice Hall, 1957

IBM's Geometry Theorem Prover

Newell and Simon had considered geometry theorem proving as a possibility before settling on logic theorem proving. At IBM, Nathaniel Rochester, who had attended some of the Dartmouth meetings, was impressed by a manually simulated program of Marvin Minsky's for proving high school geometry theorems. He set Herbert Gelernter, a young physics graduate who had joined the corporation, the task of developing something similar that would run on the 704. It turned out to be a more formidable task than had been anticipated, taking three years and finally requiring somewhere in the order of twenty thousand coded instructions. The result was known as Geometry Theorem Prover (GTP).[1]

As with Logic Theorist, the idea was to present the program with a target theorem to prove and see if GTP could construct a chain of reasoning connecting it back to already proved theorems and/or stated axioms. What made GTP interestingly different, however, was that instead of the input being written as a symbolic expression of the same general form as the facts already known, and therefore capable in principle of being derived from them via straightforward transformations, it was given in the same way as to high school students: as a diagram, or, more precisely, a diagram specified by coordinate points encoded on punched cards. From this the program was able to extract salient features such as parallel lines, equal line segments and angles, the exis-

78

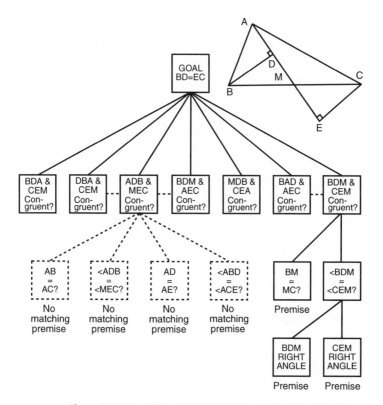

Figure 9.1 A Proof Found by IBM's Geometry Theorem Prover

tence of any right angles—the kinds of things a human would note. Figure 9.1 shows an example of a theorem given to the program and the method that was followed to solve it. Since GTP operates by working backward from the problem, the tree becomes inverted: the target is the starting point at the top, from which branches lead back in search of a path to the supplied premises.

A textbook would state the problem as requiring to prove that two vertexes (corners) of a triangle are equidistant from the median drawn from the third vertex. In the diagram, the triangle in question is ABC. A median drawn from a vertex is the line AE, drawn from A so that it passes through the midpoint, M, of the opposite side, BC. The distance to AE from the other two vertexes, B and C, are given by lines perpendicular to AE, i.e., the lines BD and CE, and the object is to show that they are equal.

Or, in summary:
Given
    Premise BM = MC
and Premise BDM and MEC are right angles
    Prove that BD = CE

One of geometry's most fruitful techniques for showing that line segments are equal is to establish that they occupy corresponding positions in two triangles that can be shown to be "congruent," i.e., capable of being made to coincide exactly if one can be slid on top of the other or flipped over and slid (like a left-hand glove to match a right-hand one). The conditions for congruence are well known and go back to before the times of Euclid. One way, then, for a program to go would be to set off, British Museum–algorithm–like, by taking every pair of triangles that contain BD and EC and applying congruence tests as indicated by the dotted paths to see if they lead to the premises. Note the first two boxes in the first row. It doesn't matter that BDA and DBA are the same triangle; an exhaustive-search algorithm tries everything in sight in a strict, systematic order. In fact, there are 144 possible pairs of triangles that meet the criteria, only 6 of which are congruent.

This is a bit like taking a brown suede loafer and trying every item in one's wardrobe in turn for a match without even taking into account whether the item is another shoe. GTP did a bit better than that by applying quick numerical checks to weed out pairs that didn't "look" right and eliminated them from further consideration—triangles ABD and CEA, for example, contain the specified line segments, but any human would disregard them on sight. Triangles BDM and CEM pass the plausibility test and are investigated further to see if a formal proof can be found to confirm the "hunch."

Two equal angles and one equal side are sufficient to establish congruence of a pair of triangles. The two angles at M are equal axiomatically; BM = MC by definition since M is the midpoint of BC; and lo, each triangle contains a right angle by construction. Hence, the goal statement has been connected to the premises, i.e., shown to follow from them.

A purely mechanical search by rote would in general involve a million combinations to arrive at a two-step proof and a billion for a three-step proof of the type shown. By inspecting a model to discard repetitions and senseless continuations, GTP was able to reduce these to 25 choices for a two-step case and 125 for a three-step—not bad at all. Eventually, the program was able to deal with proofs requiring up to ten steps (which I calculate would involve a number of combinations equal to 10,000 times the number of nanoseconds since the big bang, doing it the hard way). The main significance from the AI point of view, however, was not so much the reduction in numbers, impressive as this was, but the precedent that was set of getting a computer to express the problem in terms of an internal geometric representation, closer to the way in which people do it.

Taming Babel

THE STANDARDIZATION OF COMMON LANGUAGES

One of the reasons why the GTP project took three years was that on top of everything else, Gelernter had to invent virtually a new computer language to give the kind of representation he needed to work with. High-level languages were another aspect of the emerging discipline of computer science in general that was making rapid advances in the second half of the 1950s. IBM's FORTRAN, standing for FORmula TRANslation, developed for representing numerical and algebraic equations, was introduced during this period, and in later versions it continues as one of the most widespread programming languages used in scientific and engineering applications today.

As is usually the case with any new technology that emerges and mushrooms in a short space of time, computing appeared on a bare stage, where there were no set standards or codes of practice comparable to those governing more established industries. Early machines were built to individual designs, each requiring programming via the unique system of numeric codes that reflected its own specific set of instructions and operations. Not only was this tedious and time-consuming, but the long numeric schedules were invitations for error. The first, obvious step in making the task less onerous was to introduce more readily intelligible mnemonics like ADD and FETCH for the "source" programs to be written in, which could then be automatically translated by other programs, known as "assemblers," into the "object code" that was actually loaded into the machine and run.

(When I was introduced to assembler programming at Honeywell in England in the early seventies, it was all done on punched paper tape. Having drafted your program on special coding pads, you then used a keyboard to punch it out as the Source tape. This then had to be loaded into the computer to be assembled, which required another program called the "Loader"—computer people are, if anything, logical. But the Loader was another roll of paper tape. How did you load the Loader without getting into an infinite regress? By keying in, one line at a time via binary front-panel switches, a "Bootstrap" loader—the origin of today's term of "booting" the system—consisting of about a dozen instructions, which was just able to load a tape. The Loader then loaded the Source, followed by the Assembler, which was another reel of tape. The computer then punched out the Object program as yet another reel. Then the Object would have to be loaded in order to run.

Of course, it never ran cleanly the first time, if it ran at all, because there would be bugs somewhere. To edit required loading an Editor program, which—yes, you're getting the idea—came as another reel of tape. The edited Source was then punched out as a new Source tape, which naturally meant assembling a new version of the Object tape. Since memory was limited, these operations would probably have overwritten the Assembler, which would have to be reloaded. Then, if it still didn't work, you went around the loop again. Punched cards were an alternative to paper tape, but the principle was the same.

I remember once, when the class I was in had spent three days trying to get a simple sorting routine working, we were taken to an air-conditioned inner sanctum and allowed to gaze in awe while the same operations were performed before our eyes in seconds using the latest wonder of the age: a magnetic disk system, storing ten megabytes in a multiplatter stack about as big as the bottom section of a wedding cake, housed in a glass-topped washing machine. We were solemnly assured that in years to come, all the major installations would be using these. Last week I was looking at a laptop with one hundred times that capacity. All the same, well into the seventies, science-fiction writers were still describing scenes with starship navigation officers feeding paper tape into the flight-deck computer.)

Assembly languages took some of the hard labor out of coding, but they were still machine-specific. Transferring a problem to a different machine meant having to rewrite it in the new machine's language. A way around the inconvenience of this would be to define a standard, universal language that anyone could use to write the original program; this would be convertible to any specific machine's object code by a translator program that the machine's manufacturer would supply for the purpose. FORTRAN was such a "high-level" language. A program written in FORTRAN could be "compiled" into 700-series code by the IBM compiler, or by Univac compilers to run on Univac machines, and similarly for all the other names that were starting to appear in the industry. A variety of such languages were developed for specialized purposes, such as ALGOL, which was more mathematical, and COBOL, for business applications. BASIC was another, although it is probably better known to most people today in its "interpreter" (as opposed to compiler) form, where each command line is entered and executed individually ("Press ENTER") instead of as a complete program. The advantage of this is that it enables an interactive operation, which is far more convenient for writing and testing programs.

LIST PROCESSING, JOHN MCCARTHY, AND LISP

Understandably, the early languages reflected the needs of the applications the early machines were being used for. They assumed, for example, that all the variables involved in a program, and the data structures, such as tables and arrays, that used them would be known and defined at the beginning in the tidy, organized kind of way that a mathematician is able to specify at the start of a problem. You could think of the program as formatting an area of memory for collections of data items, like the boxes on a questionnaire form. Once set up, the pattern remains fixed, and any required item of data will be found in its proper place.

But the kinds of problems that AI work dealt with weren't like that. Unlike the situation with algorithmic programming, nobody could say for certain what quantities or relationships might need to be expressed as a result of applying different heuristics, which meant that the program needed to be capable of creating new representations and modifying them as it went along. The available languages didn't permit that.

The other principal thing that regular languages didn't do very well was express the kinds of relationships that humans use when they create chains of associations that connect objects, events, abstract ideas, and all the other concepts that minds are capable of forming, such as when a song reminds us of a place, which reminds us of a person, which reminds us of a time, which . . .

The items manipulated in conventional programs had associations with their physical addresses in memory but contained no indicators of how they related to one another.

Newell, Shaw, and Simon had produced their own answer in the form of a language called Information Processing Language, or IPL, as part of the task of developing Logic Theorist. John McCarthy, who had moved to the electrical engineering department at MIT, took some of the ideas of IPL as his inspiration for developing a general, high-level language suitable for processing "lists," as the concatenated types of associative variables characteristic of AI programming were termed. "LISP," standing for "LISt Processor" and announced in 1958, enabled associative chains to be constructed by having each data item lead to the next like the clues in a treasure hunt. In a similar kind of way to that in which a footnote reference enables a reader to jump out of a piece of text and return again, a chain could be detached and linked or inserted elsewhere by means of a few pointers, without having to shuffle everything around to make room. This also facilitated packaging and unpackaging concepts in a way that enabled attention to be directed at the right level. For example, *tools* might be subsumed into *house contents* for the purpose of looking at the world in one way, but considered as comprising *hammer, saw, drill,* and so on from the viewpoint of another.

A particularly valuable feature in view of the limited memory capacities of early machines was that a variable once finished with could be deleted and its space reassigned to new ones being created. Finally, the LISP statements that make up a program are formed from the symbols that the program operates on, which means—in principle anyway—that a LISP program can change its behavior by altering its own instructions. The intention was to produce evolving programs that would learn from experience the way people do—a pretty impressive piece of foresight for 1958. Two programs that employ self-modifying LISP structures to learn from experience—Doug Lenat's "Automated Mathematician" and "EURISKO"—are discussed in chapter fifteen.

MIT's AI Group and Project MAC

Also in 1958, Marvin Minsky joined John McCarthy in forming the MIT Artificial Intelligence Group. The partnership became legendary and for several years formed the nucleus of one of the most celebrated and active centers of early AI research, a magnet for the Cambridge area's assortment of computer-fixated science graduates, midnight hackers, uncommitted individualists, and denizens of haunts ranging from the militarily sensitive Lincoln Laboratory at one end of the spectrum to the famous MIT Model Railroad Club at the other.[2]

At Harvard, Minsky had been a student of J.C.R. Licklider, who had since become director of the Defense Department's Advanced Projects Research Agency (ARPA). Licklider's policy was to fund people that he knew and trusted, rather than projects, and the MIT AI Group received a generous flow of nonspecific grants lasting many years for the ARPA program of broad-based research into Machine Aided Cognition that became known as Project MAC. The principal means by which this objective was to be achieved was also covered by the same general charter and went under the same acronym, this time interpreted as Multiple Access Computer, the aim being to develop methods for making the computer's powers available in a distributed fashion to many users. (It seems that other people were also getting tired of waiting in line with armfuls of cards and tapes.)

These years were productive not only in terms of innovations and insights but also in bringing together many of what were to become well-known names in the field. In 1961 one of Minsky's students, James Slagel, completed a program called SAINT (Symbolic Automatic INTegrator), which applied the methods developed for Logic Theorist to problems of the integral calculus, showing that the technique was applicable in mathematics as well as logic. Out of eighty-six problems taken from MIT freshmen final exams as a test, SAINT successfully solved eighty-four. Another graduate student, Joel Moses, extended SAINT to an upgraded version known as SIN (Symbolic INTegrator), capable of solving more advanced problems, and SIN in turn grew into a system called MACSYMA, used by scientists, engineers, and mathematicians to the present day. David Waltz and Patrick Winston made milestone contributions later in the sixties to work on programming visual object recognition; subsequently, Waltz moved into the private sector, and Winston currently holds Marvin Minsky's previous position as director of the MIT AI Laboratory. Gerald Sussman also began as a graduate student studying computer vision under Minsky and is today an MIT professor. Tom Binford began at MIT in the same field and today specializes in computerized radar and visual-image analysis at Stanford. Tom Evans set about establishing the intelligence of programs the straightforward way—by writing them to perform IQ tests. Two more students of that period, Daniel Bobrow and Bertram Raphael, made early sorties into automatic natural-language comprehension, which turned out to be

a much more complex and involved business than had been generally anticipated and continues as one of the major unsolved challenges today. Joseph
Weizenbaum, an early colleague of Minsky's, now retired, became critical in
later years of moves to commercialize AI work without, as he saw it, sufficient
attention to ethical and human issues. We will be looking more closely later at
some of this work and where it has led since.[3]

THE DEVELOPMENT OF TIME SHARING

Another significant achievement by John McCarthy—as if the LISP language
wasn't enough—was the development of "time sharing" to overcome the
cards/tape bottlenecking nightmare. To a human, typing at five characters per
second seems fast. A computer capable of inputting a character, say, every ten
microseconds (i.e., allowing for some software to decode and store it), however, will sit waiting twenty thousand times as long for the next key to be
pressed. During that dead time, it could be doing things like running useful
programs, servicing other keyboards, transferring data to and from other devices, and generally keeping busy.

Working with fellow MIT computer scientist Fernando Corbato,
McCarthy devised a system for sharing a computer's capabilities among many
simultaneous users, all running different jobs and using different peripheral
equipment, yet each enjoying the illusion of having a dedicated machine. Like
a busy bartender who can keep track of the moods, conversations, and half-told
jokes, and switch demeanor from sympathetic to serious to jovial as appropriate, the time-sharing control program allots a slot of the machine's time to
each user in turn, storing details of where each job is before interrupting it and
moving on to the next. Also, it has to partition the computer's memory in such
a way as to prevent errors in one user's program from corrupting another's, for
example, by writing data into the wrong place—or from crashing the system
completely.

Although this fulfilled the multiple-access aspect of the Project MAC goals,
it was actually begun a lot earlier and presented as a working system at about
the time MAC was being formally launched. The first demonstration was on a
PDP-1 machine from a new company founded by former MIT engineers: Digital Equipment Corporation. McCarthy and Corbato then time-shared MIT's
mainframe computer, making it the first institution to own such a facility.
McCarthy, however, did not stay to witness the results, or to participate in the
flow of ARPA largess. In 1962 he returned to California to set up the artificial
intelligence laboratory at Stanford, where he remains a venerable figure today
as professor of computer science.

"Intelligence" and Search Reduction

PROBLEM SPACES

A great deal of this early research effort focused on problems of the kind that can be represented in the same way as a machine sequencing through states, a shopper visiting a series of locations, or a proof proceeding through theorems: as a tree extending into some kind of "problem space," branching out from a starting condition into multiplying possible continuations. Such a tree can be depicted as a chart, or graph. The various states or conditions that might be encountered are referred to as "nodes" and the lines connecting them as "paths." Solving the problem consists of finding a path (there may be only one) that leads to the particular node (there may be several) representing the desired goal. Solving it intelligently means rapidly and efficiently narrowing down the choices to the few paths most likely to achieve positive results. This is what we recognize in a skilled doctor zeroing in on the symptoms of a disease, an artist finding the right combination of effects to express the mood of a composition— people in general who, professionally and in their personal lives, have "got their act together." In fact, a general working definition of "intelligence" could be offered as *"a measure of a system's* (I don't see why this shouldn't include humans) *ability to learn from experience and modify its behavior in a manner appropriate to its goals."*

Note that this doesn't presume anything about what the goals are. Regrettable but true, being undeniably "intelligent" doesn't prevent behavior from being morally questionable or socially undesirable. Also, it doesn't equate intelligence necessarily with being intellectually accomplished. We've all met the cocktail-party bore whose determination to impress reduces everyone to numbed insensibility, producing precisely the opposite effect. On the other hand, there are those with little formal learning who can always adjust to the company and the occasion, who unerringly read the moods and feelings of others and are able to monitor and control their own. Perhaps they have little book learning and are short on degrees and diplomas, but in no way can you dismiss them as stupid. And then, of course, there are those usually exceptional individuals who manage to combine both kinds of competence. Nothing says they have to be mutually exclusive.

What meets the above definition is the knack for "getting it right," for "knowing what to do"—the ability to sum up quickly a situation on the basis of well-assimilated past experience, pick out the parts that are relevant, and identify a potentially effective course of action. In short, applying good heuristics for rapidly and ruthlessly thinning down search trees.

Real-life situations, however, pose immensely complicated jumbles of problems involving virtually unlimited variables in which motives constantly conflict and in which everyone can seldom agree on what the rules and the goals are. The early AI projects therefore looked to areas that compared to the-orem proving in offering restricted problem domains, clearly defined rules, and ready measurement of performance. Mathematics and geometry were clear can-didates; so were classical games and puzzles. The next chapter looks at game playing in more detail. In all these areas, cutting down on search was the first major preoccupation.

GENERATING SEARCH TREES

Computer "search" means generating successive nodes of a problem space and checking at each step to see if a solution has been produced. Algorithms—trying everything possible until the right answer is found—are practicable only where (relatively) small problem spaces are involved. When we talk about "doing a computer search" of a customer database, say, to find the record for John Smith, the term is used quite legitimately but applies in the simplest sense of progressing in a one-dimensional fashion through the sequence of records until a match is found—or shown not to be present.

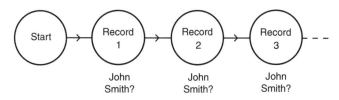

Figure 9.2 A One-Dimensional Search

Another example might be the restricted domain of a particular mathe-matical calculation, where the procedure to be followed is precisely defined by the program. Such operations characterize the regular applications of com-puters that almost everyone today has become used to.

In the more general case, where each state has multiple possible continua-tions, a node is said to be "expanded" by generating its set of successor nodes. There are two basic ways in which a procedure can go about expanding nodes:

1. Expand all nodes below a given node in the order in which they were generated.
2. Expand the most recently generated node first.

Figure 9.3 shows a series of "snapshots" of a tree being generated according to the first way. All nodes at a given level are checked before going to the next level, meaning that the tree is generated in its entire breadth at each level and then taken deeper. This is known as a *breadth-first* search. A breadth-first proce-dure is algorithmic. If a path does exist from a start node to a goal node, it will be produced eventually.

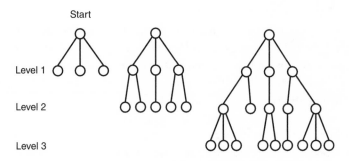

Figure 9.3 Breadth-First Search Procedure

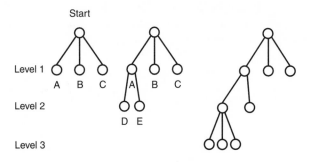

Figure 9.4 Depth-First Search Procedure

Figure 9.4 shows the same tree being expanded by the second method. After expansion of the start node (from right to left), the last node to be generated is expanded down to Level 2, then the last-generated node of that set to Level 3, and so on. The tree is followed as deep as it goes along one branch before another branch is tried. This is a *depth-first* search. A depth-first procedure is not algorithmic but could continue forever in the wrong direction without finding a solution, even though one might exist.

A depth-first search can be made algorithmic, however, by placing a limit on the depth to which the search is allowed to continue and having the program back up and repeat down the other branches before the next probe in depth is initiated. In the example shown, if the limit were set at 100, say, the left-most chain from A through D would be stopped at Level 100 and the search shifted to try the line from A through E. Only when all continuations from A, B, and C were exhausted would a probe down to Level 200 be initiated, and so on. This is known as a *bounded depth-first* search.

Both kinds of search procedure are "blind" in the sense that the order in which they expand nodes is not related to the actual location of goal nodes in the problem space. Hence, they are not heuristic search procedures.[4]

HEURISTIC SEARCHING

The problems that AI workers were tackling, however, were chosen to be more representative of the kinds of situations that humans somehow manage to deal with that involve enormous problem spaces. Heuristic methods are necessary to reduce the size of the possible search. Such rules of thumb don't guarantee finding a solution even if there is one, but, more in the way humans seem to work, are devised—we hope—to be good enough, most of the time. Thus, a detective looking for John Smith in New York doesn't start at one end of the city and begin stopping everyone in sight, either breadth-first by working all the crosstown streets in turn or depth-first by following people down the avenues. He will ask around Smith's neighborhood, check known haunts, inquire at Smith's workplace, i.e., he will apply practical rules for singling out a few possibilities that have a high probability of success. AI problems call for the same kind of thing. Rather than a specific procedure, what's programmed in is the *potential*—call it "judgment" if you will—to select from a repertoire of procedures.

Most heuristic procedures are, in effect, modifications of the bounded depth-first search, where the explored path is selected for having some inherent merit rather than by an arbitrary rule such as which node was expanded last. Typically, information about the problem is incorporated, causing nodes to be generated first that are evaluated as most likely to lie on a solution path. Thus, the search is "guided" into the most promising regions of the problem space. A node's "value" might be decided according to a *probability* calculation of its lying on a path to a goal node, a measured *difference* between certain of its properties compared to those of the goal, or an assessment of key *features* that it possesses, for example, the number of pieces owned by each side, and their positions, in a board game. In all cases, the particular method or combination of methods adopted will depend on the nature of the problem. It is possible for a procedure to be both algorithmic and heuristic. In such an instance, every possibility will be investigated eventually, but heuristics are used to try the most promising directions first.

The Very Model of a Problem-Solver General: GPS at Carnegie Tech

MEANS-ENDS ANALYSIS

At Carnegie (then still) Tech, while the thrust of most of the work going on elsewhere was directed at further developing the kinds of techniques demonstrated in Logic Theorist, Newell and Simon were already shifting their attention to a new area. Their philosophy had always been to try and find out as far as possible how humans went about solving problems and to model their approach to AI on that. While, admittedly, there was no compelling reason to suppose that "thinking" *had* to be done the way people do it—any more than counting required fingers—it seemed advisable in the absence of any better suggestion to take advantage of whatever hints could be got from the only working example nature had to offer. It seemed, however, that humans made use of strategies that Newell and Simon hadn't appreciated when they set about the design of LT.

They became aware of this through work being done at the Naval Research Laboratory by the psychologists O. K. Moore and Scarvia B. Anderson,[5] who had also been using logic-theorem proving as a tool to investigate human problem solving. One of Moore and Anderson's methods was to have subjects give a talking commentary as they thought their way through a problem in order to obtain a trace of the reasoning processes being applied. An example would be, "Well, my first feeling is that we want to get R over to the left, and somehow invert P and Q. So . . ." What was going on, they realized, was an identification of the difference between the situation as it exists presently and the situation as it is desired to be, and the kind of action that typically would be expected to reduce that difference. They called this technique *means-ends analysis*. What it amounts to is saying, "This is the end I want to achieve. These are the means that would normally get me there. Can I apply them in the situation I'm in? If not, what's the difference between the situation I'm in and a situation where I could apply them?" And that becomes a new subproblem that gets me closer to solving the original one. Newell and Simon give the following example from daily life in *Human Problem Solving*:

> I want to take my son to nursery school. What's the difference between what I have and what I want? One of distance. What changes distance? My automobile. My automobile won't work. What is needed to make it work? A new battery. What has new batteries? An auto repair shop. I want the repair shop to put in a new battery; but the shop doesn't know I need one. What is the difficulty? One of communication. What allows communication? A telephone. . . .[6]

These ideas were implemented in the successor to LT, the General Problem Solver (GPS), which first ran in 1957. In its various versions and extensions, it remained the focus of Newell and Simon's efforts for the next ten years. *Human Problem Solving* is a comprehensive 920-page report of that work.

As its name implies, GPS was aimed at providing a general problem-solving capability, as opposed to something special-purpose like LT, which had been specifically written to prove logic theorems. It was thought that humans had a general reasoning ability that they were able to apply to different situations. Following this model, the idea of GPS was to separate out the reasoning heuristics that were believed to apply broadly and encode them as a task-independent "core" of a general system capable of dealing with a variety of problem types; then, to deal with a particular case, it would only be necessary to supply the task-specific component—much in the way that a single-motor unit drives an array of power-tool attachments. In essence, GPS attempted to reduce the chore of having to spell out in every detail what the computer was to *do* to one of specifying only what it needed to *know*. Given a body of knowledge about some aspect of the world, its general reasoning capability would enable it to handle a problem that pertained to that context.

DIFFERENCE TABLES AND OPERATORS

The required information was supplied to GPS in the form of "difference tables," specifying the ways in which the given situation differed from the desired goal, and actions termed "difference operators," which had the effect of reducing those differences. To specify the problem, all the programmer had to do was construct the relevant difference tables and operators. GPS would then take over via means-ends analysis.

Another way to think of the principle would be as Norbert Wiener's feedback engineering expressed in software. Essentially, GPS operated in three steps:

1. Evaluate the difference between the current situation and the desired goal state.
2. Find an operator that typically reduces that kind of difference.
3. Determine whether that operator can be applied in the present situation.
   —If it can, then apply it.
   —If it can't, then determine a situation that the operator could be applied to. This becomes the new subgoal. Return to Step 1.

SUBGOALS AND PLANNING

An example of the kind of problem given to GPS was the classical monkey-and-the-banana: The monkey is alone in a room with a banana hanging out of reach and a chair high enough to put the monkey within range, provided it has enough sense to move the chair to the right place and climb onto it. Most monkeys are smart enough to figure it out. Is this GPS?

The problem was defined via difference tables giving the spatial coordinates of the monkey, the banana, and the chair. Certain actions were specified that could reduce these differences, for example, "Reach," "Jump," "Climb," "Move self," and "Move chair." Further, some actions couldn't be performed without certain conditions being fulfilled; for example, before the chair could be moved, both it and the monkey had to be in the same place. Hence, once "Move chair" was identified as a subgoal of "chair under banana" after reaching and jumping were found not to work, "Move self" in turn became a sub-subgoal of achieving it. Application of the operators in the right sequence to reduce to zero the various coordinate differences given at the outset signified the successful solution of the problem.

In addition to introducing means-ends analysis, today established as a standard AI technique, GPS exhibited the rudiments of being able to formulate *plans*—by identifying subgoals, it had its broad strategy roughed out before plunging into details. And it lived up to its title of being "general," finding successful application not only in logic but across a range of games and puzzles as well. As Simon remarked about those years, "We learned more than most people want to know about Missionaries and Cannibals, cryptarithmetic problems, chess, and the Tower of Hanoi."

I met Herbert Simon at an AI symposium at Carnegie Mellon University in October 1996 that was being held in honor of his eightieth birthday. (Allen Newell died in 1992.)[7] Simon still holds professorships in the departments of psychology and computer science and maintains a busy teaching schedule in both faculties.

An Example of Subgoals: The "15 Problem"

The effectiveness of designing a system to identify subgoals along a solution path and search for connections from one subgoal to the next was recognized by other researchers too. John McCarthy expressed the principle in terms of needing to drive to a distant destination ("The San Diego Problem") when equipped with only a local gas-station-supplied road map covering a thirty-mile radius. The tactic was to realize that other, similar-brand gas stations were marked on the map, and you can buy a map of the adjoining sector from one at the edge, thus building a series that will get you where you want to go. This is sometimes referred to as the "milepost" paradigm for constructing plans.

A good illustration of applying the milepost paradigm is a program written by Ashok K. Chandra of Stanford University at McCarthy's instigation[8] for solving the classic "15 Problem"—see Figure 9.5.

This puzzle is commonly encountered as an amusement consisting of fifteen numbered plastic tiles constrained to slide vertically or horizontally in a frame, and one blank empty space that any adjacent tile can move into. (Moving a tile, of course, moves the space in the opposite direction.) The problem is to find a sequence of moves that will transform the initial tile configuration into a goal configuration.

As before, each possible configuration can be depicted as a "state" in problem space, the various states being connected by paths representing the transformation moves. A state with the blank in a center square can generate four possible successor states; with the blank in a center-edge square, three; and in a corner square, two. It doesn't sound too bad, does it? . . . But remember the shopping trip.

Altogether there are 16! (16 factorial) possible states in the complete

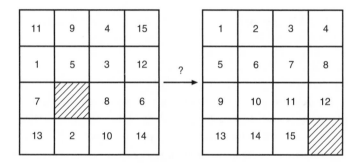

Figure 9.5 A 15 Problem

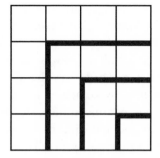

Figure 9.6 Gnomons

problem space, which turns out to be equal to 20,922,789,888,000. Only half of them, however, can be reached from a given starting configuration. The other 10.5 trillion are impossible to get to by any sequence of transformations.

Chandra's program established as successive subgoals the correct placement of tiles in three progressively contracting boundary regions termed "gnomons"—see Figure 9.6. The program begins by completing the outer gnomon, which involves just seven squares, and, when accomplished, leaves as the remaining problem space a 3 × 3 grid with 9! = 362,880 possible states—a huge reduction from 16! This is repeated to fill the next gnomon inside that, with corresponding simplification, and then the last.

In a series of three hundred randomly generated 15 problems, Chandra's program solved those for which a solution path existed in an average of ten seconds. In the process, it needed to expand less than a thousand nodes of the total problem space. That has brought us a long way from the British Museum monkeys.

Successors to GPS

SWITCHING BETWEEN PROBLEM SPACES

GPS introduced several powerful ideas that became part of the standard tool kit of concepts for designing AI planning systems. Two of the most important were means-ends analysis and automatic subgoaling. The first viewed the solution of a problem as a goal state to be achieved by applying a series of transformations ("operators") to some initial state in such a way as to "move" it closer through the corresponding problem space. The second enabled the system to create a new subgoal to direct its efforts at instead, when none of the options open to it immediately would get it any closer to the main goal.

Further experience, however, as would be expected of a new field where almost nothing is known and everything is speculative and experimental, showed that GPS also had its limits. Allen Newell once voiced the belief that the way to make progress was to maintain a state of maximal confusion between cognitive psychology and engineering.[9] This was his way of reiterating that the goal of the work as he saw it was as it had always been, to model the full range of human problem-solving abilities by computer techniques. Keeping to their original practice, he and Simon continued their studies of the ways in which human subjects actually went about solving problems—in contrast, as it frequently turned out, to the ways they were generally believed to. By the late sixties it was becoming apparent that the control structure of GPS was too inflexible to capture the variability of human behavior. The difference tables underlying means-ends analysis represented only part of the knowledge that human subjects used. Humans—for the most part, anyway—don't live in a compulsive, zombielike trance in which every movement is directed unerringly toward a single overriding goal. Very often they make use of knowledge that they know from experience is useful in the situation, even though it may not be immediately directed at the goal as stated or even related to the problem space in which the goal is framed.

Suppose, for example, that the objective is to get from New York to San Francisco. The problem space models physical space and consists of all the locations in the world. The operators are actions such as walking, driving, or taking a bus, cab, train, plane, or ship, which transform one location into another. GPS would first compute the difference between the actual state (New York) and the goal (San Francisco) and then select the operator that best reduces the most important difference. In our case, for the distance involved, this would most likely be to take a commercial airline flight. But we're in an office in Manhattan, and planes don't leave from offices, so we can't apply that operator immediately. In such a situation, GPS would consider the inability to apply the indicated operator a subproblem and attempt to solve it by using the same method to get itself to the airport, perhaps finding that in this reformulated version taking a cab is the operator of choice, but cabs don't come to offices either, so it would first have to get out to the sidewalk, which would require getting down there in an elevator, which would require walking down the hall, and so on, applying the same procedure recursively to recognizable subgoals of the original problem.

But when it finally gets to the airport it finds it can't catch a plane to San Francisco because it doesn't have the money to buy a ticket. Solving this as a subproblem requires a completely different problem space with its own goal of "get money," which involves operators having nothing to do with moving physically nearer San Francisco. Determining the appropriate problem space was an issue never really resolved with GPS. Even in cases where it was directed toward identifying the right set of substates and suboperators, the overall order of applying them was likely to be all wrong, perhaps entailing something comparable to coming all the way back to the bank next door to where the journey started. Or maybe the flight was full or canceled, or the bank wasn't open that day, after a trip all the way back into town. Humans (most of them, anyway) don't get caught in such situations because they "know" to check the flight and make a reservation before leaving, to have enough cash, a credit card, or a checkbook on hand before leaving, and so on.

But neither would a human need to have all this solved in detail before proceeding to the final stage of the problem at the more general level either. We tend to plan out a rough strategy and verify it—check to see if there's a flight, have an idea of how we'll proceed at the other end, such as whether someone can meet us at the airport, and then come back to take care of such details as buying the ticket. GPS was extended to a system called PLANNING GPS, implemented by 1972, that did confer some ability to work in this way, but it was never able to match the flexibility with which humans are able to switch back and forth between different levels of abstraction, guided by their knowledge of which details could wait and which could not. A way was needed to provide the pieces of ad hoc information, in no way derivable from the bare facts of the situation, that enable humans to do this.

PRODUCTION SYSTEMS

In 1943, mathematician Emil Post described what he termed a method of "production systems" based on "production rules," or "productions," for stipulating conditions in problems of symbolic logic.[10] Borrowing the term, Newell and Simon introduced a system of supplementing GPS's task knowledge by means of rules in the form of *if . . . then . . .* This was precisely the kind of approach they had observed human problem solvers applying: "*If* I see this situation [e.g., intention to fly somewhere], *then* I do that [check available funds]." The behavior of the human subjects in fact changed from a search-intensive mode in which virtually random trial and error might predominate to begin with, to faster, surer zeroing in on the right method with no searching around at all as experience accumulated. Existing representational systems were not suitable for encoding this kind of information, and through the early to mid-seventies Newell developed a variety of production-system languages culminating in the series known as OPS.

THE INSTRUCTABLE PRODUCTION SYSTEM

This work led to the question of whether a system could be programmed completely in terms of production rules, which was the same as asking if very large systems made up of thousands or even tens of thousands of production rules could be built and operated successfully. The outcome was the Large Production System Project in 1975, which met the challenge head-on by having all knowledge acquisition take the form of rule-based instruction. This was known as the Instructable Production System, IPS. Although the project yielded much research information and the language developments mentioned above, the several systems that grew under it were never able to grow to a reasonable size, and Newell described the whole thing as "a first-class failure."[11]

The major cause was that the methods supplied to IPS to accomplish one task tended to be too task-specific to enable it to perform the next task, the usual symptom of which was that IPS would come to a halt. Between them, a variety of tasks defined a huge problem space of task situations, but each set of production rules supplied covered only a small region of it. The clusters were like a scattering of dots through this space, and a new task that arose would rarely happen to coincide with a dot where rules existed to tell IPS what to do. Going back to our illustration, it was as if rules were there that would get you to San Francisco if you happened to be in New York, Chicago, or Atlanta, say, and maybe a hundred other places too. But not if you were in Warrington, Florida, or Clifton, Colorado, or any of the thousands of places that did not have convenient airports.

KEEPING MOVING WHEN
THERE'S NO OBVIOUS PLACE TO GO: "WEAK METHODS"

So IPS died. But the problem that it had revealed was still a potential obstacle to the large-scale use of production rules in the future. Newell and John Laird, who joined the project later, reasoned that what the system needed was a less-directed, more general pattern of fallback activity that it would resort to in the event that nothing specific to the particular situation presented itself. This meant having rules in reserve that would have wide applicability anywhere, to keep things moving in a direction at least likely to prove more fruitful than doing nothing when there was no definite pointer toward anything better. Examples might be to go to a depth-first search to probe further ahead or cast wider with a breadth-first search. Another possibility, in cases where the problem space can be represented as a mathematical surface whose higher ground indicates improvement of some kind, might be to explore the surrounding terrain and apply "hill-climbing," a method of applying an operator to follow the slope upward. For instance, a pattern of humps and dips could represent the profit made on a product as the price varies in one direction and the quantity produced in the other. Collectively, these are known as *weak methods*—weak not because they're ineffective or fail to constrain the search tightly but because they make weak demands on knowledge specific to the task being performed—all manner of different tasks can usefully employ hill-climbing, for example.

GPS + IPS: The "Soar" Lineage

Weak methods are exactly what is required when there is no "strong" knowledge available to point to a solution directly. Hence, they are methods of last resort, but also the means of providing robustness in the face of novelty.

Alone, neither GPS or IPS had been able to provide the generality that had been sought. But their joint legacy left as a clear goal the suggestion of bringing together what had been their strengths into an architecture that would support multiple problem spaces operating a range of weak methods, with task-specific "strong" knowledge representation supplied in the form of production rules. This integration came about in the system designated "Soar," the first version of which dates from 1982.[12] Other systems to emerge at Carnegie Mellon University during the eighties, based on architectures and concepts similar to Soar, were John Anderson's Act* (pronounced "Act Star") and Prodigy, by Steven Minton, Jaime Carbonell, and others.

We shall have more to say about Soar in a later chapter, when we deal with common sense and machine learning.

1. Gelernter. Also Gelernter, Hansen, and Loveland.
2. Crevier gives a comprehensive and colorful account of the early days of the AI group at MIT.
3. Pamela McCorduck's *Machines Who Think* has become a classic for intriguing character sketches of just about all the leading names in the field through the late seventies.
4. See Knuth for a general introduction to algorithms and algorithmic methods for optimizing searches.
5. Moore and Anderson (1954a), (1954b).
6. Newell and Simon, p. 416.
7. For a tribute and assessment of Newell's work, see Laird and Rosenbloom (1992).
8. Jackson, p. 104.
9. Crevier, p. 258.
10. Post.
11. Laird and Rosenbloom (1992), p. 29.
12. Laird and Rosenbloom (1996).

Occam's Chain Saw

HACKING AWAY AT GAME TREES

Gamesmanship: The Art of Winning Games Without Actually Cheating.
—Stephen Potter, Book title (1947)

Laboratories of Life

Problems encountered in real life tend to be complex and ill-defined. Everything we do seems to involve endless threads of relatedness in which something else needs to be taken into account that we didn't think of. Nobody agrees on the rules, the goals are obscure, and as likely as not we've no clear way of knowing if we've achieved them. The risks of failure are real, nevertheless, and can be catastrophic, even fatal. We have evolved ways of muddling through to the end of a reasonable life span regardless, which some people call "intelligence" and would like to emulate by machine.

Games, by contrast, offer restricted problem domains where the basic elements involved are few, the rules are clearly defined, and performance is easily assessed; nevertheless, the methods of solution that they call for are nontrivial, and penalties may be more than just tokens. They can be chosen to include an element of chance or not, and players may share the same information or play according to different levels of knowledge, which the aim may be to acquire. Beyond being sources of amusement, from the beginnings of history games have provided training grounds for life—both for the young, who are newcomers to all of it, and via such devices as war games and management games for novices in specialized aspects of it. Their simplified worlds supply relaxing diversions from life and, in extreme cases, what virtually become substitutes for life.

For all these reasons, games offer natural laboratories for the study of human motivations, problem-solving strategies, and competitive behavior in general. The importance attached to games may be judged from the comprehensive *Theory of Games and Economic Behavior* by Oskar Morgenstern and John von Neumann, published in 1944, a work said to have made Herbert Simon envious for years.

Finally, the ease of creating repeatable conditions, coupled with quantifiable measures of improvement, also make games an ideal medium for experimenting with ways of reproducing in machines that other quality which is perhaps the strongest characteristic of intelligent behavior: the ability to learn from experience.

Early Game-Playing Programs

FIRST ATTEMPTS AND SPECULATIONS—
TURING AND SHANNON

Attempts at game-playing programs began appearing almost as soon as the first computers did. Alan Turing had always exhibited a playful streak—the Turing test itself was an adaptation of an English parlor game—and in 1947–1948 he devoted some time and thought to experimenting with chess playing on the successors to Britain's wartime code-breaking machines. Turing's program was not the result of systematic studies of human problem-solving methods in the fashion that would become standard when the AI movement became established a decade later, but instead attempted simply to capture introspectively his own thought processes when playing—and applied them with considerable simplification. It tended to overlook the same things he overlooked, pick the same kinds of moves, and make the same mistakes—Turing was not an especially strong chess player. He described its game as a caricature of his own. The MADM Machine that he was involved in building at Manchester became the first computer to be capable of playing a full game of chess, although not a very good one, and it was excruciatingly slow. The Manchester group also tackled computer ticktacktoe, one of the simpler game problems, and checkers as an intermediary between that and chess.

In the United States, Claude Shannon, who had applied two-state Boolean algebra to relay-switching networks at Bell Labs and quantified information theory into a science, had moved to MIT by 1950, when he published a paper in *Scientific American* entitled "A Chess-Playing Machine."[1] This was where he made his oft-quoted estimate of the total number of possible chess games as 10^{120}.

An early misconception that was widely prevalent around this time, cited airily by many commentators eager to expound about the new machines, was that programming computers to play chess was a straightforward enough matter since with their speed they could simply examine all continuations and pick the best. These assurances were no doubt based on intuitive appreciation of the treelike structure of a chess game, but unfortunately no one bothered to check with anybody who might have given a quantitative indication of the tree's extent. We'll look into this a little more closely below. Shannon's purpose was to draw attention to the computer's potential for performing operations on symbols that could represent anything, not just numerical calculations—a point that was still far from being generally appreciated at the time.

It's interesting to speculate on how much the adoption of the somewhat restrictive term "computer" may have contributed to this. Prior to the advent of programmable, electronic, general-purpose, symbol processors, "computer" was a term applied to humans to describe a specialized occupation—literally, a "person who computes." The operators on the numerical mass-production line set up to produce trigonometrical tables for the grand project of the new French Republic at the end of the eighteenth century were computers that worked by hand. By the middle of the twentieth century, "computers" sat in offices equipped with electromechanical desk calculators, and Turing in his 1950 paper refers to them as such. Viewing "computation" as being by definition what "computers" do—and by implication all that they *can* do—has colored debates on the practicability of AI in principle that have continued to the present day.

It's tempting to wonder what differences in attitude might have been engendered by the use of a less restrictive-sounding term at the outset. "Symbol processor" sounds a bit vague, and most people would have a hard time accepting that what goes on in their heads is symbol processing, anyway. Leibniz proposed calling his envisaged logical calculator a "ratiocinator," but that probably wouldn't work either because most of the minority able to pronounce it probably wouldn't know what it means. (To me it suggests something that cremates dead rodents.) Perhaps something like the more generic "processor" would have helped keep minds and opinions a little more open. Then things like "vision processor," "speech processor," and so on would have been added as applications diversified from the initial "numeric processor," and "general processor," with its connotation of being able to do anything, might have followed naturally in due course.

Shannon also constructed a special-purpose chess player that was a machine, not a program, as well as an electronic "mouse" that learned to navigate through mazes. The methods were not extendable to more general domains, however, and Shannon pretty much withdrew from the AI scene to remain an interested spectator.

Checkers and Chess at IBM

ARTHUR SAMUEL'S FUND-RAISING TRIVIALITY
Serious proposals for developing game-playing programs—based, it turned out, on utterly naive impressions of what was involved—were being floated even

before Alan Turing's first exploratory forays and Claude Shannon's theoretical studies. In 1946, Arthur Samuel moved from Bell Labs, where he had been an expert in vacuum-tube technology, to take a teaching position at the University of Illinois.[2] His work at Bell had convinced him that computers were the way of the future, and he persuaded the board of trustees that becoming one of the first universities to acquire a machine of its own would constitute an invaluable investment. Nobody was yet in the business of producing computers for sale, and $110,000—a respectable amount indeed for those days—was voted for building one. Although this was actually more than Samuel had asked for, his later budgeting after talking to the people at the Moore School of the University of Pennsylvania, who had built the ENIAC, told him it would be insufficient for such a task. Loathe to have to go back, Oliver Twist–like, asking for more after the board's display of confidence and generosity, he looked for ways of possibly attracting government funds to supplement the university's grant.

As it happened, the world checkers tournament the following year (1947) was due to be held at Kankakee, Illinois. So an obvious and simple plan presented itself. Samuel knew that people like Shannon had been talking about machines playing chess; checkers, he felt, would be trivial by comparison. What they would do, then, would be to build a small computer and program it to play checkers; then, at the end of the tournament, they would challenge whoever had won, beat him, and thereby attract lots of attention and publicity, with copious flows of further development funding sure to follow. Thus blithely resolved, and knowing nothing about actually programming computers, Samuel embarked on the double task of learning how and trying to apply his new knowledge while he was acquiring it. At the same time, no actual computer on which to test his ideas existed, for the engineering group was simultaneously trying to design the machine and build it under the instruction of experts from the wartime projects.

To the unlikely surprise of anyone with today's hindsight, neither machine nor program came even close to being completed on time, and the new world champion walked away with his image untarnished. (The idea, however, was an interesting instance of history repeating itself. Charles Babbage and his accomplice, Lady Lovelace, had contemplated getting a cut-down version of the Analytical Engine to play ticktacktoe—and even chess—as a publicity stunt to attract funds after the British government's support evaporated. What the waiting time might have been for a steam-driven mechanical chess player to perform any reasonable search at all boggles the mind.)

For Samuel, the episode proved to be that road-to-Damascus experience that many from around that time onward have been smitten by, otherwise known as being bitten by the computer bug. His future, he decided, was not in a university engineering department, where he would be permanently pigeonholed as a specialist in vacuum tubes. In 1949 he joined IBM, which had been involved in building the Harvard Mark I and was just developing the small plug board computer designated the 604—predecessor of the 701 mentioned in chapter eight, which would be announced in 1951. Ironically, it was mainly on account of his vacuum-tube expertise that he was hired, yet one of his major efforts initially was devoted to dissuading the company from going ahead with plans for setting up a manufacturing line for its own design of tubes. His experience at Bell told him that such a venture would become reality just in time to become obsolete; the transistor was already in sight.

Through all this time, Samuel's fascination with the checkers project that he had begun at the University of Illinois persisted, and one of the first programs written for the 701 was an adaptation of the intended world-champion-beater that he had begun developing for the machine-that-never-was. It proved very suitable as a test routine for checking out production machines before they were shipped.

Samuel spent some time scouting around Europe for IBM and found that his checkers-playing program gave him negotiating capital to serve as the basis for many useful exchanges of information with curious researchers whose attitudes might otherwise have been less receptive. All in all, Samuel was to work for another dozen years on the problem that he had misjudged as "trivial" before he was able to produce a program that could play at championship level. Back at IBM in the States, and then later at Stanford after he retired from IBM, he continually refined and added to it. Never especially fond of the game himself, he found neither extensive reading nor protracted attempts at getting masters to describe what went on in their heads proved effective in instilling an insight into the deeper strategies that an effective program somehow had to capture. Like the economics texts that Herbert Simon had found fanciful, the books either expounded theories that didn't reflect reality or else merely recorded reality without explaining it. Human experts proved hopeless at trying to articulate processes that, to a large degree, were probably never registered consciously to begin with. Like pianists, typists, and observers of quantum events, the very act of trying to focus on the process disrupted it.

Finally, Samuel incorporated what was to prove the decisive feature—the ability for the program to recall details of its past games and learn from them.[3] When his program began beating him regularly, he knew he was on the right track. By 1961 it was playing at master level, and the following year it beat Robert Nealy, the former Connecticut state champion. In a return series, however, Nealy revenged himself. Samuel's Checkers Player finally lost its title of reigning machine champion in 1977 to a program called Paaslow, written by Eric C. Jensen and Tom R. Truscott of Duke University.

ALEX BERNSTEIN: GETTING THE
FIRST TRUE MEASURE OF THE PROBLEM

Unlike Arthur Samuel with his largely indifferent aptitude for checkers, Alex Bernstein had shown a flair for chess from an early age. He began playing at the age of ten and was soon seriously engrossed, becoming captain of the Bronx Science High School chess team. He became acquainted with computers when working in a research and development unit of the army Signal Corps and from 1953 to 1955 was involved with simulations of the air-defense system around Washington—interestingly, at just about the same time as Allen Newell was computer-simulating air defenses with Rand in California. After leaving the army, Bernstein accepted an opportunity to join IBM and there met a young computer expert called Hal (an interestingly coincidental namesake) Judd, who became interested in Bernstein's chess proficiency and suggested a joint effort at trying to develop a chess-playing program. Judd was transferred away almost immediately, but the idea had taken root with Bernstein, who succeeded in getting management approval to spend half of his time at IBM's Scientific Center (later, Service Bureau) in Manhattan on the chess project.

Whereas Samuel had made stalwart attempts to master the principles of what he readily admitted was not, for him, an art that came naturally, Bernstein was thoroughly versed in chess theory. He spent six months analyzing five hundred chess openings, working out ways to assign measurable values to such abstractions that experienced players assess instinctively, such as strengths and weaknesses of position, mobility of pieces, control of board area, security of the king's position, trying to code it into usable heuristics to narrow the choice down to a few sensible continuations the way humans do. And at the end of that time and effort he found himself on the verge of being ready to give up. Whatever humans really did, it was subtle and elusive beyond all expectations. He was unable to make any sense of it.

Shaken though Bernstein might have been, a quitter he was not. At this point he widened out from the traditional notions of strategy that he had been concentrating on and immersed himself in the ideas of more modern schools of thinking. Taking stock of approaches to computer chess that were being pursued elsewhere, he read up on what had been published in the field and visited Shannon at MIT. Newell, Simon, and Shaw had produced an experimental chess-playing program at Carnegie Tech,[4] but it was of mediocre performance and never won against a human player. The chess master and writer Edward Lasker introduced Bernstein to Stanislaw Ulam and a group who were programming chess on the MANIAC computer at Los Alamos.[5] (I once asked Isaac Asimov over dinner why he thought there was this obsession for giving early computers names that ended in IAC. His reply was, "They named them after the smartest one: ISIAAC.")

The outcome, after two years of intensive effort to understand and emulate human techniques as closely as could be achieved, was that the program was able to play what Bernstein described as "a respectable beginner's game." And every once in a while it made a move that was "remarkably good."[6]

Measured against the original hopes and expectations, it had to be admitted that the result, while successful in the sense that it worked, was modest. One wouldn't have thought so from the extensive publicity that the achievement received, which included invitations for Bernstein to address numerous scientific meetings and international coverage in *The New York Times*, *Scientific American*, and *Life*.

Thomas J. Watson, IBM's president, was less than happy with such portentous events, however, especially when Samuel's checkers project and Gelernter's Geometry Theorem Prover began getting coverage too. IBM's marketing policy maintained staunchly that the company was in the business of supplying business systems to businessmen with serious needs, and shareholders were demanding to know why all this money was being squandered on playing games. Things became more alarming when management began reporting sales resistance on the part of prospective customers, which, rightly or wrongly, they attributed to negative psychology brought about by this image the media was creating of the computer as a threat that would take over their decision-making functions and reduce them to button pushers. From then on, the corporate message, echoed through every sales presentation and other outlets at the company's command, was that computers were simply dumb and obedient servants that did what they were told and nothing more—Lovelace reiterated with the voice of authority. AI work was wound down—or at least put on a tight rein. That was when Samuel was sent to Europe. Bernstein eventually became a psychiatrist, and Gelernter went back into physics.

Games in General[7]

The kinds of games that computers lend themselves to are those known as "games of strategy," characterized by having well-defined rules and objectives that the players endeavor to achieve. Of course, these are not the only games that exist. A major purpose served by games is enjoyment, and many games are played purely for the fun of it with no clear goal—and frequently with few, if any, discernible rules. Until—indeed, if ever—computers, or whatever their successors might be termed, become more capable of enjoying themselves, the question of their participating in games of that sort doesn't really arise.

The distinguishing thing about games of strategy is that they are played to win a profit expressed as a payoff of some kind. They can be two-player or multiplayer. Note that just because a payoff is involved, it doesn't mean that a game is necessarily competitive. The satisfaction might come from developing a cooperative strategy aimed at maximizing the payoff to all players—doing a jigsaw together or climbing a mountain with a team might qualify, although these activities are not carried out within frameworks of formal rules. At the other extreme, a "zero-sum game," where one player's gain can only be realized through a matching cost to others, is strictly competitive. (It's called zero-sum because a positive gain, or "credit," to one player represents an equal negative gain, or "debit," to somebody else, and the sum of all positive and negative gains is zero.) Poker is a prime example. Chess, checkers, ticktacktoe, and the Japanese game of Go are all zero-sum games. Chess and checkers are also examples of perfect-information games, where both players have full knowledge of everything that has gone before and the options currently available. Monopoly is a multiplayer game of perfect information. Bridge and poker are instances of multiplayer, imperfect-information games, where some of what each player knows is hidden from the others. Bridge is also a game that involves partnerships, although situations can arise in poker where the best strategy for two—or maybe more—players might be to temporarily ally against another.

The games that feature most commonly in AI work tend to be in the two-player, zero-sum, perfect-information category, usually without any chance element. Naturally, every one of these generalizations has its exceptions.

Game Trees and Searching

STATE TRANSITIONS AGAIN

Let's consider a game of the typical two-player, zero-sum kind where the players take turns at making moves directed toward achieving a win. At the beginning, the game can be said to be in its opening "state." The first player's move transforms it to a different state, the second player's reply puts it in another state still, and so on. Eventually, the game ends in a win for one side or the other, or possibly in a draw, in one of a number of possible final states, states that have no further continuations. As this terminology of states suggests, games too can be modeled using the same representation that we've met already: a tree structure of nodes, one for each state, connected by the possible transitions between them. The principal difference between games and the decision trees we've met before is that in games the players alternate in deciding which transition will apply to the current state. Hence, neither has full control over how the path will unfold from beginning to end. Figure 10.1 depicts in tree form the opening of such a game. Note the use of two distinct shapes for the nodes as a convenience to indicate whose move it is.

A tree is not the only way in which a game may be represented. It often happens that different sequences of moves will result in the same position, meaning that what are shown as different nodes on a tree are in fact identical states or "positions." This kind of information is given more readily by a "state-space graph." Three different paths, for example, will bring the game to a state 3. State-space graphs are better for showing loops and symmetries.

BACKING UP

One of the first principles of chess that's impressed upon novices after they have learned the basics is always to ask before considering the next move, "What is he threatening?" It's easy to get carried away by one's own plans and

GAME TREE

STATE - SPACE GRAPH

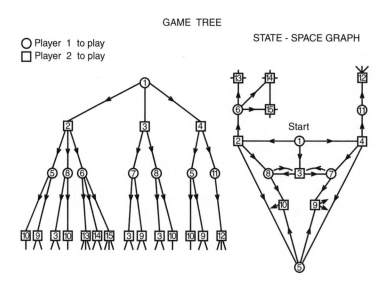

**Figure 10.1 Tree for the Beginning of a Hypothetical Game,
Together with the Corresponding State-Space Graph**

visions of victory to the point of forgetting that the opponent has plans too. What makes games different from the kind of problem and puzzle solving that we've looked at so far is that evaluations of the worth of a continuation will vary depending on who is doing the evaluating. What's judged as good by one player is unlikely to be good for the other and vice versa. Any player, machine or human, to have any hope at all, must exhibit some form of awareness of this.

Let's take a simple case where the payoff being played for is winning as opposed to losing, or maybe having to settle for a draw, and suppose that after some number of moves the game has reached the position represented by node A in Figure 10.2. It's Player 2's turn (indicated by a square), and the two possible continuations lead to the outcomes shown.

Another principle of sound chess is that you don't make risky moves and try to act nonchalantly, hoping that the other player won't see an opportunity. Always assume that the opponent will make the best move available, and plan accordingly. Applying this principle means that if Player 2 makes the move leading to node B, then Player 1 will go for the win. Node B, therefore, has the "theoretical value" of a Player-1-win—the outcome of the game in that position is determined by Player 1's having control and the assumption that the option most advantageous to Player 1 will be chosen. The best that Player 2 at A can do, therefore, is go for the draw, which by the same reasoning as before gives node A the value of a Draw. Thus, A and B are terminal nodes—the end of their particular branch of the game tree.

In Figure 10.3, this branch has been extended backward to node C, which

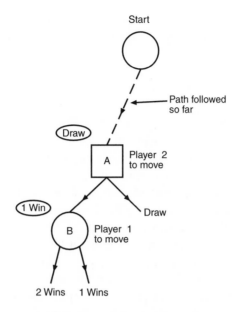

Figure 10.2 "Values" of Positions

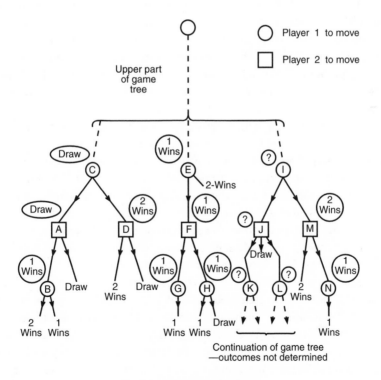

Figure 10.3 Backing Up Values

also shows Player 1 as having the option to go to node D. Although D also leads to a possible Draw, we assume that Player 2 won't choose it, which gives node D the value of Player-2-win. All of the successor nodes (in this case only two) to node C have thus been evaluated, and since Player 1 has control at C, we can say that the path to A will be chosen. The Draw value that we obtained for node A can thus be "backed up" to give a Draw value for node C.

Again, at node F, Player 2 has no choice but Player-1-win successor nodes. The value of node F becomes a Player-1-win and backs up to node E.

The game path to node J continues via K and L to branches whose outcome is not yet determined, and therefore no value can be assigned to J. Given the choice, Player 1 at node I would choose something better than the Player-2-win of node M, and so the value of node I is unknown also.

In theory, all the terminal nodes could be evaluated and their values backed up through the tree in this fashion until it was possible to assign a value to the Start node. At that point, the game would be totally determined. If the Start node had a Player-1-win value, it would mean that a path (or maybe several) exists whereby Player 1 can always steer the game to a winning position no matter what Player 2 does. Conversely, it might happen that the advantage is with the second player and no opening by Player 1 can avoid losing if Player 2 plays correctly. Or it might be that the best either can achieve is a Draw.

Such complete knowledge would make the actual playing of the game pretty pointless. Indeed, some simple games such as ticktacktoe, nim, and hex have been completely determined, and the outcome of playing against a computer programmed with such "global" representations is totally predictable. Computer programs have also been written for the game Othello that have never lost to a human player. In Othello (also known as reversi), players take turns at placing counters on an 8 × 8 board. The counters are black on one side and white on the other. Placing one so that it and other, already-placed counters of one's own color straddle an opposing counter, or groups of them, cause all the intervening ones to be flipped over to become one's own color. A counter can flip repeatedly to change color many times in the course of a game, and the object is to end the game with the majority. Positional judgment is required only in the earliest stages. After a few moves, the computer is able to latch onto a winning path through the tree. Three-dimensional ticktacktoe on a 4 × 4 × 4 board has also been completely solved, shown by Oren Patasnik of Bell Labs in 1980 to be always winnable by the player with the first move.[8]

But for the more interesting types of games that provide typical subjects for AI research, analysis is attempted only of a portion of the game tree lying immediately beyond the position currently reached. This is referred to as "local" representation. It is done not to introduce a component of unpredictability as an artificial challenge but because when we get beyond the realm of simple games like the ones mentioned above, mapping of the entire state-space rapidly becomes impracticable. A few numbers will show why.

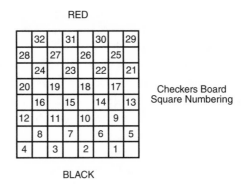

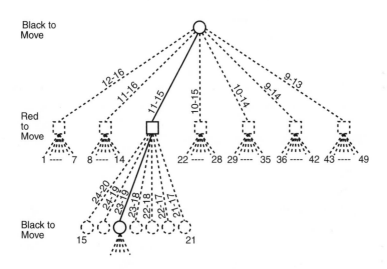

Figure 10.4 Opening Moves for Checkers

NOT SO TRIVIAL: A CLOSER LOOK AT CHECKERS

Figure 10.4 shows the options for the first two moves of a checkers game. Black begins with seven possible opening moves to choose from. For each of them, Red has seven possible replies. Thus, in the tree of all possible games, we have forty-nine branches already at the second level. The actual moves selected for the illustration are 11–15, to which Red replies 23–19. Black can respond in five ways, and if this were so for all of Black's possible responses (I haven't plodded through them all to verify if it is), we would have 245 branches for Black's second move.

Taking 6 as a guess for the "branching factor," B, the average number of branches from a node through a typical game, and thirty moves per side to give an average "Depth," D, of sixty levels, an estimate for the number of possible games, i.e., the number of terminal nodes to the complete tree, is given by:

$$B^D = 6^{60} \text{ i.e., approximately } 5^{46}.$$

It can also be shown that with the same parameters, the total number of nodes in the tree is approximately:[9]

$$(B^{D+1})/(B-1) = 6^{61}/5 \text{ i.e., about } 6^{46}$$

There are around 3.15 billion seconds in a century. On the basis of the above figures, a machine capable of analyzing a billion checkers positions a second would take something like 2^{38} centuries to complete an exhaustive search. The age of the universe is reckoned to be less than 10^{11} years, or 10^9 centuries. That means that had the machine been running that long, the fraction of the calculation that it would have gotten through by now is given by 1.3×10^{-30}, which is close to one divided by (one followed by thirty zeros). Yet checkers is played on only half the squares available on the board. Claude Shannon's 10^{120} for the number of possible chess games makes the above figure insignificant, and that in turn shrinks into utter negligibility against the 10^{760} that has been estimated for Go. If this can be so of the artificially limited domains of games, what, then, of life?

The combinatorial explosion again. We did say that once you start getting out of the restricted areas typical of the more familiar kinds of computer task, it crops up everywhere. Clearly, there is no chance of representing such trees globally. We have another case for heuristics.

MINIMAXING

Taking our two-player, zero-sum, win-lose-draw game of Figure 10.1 again, let's assume that it belongs to the "interesting" category, which means that complete knowledge of the state-space is impossible. Hence, in the early stages and usually well into the play, the game can go any way—which, after all, is the whole point of playing it. This is another way of saying that unless the path being followed is close to a terminal situation, it's seldom possible to say for sure what kind of ending a given move will lead to. The next best thing, then, is to evaluate in some way the various choices presenting themselves at any given point according to their likelihood of leading to better or worse chances as our experience tells us. This, of course, is what humans do all the time. Evaluating choices means looking ahead to some degree and assessing the situations they lead to. People call it exercising foresight—a good faculty to try to understand better and emulate in any study of intelligence.

Figure 10.5 shows a portion of a game tree in which the positions across the bottom have been given values as can best be judged according to some hypothetical scale from 0 to 10. Let's suppose that the evaluating is from Player 1's point of view, i.e., the higher the value, the better the game looks. It follows that from Player 2's point of view, the lower the number, the better.

Consider the position represented at position X, where Player 2 is to move. The choices available lead to positions valued at 3, 9, and 4 by whatever method we've adopted to judge a position's worth. Since a smaller number is more

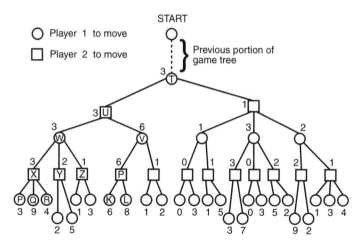

Figure 10.5 Minimaxing Procedure

favorable to Player 2, the *minimum* value available will be chosen, in this case 3, and it becomes the value for position X. Similarly, the minimums of the choices available at Y and Z give values of 2 and 1, respectively. And the same applies for all of Player 2's other moves at this level.

Player 1 arriving at position W will therefore be faced by three possible moves leading to values of 3, 2, or 1. Since a higher number favors Player 1, the *maximum* value available will be chosen, producing a backed-up value of 3 for W. In the same way, Player 1 will opt for 6 at position V. This is repeated, choosing minimum and maximum values alternately at successive levels and arriving finally at a value of 3 for position T, the root node for the portion of the game tree being considered. This procedure is known as *minimaxing*. As we saw earlier, the values tend to become more accurate toward the terminal part of a branch, where outcomes are known precisely. In the early and intermediate stages of win-lose-draw types of games, the numbers assigned are, in effect, estimates of the various positional strengths according to whatever criteria are adopted. In general, however, we did say that the object of strategy games is to maximize some kind of payoff. In other games the value might be a direct expression of the profit or loss calculated to result from a position, for example, Monopoly. The basically very simple principle of minimaxing accounts for much of the success of game programs.

THE ALPHA-BETA TECHNIQUE

Obviously, anything that reduces the amount of the tree needing to be analyzed is an asset. The following is a method first investigated by John McCarthy and his students for identifying nodes that can have no effect on the value of nodes above them in the tree. Therefore, no time need be wasted looking at any branches further below them.

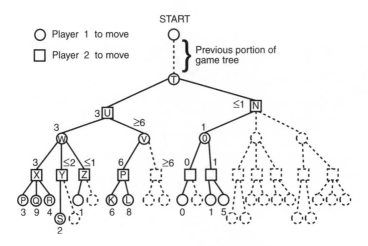

Figure 10.6 Alpha-Beta Tree Reduction

Figure 10.6 shows again the same part of the tree that we looked at in Figure 10.5. Imagine that the program has evaluated P, Q, and R to arrive at a value of 3 for node X. It then moves to the continuations from Y and determines 2 as the value for S. Since Player 2 will always choose the lowest value available, we can safely conclude that the final value for node Y will be 2 or less. Hence, there is no chance of Player 1 (who looks for the maximum) at position W choosing the continuation to Y since its value can't be higher than the 3 at node P, which we already know is available. Therefore, node Y can't have any effect at W, and no further continuations from Y need be considered. In exactly the same way, as soon as the first successor from Z is shown to have a value of less than 3, Z can be discarded as irrelevant.

Next, the program evaluates K and L and selects the minimum, 6, for the value of P. We can now say immediately that the final value for V will be 6 or higher because Player 1 at V already has 6 but will go for more still if further choices permit. But none of it matters because Player 2 at U already has a choice of 3 available, which is less than 6. Hence, no further nodes below V need be considered.

Similarly again, as soon as 1 has been established for node O, we know that the value for N must be 1 or less. Since Player 1 at T will choose U, nothing further below N needs evaluating.

The alpha-beta technique is essentially a way of endowing the program with a bit of common sense. Its effectiveness is highly dependent on the order in which nodes are examined, but with the application of heuristics to raise the likelihood of the more critical nodes being evaluated first, the savings can be enormous. With a good ordering method, the depth to which a tree can be analyzed below a given node, using the same number of evaluations, can be almost doubled.

A variety of methods has been developed for deciding the order in which nodes are to be analyzed. One is to conduct a "shallow search" beyond each of the successor nodes, possibly using its own evaluation criteria, in an effort to get some kind of a "feel" for the game likely to follow before committing the resources for a regular in-depth search. Another is called "forward pruning," which seeks to identify indicators of "implausibility" in order to eliminate from further consideration games with an appearance of being simply unsound or unwinnable. The problem, of course, is that unexpected changes of fortune can be hidden in portions of the game tree pruned off in this manner. Continuations in chess, for example, where a queen sacrifice leads to a forced mate five moves later can easily be thrown away. This is the reason it's so difficult to produce programs with the flair that earns triple exclamation point (!!!) ratings in the chess books.

Learning

A human newborn arrives knowing nothing but with a capacity to learn that can only be described as astounding. Within days, the process of interpreting patches of color and shape into objects existing in space, encoding mental constructs into strings of sounds capable of activating similar constructs assumed to exist in the minds of others, and using abstract properties extracted from the world as accurate predictors of its behavior has begun. What are the ground rules, presumably built-in neurally, responsible for initiating this process? Finding out how to program a machine to learn for itself was one of the earliest goals of AI research. Much work done by humans is trivial and repetitive, yet it requires some learning. Automating such tasks offered the prospect of freeing people for more creative and, one hopes, more rewarding lives. Also, the need to spell out a machine's operations in minute and exact detail can be tedious, time-consuming, and costly. Again, tremendous advantages stand to be gained from machines programmed with at least the rudiments of an ability to measure their own performance and experiment with ways of improving it.

Study of machine learning had from the start been one of the main motivations behind Arthur Samuel's Checkers Player. Throughout the twenty-two years of its reign and continual improvement from its inception in 1955 to eventually succumbing to the Jensen-Truscott program in 1977, Samuel resisted the temptation to boost its superficial performance by the brute-strength means of exploiting newer, faster hardware. Instead, he concentrated meticulously on the *technique* that it had always been his purpose to investigate. Essentially, it used a minimax search, later modified to alpha-beta, using forward pruning. We'll look briefly at two types of learning that Samuel explored: rote learning and learning by generalization.

ROTE LEARNING

This was the form that Samuel described as the most elementary. Basically, the idea is that the program saves all of the positions that it encounters during its various games, along with their computed evaluations, and retrieves the information instead of having to recompute it if the same position is encountered again. In fact, the method proved more beneficial than just saving time in the way that might be at first imagined. This is because the saved evaluations from previous games provided, effectively, a deeper "look ahead" into the search tree than would normally be attainable using the bounded depth-first limit programmed into the system. Figure 10.7 shows how this comes about.

The program varied the look-ahead that it would use in a given instance according to board conditions. For example, in a "jump" situation, the static evaluation of the position didn't really mean anything because the next move was forced, and the program would probe deeper for meaningful evaluations. Let's take the typical number of levels to which the program will search as three. From the position indicated as A, the program would normally base its evaluations on positions analyzed three levels deeper as indicated. However, when it comes to evaluate node X, it finds that it has encountered this position before and stored a value associated with it that resulted from the previous search taken three levels further. Hence, without doing any further work,

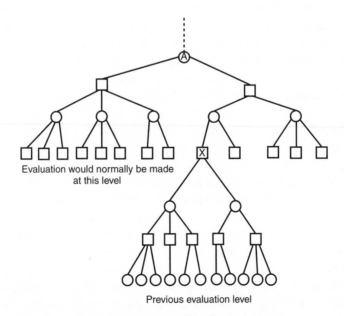

Evaluation would normally be made
at this level

Previous evaluation level

Figure 10.7 Increase of Effective Look-Ahead

although the current position being evaluated is A, the program is able to incorporate information previously computed from three levels deeper than its present search limit. A will thus be assigned a new value, and that value in turn will have the effect of influencing the next three nodes above A. Should that position arise again, the farthest above A will have received information from nine levels down. In this way, the program is able to accumulate information with experience and improve its game. A further source of learning is that the program can compare its static evaluation of a node—its previous estimate of the kind of game that X would likely lead to—with the worth of the position actually arrived at and revise its evaluation procedure accordingly.

In spite of these provisions, several additional features had to be incorporated to overcome certain residual weaknesses. A salient one, for example, was the program's frequent inability to press rapidly toward a win once it had an unquestionably winning position—a difficulty experienced by many novices. A situation of two kings against one king, for instance, is a won game from just about any board position, but a novice will often chase the lone king around the board endlessly through want of a clear notion of how to corner it. In the program's case, such a situation presented itself as equal evaluations for every continuation, supplying no indication of which one to follow and resulting in games that lost direction and protracted aimlessly. The solution was to store the level number in addition with each evaluation so that the program could select the path to an ending that was shortest. (Assuming it was the program that had the win. Otherwise it would stall by selecting the longest.) Many of the early attempts at learning programs failed through not taking sufficient account of the importance of this need to maintain a sense of direction. It comes to mind as a rather common human failing also.

LEARNING THROUGH GENERALIZATION

An obvious way to decrease the amount of memory work involved in utilizing past experience is to draw general conclusions on the basis of that experience and save just the generalizations, not every experience in detail. Again, this sounds like a pretty close description of what people do. The principal way in which Samuel's checkers program endeavored to implement this was by allowing for the program to modify its own evaluation function.

So far, we haven't said very much about the way positions are actually evaluated, we've simply assumed that the program somehow takes stock of the general board situation and comes up with an assessment. In reality, of course, a program needs to have specified to it just what it's supposed to assess and how.

The method that Samuel employed was to represent each board position as a "linear polynomial." This needn't be as intimidating as it may sound. A polynomial is a number consisting of a series of terms. Linear means that the terms are added together. Each term represents some aspect, or property, of the position that is considered as contributing to that position's worth—for example, the relative number of pieces possessed by the two sides or the number of squares they are free to move to. A term is made up of two parts: first, a "variable" measuring the current value of the property in question, and second, a "coefficient," or multiplier, which weights the strength of that variable relative to the others in determining the value of the polynomial as a whole.

Suppose, for example, that three factors influence my evaluation of whether to go to the beach today:

W—the weather
C—the importance of other chores that need to get done
K—the level of insistence being exhibited by the kids

All of these can vary from one day to another, and so they are variables. They don't, however, all weigh equally in my decision. If an important chore needs to be done, and this is the only time available, then that tends to come first, and the answer might be "sorry, not today," even if the sun's up there and the kids are restless. But we'll factor them into the equation as second in importance and take our chances with the weather, making it the lowest. These priorities could be reflected in defining three coefficients, C_c, C_k, and C_w, and establishing their relative strengths by setting them at:

$C_c = -5$ (negative since it counts *against* going)
$C_k = 3$
$C_w = 2$

The value of the "going to the beach" option, GB, is given by the polynomial:
$$GB = C_k.K + C_w.W + C_c.C \text{ (the "." meaning "times")}$$
or $3.K + 2.W - 5.C$ for whatever today's measures of K,
W, and C happen to be.

Let's say that our decision criterion is that if the value comes out positive we go, if it comes out negative we stay at home, and if it comes out zero we flip a coin. Now let's apply our evaluation function to two different days.

(1)	Weather cool and cloudy	$W = 2$
	Promised to put up shelves	$C = 4$
	Kids just as happy to watch movie	$K = 2$

Hence GB = $3 \times 2 + 2 \times 2 - 5 \times 4 = 6 + 4 - 20 = -10$
$\qquad\qquad\qquad\qquad\qquad\qquad\qquad$ We don't go

(2)	Weather clear and sunny	$W = 6$
	Still haven't put up shelves	$C = 4$
	Kids insistent	$K = 5$

Hence GB = $3 \times 5 + 2 \times 6 - 5 \times 4 = 15 + 12 - 20 = 7$
$\qquad\qquad\qquad\qquad\qquad\qquad\qquad$ We're packing

In Samuel's system, criteria that related as intermediary goals to the larger, more important criteria had smaller coefficients. Achievement of these intermediate goals indicated that the machine was steering in a direction so that these larger terms would eventually increase. If the machine was too far from a terminal position, an intermediate goal to pursue might be to search for advantageous piece ratios in the tree below, i.e., to look for opportunities to force a capture. If that was not possible within the depth limit being examined, it might look for positional strengths, and so on. Evaluation of piece ratios took account of the well-known checkers principle that it is to one's advantage to trade pieces when ahead and to avoid trades if behind (an example of a practical rule-of-thumb heuristic).

In practice, Samuel's evaluation polynomial had sixteen terms, which the program itself selected from a set of thirty-eight measured parameters. The program was thus able to change the polynomial to suit as different parameters took on more or less importance at progressive stages of the game. The program was also able to experiment with various strategies of assigning varying importance to these parameters by "twiddling" their multiplying coefficients to set their relative contributions to the whole.

Learning experience accumulated both from games against humans and from having the machine play itself. In the latter case, it used polynomial-modifying procedures when playing one side but kept the same fixed polynomial through the game when playing the other. This provided a standard for monitoring occasional bad choices that sent it the wrong way or spotting when, as sometimes happened, the machine was getting trapped on some local peak of improving performance, requiring needed manual intervention to give it the "kick" needed to find its way back to the main slope. Its performance was also assessed by comparing its selections with approved "book" moves from games analyzed and appraised by masters.

The two approaches to learning turned out to complement each other well, in that rote learning proved effective in the openings and at pressing home winning advantages to a close but was weak in the middle game, whereas generalization learning was weaker in the openings but better at handling the more complex situations of the middle game.

As has been mentioned, the performance of the program improved steadily until it could win against its creator every time, and at one time it beat a state champion. Yes, eventually the Duke University Paaslow program bested it and made the headlines—but in a spirit more akin to employing earthmoving machinery to tend a Japanese garden. Paaslow was an exhaustive search program that investigated about a million positions every two minutes, looking ahead seven moves in the middle game and ten moves by the end game. The remarkable thing about it was how little chess strategy was programmed in. Basically, it knew that winning material is good, making kings is good, and blocking the opponent from the kingmaking rank is good. Beyond that, it relied totally on its ability to explore exhaustively every continuation for at least seven moves ahead of a given position. Samuel's approach is more instructive when it comes to revealing something of the subtleties and finesse involved in intelligent reasoning and is the more fondly remembered by AI workers on that account.

For those who might be curious, the game in which it defeated Robert Nealy in 1962 is reproduced below.

	32		31		30		29
28		27		26		25	
	24		23		22		21
20		19		18		17	
	16		15		14		13
12		11		10		9	
	8		7		6		5
4		3		2		1	

Move	Black (Program)	Red (Nealy)	Move	Black (Program)	Red (Nealy)
1	11-15		28		27-23
2		23-19	29	15-19	
3	8-11		30		23-16
4		22-17	31	12-19	
5	4-8		32		32-27
6		17-13	33	19-24	
7	15-18		34		27-23
8		24-20	35	24-27	
9	9-14		36		22-18
10		26-23	37	27-31	
11	10-15		38		18-9
12		19-10	39	31-22	
13	6-15		40		9-5
14		28-24	41	22-26	
15	15-19		42		23-19
16		24-15	43	26-22	
17	5-9		44		19-16
18		13-16	45	22-18	
19	1-10-19-26		46		21-17
20		31-22-15	47	18-23	
21	11-18		48		17-13
22		30-26	49	2-6	
23	8-11		50		16-11
24		25-22	51	7-16	
25	18-25		52		20-11
26		29-22	53	23-19	
27	11-15				Red concedes

Figure 10.8 Samuel's Checkers Player Versus Nealy

World-Champion Class

HANS BERLINER'S BACKGAMMON PROGRAM

Two broad approaches to game playing emerge from the foregoing. One is the search-intensive method of plunging as deeply ahead into the game tree and considering as many of the alternatives as time and other resources permit. This is the power-tools, heavy-engineering philosophy. Faster hardware and horsepower are what get results. The other approach is evaluation-intensive: endeavoring to understand and analyze the game-strength potential implicit in a given situation sufficiently clearly to be able to encode it. While at least a rudiment of both is indispensable, either may dominate in a particular implementation, or they can be combined to make varying relative contributions. It can probably be said that the principles of further improving the search-intensive approach are sufficiently well understood for it to be essentially a matter of engineering. For true AI research, however, concerned more with unraveling those insights and hunches that guide humans through mazes of daily complexities that no conceivable search engine running for the lifetime of the universe could hope even to scratch the surface of, the challenge lies in more reliable evaluation.

These were the considerations motivating Hans Berliner, a psychologist turned AI researcher, who by the late 1970s was working at Carnegie Mellon University on evaluation methods. Berliner was also a onetime world correspondence-chess champion, so he not unnaturally turned his attention to games in search of a suitable vehicle for conducting studies. Finally, he settled on backgammon as ideal for his purpose.[10]

Like many board games, this is a stylization of combat in miniature, deriving its name from the Welsh *bac gamen*, which means "little war." The board has twenty-four landing areas that act as staging posts for the two players to move their armies of fifteen men each around the board to a final lodgement space and thence off the board. The first one to complete this process wins. The roll of a pair of dice determines the places that men can be advanced to, the two numbers showing either being played separately or combined to move one man. The conflict lies in the competition to occupy landing areas and deny them to the other side and in finding moves to send an inadequately defended opposing man back to the start. It is fought out as the two armies entangle on their way past each other, moving around in opposite directions. Since the dice obviously introduce an element of luck, backgammon matches are always arranged as a series of games.

It was this chance element that made backgammon suitable, as it generated too many possibilities for any search-intensive procedure to handle. With two dice able to roll twenty-one different ways and twenty choices of how to play each roll, the branching factor is 420 at each move, compared to something like

30 for chess. By the time each player has moved ten times, this will already have generated a thousand billion times the number of possibilities contained in the entire tree for checkers. Moreover, none of the twenty-one–way branchings at the dice throws can be pruned by any plausibility criteria because they are selected by pure chance.

In July 1979, Berliner sat in the Winter Sports Palace in Monte Carlo, facing Luigi Villa, an Italian who the previous day had become the new world backgammon champion. With Berliner was Villa's actual opponent, a three-foot-high robot that was quickly dubbed "Gammonoid," linked via satellite to a computer running Berliner's program back at CMU in Pittsburgh. The result was that the program won by a devastating six games to one. Villa's feelings so soon after his triumph can't have been helped by the comic antics of the robot, whose erratic mechanical behavior made it continually bump into things. It also managed to get itself tangled up in the curtains when it made what was supposed to be its dramatic entry onstage to the accompaniment of the theme from *Star Wars*. The spectators, who had thought the event would be good for laughs if nothing else, were stunned and the reporters maniacal in their excitement. It was the first time a machine had defeated a reigning world champion in a substantial game of wits and strategy.

Berliner's next task was to incorporate into the program a means whereby it would be able to develop an overall profile of an opponent's playing style and play an anticipatory game accordingly. This kind of mechanism could perhaps be incorporated into a bridge-playing program to capture something of the tactics for misleading and deception that humans can be so adept at, especially in the bidding phase.

Random Element

COMPUTERS DON'T HAVE MINDS
BUT MAY SOMETIMES READ YOURS

As an interesting side note, it turns out that computers can be surprisingly good at games in which the play is completely random. An example is SEER (SEquence Extrapolating Robot), developed by D. W. Hagelbarger of Bell Labs in the late seventies,[11] which wins against humans 55 to 60 percent of the time in guessing the other player's secret call for the simple flip of a coin. It seems that it is impossible for humans to play purely randomly, and since that can be shown mathematically to be the best strategy, the machine has an edge. A program that merely made random guesses and let its opponent lose by inferior play, however, wouldn't be exactly challenging or informative. Beyond that, SEER spent much time analyzing its opponent's play for deliberate or unconscious patterns, such as statistical distributions or correlations between the number of the turn and the guessed call, and basing its own guesses on that information in preference to playing randomly. (Randomness is the best play against a series that contains no information—which is what a random sequence is—but one can obviously do still better given an element of predictability.)

It's hard to say if such developments might point the way to the emergence, one day, of computers as competent psychologists. What they *do* demonstrate is that there are areas that pure search methods will never penetrate, for which amazingly effective evaluation techniques can be devised. This should come as a reassurance to those who dismay at the successes of "brute force" and insist that strategy and "guile" are what AI should be concerned with.

1. Shannon (1950b). See also Shannon (1950a).
2. McCorduck, pp. 148–53.
3. Samuel.
4. Newell, Shaw, and Simon (1958).
5. Kister et al.
6. McCorduck, p. 158.
7. Jackson, pp. 117 *ff.*, contains a good general introduction.
8. "Force v. Guile."
9. Jackson, p. 127.
10. Berliner.
11. "Force v. Guile."

Top Gun

BLACK HAT AND WHITE HAT:
THE CHESS FIGHTERS

"In building a path-breaking, successful program, the IBM team has definitely demonstrated artistry that is impressive and moving. But the artistry is on display in the code, the program they wrote, more than in the chess game played by the computer."

—David Gelernter[1]

The Early Program Duels

MACHACK FROM MAC

We have covered a lot of ground on the ideas behind game-playing programs since we left Alex Bernstein's project at the end of the fifties and IBM worrying that stories of "giant electronic brains" were becoming psychologically threatening to potential customers. For a while, game playing took something of a backseat in AI research. In the early sixties, a program that was begun at MIT and further developed at Stanford lost the first computer-chess-by-mail match to an opponent written at the Institute of Control Sciences in Moscow.[2] Then, in 1967, Richard Greenblatt, one of Marvin Minsky's students at MIT, wrote "MacHack," the first program that would compete respectably against human opponents in chess tournaments. The "Mac" part was in celebration of Project MAC, which was still going strong at the time, and the "Hack" was no doubt in recognition of "hackers," the name given to compulsive programmers manifesting the first symptoms of addictiveness, then becoming apparent in the MIT underworld.

MacHack employed a sophisticated tree-searching method that used a set of plausibility heuristics to extend the depth and analyze more intensively where suggestions of a particularly promising line of play were identified—an attempt to capture what humans do. Basically, it evaluated a move by comparing the positions and attacks available after the move with the ones that existed before it, taking account of changes in the blocking and unblocking of pieces, attacks on weaknesses such as pinned pieces, and such general guiding principles as "it's bad to position pieces in front of center pawns that are still on their original squares." Moves were ordered according to the score assigned by the plausibility generator and subject to an alpha-beta pruning process throughout, estimated as reducing the required computation by a factor of 100. The search terminated at varying depths, which depended on the configurations encountered, being pursued until what is known as a "dead" position was reached—a position free of moves that involve no choice, such as a jump opportunity in checkers or a check in chess, where the implications that would normally follow from evaluating the position are invalidated. Like Samuel's program, MacHack kept records of previously encountered positions and their evaluations and, in addition, contained a library of standard "book" openings.

Although undeniably designed to embody "skill" rather than force, MacHack was not a learning program. Its level of skill relative to that attainable by humans was not as great as that achieved by Samuel's Checkers Player. On the U.S. Chess Federation scale, its score in 1967 was given as 1,400, which puts it at the top of the 1,200 to 1,400 Class D category, and in April of that year it won the Massachusetts Class D amateur trophy to become the first chess program to win against a human in tournament competition and an honorary member of the USCF. (For comparison, Class E, below D, is rated as 100 to 1,200; classes C, B, and A cover 200-point-wide rating categories from 1,400 to 2,000; 2,000 to 2,200 is "Expert"; 2,200 to 2,400, "Master"; and above 2,400 "Grand Master" to the world champion rating, 2,800. The scale is calculated in such a way that for two players rated 200 points apart, the one with the higher rating will win 75 percent of the time. Tournament players average 1,800; all U.S. players, good, bad, and indifferent, about 900.)

MacHack went on to play in the Class C category with a rating between 1,400 and 1,500, not far below the USCF members' mean of 1,537. This provided inspiration for a revival of interest in chess-playing programs throughout the AI community to the degree that in 1968 the Scottish international master David Levy offered a bet that no computer would win against him in a match of an even number of games within the next ten years. John McCarthy and Donald Michie, founder of the major AI facility that had grown at Edinburgh University, accepted at 250 pounds each and in 1971 were joined by Seymour Papert, who had joined Minsky and MIT, and Ed Kozdrowickie of the University of California at Davis for the same amounts. Nineteen seventy-two was the year that Bobby Fischer won the world championship from the U.S.S.R.'s Boris Spassky and triggered a chess fervor in the United States. The Association of Computing Machinery (ACM) organized an annual computer-chess tournament,

Move	White (McHack)	Black (Human)	Move	White (McHack)	Black (Human)
1	e4	c5	12	Qxd6	Bd7
2	d4	cxd4	13	Bh4	Bg7
3	Qxd4	Nc6	14	Nd5	Nxe4
4	Qd3	Nf6	15	Nc7ch	Qxc7
5	Nc3	g6	16	Qxc7	Nc5
6	Nf3	d6	17	Qd6	Bf8
7	Bf4	e5	18	Qd5	Rc8
8	Bg3	a5	19	Nxe5	Be6
9	O-O-O	b5	20	Qxc6ch	Rxc6
10	a4	Bh6ch	21	Rd8mate	
11	Kb1	b4			

Figure 11.1 First Game Won by a Computer in Tournament Competition Chess
(Game 3, Tournament 2, Massachusetts State Championship, 1967;
Human opponent's rating: 1,510)[3]

and in 1974 a world championship event was held in Stockholm, supervised by the International Federation for Information Processing. Sadly for the Western effort, the title went to the Russian program Kaissa, which had won the chess-by-mail match with Stanford earlier.

Automatic Weapons

NORTHWESTERN UNIVERSITY'S "CHESS" SERIES AND BELL LABS' "BELLE"

John McCarthy is reputed to have summarized the flair that we call human intuition with the observation "General principles apply, except when they don't." Napoleon said that luck isn't really so unusual; it's just that few people know how to recognize it when it happens. The unexpected bursts of brilliance that can invent things proved to be impossible, solve the insoluble, and turn lost battles or games into stunning victories are often the result of breaking all the rules when everyone else is being slavishly bound by them. If such insights consist in part of being able—not necessarily always consciously—to see through, or around, or beyond the rules, then it will be a while yet before AI can produce any geniuses; one must first know what the rules are.

The problem with the evaluation-intensive strategies attempted by the programs we have talked about was an inability to spot the outrageous when it presented itself. Perhaps part of the human answer to this lies in our urge to explore, to experiment, to play. Since the rules programmed into the selective search procedures reflected the best that could be distilled of general principles, lines violating those principles would typically be rejected without further consideration. And in general this produced the solid, competent play that characterized the performance of these programs for most of the time. Lacking was an instinct to pounce upon those subtle opportunities that arise from time to time, the ones that call for defying the rules. Worse still, when the opportunity presented was the other way around and the machine missed it, the result was an outright blunder of a kind that a human player of the machine's level would seldom, if ever, commit.

In 1973, Lawrence R. Atkin and David J. Slate of the Computation Center at Northwestern University, who had produced a formidable chess player called "Chess 3.0," along the lines of Greenblatt's MacHack, came to the conclusion that the answer was simply to explore more possibilities more deeply—even at-first-sight dumb ones—before tossing them out too soon. Although employing an alpha-beta method to prune out the more extreme implausibilities, along with a mechanism for recognizing repeated positions, the philosophy of the redesigned system, "Chess 4.5," was basically to exploit the faster processing speeds and larger memories that were becoming available by pushing its analysis rate to 3,600 moves per second. And it paid off. In 1976, Chess 4.5 gained the North American Computer Chess Championships (NACCC) and in March 1977 won the Minnesota Open Championship, achieving a rating of 2,070, which qualified it at the "Expert" level. It should be added that—as would be expected from an approach based on deep and intensive searching from the current position—this performance was a result more of dazzling shorter-term tactics rather than long-term strategic planning, which remained mediocre. But it is precisely this kind of "feel" for the more remote qualities of a game that sets world-class human players apart. Such a profile would therefore give the program an edge against typical middle-of-the-league players, perhaps, but would not be expected to gain entry to the top divisions.

Nevertheless, it was the best chess player yet devised and seemed a promising-enough contender, at long last, to consider taking David Levy up on his 1968 bet. The first game of the match was played in the spring of 1977 at Carnegie Mellon, where Donald Michie was visiting, with Chess 4.5 running on a Control Data Corporation Cyber 176, then reckoned to be the world's most powerful commercial computer, linked in via phone line from Minneapolis. After what was described in reports as "A Good Try,"[4] Chess 4.5 resigned on the forty-third move—or, to be precise, the game was conceded by its designers. All the same, Chess 4.5 kept its reputation reasonably intact by going on to beat the Russian entry at Toronto during the 1977 Conference of the International Federation of Information Processing Societies and gain the world computer chess crown.

The following summer, Levy collected on his bet by winning $3\frac{1}{2}$ to $1\frac{1}{2}$ when the final games of the match were played at the Canadian National Exhibition, again in Toronto, this time with an improved version of the program, Chess 4.7. After winning the fourth game in what the match commentator, George Koltanowski, described as "masterly fashion," the machine was doing well in game five when it was smitten by a technical problem and, after lying

Black
Levy

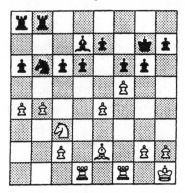

White
Chess 4.5

Position after 26. a4??

Move	White (Chess 4.5)	Black (Levy)	Move	White (Chess 4.5)	Black (Levy)
1	e4	c5	23	Rb1	Nb6
2	Nf3	d6	24	R/f3-f1	Rf8-b8
3	d4	cxd4	25	R/b1-d1	f6!
4	Nxd4	Nf6	26	a4??	a5!
5	Nc3	g6	27	b5	cxb5
6	f3	Bg7	28	axb5	Rc8
7	Be3	0-0	29	Rd3	Rc5
8	Qd2	Nc6	30	Rg3	R/a8-c8
9	Bc4	a6	31	R/f1-f3	a4
10	Nxc6?	bxc6	32	h4	a3
11	0-0	Nd7	33	fxg6	hxg6
12	f4	Nb6	34	Re3	Be6
13	Be2	Be6	35	h5	g5
14	b3	Nc8	36	Na5	a2
15	a3!	Qa5	37	Ra3	Bxd5
16	b4	Qc7	38	exd5	Rxc2
17	f5!	Bd7	39	Bd1	Rd2
18	Bh6	Qb6ch!	40	Kh2	Rc1
19	Kh1	Qd4	41	Bb3	a1=Q
20	Qxd4	BXd4	42	Rxa1	Rxa1
21	Rf3	Bg7	43	Resigns	
22	Bg7	Kg7			

Levy won the toss of the coin and elected to play Black. His response to the opening, e4, is a version of the well-known Dragon variation, which normally leads to a good battle.

In its early moves, the computer chose from a stored "book" of standard openings. Move 9, Bc4, was added to the book just before the match because the more common move 0-0-0 had occasionally given the machine trouble.

The capture of Levy's knight on Move 10 was a serious error because it strengthened Black's center.

Move 15, a3, was awarded an exclamation point for correctly anticipating and blunting the effect of Levy's threat in moving ... Qa5.

By the 17th move Chess 4.5 had gained a slight upper hand. With Move 18, however, Bh6, it misjudged the situation and allowed the exchange of queens two moves later, relieving Levy's position. At this point the game was even. Chess 4.5 could have retained its advantage at 18 by moving Rf3, thereby preparing the way for a strong attack with Bh6.

On the 26th move Chess 4.5 made a fatal error which ruined the pawn structure on the queen side. After that, the outcome was no longer in doubt, and Levy confidently capitalized to force a resignation.

Figure 11.2 Chess 4.5 versus David Levy: Spring 1977;
Comments Taken from Analysis by Hans Berliner

dead for an hour, lost on time. Koltanowski expressed sympathy but declared himself convinced that computers would be taking on grand masters within ten years, which turned out to be pretty close. Undeterred, Levy renewed his bet for another six years.

For the interest of chess enthusiasts, the first game between Levy and Chess 4.5 is reproduced in Figure 11.2.

By this time the challenge being posed by computer chess players was unmistakable and beginning to attract serious attention. In 1979 a Dutch software company called Volmac offered $50,000 to anyone producing a program that could defeat the former world champion Max Euwe by January 1, 1984. The prize was not collected. In the same year, Edward Fredkin, an MIT professor and inventor, announced an offer of $5,000, with no time limit, for the first chess program to achieve master rating in tournament play against humans; $10,000 for the first to reach international grand master and $100,000 for the first to beat the reigning world champion.

In what can only be described as a case of poetic justice, Chess 4.7 was eventually unseated when its own philosophy was taken a stage further and turned back upon it. In the early eighties, Ken Thompson and Joe Condon of Bell Labs incorporated the Northwestern style of "fast-and-dirty" board-crunching procedures into specially designed hardware chips capable of processing 150,000 positions per second. The result was "Belle," a dedicated (i.e., chess only), portable machine that in August 1983 rated in at 2,200, earning itself the first-ever computer "Master" title and collecting the first Fredkin prize.[5]

THE CRAY BLITZ: SUPERCOMPUTERS ENTER THE ACT

By this time, the challengers were appearing from all directions like black-hat contenders for the title of fastest-gun-in-town in a Western movie—and with about comparable life expectancy. Within a few weeks of becoming the first-ever machine chess master, Belle lost the world championship in New York to a 28,000-line program called Cray Blitz, the result of 32,000 man-hours of programming effort, running on a Cray XMP-48 multiprocessor supercomputer. Written by Bob Hyatt and Albert Gower from the University of Southern Mississippi and Harry Nelson of the Lawrence Livermore National Laboratory in California, it prevailed over twenty-one teams from eight competing countries. In April 1984 the indefatigable David Levy took it on in a telephone match from London and won comfortably, putting it in its place as he had Northwestern "Chess" and letting the world know that carbon chemistry still ruled. To make the point further, he announced that he was ready to bet £100,000 (about $160,000) that no computer would beat him or any player appointed by him for the next ten years. This time there were no takers.

Cray Blitz still had a firm hold on the world title for machines, however, and in 1986 successfully defended its title in Cologne, Germany. But it represented the end of the line for world-championship-level chess running on pro-grammable, general-purpose computers. In the future, all the winners would be special-purpose machines designed specifically for the job, following the pattern set by Belle.

LEAN, MEAN MACHINE: HANS BERLINER'S HITECH

Cray Blitz's demise came with a creation by Carnegie Mellon's Hans Berliner, himself once rated among the top twelve U.S. chess players, the same man who had already notched a world champion with his backgammon program in 1979. Designated "Hitech," it combined dedicated chess-position-processing circuits with an elaborate evaluation program called Oracle, which applied judgment derived from Berliner's extensive chess knowledge. Average look-ahead was eight moves, but in situations that seemed worth pursuing moves could be extended to as many as fourteen.

The principle that the special hardware worked on was to carry out multiple searching operations in parallel, i.e., at the same time. A chess move (apart from castling, which only happens once at the most per side in a game) involves the transfer of one piece to one square. Therefore, the possible continuations can conveniently be divided into sets consisting of all the legal moves that can result in a piece landing on each of the board's sixty-four squares. Hitech's special circuitry contained sixty-four processor chips, one doing the computations for each square and examining the continuations as it judged fit. Meanwhile, the remaining processors were examining the other games that would follow from moves to the other sixty-three squares. This enabled Hitech to rattle through board positions at an unprecedented 175,000 per second. In 1986 it was rated at 2,300, making it the world's first computer international master.

This performance becomes even more impressive when one bears in mind that it was implemented on a breadbox-size special-hardware unit connected to a $20,000 Sun workstation, whereas the Cray supercomputer that Blitz was written for weighed in at a whopping $14 million. Admittedly, Hitech was no good for anything else.

The shoot-out between Hitech and Cray Blitz took place at the North American Computer Chess Championship held at the annual ACM meeting in October 1985 at the Radisson Hotel in Denver.[6] The tournament featured matches between ten contenders that year, out of which the chess cognoscenti who were present seem agreed that the most interesting was one that Cray Blitz lost to a dedicated chess machine called Bebe, a product of private enterprise in the form of SYS-10 Inc. of Hoffman Estates, Illinois. Bebe, which finished second in the tournament after Hitech, examined 20,000 boards per second with a seven-level look-ahead. Third place, interestingly, went to "Intelligent Software," entered by David Levy, running on nothing more sophisticated than an Apple IIe with an accelerator card, processing five hundred boards per second with a seven-level look-ahead. Presumably, then, Levy had made good use of his formidable chess knowledge in developing a remarkably effective evaluation scheme. But it was to be a last fling for evaluation-oriented bids at the top titles. For chess, at any rate, being fastest with the mostest was what was getting the results.

In 1988, Hitech became the first computer to defeat a grand master, besting former U.S. champion Arnold Denker in a four-game match.

The AI Effect

AI researchers talk about a peculiar phenomenon known as the "AI effect." At the outset of a project, the goal is to entice a performance from machines in some designated area that everyone agrees would require "intelligence" if done by a human. If the project fails, it becomes a target of derision to be pointed at by the skeptics as an example of the absurdity of the idea that AI could be possible. If it succeeds, with the process demystified and its inner workings laid bare as lines of prosaic computer code, the subject is dismissed as "not really all that intelligent after all." Perhaps, true to the tradition of indignation and hostility that greeted Copernicus (we're not the center of everything after all), Darwin (we're not particularly special here), and Freud (we're not even rational), the real threat that we resist is the further demystification of ourselves.

It seems to happen repeatedly that a line of AI work originally pursued to uncover something of the mysteries of human intelligence finds itself being diverted in such a direction that, while the goal as originally stated remains elusive, the measures that were supposed to mark its attainment are demonstrated brilliantly. Then, the resulting new knowledge typically stimulates demands for application of it and a burgeoning industry, market, and additional facet to our way of life comes into being, which within a decade we take for granted; but by then, of course, it isn't AI. Maybe the reason why we keep failing to find hidden inner mysteries is that what's in there to be found isn't really as mysterious as we wanted—and to a large degree would prefer still—to believe.

To begin with, chess offered what seemed an opportunity to probe into processes involving some of the most subtle and intuitive qualities in the human mental repertoire—it has been said that genius expresses itself in three basic ways: through music, chess, and mathematics. Somewhere along the way it became acknowledged that, however else humans might achieve it, if the aim is to get excellence of performance in terms of measurable results, there are methods that are more appropriate to machines. As soon as the ultimate goal of wresting the world championship itself from humans appeared on the horizon as a distinct possibility, mutterings began to be heard, including some from within the AI community itself, that chess wasn't really an indicator of "intelligence" after all. In the meantime, the results from the frenetic activity of the seventies and eighties innocuously crept in through the back door of our lives to appear in schools, shopping malls, and children's birthday packages. Special-

Black
Bebe

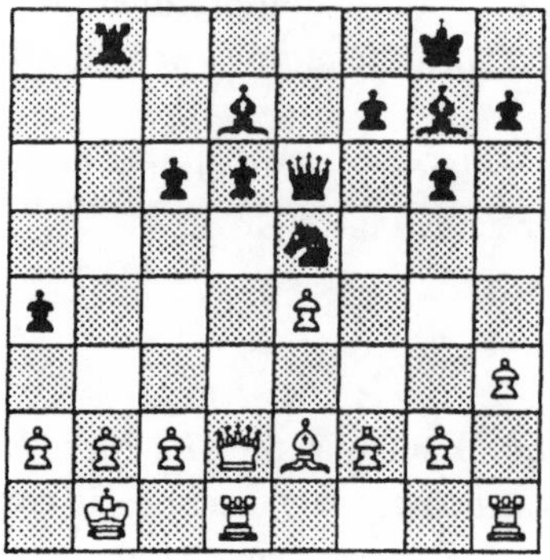

White
Cray Blitz

Position after 21. .... Rb8

Move	White (Cray Blitz)	Black (Bebe)	Move	White (Cray Blitz)	Black (Bebe)
1	e4	c5	27	Qc2	Qf6
2	Nf3	d6	28	Bc4	Qa1ch
3	d4	cxd4	29	Kd2	Qxa2
4	Nxd4	Nf6	30	Qxa2	Rxa2
5	Nc3	g6	31	Kc1	d5
6	Bg5	Bg7	32	exd5	cxd5
7	Qd2	Nc6	33	Bxd5	Bb5
8	O-O-O	O-O	34	Rhe1	Nd3ch
9	Nb3	Re8	35	Rxd3	Bxd3
10	Bc4	Ng4	36	Re8ch	Bf8
11	h3	Nge5	37	g4	Kg7
12	Bb5	a6	38	Re3	Ba3ch
13	Be2	a5	39	Kd1	Ra1ch
14	Bb5	Be6	40	Kd2	Bf1
15	Nd5	a4	41	Kc3	Rc1ch
16	Nd4	Bd7	42	Kd2	Rc5
17	Nxc6	bxc6	43	Ke1	Bxh3
18	Nxe7	Rxe7	44	Bc4	h5
19	Bxe7	Qxe7	45	gxh5	gxh5
20	Be2	Qe6	46	Kf2	h4
21	Kb1	Rb8	47	Rd3	Bf5
22	b3	axb3	48	Rd4	h3
23	cxb3	Be8	49	Rh4	Rc7
24	Kc2	Nd7	50	Rh5	
25	f3	Ra8		Resigns	
26	Kc1	Nc5			

Move 10. Black played ... Ng4 intending ... Bxc3 on the next move, maybe thinking that 12. bxc3 is forced because 12 Qxc3 would allow the fork with 12. ... Nxf2. But Black changes its mind, for after 12. Qxc3! Nxf2, either White rook to f1 thwarts the attack since a White bishop check at f7 would be fatal.

After Move 16 White's situation is dangerous. The Black pawn (a4) threatens to weaken White's king's position.

The position after Move 21 is shown opposite. Black threatens 22. ... Rxb2 ch, and after 23. Kxb2, Nc4 ch, winning White's queen.

Move 29. An even stronger move would be 29. ... Bc3 ch, followed by 30. Ke2 Rxa2 ch!

After Move 34, Black's material advantage of one piece is about to be increased by another exchange. In human tournament play, White could reasonably resign at this point.

Figure 11.3 Machine Against Machine: The Last of the Big Programs;
Cray Blitz versus Bebe, Denver, 1985

purpose chess machines are now commercially available that range in price from under a hundred dollars to thousands, including some that play at grandmaster level and others that will talk to you and offer hints and instruction, or even taunts at a foolish move. By 1991 the market for chess software was already estimated at $100 million and today lists product names that have become household words. The U.S. Chess Federation markets its own stand-alone game called Chess Academy for interactive instruction and practice.

All this was the result of the fruits reaped behind the advancing battle lines. At the front itself in this same period, fresh assault divisions had been wheeling up the heavy siege artillery to the final fortress.

Tank Warfare

THE ARRIVAL OF THE CHESS ENGINES

After the emphasis on evaluation and the embodiment of knowledge that had been set by the work of such people as Herbert Simon and Hans Berliner, it is perhaps strange to record that the next major development, firming the commitment to speed, special hardware, and intensive search, took place at Carnegie Mellon. Deep Thought, as the design was named, began as a project undertaken by a group of graduate students, Feng-hsiung Hsu, Murray Campbell, Thomas Anantharaman, and Andreas Nowatzyck. Making no pretense at trying to imitate whatever humans do, its first version analyzed 750,000 positions per second using 250 chips and two processors on a board the size of the chessboard itself and could project ten moves ahead along the most promising lines of play. The prototype, which at that stage contained only half the number of dedicated circuit chips planned, won the North American Computer Chess championship in 1987. The following year it achieved a rating of 2,500, earning a rank of international grand master and winning the second Fredkin prize. This put it above all but about two hundred human players worldwide. With $100,000 as a lure on top of all the other factors, a challenge to the world champion was inevitable.

The two-game match took place on October 22, 1989, in the New York Academy of Art and featured the full six-processor version of Deep Thought. Representing the humans was the Armenian Garry Kasparov, who three years before had become the youngest world champion at twenty-two and whose play was rated at 2,800. In 1970 people had come to chess tournaments featuring computers to poke fun at the machines and maybe to find reassurance as to their own superiority. This time they came to marvel—in some cases with undisguisable nervousness. But they were able to go home again breathing easier—for a while longer at least; Kasparov took both games comfortably. Nevertheless, Kasparov prepared assiduously for the match by studying fifty of Deep Thought's previous games and refraining from the displays of daring and aggressiveness for which his play was noted—unlike the aplomb with which David Levy had sat down to play Chess 4.5 only twelve years previously. And in further contrast to that event, in spite of Kasparov's win, everyone involved seemed to come away with the idea that the writing was clearly on the wall. The match organizer, Shelby Lyman, commented, "The real drama here is that Garry is facing his fate."[7] He put the time that the world champion would yield to a machine at five to ten years. Hans Berliner thought four. Kasparov himself, who should have had a better feel than anyone for what was involved, estimated that he might be able to stave off the day, "perhaps to the end of the century."

Meanwhile, the howitzer shops were tooling for even heavier munitions. Campbell and Hsu were taken on by IBM and installed at the Thomas J. Watson Research Center at Yorktown Heights, New York, to form a team with A. Joseph Hoane, Jr., Gershon Brody, and Chung-Jen Tan dedicated to further enhancing Deep Thought. The goal was to shrink the original pizza-size circuit board to the size of a single chip and stack a thousand of them together in parallel to enable analysis at the rate of one billion chess positions per second. It should be noted that this is still a long way short of the totally nonselective "pure brute force" method that some people imagine these machines use. An immense amount of tree pruning is still applied. Incredible as it may seem, even at a billion positions per second, a twenty-level search depth with an average of twenty branches per level would require over 300 million years to process exhaustively.

By the time of the 1990 NACCC tournament, Monroe Newborn, professor of computer science at McGill University in Montreal, who had been organizer of the championship since its inception, estimated that there were probably no more than forty to fifty players left in the world who were better than the machines.[8] The lineup that year included Belle, brought out of retirement for appearance and nostalgia's sake, Hitech again, a machine called Mephisto-Portorose, developed for commercial marketing by the German firm Hegener & Glasser, and Deep Thought II, now weighing in at 10 million boards per second. For the first time, the contest ended in a draw, with Deep Thought II and Mephisto sharing the title.

Mephisto also had the distinction, again in 1990, of becoming the first machine to beat a former world chess champion by defeating Kasparov's predecessor, Anatoly Karpov, in an exhibition. It should be added that Karpov was playing twenty-three other opponents, all humans, simultaneously at the time. Perhaps it should also be added that all the humans lost. The tolling of the bell could be heard all the more ominously when Deep Thought II, on behalf of the machines, settled the score with David Levy by achieving a perfect winning score of four games to nil.

Nineteen ninety-one saw a computer solve a long-standing chess conundrum. Lewis Stiller from Johns Hopkins University wrote a program running on powerful parallel processing hardware that proved that a king, rook, and bishop can defeat a king and two knights. The winning line requires 223 moves, and its proof involved analyzing more than 100 billion positions.[9] In August 1993 the current version of Deep Thought defeated Judith Polgar, the youngest grand master in history and the world's strongest female player, and in 1994 won the title of International Computer Chess Champion.

HUMANS 4, MACHINES 2: KASPAROV AND DEEP BLUE, 1996

Finally, in February 1996, in what became a media sensation in itself with $400,000 in prize money for the winner and $100,000 for the loser, Kasparov faced Deep Thought's successor in a six-game match at the fiftieth anniversary celebration of the Association for Computing Machines, held in Philadelphia.

Deep Blue is described in IBM literature as "a RISC System/6000 Scalable POWER parallel Systems (SP) high-performance computer." What this is meant to convey is that the latest iteration of the machine consisted of a thirty-two-node (input/output channel) IBM PowerParallel SP2 high-performance computer, each node connected to a microchannel card containing eight dedicated chess processor chips—256 in all—having a speed of 2 to 3 million positions per second each. The programming code was written in C and ran under the AIX operating system. In addition, Deep Blue fielded a database of openings from every grand-master game played in the previous one hundred years and a database of billions of endgame situations, activated when the number of pieces on the board falls to six. The designers stated that this array of starship *Enterprise* weaponry endowed Deep Blue with a thousand times the power of its predecessor, which had lost to Kasparov in 1989. The second confrontation was followed by an estimated billion people around the world and became the largest World Wide Web event ever. Over a million hits were registered on the official web site covering the event, which was set up by IBM at the invitation of the ACM.

In the first game, Deep Blue stunned the world by turning a retreat into an attack that resulted in Kasparov's ceding defeat on the thirty-seventh move. Visibly shaken, Kasparov left the game site in the Philadelphia Convention Center without a word. The result came as a surprise to both chess grand masters commentating on the event and to the IBM design team, all of whom had thought that Kasparov's strong attack in the early phase would give him the day. Perhaps the message was that Kasparov's gamesmanship and penchant for rattling opponents with audacious, unexpected moves is lost on computers. C. J. Tan, the manager of the IBM Deep Blue Research Project, commented that Deep Blue was far from being the perfect chess player and had certain limitations; at the same time, he declined to reveal what they were.

In the second game, Kasparov rebounded and in a triumphant display of long-range strategic thinking put the machine down in a grueling duel of seventy-three moves that went on for five hours, forty-five minutes. Afterward, Kasparov felt that he had found a strategy for outmaneuvering the machine, which he referred to as "the monster." By playing safely rather than adopting an overt offense, he could lull the machine into opening up its position. "If you threaten, the machine will counterattack," he said, maybe somewhat wryly after his experience in the first game. "But if there is no threat, the machine will go about its business and eventually give you an opportunity."[10]

The third game, which coincided with the University of Pennsylvania's celebration of the fiftieth birthday of ENIAC, ended in a draw after thirty-nine moves. The game on the following day, a Wednesday, also resulted in a draw when the IBM team's Campbell made the offer at Move 50, leaving the score so far a tie at 2–2 (chess games are scored 1 for a win and $1/2$ each for a draw). Kasparov had made a similar offer after Move 41, which was rejected. "I'm really tired," Kasparov said afterward, with two games left to play on Friday and Saturday. "If I were playing a human, they would be too. I feel pressure. The computer does not."[11]

Game five was the turning point. After offering a draw and being rejected, Kasparov rallied dramatically, responding with some strong moves to a couple of mistakes on Deep Blue's part and forcing a resignation after forty-seven moves. This left Kasparov in the situation of facing at worst a drawn match if Deep Blue won the final game. For Kasparov, on the other hand, either a win or a draw would carry off the prize.

The traditional reaction here would be to play safe and make do with the draw. Kasparov, however, returning with confidence now to his own style, attacked from the outset and quickly took control of the board to press home a win when the machine's pieces became hopelessly trapped and in each other's way, unable to stave off a mating threat. For those who knew what to look for, signs of the end came just before Kasparov's fortieth move, when he picked up his watch from the table and put it back on his wrist. "The watch!" international master and commentator Maurice Ashley cried. "The watch!" In an adjoining room to the match, six hundred spectators who were watching on closed-circuit TV burst into laughter.[12] It had long been recognized as one of Kasparov's personal quirks—deliberate or unconscious—to put his watch back on when he feels he has a game clinched. Sure enough, the IBM scientists resigned from the game three moves later.

So, a respite for carbon and proteins for a little while longer. Yasser Seirawan, another commentator and international grand master, found himself astounded nevertheless. "I was stunned by its depth of analysis," he said. "It was unnerving. You want to say, 'Can't you even show a bead of sweat?' "[13]

Although Kasparov had clearly figured out how to gain momentum as the tournament proceeded, he was emphatic about the IBM scientists' achievement and profuse in his congratulations. "This was a serious opponent," he said, rating the match as demanding as the one he had played the previous fall against Viswanathan Anand, a human challenger for the world championship. "As tough as the world championship," Kasparov said. By the estimation of all the grand masters who had been following it, the match was surprisingly competitive. Few, if any, had given Deep Blue a chance. Several had predicted a straight 6–0 rout by Kasparov.

What the match perhaps illustrated most of all is the human capacity for what we maybe do best: learning much from a little experience. Kasparov consistently sought positions in which he had discerned from the early games that the computer had trouble—where the short term was cloudy, with no immediate tactical opportunities that intensive searching would zero in on—and he could catch it in a delicate web of forces that it was evidently unable to see. It has long been noted that players of grand-master caliber take in the game in larger chunks of meaning than the average player is able to identify, whole board-patterns that they recognize from countless examples as requiring a subtle variation in emphasis or aims. It was this lack of positional comprehension that Kasparov was able to identify and exploit. In his own words, "You have to limit its unlimited potential. You have to be careful not to create weaknesses in your own position, not to leave hanging pieces, not to leave a king threat. You have to play solid, positional chess because any mistake will be punished by the machine more severely than by any human player."[14]

The IBM scientists apparently saw things the same way. When I talked with Murray Campbell later that year at an AI symposium held at Carnegie Mellon, he was skeptical about the value of ever-deeper searching. Beyond a certain point, he said, deeper searches provide less of a return per level, and a greater percentage of computing effort is wasted on worrying about situations that never come close to happening. It would be more profitable, he felt, to devote more of the chip power to evaluation.

Kasparov issued a rematch challenge for 1997, and IBM promptly accepted. The return match was scheduled to take place in New York City in May.

(The old policy that had affected Samuel and Bernstein still seems to be the guiding rule at IBM today. After I met Campbell, I called the publicity department at Yorktown Heights to ask for an information package that he had recommended, explaining that I wanted it for background information for an AI book I was working on. In a return call, I was informed that Deep Blue "is not AI" and that IBM had no relevant information to offer. I should add that I can see the company's point. Campbell had stressed that chess was being used as a vehicle to explore the potential of technologies suitable for producing high-performance "computation engines" for application in such areas as astrophysics and molecular dynamics, not for any insights to human or humanlike intelligence. I called Campbell back to plead that whatever one chooses to call it, a machine that can take on the world champion would be rather conspicuous by omission if not included in a book on AI. Campbell agreed heartily and intervened, and to give thanks and credit where it's due, the company had the information to me by Federal Express the next morning.)

Game 1

Move	White (Deep Blue)	Black (Kasparov)	Move	White (Deep Blue)	Black (Kasparov)
1	e4	c5	20	Nxb6	axb6
2	c3	d5	21	Rfd1	f5
3	exd5	Qxd5	22	Qe3	Qf6
4	d4	Nf6	23	d5	Rxd5
5	Nf3	Bg4	24	Rxd5	exd5
6	Be2	e6	25	b3	Kh8
7	h3	Bh5	26	Qxb6	Rg8
8	O-O	Nc6	27	Qc5	d4
9	Be3	cxd4	28	Nd6	f4
10	cxd4	Bb4	29	Nxb7	Ne5
11	a3	Ba5	30	Qd5	f3
12	Nc3	Qd3	31	g3	Nd3
13	Nb5	Qe7	32	Rc7	Re8
14	Ne5	Bxe3	33	Nd6	Re1 ch
15	Qxe2	O-O	34	Kh2	Nxf2
16	Rac1	Rac8	35	Nxf7 ch	Kg7
17	Bg5	Bb6	36	Ng5 ch	Kh6
18	Bxf6	gxf6	37	Rxh7	Resigns
19	Nc4	Rfd8			

Game 6

Move	White (Kasparov)	Black (Deep Blue)	Move	White (Kasparov)	Black (Deep Blue)
1	Nf3	d5	23	Qd3	g6
2	d4	c6	24	Re2	Nf5
3	c4	e6	25	Bc3	h5
4	Nbd2	Nf6	26	b5	Nce7
5	e3	c5	27	Bd2	Kg7
6	b3	Nc6	28	a4	Ra8
7	Bb2	cxd4	29	a5	a6
8	exd4	Be7	30	b6	Bb8
9	Rc1	O-O	31	Bc2	Nc6
10	Bd3	Bd7	32	Ba4	Re7
11	O-O	Nh5	33	Bc3	Ne5
12	Re1	Nf4	34	dxe5	Qxa4
13	Bb1	Bd6	35	Nd4	Nxd4
14	g3	Ng6	36	Qxd4	Qd7
15	Ne5	Rc8	37	Bd2	Re8
16	Nxd7	Qxd7	38	Bg5	Rc8
17	Nf3	Bb4	39	Bf6 ch	Kh7
18	Re3	Rfd8	40	c6	Bxc6
19	h4	Nge7	41	Qc5	Kh6
20	a3	Ba5	42	Rb2	Qb7
21	b4	Bc7	43	Rb4	Resigns
22	c5	Rde8			

**Figure 11.4 Silicon Physics versus Carbon Chemistry;
the First and Last Kasparov–Deep Blue Games, February 1996**

THE CITADEL FALLS: 1997

With the relentlessness of the machines bearing down on the last human
stronghold in a *Terminator* movie, the inevitable finally happened at the Equi-
table Center in midtown Manhattan on Sunday, May 11, 1997. After Kasparov
took the first game, Deep Blue the second, and Games 3, 4, and 5 were draws,

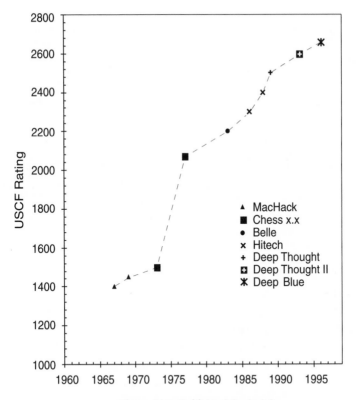

Figure 11.5. Twilight of the Gods?
The Advances in Computer Chess Ratings

the score was 2.5 each with everything depending on the sixth game. The makings were there for a tussle worthy of going down in history as the Armageddon of silicon versus carbon. And then the champion for humanity, assessed as the most formidable player that our kind has ever produced, suddenly crumpled and resigned on the nineteenth move after less than an hour of play.

The media went into a frenzy, of course. And let's not be tempted to disguise or belittle what was a magnificent achievement. A human one. For it was humans who designed and programmed the system, and they deserve credit in the same way as the engineers who created the Saturn V rocket that put humans on the Moon or the design teams who produced the 747. But was it really an indicator that the ultimate in human mental ability had finally been artificially matched? There was no huge rush to proclaim so. The AI Effect seemed to excel itself.

Kasparov began with the philosophy that he had developed in the course of the 1996 match for what would constitute good anticomputer strategy: avoid early confrontations; play a slow, solid game; try to force positional mistakes. And it worked perfectly for the first game. What threw Kasparov was the change that appeared to have come over Deep Blue by the time they met for the

GAME 6

White	Black	White	Black
D. Blue	Kasparov	D. Blue	Kasparov
1 e4	c6	10 Bg6	Kd8
2 d4	d5	11 Bf4	b5
3 Nc3	dxe4	12 a4	Bb7
4 Nxe4	Nd7	13 Re1	Nd5
5 Ng5	Ngf6	14 Bg3	Kc8
6 Bd3	e6	15 axb5	cxb5
7 N1f3	h6	16 Qd3	Bc6
8 Nxe6	Qe7	17 Bf5	exf5
9 O-O	fxe6	18 Rxe7	Bxe7
		19 c4	Resigns

The Caro-Kann Defense is an unusual opening for Kasparov to play.

The moves through to 7. N1f3 are the standard "book" line, played in thousands of games before. 7. ... h6(?) came as a surprise to all commentators. The normal move is 7. ... Bd6 (first!) 8. Qe2 h6 9. Ne4 Ne4 10. Qe4 Nf6 Black's seventh move as played permits the Knight sacrifice 8. Ne6, from which White is able to gain an advantage.
If 8. Ne4 Ne4 9. Be4 Nf6 10. Bd3 c5, Black does fine since he hasn't yet moved his f8 bishop, and the freeing break ... c6-c5 followed by Bf8-c5 comes without losing a tempo.
In transposing the move order, Kasparov apparently walked into a well-known book trap.

Figure 11.6 Deep Blue vs. Kasparov May 1997

second game. In Kasparov's own words, from an article that appeared in *Time* two weeks later (May 26, 1997, p. 66): "The decisive game of the match was Game 2, which left a scar on my memory and prevented me from achieving my usual total concentration in the following games. In Deep Blue's Game 2 we saw something that went well beyond our wildest expectations of how well a computer would be able to foresee the long-term positional consequences of its decisions. The machine refused to move to a position that had a decisive short-term advantage, showing a very human sense of danger."

What a rattling experience that must have been. Just how much is shown by the fact that Kasparov eventually resigned the game in a position where he failed to see that he could have forced a draw through the chess technicality known as "perpetual check." Although most commentators agreed with Kasparov's decision at the time, a midwestern philosophy professor amid the hubbub of the chess chatroom discovered the sequence of moves that could have saved Kasparov from defeat. So how had the world champion, generally held to be the best player in history, missed it? Apparently, through being unnerved to the point of dismissing such a possibility on the grounds that if it existed, Deep Blue would have found and countered it. "I do not understand how the most powerful chess machine in the world could not see simple perpetual check," he said afterward. Well, it was surely not for the same reason that Kasparov didn't.

The following three games were drawn, grueling and heavy with emotional portent for the man, but just more-of-the-same shuffling bits through registers for the machine. The abrupt collapse in the sixth game showed all the signs of nervous and psychological exhaustion. Playing Black, Kasparov made a known mistake on the seventh move into the game that develops from the opening known as the Caro-Kann Defense, which the machine instantly exploited by consulting its reference library—there was no calculation load at this point at all—and quickly obtained a winning position. Was it an inexplicable slip on the part of a player of such caliber, or a wrongly concluded belief that he had found a way around the standard pitfall? The mortified expression on Kasparov's face immediately afterward suggests the former. Grandmasters and computer experts alike went from praising the match as a great experiment to smacking their foreheads in amazement and near-speechlessness. The most widely heard reaction was to deplore the standard of play on both sides. "This wasn't serious chess," said Lev Alburt, the former U.S. champion, who believes there are a hundred grandmasters who can beat Deep Blue, while to the American grand-master Patrick Wolff the computer in some situations played like a "numskull." "He [Kasparov] didn't try his best," was the verdict of Susan Polgar, the women's world champion, who immediately after the match issued her own challenge to IBM to take on Deep Blue herself. It's telling, perhaps, that in his rematch challenge to IBM, Kasparov proposed a match of 10 games over 20 days, played on alternate days, and to be held in the fall, when he could be at his best after the summer's vacation. Then, he promised, "I personally guarantee you I will tear it to pieces."

So what was the big difference? What changed so much in the second game to upset the equilibrium of a player like Kasparov to the point that he remained off balance for the remainder of the match? Murray Campbell had already said (see the Kasparov, 1996 section above) that he didn't place great faith in putting much more effort into improving the machine's sheer, brute-force calculating power. And, indeed, we saw that even systems with far more power than Deep Blue (200 million positions per second at the time of the 1997 match) could never explore more than an insignificant part of the game tree. Huge parts still have to be discarded "on sight"—which is the part humans do that becomes all but impossible to describe.

Frederick Friedel, who is Kasparov's computer adviser, explains the point with an anecdote in which he once asked the former world champion Max Euwe about a particular position in which both sides had the same number of pawns and pieces and controlled the same numbers of squares. Any amateur would have said that the position was a draw. But when Euwe was asked, he said, "White's winning. It controls more squares." When Friedel proceeded to count them and show they were the same, Euwe pointed and said, "Yes, but those don't count. They're not important."

Exactly why this is, is the kind of information that remains too subtle to elu-cidate and program. Although substantial hardware upgrades were made in the interim since the 1996 match, it's doubtful if they constituted the major factor in bringing about humanity's change of fortune. More important was the effort that went into programming, making the system far more amenable to fine-tuning between games, and the incorporation of a vast amount of human experience into its database—five grandmasters were enlisted to advise the IBM team during the preparatory period. It was the flexibility of style that these measures made possible that threw Kasparov. He had come prepared to play a machine. What he found himself up against had been programmed to respond like a grandmaster.

So does this represent the permanent unseating of the human race from a throne once believed to be uncontestable, that we're simply going to have to get used to? Or will the disgruntled grandmasters, including Kasparov himself, who insist, Paula Jones–style, that they haven't yet begun to fight, be able to put that day off for a while longer—some assert, now they've a better measure of the opposition, indefinitely? I'm not going to attempt calling that one. But it is reassuring in a way to note that the best hopes for the machine's consolidating its position seem to lie in attending more to evaluation and those subtly human things, rather than blindly adding more and more brute force.

Arthur Samuel would not doubt smile and nod.

So Is This Intelligence?

INTELLIGENCE EVERYWHERE

I suggested earlier that a good working definition of intelligence might be a measure of a system's ability to learn from experience and modify its own behavior in a manner that's appropriate to its goals. If information coming in from the outside world constitutes "experience" within the narrow problem domain defined by the game, I don't see how you could have a better demonstration of appropriate behavior modification than playing at world championship level. After all, nobody programmed in the specific response to be given to any and every move of every game in the way seemingly implied by the objection that computers can only handle situations foreseen by their programmers. "Ah, but the general rules had to be programmed in. The computer didn't figure them out. And despite all the talk about it applying chess 'knowledge,' the knowledge was put in there by people." Yes, that's true. But you could say the same about humans also. They all come into the world knowing nothing and possessing only the "ground rules" that were put there by God or by nature, depending on one's beliefs. And most of what they learn after that comes through language, books, teachers, and example. Trying to find ways of getting machines to do something comparable is what AI research is all about.

This is where debates over questions of this kind tend to get hung up over the meaning of vaguely defined words such as "think" and whether things like "awareness" and "consciousness" are implied—exactly what Turing was trying to avoid by proposing his test. The result in every exchange that I've witnessed has been a deadlock or interminable wheel spinning that leaves every participant holding the same views that they entered with. I think, however, the question can be answered without getting into all that, in a way that's consistent with the sense in which we've been using the word "intelligence," which could be summed up as describing behavior purposefully and efficiently directed toward achieving a nontrivial goal. The behavior of a well-trained fire-fighting or paramedic team in dealing with an emergency situation would surely have to be described as intelligent compared to a panicking crowd running in circles, or the way that the crew of a nuclear submarine or the workforce building a bridge or a high rise goes about its business compared to a mob staging a riot. So if the ability to apply purposeful and effective solutions to complex problems is an acceptable measure of acting "intelligently," then in that sense, yes: Deep Blue—and many other programs that have been produced for purposes other than chess playing—qualifies. "Yes, but then 'it' isn't what's being intelligent. It's only playing back stored human intelligence." Okay, if you want to think about it that way. But the same could be said of DNA. It should come as a reassurance to those who find the thought of intelligent machines threatening. It doesn't make them potentially any the less useful.

What I'm really suggesting here is that for our present purposes—and as far as I can see, what will be the concern of the subject for a long time to come— "intelligence" can be separated from the other concepts that cause all the trouble. Perhaps it's only a hangover from Victorian preoccupation with intellect that causes them to be regarded as synonymous in the first place. In the days when it seemed unquestionable that the whole purpose of recently formulated evolution had been to produce eminent Victorians, the intellectual pursuits that they felt distinguished them had to be an expression of everything that it meant to be human, at its highest, and since humans were unique in their experience of conscious awareness, obviously consciousness and intelligence were the same thing. (A frequently expressed belief of the times was that laboring and servant classes actually had a lower sensitivity to physical pain and emotional anguish and a greater inherent hardiness for toil. This conveniently justified placing them in an intermediary position on the scale, filling the gap, as it were, between draft animals and the eminences. The further implication, of course, though not often openly expressed, was that they weren't "completely" human.)

But when we start to look about us, I submit that there are all kinds of intelligent processes going on that don't require consciousness at all, eminently Victorian or otherwise. I remember flying in a helicopter above Boston once and suddenly being struck by the intricacy and complexity of the traffic patterns flowing in the streets and highways below. The collective impression was of a single organism adapting to changing conditions as it pursued its own ends. Suppose that the ultimate bureaucratic totalitarian state were one day to become fact and the Ministry of Personnel Transportation required a form to be submitted from every person once a week detailing all the journeys he or she desired to make for the seven-day period beginning the following week. (Changes of plan? Unexpected emergencies? Sudden impulses? You've got to be joking.) Then all the forms, containing all points of origin, destinations, and requested times of day, are processed so the Weekly Urban Traffic Plan can be issued, and you receive your personal schedule of routings in due course. Of course, it wouldn't work; no department of planners with or without mechanized help could solve such a problem in the time span allotted. And yet such problems *are* solved daily, moreover, in real time—and despite the snarl-ups and frustrations at times, in the main, tolerably effectively—in thousands of places all around the world. Well, behavior that manages to solve problems of such complexity qualifies to be called "intelligent," doesn't it? The behavior I'm referring to is that of the whole system, not of the individual drivers, none of whom would be capable of solving the whole problem. We have another example of an emergent property manifesting itself from the collective action of many essentially simple units, each concerned only with its own local conditions and interacting according to a few basic rules. I don't think anyone would see a need to invoke some collective, citywide consciousness to explain it. The two concepts—consciousness and intelligence—are distinct and separable. By the same token, we could say that national and global economic, political, and social systems—entities that every day manage and solve, with varying degrees of success, extraordinarily complex problems, given the eccentricities of the basic material they're supposed to work with (us)—exhibit amazing levels of behavior that deserve (all the usual jokes acknowledged but notwithstanding) to be called intelligent.

Neither is it necessary to confine attention to the world of human activities to see such effects in action.[15] A few termites, given some pellets of the material they use for building, act as if they are confused or only partly functional. They'll push them around, perhaps put a couple on top of each other, in a way that seems to say they know they're supposed to do something with them but aren't sure what. Increase the numbers, and the behavior becomes more coordinated and purposeful. Finally, at the population size of a full colony, they are able to organize themselves into work teams that somehow know when to start curving two parallel-rising columns toward each other to meet, producing arches that would have delighted the architects of any Gothic cathedral, eventually producing those World Trade Center–height mounds with their systems of chambers, galleries, and ventilation shafts that astonish us. It has been said that a colony of social insects does, in fact, compose a single, distributed organism, formed from freely mobile "cells" that communicate primarily chemically, as opposed to consisting of fixed units hard-wired in place.

And one doesn't have to look only at complete organisms. The coordination and complexity of, say, the human immune system enables it to adapt and modify its behavior in response to new situations in ways that would be heralded as a work of genius if devised by a human chemical engineer. Or the circulatory system, or the thermal regulation system, or the astounding cycles of feedback and regulation taking place in the metabolism of any cell. All of these are instances of extraordinarily complex problems being solved in ways that can only be described as highly purposeful and efficient when compared, say, to anything that the same materials would be capable of after being put through a sausage machine.

Some would insist that even if we accept this as "intelligence," it has to be evidence of a consciousness existing somewhere else. Evolutionists say no, it can arise by itself. That's something else I'm not about to get into here. But suppose that for the sake of argument we agree, isn't this saying that the intelligence that directs the assembly of proteins into elephants is valid enough, even if the consciousness responsible operates indirectly through the authoring of DNA? Why, then, shouldn't we grant the same credit to behavior arising via a differently authored kind of DNA that can direct a machine in plausibly taking on the world chess champion?

So if this is intelligence, it abounds everywhere in nature and doesn't demand the presence of immediate and overt consciousness. Looked at in this way, the suggestion that intelligent behavior might also be reproduced through machines—just as so many other aspects of nature, from generating heat and light to moving heavy objects and self-propulsion, have been reproduced through machines—perhaps becomes an easier notion to go along with.

WHY 747S DON'T HAVE FEATHERS

There is a rather sobering implication to all this. For many years—centuries, in fact—men dreamed of artificial flight[16] and sought to achieve it by constructing all manner of contraptions that flapped, beat, heaved, and usually fell to pieces, in some cases even going to the extent of creating imitation feathers. (One intrepid attempt even carried a faithfully reproduced beak. "Well, we *think* it's the wings that do it, but you never know.") Finally, the meticulous research of the Wright brothers led them to the way of tackling flight that was *appropriate* to engineering methods. And once the right principles were grasped, the progress we've seen in less than a century became unavoidable. In the particular areas of performance that were of human interest, it quickly became possible to outstrip nature. Nothing in the natural world can lift loads of hundreds of tons across global distances, flying close to the speed of sound on the fringes of the atmosphere. And nothing even sets the precedent of going out into space.

Nature's way of doing things might not be the only way—or necessarily the best way—for our purposes; in some cases, one is tempted to say, not even for its own. There are potentials that nature never hit upon or was unable to develop into anything practicable. The wheel is a wonderfully efficient device, but naturally occurring free rotation is found only in the flagella of a few protozoans, presenting insurmountable problems for evolution to have taken further. The comparative fragility of organic molecules makes it impossible to generate the temperatures, and hence utilize the energy densities, that are attainable from direct combustion. No currents in natural nervous systems can be made to oscillate fast enough to take advantage of radio waves. And so on.

It could be that trying to give silicon circuitry the same kind of intelligence as that displayed by protein-based systems simply isn't the way to go. Even more so if the particular traits we try to imitate turn out to be "fixes" adopted by nature to overcome some shortcoming that an engineering approach starting from scratch doesn't have to be stuck with in the first place—the acute limitations of human short-term memory, for example. What this is saying, in effect, is that once we hit on the right approach that "takes off," we could very soon find ourselves dealing with intelligences that compare with human problem-solving capabilities in about the same way a 747 does to a pigeon. (I know that a 747 can't lay eggs. But building a gas-turbine-powered behemoth would be a strange way to go about making eggs when we've already got chickens.)

Some people will perhaps find such a prospect daunting—and it's understandable why. But is it really so different from the various other ways in which, through application of our own natural intelligence, we have devised things like telescopes, microscopes, telephones, bicycles, cranes, and automobiles to enhance and extend our own limited faculties? It's often said that many of our current problems arise through our ability to create complications faster than we can find solutions. Well, if that's so, then maybe having some high-power problem solvers to draw on wouldn't be a bad idea.

As too many stories of wars, unnecessary famines, economic collapses, and political debacles illustrate, we could use help managing our affairs in a number of departments. Our tendency has always been to shrug such things off resignedly as realities of life that nothing can be done about. Perhaps that won't always be true, any more than it was true that bubonic plague and 70 percent infant mortality were realities we could do nothing about.

And there's no reason why humans should feel somehow belittled or cease to enjoy their uniqueness as a consequence. After all, have we ceased holding the Olympics because the weightlifting champion would be trounced by a forklift or the gold medalists for the track events left standing by the family automobile?

As a footnote, it's interesting to speculate on what manner of game might result from Deep Blue and Kasparov playing in consultation, on the same side. Perhaps that's more the kind of way in which humans and machines should be viewing the future.

1. From Weber (1996a).
2 See Crevier, pp. 223 *ff.*, and McCorduck, pp. 161 *ff.*, for more of this early history.
3. Jackson, p. 149.
4. "Good Try."
5. "Chess 4.7 v. Belle."
6. Dewdney.
7. Crevier, p. 233.
8. Cody.
9. *New York Times*, February 18, 1996.
10. Associated Press WWW news service.
11. Ibid.
12. Weber (1996b).
13. Associated Press WWW news service.
14. Weber (1996b).
15. For a fascinating chapter on such things, see Thomas.
16. Hayes & Ford supplied this wonderful metaphor.

12

Adventures in Toyland
DISTILLATIONS OF REALITY

"Each model—or 'micro-world' as we shall call it—is very schematic; it talks about a fairyland in which things are so simplified that almost every statement about them would be literally false if asserted about the real world."
> —Marvin Minsky and Seymour Papert, from their proposal for the Blocks Micro Worlds project

Computers have proved immensely effective as aids to clear thinking. Muddled and half-baked ideas have sometimes survived for centuries because luminaries have deluded themselves as much as their followers or because lesser lights, fearing ridicule, couldn't summon up the nerve to admit that they didn't know what the Master was talking about. A test as near foolproof as one could get of whether you understand something as well as you think is to express it as a computer program and then see if the program does what it's supposed to. Computers are not sycophants and won't make enthusiastic noises to ensure their promotion or camouflage what they don't know. What you get is what you said.

A World of Knowledge

GENERALIZING FROM EXPERIENCE
Getting computers to play games effectively seemed a good way of getting closer to how humans think. It involved planning, strategy, adaptation, and goal seeking while at the same time avoiding the horrendous complications of the real world. The result, however, was that the most effective realizations ended up as purpose-designed, dedicated game players. While these will doubtless

prove of inestimable value as test beds for Murray Campbell's "computation engines," the original goal of modeling general, human-style "thinking" somehow seems to have been lost along the way. In a way, the story recapitulates the earlier experiments with the Logic Theorist and Geometry Theorem Prover, which, while providing the groundwork for a powerful assortment of logical and mathematical analyzers used today, diverged off the more general road to thrive in their own specialized evolutionary niche.

The Newell and Simon General Problem Solver we left in chapter nine envisaged a broad problem-solving capability that would be given problem-specific information in the form of a difference table and apply means-ends analysis to reduce the differences and eventually achieve whatever final goal was stipulated. The assumption was that a common set of problem-solving techniques would be shown to be valid, independent of content. And, indeed, GPS was applied successfully to a range of familiar puzzles and problems of various kinds. But as some workers began to note, compared to what a real, general-problem-solving intelligence does when confronted by needs and an environment—a human, for example, or a monkey staring up at a dangling banana—an inordinate amount of the solution was not being generated by the program but supplied for it by the programmer.

Let's take the monkey-and-banana as an example. Yes, when given a table specifying the differences in coordinates of different objects and a set of operations such as "move chair" and "climb chair" that could change those values, GPS would eventually produce a sequence of operations that reduced the goal difference to zero. But a real monkey doesn't start with its actions restricted to a few, preselected for their relevance to the problem; it has available to it a virtually limitless repertoire of things it might do—turn cartwheels, scream at the chair, put the chair on its head—but which it rejects instinctively as inappropriate, just as Kasparov ignores all but two or three of the available moves. What the programmer was having to supply was knowledge about the world—knowledge that a monkey has been acquiring, testing, and organizing since its birth. A real-life problem solver, in other words, doesn't construct solutions by applying some all-around capability in a vacuum. It arrives at them by connecting and relating new information to what it already knows.

RECOGNIZING BY STEREOTYPE: TEMPLATE MATCHING

The first experiments at programming computers to deal with new information according to preexisting knowledge, instead of being told explicitly what to do with it, used the somewhat rigid approach of comparing the input against a set of stored reference standards and seeing which came closest. Such *template matching* methods were tried out in areas that included character and image recognition, linking of concepts, identifying logical and algebraic relationships, and categorizing simple English-language sentences. Nobody was claiming that brains work in such a fashion, but it was a way of at least getting a measure of the problems involved.

An early creation known as the Conversation Machine matched typed input against a set of key words that it looked for and, depending on whether it decided it was being asked a question or invited to comment on a remark, was able to put together a passable response, most of the time, from a stored assortment of facts.[1] Thus, given the input "I don't like rain in July," it could reply chattily, "We don't usually have rainy weather in July, so you probably won't be disappointed." Not a bad performance, perhaps—but only if one confined oneself to the weather. "Baseball," by Bert Green at the Lincoln Labs, accepted simply phrased questions about American League teams, scores, places, and times of events and answered them from stored data in regular, though very restricted, English. These programs and others of a similar nature at the time made no analysis of semantics (the meaning of a sentence) but attempted to assign a code based on the simple structural components, which it matched against the codes of data items stored in memory. They were particularly prone to being confused by ambiguities in the question posed.

SAD SAM, the work of Robert K. Lindsay, a student of Newell and Simon at Carnegie, went a step further in building an internal model of its knowledge base and being able to infer from it facts that had not been specifically spelled out. Its subject was family kinship relationships, and it accepted new information or questions in ordinary English. Given that "Jim is John's brother" and "Jim's mother is Mary," for example, it would infer that Mary was also John's mother and build the information into its growing genealogical tree. In a sense, then, SAD SAM could be said to show the beginnings of "understanding." Missing, of course, if we compare it with general intelligences like the one that knows chairs can be climbed on even if it hasn't seen one before, were the kinds of links that would enable us to say that Jim and John quite likely resembled each other, almost certainly spoke the same language, had many friends in common, and were familiar with the same neighborhood. We understand more than we are told.

It sometimes seems that half the AI world that would come into being over the next twenty years began as Marvin Minsky's graduate students. In 1963 one of them, Tom Evans, produced a program called ANALOGY[2] that set out to explore the kind of thinking that goes on when we perceive two objects or experiences to be not identical but similar, or two sets of objects to be related in a similar kind of way. Evans used as his vehicle the questions posed in IQ tests set by the American Council on Education. Figure 12.1 shows an example.

The program had first to discover a transformation that would turn A into B and then apply the transformation to C to obtain one of the choices one to five. More than simply matching what it was given against a set of references stored internally, therefore, it created the "templates"—transformation procedures—that it used.

A is to B as C is to which of 1 to 5?

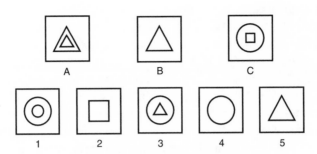

Figure 12.1 Typical ANALOGY Problem

There is actually more involved than might appear at first sight. Although "Remove inner triangle" does indeed transform A into B, it couldn't be used on C since C doesn't have an inner triangle. The program would have to discover "Remove inner object." Further, C might have contained an inner triangle as well as an inner square, in which case either "Remove inner triangle" or "Remove all inner objects" would transform A into B, but only one of them applied to C would yield one of the target figures. Sometimes, more than one rule could be found that satisfied the problem. To accommodate such cases, rules had to be incorporated to decide which "made the most sense"—a source of disputes over IQ testing that continues among humans.

Two more of Minsky's students produced efforts aimed at exploring internal computer representations of verbal information expressed in English. Daniel Bobrow's STUDENT (1964)[3] solved algebraic problems expressed as popular conundrums taking the form "If Bill's father's uncle is twice as old as Bill's father, two years from now Bill's father will be three times as old as Bill, and the sum of their ages is ninety-two, what is Bill's age?" In the same year, Bertram Raphael produced SIR (Semantic Information Retrieval),[4] which dealt with such ambiguities as part-whole and ownership relationships, for instance, those involved in sorting out from other given facts whether "John has ten fingers" means that the fingers are parts of him as opposed to things that he owns.

The object of these exercises was not conversational ability but groundwork on data structures that might form a later basis for it. Both systems simply scanned for matches to stored sequences containing predefined keywords. When STUDENT, for example, encountered *the sum of __ and __*, it would add together whatever was indicated by the blanks; similarly, with *__ times __*, it would multiply them. And this it would blithely attempt to do in cases like "the sum of costs and overheads . . ." or "the number of times it rained . . ." with the consequences to be expected.

These early experiments showed that figuring out the data structures for representing knowledge, the rules to apply to them, and what to do in cases where no rule seemed to fit—or maybe where several could—was going to be a complicated business.

NOT SO ELEMENTARY, WATSON: THE LIMITATIONS OF DEDUCTION

A key need identified by AI workers of the early sixties was to endow programs with the ability to originate their own information. Devising efficient search-reduction heuristics was a start, but it didn't provide any basis for a system to discover new and better heuristics for itself—surely the essence of intelligence. As exemplified by their achievements in areas like logic and mathematical theorem proving, AI programs were very strong on deducing consequences from the information given. Deductive logic, however, is totally noncreative in that its conclusions, while they may be far from obvious, are fully contained in the premises. Deduction can add nothing new, or show anything to be true in the sense of conforming to real-world experience. It merely makes explicit the implications of whatever is assumed. Where AI programs were weak was in the area of the inverse process: induction—drawing general conclusions from limited examples. Instead of starting with assumptions and deriving statements that *must* follow from them, we start with a few statements and make an assumption that we think *probable*. Thus, although there's no way to prove rigorously that every hornet will sting, after a couple of mishaps we leave them alone. A long, curvy yellow thing with segmented sides is most likely a banana; hollow-built structures of what looks like wood are probably movable, and a shove or two will tell if they collapse, and so on. Forming theories about the external environment and testing them sounds more like the operations of everyday intelligence. Another way to describe it would be making sense of the world: adding to and integrating with the existing store of world knowledge. Or, in a word, learning.

College Course or Trade Apprenticeship?

TOP-DOWN AND BOTTOM-UP

Two basic philosophies emerged on how to instill new knowledge and integrate it into the computer's representation of the world. The first, known as "top-down," seeks to educate through sufficiently rich and versatile formal language structures. In other words, rather than have to wait billions of years for the right representations to come about through the shuffling and redealing of hands of genes, why not take advantage of the accumulated results by using the intelligence that already exists to spell out and connect what the computer needs to understand? And as a bonus, we might even be able to improve matters in areas where evolution's choices seem to have taken a less-than-optimum turn (small short-term memory) or left us stuck with adaptations that might have been useful once, but the conditions that favored them have changed (emotional overrides, predatory urges). On the other hand, we might add in abilities that the natural world never provided reasons to develop, such as fast, precision calculating. John McCarthy has remained one of the staunchest advocates of the top-down approach. In 1958 he identified as the key problem in artificial intelligence a way to express formally the information that is normally conveyed by ordinary language and by experience. The predicate calculus (see chapter four) possesses the kind of richness necessary to capture highly complex logical relationships, and his development of LISP provided, essentially, a means of expressing its statements as machine-communicable procedures. The attempts at developing further, more powerful languages have formed a significant part of his work since he came to Stanford.

The "bottom-up" approach takes the view that rather than being carried away by possibly misleading ideas of our own, we should be guided by the only process we *know* of as being capable of producing working, general intelligences, namely, the one that produced us—that is, interacting with the world and learning by exploring it. As skills like riding a bicycle or swimming attest, no amount of study or verbal instruction can substitute for *doing*. It's "doing" in the world that produces knowledge and understanding of it, the bottom-up advocates argue, nothing else. This is the really hard part that matters, and it took nature a billion years to figure out. But once you've got it right, then intellect, language understanding, logic, theorem proving, and all the other "higher" things follow fairly easily.

Even if so, the top-downers point out, appropriate structures for organizing and associating still have to exist for any action to take place at all and for new information to fit into them. It's no good putting a bucket of primordial soup in a room with a banana and expecting something interesting to happen. Somebody is still going to have to supply the ground rules that evolution hardwires in.

But look at what's involved in even basic behavior, comes the retort. Insects manage to do the most amazing things with just a few hundred neurons, and we haven't the faintest idea how. If we don't understand that yet, how can we expect to comprehend something as complex as human cognitive processes in sufficient detail to turn them into computer code?

"We don't want insects. We want something that can think."

"But something as involved as thinking has to be based on a foundation of simpler fundamentals."

"That's fine. But we don't have to wait for a fortuitous combination of unguided processes to create it. We can put it there to begin with."

And so the debate went in the early years, and it still continues.

But it wasn't necessary, right at the outset, to produce a fully competent, all-round rationality on the one hand or to take on the complexity of the real, natural environment on the other. Not even humans are expected to do that. Regardless of which direction was adopted, perhaps it would be possible to imitate what we do and begin with something simple that could grow.

NURSERY SCHOOLS FOR COMPUTERS: MINSKY AND PAPERT

Children don't start out with command of formal grammars and complicated representational structures. They begin by learning to communicate primitive elements of *meaning* ("Cat fall pool, Mommy") and develop sophistication as their needs and their abilities grow. Young mammals develop their coordination and skills in mock fights and play before going out to face serious hazards and foes. In World War II, the flight simulator came about as a way of getting fighter pilots through their early combat experiences artificially after it was discovered that 80 percent of the fatalities happened in rookies' first five missions. Perhaps computers could be introduced to reality gradually in the same way— by simplifying the world down to essentials as it is in physics problems, getting across the basic principles without the distractions of extraneous detail. Let the new, artificial intelligences discover the world a bit at a time as natural ones do—beginning in artificial playpens furnished with symbolic toys.

This approach came about largely as an outcome of the meeting of two minds that came to England in 1961, one from the center of the American AI community that had taken shape in the late fifties and the other from an unexpected, and geographically almost literally opposite, direction. Seymour Papert was a South African who in the 1930s had spent much of his childhood in camps and trucks in the African bush as the family traveled with his father, an entomologist, on field tours and research missions to study such subjects as the tsetse fly.[5] His own interests lay more in the direction of thinking and logic, and they led him to attend seminars on the subject at the University of Johannesburg. One of the questions argued endlessly there was whether logic could be formalized, and, in a fashion reminiscent of the project that Leibniz had envisioned, Papert built a small machine with lights and buttons that could represent logical syllogisms. At that time he had no notion that similar machines might exist elsewhere, and he discovered them through reading Claude Shannon's thesis describing the use of Boolean algebra to design switching circuits.

He first studied philosophy, but, deciding that it was too abstruse, not tangible enough to real-world problems for his tastes, switched to mathematics, earning a Ph.D. at the University of Witwatersrand in 1952, then moving to England to gain a second doctorate at Cambridge when he was thirty. His main interest, however, continued to be the mechanisms and formal representation of thinking, and this, in 1958, brought him to Geneva, Switzerland, to work with the child psychologist Jean Piaget, whom he had met at conferences in Paris. Piaget was investigating the development of mental faculties in the growing child, in particular the abilities that are inborn and those that have to be developed through trial-and-error experience.

One of Piaget's main findings was that real thinking doesn't resemble the orderly chains of polished reasoning presented by theorists after they have unscrambled their notes and seen with hindsight the procedure they *ought* to have followed—often to the inner despair of students forced to the realization that their own thought processes don't take place anything like that. Rather, thinking abilities come together as links between, and assemblies of, simpler, building block–like units that Piaget termed "mother structures," which first have to be properly formed and assimilated. Moreover, it seemed that in many cases these components formed when they were ready to at a characteristic age, and prematurely attempting to induce a child to exhibit the competence that required them was as pointless as trying to teach a bird to fly before it develops wing feathers.

For example, from experiments that track an infant's gaze as it anticipates the emergence of a toy from a tunnel after it has entered the other end, it becomes evident that the concept of an object's continuing to exist when it is out of sight is something that forms at a definite stage of development. Trying to entertain by inventing games of hiding things before that stage is reached won't be very productive. Again, one of the first clues that is registered as to the relative sizes of objects is height—possibly as an important early-warning device reflecting the hazards that falling presents to large animals. (Compared overwhelmingly to most species, humans are large.) Hence, a young child will judge that a tall, thin glass contains more liquid than a shorter, fatter one, even though the tall one was just filled from the short one before the child's eyes. The concept of "conservation"—that quantity stays the same regardless of the container—forms later. Until it does, you're not going to get very far trying to impress an early grasp of "number" in the hope of impressing equally shallow friends and relatives. And so on.

Not surprisingly, from the interest in logic and simulation that he had shown earlier in South Africa, Papert was convinced that computers offered the ideal medium for modeling and studying such processes. This was still in the late fifties, when computers were extremely rare, and, to test his ideas practically, Papert began traveling back to England to use the ACE machine that Alan Turing was working with at the National Physical Laboratory in Teddington, just west of London. He recounts a story that at one point Turing was having trouble with his bicycle, which persisted in periodically losing its chain. The period turned out to occur at regular intervals, and Turing learned to count the precise number of turns of the pedals that he could get away with before having to jump off and readjust the chain. This became tiresome, so the intrepid computer designer contrived a handlebar-mounted device to do the counting for him. The problem was due to a faulty link that eventually coincided with a bent spoke and could have been fixed by a mechanic in minutes.

Turing, apparently, didn't think that way. Or maybe he just preferred the challenge.

At NPL, Papert came into contact with American AI researchers, in particular Marvin Minsky, whom he met at a symposium in 1961. They soon discovered that they shared many views on the subject of learning, had common interests in computers and mathematics, and in fact had independently discovered the same theorem in an area of probability theory. Piaget, on the other hand, was less enthused about computers, which was probably a leading factor in the end of his collaboration with Papert after five fruitful years. Warren McCulloch, who with Walter Pitts had published the groundbreaking work on computation by neurons mentioned in chapter five, invited Papert to work in the United States, and, after some delays due to immigration hassles over anti-apartheid activities that Papert had been involved in during his student days, Papert joined Minsky's group at MIT in 1963. So, a year following John McCarthy's departure for Stanford, Marvin Minsky was once again part of a partnership that would become famous in AI circles.

Like Dewey and Montessori, Papert had come to the conclusion that the most effective way for children to learn is not by rote memorizing or by being told but by *doing* and—equally important—*thinking about* what they are doing. Left to themselves, children find out about the world by exploring it; by looking, touching, finding what moves, bends, breaks, or doesn't; by taking apart—and maybe even managing to put back together again. These views accorded well with the ideas Minsky had been having about how to introduce world knowledge to barely postembryonic computer intelligences. Together, they produced the concepts and design for a series of experiments to bring together findings from research in computing, perception, robotics, and child psychology, which became the guiding theme that would shape most of MIT's AI research effort in the late sixties and early seventies. In 1968 the MIT Artificial Intelligence Group officially became the Artificial Intelligence Laboratory with Minsky and Papert as codirectors.

Papert kept his focus within the field of education rather than in becoming a central figure of AI. One of his better-known and commercially successful creations was a system called LOGO, a simplified computer language designed for children that enabled them to *discover* mathematics by creating geometry dynamically on a screen and interacting directly with the functions generating the forms. The aim was to encourage creativity, curiosity, and experimentation in place of notions of "failure" and the ensuing self-doubt. These, Papert always felt, were the key to all effective learning. Many adults who emerged from the regular educational process with a phobia of numbers and mathematics that followed them through life would probably agree.

In 1985, Seymour Papert joined the MIT Media Laboratory, where he remains today, concentrating on the development of computer-oriented, interactive educational environments.

Playpens for Programs:
The Blocks Micro Worlds Project

The basic philosophy Minsky and Papert proposed was to create simplified worlds in which the fundamentals of interacting with an environment—perception, coordination, and prediction—could be removed from the needless confusion of real-world complexity. Once the principles were understood, the methods embodying them would be progressively upgraded to broader levels of generality. This became known as the Blocks Micro Worlds project, and it accounted for the bulk of the MIT AI lab's effort through the late sixties and into the seventies. In cartoonlike, Platonic worlds inhabited by pure geometric forms, assorted robots and programs peered out through TV cameras, interpreted what they saw, manipulated physical forms in space, moved themselves around, and described their perceptions and the problems they were encountering.

THE BEGINNINGS OF ARTIFICIAL VISION
An obvious area to tackle first for putting computers in touch with their spatial environment was getting them to see. It's estimated that something like 60 percent of the human cerebral cortex is devoted to processing visual information; hence, artificial intelligences able to share the visual world have in common with us the greater part of our perceived reality, a pretty basic prerequisite for any form of meaningful and productive communication later. Furthermore, communicating with computers able to perceive the world directly through vision is far more flexible and interesting than doing so via restrictive and dull-to-use keyboards that have provided the standard channel so far. The prospect of better communication with computers also has the commercial attraction of making them more widely accessible and opening up all kinds of new applications and markets. It remains a significant point today that while communicating with computers via simplified interfaces such as click-on icons, menu selections, and so forth has become almost universal, the proportion of users/owners who actually *program* them is quite small. Finally, there was an enormous potential market for devices that could input information directly as text, documents, and other visual forms, obviating the need for the vast rooms full of clattering keyboard data-entry machines that filled the lower floors of most commercial establishments. Data entry via keyboard, especially given the monotony of the job, was notoriously error-prone.

FINDING SHAPES
Three basic processes, broadly speaking, are involved in viewing a scene. First, light from some source such as the sun, reflected and modified (e.g., by having some wavelengths absorbed to a greater or lesser degree than others, which is what gives the reflected light its color) by objects, is collected in the eye and turned into raw sensory data. Second, the raw data are processed to build an

internal representation, a symbolic structure of some form that encodes what was seen. Third, cognitive processes, operating at a more abstract level in ways that are still not understood, interpret and make sense of the representations in terms of what the representations represent.

Minsky was of the view, and remains strongly so today, that putting effort into duplicating what are essentially functions of the sensory system, not the thinking entity that the senses serve, would simply be reenacting a lot of irrelevant evolution and missing the point of what an artificial *intelligence* project should be doing. Blocks World was essentially a top-down approach, meaning that the aim was to develop enough understanding of the high-level cognitive processes to define them precisely. Computers could simulate the representations normally supplied by the visual processing centers, which is just the kind of thing that computers are good for. The hard work, the really tricky stuff, lay in trying to figure out how the cognitive centers make sense of things from there. The early work, therefore, was concerned with analyzing representations of regions and boundaries in a scene and recognizing them as objects. In keeping with the general Blocks World philosophy, the objects, to begin with, were very simple.

As early as 1961, Larry Roberts at the Lincoln Laboratory had begun working on a program that searched for objects in a digitized representation of a line drawing, i.e. the drawing was encoded and supplied as a set of numbers, not presented to a camera as an image.[6] In principle, an imaging system could have generated the same numbers. Not having to bother with scanning pictures or processing camera outputs or correct for system noise, irregular lighting, shadow effects, and all kinds of other complications that have no direct bearing on interpretation was the whole point of the top-down strategy.

Roberts's program used local operators to transform the digitized input into representations of regions separated by lines and lines coming together to form vertexes (corners). It then assembled these elements into list structures, associating each vertex with descriptions of the regions surrounding it. A set of similar list structures containing the same kind of information about the three basic forms that the program could recognize—cubes, wedges, and hexagonal prisms—was stored. The program would first look for a preliminary match to select one of these descriptions and then apply projective geometry transformations—effectively rotating it various ways in space—to compute the best fit between each portion of the drawing and the corresponding object. The method was thus essentially template matching, but with the refinement that the stored templates were used as the source for dynamically generating a potentially infinite variety of references to compare the inputs against, instead of merely forming a library to be selected from statically. However, it required precise internal models of the objects to be recognized, an approach that was incompatible with the more general need of being able to make sense of new objects.

Adolfo Guzman produced the first program, called SEE, that could identify objects in a scene without matching them against stored descriptions.[7] Input to SEE was in the form of information relating *regions, vertices,* and *background—* again of a building-blocks landscape similar to the one that Roberts's program lived in. For example, the simple scene shown in Figure 12.2 would be conveyed as a specification that there are five regions, 1 to 5, and a background, 6, meeting at eleven vertices, A to K, with their positions; in addition, SEE would be given the connecting relationships, so that the neighbors of region 2, reading counterclockwise, are 3, 4, 6, 1, and 6, and the boundary of region 2, again reading counterclockwise, connects vertices D, E, A, C, and K. From this information, SEE would apply heuristic rules to find evidence for grouping the regions into surfaces of separate objects.

Note that from a single description of such a scene, it is impossible to *prove* that any group of surfaces must belong to the same object. Every region could, for instance, be the base of a pyramid oriented so that the other faces are hidden from view, in which case none of the visible regions would be associated. Thus, any program that attempts this type of resolution must be guided by notions of plausibility in real-world settings, i.e., heuristics. SEE classified evidence as "strong" or "weak," enabling conjectures to be formed on a most-likely-first basis. Thus, only when strong evidence could not be found for a high-confidence solution would the program fall back on a more tentative one.

Figure 12.3 shows an example of a more complicated scene that SEE was able to interpret successfully. The positional coordinates of the vertices were used to deduce the alignment of line segments and hence infer the likelihood of one object occluding another.

In general, mistakes tended to be conservative in not grouping together regions that humans would plausibly take as surfaces belonging to the same object. In Figure 12.4, for example, the program would report regions 1 and 2 as belonging to different things.

Although this was impressive, in complex scenes with many overlapping objects and hidden vertices, achieving an acceptably unambiguous solution became impossible; there were simply too many ways in which the elements

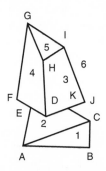

Figure 12.2 A Representation for SEE

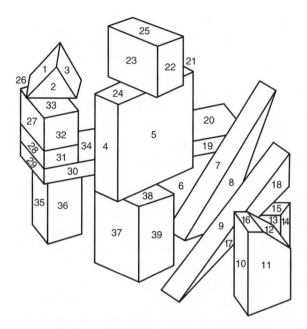

Figure 12.3 Scene Resolved by Guzman's Program

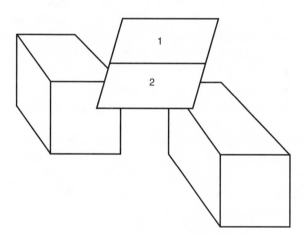

Figure 12.4 Example of Unresolved Ambiguity

could be combined. Routines were also added that could generate the lists of region and vertex relationships from the photographic image of an actual scene. But it was necessary to cheat a little by painting the blocks black and outlining the edges in white.

By the beginning of the seventies, several people were working on extensions of these ideas. M. J. Clowes constructed a "picture syntax," which sought to define rules that machines could apply for inferring interpretations that make sense in the same way that grammar defines which streams of words make sense.[8] D. A. Huffman used the same theme in a paper entitled "Impossible Objects as Nonsense Sentences."[9]

David Waltz—another Minsky student—also made use of the fact that simply being expressible in "language"—as a plane-figure representation— doesn't necessarily make a statement meaningful in the real world to which the language pertains. We've all seen drawings—and even unlikely contrivances photographed from just the right angle—of impossible objects that couldn't exist physically in space as what they appear to be. Waltz placed further constraints on the possible interpretations of a scene by considering vertices not in isolation but taking into account the implications of the other vertices they connect to. With an edge defining an indented corner, for example, the line formed where the base of a wall meets the floor can't suddenly become a projecting corner formed by the top of a wall and a roof. Thus, there are restrictions on the kinds of vertex ("fork," "arrow," "T," etc.) that a given vertex can plausibly connect to, and limiting the program to such combinations will save it a lot of grief and wasted labor in trying to construct objects that can't exist. Once one of the possible interpretations of a particular vertex had been singled out and fixed, it set further constraints on what types of other vertices connected to it might be. Constraints originating in one area of the scene thus caused further constraints to be imposed elsewhere, and the method was known accordingly as "constraint propagation."[10]

A problem with all the vertex- and edge-analyzing approaches was handling curved surfaces and objects that contained holes. Waltz's work included ways of dealing with shadows, which could confuse things by obscuring key elements.[11] The aim was to reduce the dependency of these programs on perfect drawings or information.

SEEING STRUCTURES

Identifying objects visually would be an insoluble problem if everything had to be recognized by a unique combination of features such as color, shape, locations of corners, angles formed by edges, and so on. We probably recognize most of the things that exist in the real world mainly because they are composed of simpler objects, and pay little regard to the defining features of the component objects themselves. Thus, four walls, a roof, a few windows, and a door make a house, and whether the door is brown or green, or the windows square or arched, doesn't come into it; a train is a train whatever its composition of flatcars, boxcars, and tank cars, and so on. We have a highly developed faculty, in other words, for recognizing *structures*.

The parallel between physical structures and language structure has already been alluded to and probably has deep significance, as we'll see later. The same similarity struck Patrick Winston, who at around the end of the sixties noticed that the semantic networks being created by the researchers trying to represent the relationships conveyed by a language sentence could also describe the relationships between objects forming a structure.

Winston's program used vertex and edge information as it was discussed above to recognize objects, but in addition, it was able to use such relationships between them as *above, supports, in front of, right of,* and *left of* to determine larger-scale configurations that the objects formed.[12] From the diagrams in Figure 12.5, the program would identify the component objects and then go on to relate them in a description corresponding to the graphlike illustration.

A large part of Winston's program was devoted to comparing description graphs of various scenes with each other, and from their commonalities, developing more general descriptions of *groups* of scenes having certain properties in common. From these it was able to construct notions of structures of a "kind of" type, or class, which subsequently encountered examples it could be recognized as belonging to. It was thus, in a very real sense, also a learning program. In fact, it even went further to develop a description graph from examples that it was told were or were not instances of a particular pattern. For example, on being shown the groupings in Figure 12.6 and told which classified as "arch," it learned to distinguish as "arches" new structures that it hadn't been presented with before.

Similarly, the program was able to learn other structures such as "column," "house," "pedestal," "tent," "table," and "arcade."

Although a learning program, it did require a teacher (but then, so do people). Winston's thesis had a lot to say about teaching, which probably contributed to the work's being exceptionally well received by Minsky and Papert (so much so, in fact, that they appointed him their successor as director of the AI lab). In it, he stressed the value of giving the computer "near misses," in the case of arches, for example, ones like the two instances shown in Figure 12.6. As in a controlled experiment in which, ideally, everything is held constant save a single variable, a near miss is an example that fails to meet the pattern rule in only one condition—for the two nonarches shown, it is that the top must be *on* the sides in one case and, in the other, that the sides must be separated by a *gap*. (Anyone who thinks that should be obvious has never programmed a computer.) Near misses enable the program to spot the discrepancy that makes the difference, whereas three pieces scattered about the floor, say, with the comment that they

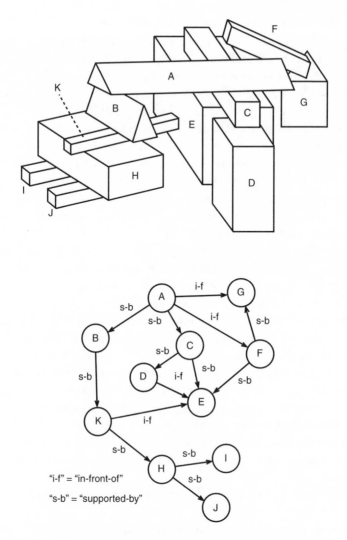

Figure 12.5 Arrangement of Objects and Relationship Graph

did not constitute an arch wouldn't be very illuminating. The number of ways it could be wrong are too large to convey any useful information—a bit like being told that two apples and a walnut don't make an elephant.

The program was able to recognize the entire group of objects shown in Figure 12.8 as a "kind of" arch. In fact, it found no fewer than five "kind of" arches in the structure. Are they immediately obvious to the reader?

As a final note of interest, the program could also solve analogy problems similar to those tackled by Evans's program, mentioned at the beginning of this chapter. Figure 12.9 shows an example. When asked to pick the figure that is to C as B is to A, the program would correctly identify 4.

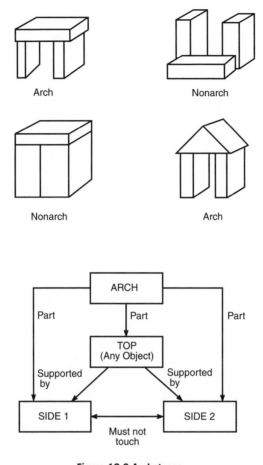

Figure 12.6 Archetypes

Toddler Talk:
Communicating with the Micro Worlds

Seeing the world is only a prerequisite for learning about it. It then must be taught. And teaching implies being able to communicate.

As well as creating programs to perceive microrealities, the Micro Worlds project also investigated ways of enabling programs to interpret ordinary language input and extract information that could be used to extend their world knowledge. Simplified and restricted languages relating to their own miniature domains of meaning were used. In keeping with the project's general spirit, Eugene Charniak's doctoral thesis in 1972 described mechanisms for inferring facts not explicitly stated from information conveyed through the medium of children's stories.[13]

A story might begin:

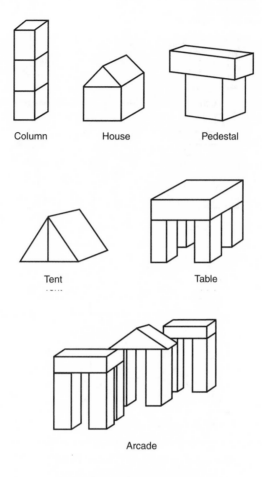

Figure 12.7 Some Basic Structures

Fred was going to the store. Today was Jack's birthday, and Fred was going to get a present.

The program would then answer questions put to it along such lines as "Who is the present for?" and "Why is Fred buying a present?" Pretty easy for any four-year-old, you might say. True, but the point was that the kind of information the questions asked for hadn't been given explicitly and couldn't be arrived at by any process of deduction from what the story actually said. Answering them required a certain amount of knowledge about the way the world is—or, at least, the microworlds conjured into being by Charniak's stories—such as, that things "got" at stores are usually bought, that presents typically come from stores, and so on. The problem turned out to be extraordinarily difficult, as we'll see when we get to chapter fourteen, which deals specifically with language comprehension.

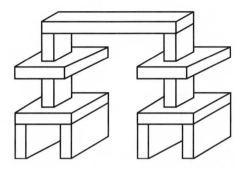

Figure 12.8 A "Kind of" Arch, Including Variants

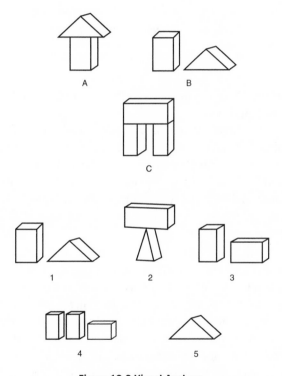

Figure 12.9 Visual Analogy

TERRY WINOGRAD'S "BLOCKS WORLD"

One of the best-known programs from this era is called SHRDLU (Figure 12.10), which was created by Terry Winograd, a student of Seymour Papert's.[14] Although SHRDLU's world was again one of simple geometric shapes, their function was not to provide objects for perception or manipulation but to serve as a subject for the program to converse about with humans. In fact, it would be truer to say that the blocks and pyramids existed as simplified representations

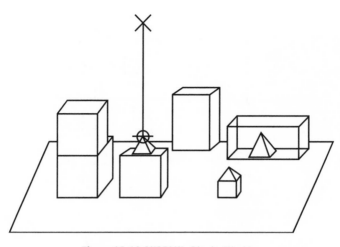

Figure 12.10 SHRDLU's Blocks World

for the humans' benefit of the internal symbolic structures and operations that SHRDLU was talking about.

SHRDLU's world consisted of a model inside a PDP–10 computer, which was depicted on a screen as a tabletop, a storage box, and an assortment of blocks and pyramids of various sizes and colors. By means of a simulated robot arm, SHRDLU could move blocks around and assemble structures of blocks in response to directions typed in through the console. It also used the screen to answer questions about what it was doing and, if necessary, to ask for clarification or more specific instructions.

Winograd's intention was pure research, not practical language-understanding applications. Nevertheless, his program had substantial influence on subsequent work. For one thing, it analyzed the syntax and grammar of input sentences—a far more sophisticated achievement than anything based on blind template-matching. But more, SHRDLU was the first program to integrate language competence with a capacity for reasoning about the world. Winograd took the position that the meaning of a sentence is inextricably embedded in its structure, not something that can be looked up independently in parts or found by matching against stereotypes. There was no dictionary of set definitions to be referred to. The operator's words and phrases were interpreted as procedures that could be tested against the conditions actually existing in the world to see if they made sense, surely a step closer to what people do. For example, if given the command "Put the blue pyramid on the green cube," a first, provisional attempt at parsing the sentence (analyzing it into its correct grammatical parts) might have identified "the blue pyramid on the green cube" as an object to be "put" somewhere, the somewhere to be specified later on in the sentence. The sentence, however, then terminates, which means that there is no further "somewhere" to be looked for, and this causes an alternative interpretation. The program then arrives at the conclusion that "the blue pyramid" is all that is to be "put," and "on the green cube" then becomes the sought-for "somewhere" to put it.

Having assessed that much, SHRDLU would then check the green cube to see if its top was clear or occupied by another object. If it was occupied, a sub-program, CLEARTOP, would be activated to take care of the situation by finding spaces elsewhere for however many objects needed to be moved and then finally calling up another subprogram called STACK, which contained the sequences necessary to perform the required operation. SHRDLU would continue in this way through more complicated inputs, converting the requests to detailed procedures for producing the desired conditions. An example of a dialogue between SHRDLU and the operator is reproduced below.

Pick up a big red block.
OK.
Grasp the pyramid.
I DON'T UNDERSTAND WHICH PYRAMID YOU MEAN.
Find a block which is taller than the one you are holding and put it in the box.
BY "IT" I ASSUME THAT YOU MEAN THE BLOCK WHICH IS TALLER THAN THE ONE I AM HOLDING.
OK.
What does the box contain?
THE BLUE PYRAMID AND THE BLUE BLOCK.
What is the pyramid supported by?
THE BOX.
How many blocks are not in the box?
FOUR OF THEM.
Why did you pick up the green pyramid?
TO GET RID OF IT.
Why did you do that?
TO CLEAR THE RED CUBE.
Why did you clear the red cube?
TO PUT IT ON THE LARGE GREEN CUBE.
Why did you do that?
BECAUSE YOU ASKED ME TO.

SHRDLU was written in a version of a LISP-based language called PLANNER that others at MIT had developed for automating some of the more tedious tasks encountered in writing large list-structured programs. The solutions produced took the form of fragments of code activated from within other fragments through various levels with no overall supervisory function that contained all the knowledge pertinent to a problem—a tangle of linkages forming and dissolving, cooperating to meet the needs of the moment and defying tidy explanation. Certainly, SHRDLU had its limits, in particular that its understanding was confined to one extremely narrow world. Its language was restricted to fairly simple English, frequently stumbling over elementary constructions and probably achieving an overall fluency somewhat less than that of an average four-year-old.

On the other hand, its principles may have looked ahead to something more general. Marvin Minsky today feels that it had more potential than was explored at the time. In a way, it recalls the hierarchies of independent agents that the cyberneticists had identified in complex biological systems. As we shall see later, it could also be viewed as anticipating some of the later findings on how minds seem to be organized.

1. McCorduck, p. 243.
2. Evans.
3. Bobrow.
4. Raphael (1964).
5. McCorduck, pp. 288 *ff.*
6. Roberts.
7. Guzman.
8. Clowes.
9. Huffman.
10. Detailed in Waltz (1982).
11. Waltz (1972).
12. Winston.
13. Charniak.
14. Winograd (1971), (1972).

13

"Bottom-Up" AI

COMPUTER VISION AND ROBOTICS

"It may well be that the way to build an intelligence is just to get your hands on dirty engineering problems. We don't have a theory of automobiles. We have good cars, but there are no fundamental equations of automotive science." —Hans Moravec

There is a story, repeated innumerable times in AI circles and literature, that Marvin Minsky once assigned the problem of getting a computer to interpret TV images to an undergraduate student as a summer project. That was in 1966, and the student's name was Gerald Sussman. Sussman is still at MIT today as a professor. The problem of artificial vision is still far from solved.

As mentioned in the last chapter, vision had early on been identified as a fundamental need if computers were to learn about the world. Minsky himself was more interested in tackling the higher-level interpretation of visual representations, which was generally presumed to present the more challenging theoretical problems. Accordingly, he sent proposals to various other research organizations, suggesting projects to handle the actual vision part. These groups in turn submitted funding proposals to ARPA, which arrived at ARPA at about the same time. The somewhat ironic result was a decision to let Minsky do the work at MIT instead of spreading it around in small parcels since his name seemed to figure centrally in what they were all talking about.

Sussman had wandered into the AI group's laboratories on Technology Square out of curiosity to see their new Digital Equipment PDP–6 computer and ended up playing with it from one of the terminals, writing a program that simulated teaching a neural network to play ticktacktoe. Minsky, one of the lab's directors, stopped by to ask who he was and what he was doing. These days, in an installation representing a comparable investment to what a PDP–6 did then, it's not unlikely that Sussman would have been asked to leave, as he lacked the appropriate clearances and authorizations. Instead, Minsky hired him.

Neural Nets and Perceptrons

Sussman's neural-net interests reflected work on direct modeling of the nervous system that had continued since the mid-fifties. Although the main AI thrust had switched at around that time to using digital computers to simulate the symbolic manipulations that the brain was believed to support, investigation of networks of artificial neuronlike devices had not been discontinued. In the early forties, McCulloch and Pitts (see chapter five) had published their paper proposing that networks of neurons in the brain were no less capable of computation than Claude Shannon's systems of switching relays. In 1949, Hebb had suggested a mechanism to account for their ability to learn, whereby initially unorganized systems of neurons are able to evolve coherent action in response to repeated stimuli.[1] A line of research pursued through the fifties and into the sixties sought to construct networks of artificial devices that could be "trained" to become proficient at set tasks in the way that biological neurons were believed to do. One of the best-known of such devices was known as the "Perceptron." The immediate field of application envisaged for it was artificial vision.

The Perceptron resulted from the work of a group at Cornell University led by Frank Rosenblatt, a former classmate of Marvin Minsky's at Bronx Science High School in New York. The principle was essentially a simple one, although tinkering and tuning to try and improve performance could lead to virtually limitless variants. A layer of photodetectors formed a light-sensitive surface analogous to the retina of the eye or the film in a camera, upon which an image was focused. The signals from the detectors were passed to a layer of McCulloch-Pitts cells interconnected with the detectors in such a way as to implement a decision based on the inputs from groups of them, similar to the manner in which a biological neuron fires according to the pattern of inputs it receives from other neurons. A third layer of switching units translated the combinations of signals from the artificial neurons into final outputs.

Learning was accomplished by adjusting the "weights" of the contributions that each detector made to the decision effected by the neural cell it was connected to (i.e., giving it a greater or lesser voice in the joint vote of the detector group, just as weighting coefficients determine the relative contributions of the terms in a polynomial). From an initial random state, the coefficients would be selectively varied to strengthen or weaken the connection paths through to the outputs in ways that encouraged correct response associations with the input stimuli being taught. To recognize letters of the alphabet, for example, the weightings would be set so that every letter, when presented to the detector array, caused a corresponding lamp to activate uniquely.

Similar projects were in progress elsewhere. At Stanford, Bernard Widrow extended the neural-net principle to adaptive and multiple neurons, closer in concept to the workings of the real thing, which could recognize visual patterns and spoken words. In Germany, Karl Steinbuch described a device called the "Learning Matrix," which could be taught through learning procedures similar to those Rosenblatt employed. Minsky had always retained something of a fascination for neural-net devices—the Snarc had represented a personal first stab in that direction, and in 1961 he presented a paper on a Perceptron-like device in England, where he met Papert. Rosenblatt, however, while coming across as colorful and enthusiastically forceful to some, gained something of a reputation for making exaggerated claims to attract publicity. This invited counter-reactions, which appeared in a book by Minsky and Seymour Papert entitled *Perceptrons* that pointed out some serious limitations inherent in the approach.[2] The effect was devastating, and it seriously retarded further work in the field for something like fifteen years. This was probably an overreaction, perhaps partly due to the high standing the authors commanded at the time. A lot of potential remained to be explored, in particular the fact that the perceived limitations turned out to be surmountable when the number of layers was increased. Work on neural nets was revived in the 1980s under the general heading of "Connectionism" and is being vigorously pursued today. We'll have more to say about it later.

Vision Basics

A PERSPECTIVE ON THE PROBLEM

The optimism with which prospects for artificial vision were regarded was characteristic of the earlier attitudes prevailing within AI. Duplicating abilities that seemed to involve no mental effort was expected to be easy compared to intellectual feats that required judgment, decision making, and reasoning. Programs to prove theorems and solve mathematical problems were advancing in leaps and bounds; computers were already playing quite passable chess, and some believed world-championship performance to be less than a decade away. By comparison, something like basic vision should, it was thought, present few major hurdles. As has often proved the case in AI, the reality turned out to be the other way around.

The amount of information contained in even a static real-world image of reasonable interest is huge. The human retina consists of a dense array made up of two kinds of cells: "rods," which respond to the brightness of incident light, and "cones," which respond to color. It contains somewhere around a hundred million of them, plus four other layers of neurons, every one firing roughly a hundred times per second. That's the equivalent of 10 *billion* calculations per second of image preprocessing, before any visual information even reaches the brain proper. Inside the cerebral cortex, over a dozen vision centers are devoted to processing it, and these are estimated as taking up something like 60 percent of the cortex.

What this means is that if vision seems effortless, it isn't because what goes on is simple—to put it mildly. Rather, the whole massive computation is handled unconsciously by dedicated circuits that nature has hard-wired into the optical system and the brain—specialized "vision-processing engines," analogous to IBM's battery of dedicated chess-playing chips that give Deep Blue its power.

What's going on here, however, is a lot more subtle than anything in Deep Blue. Anyone who has put jigsaw puzzles together knows how slight variations of shadow and lighting can render a blob of color completely meaningless until it finds its correct place, upon which it suddenly assumes a significance that depends not on any innate qualities but that is imparted by the surrounding context. The raw retinal image is very different from the smooth, cleaned-up scene that the conscious mind eventually perceives. In fact, it's a mess. The quality of the light reaching a particular point on the retina—reflected from a part of the surface of a leaf, say—is determined not only by the "natural" color and texture of the leaf but by its orientation with regard to the lighting, the color of the light, the transparency of the air in between, the effects of shadows, and so on through a whole list of factors that make the result highly variable. Further confusion arises from distortions induced by the far-from-perfect optical system itself and the background noise effects of cells firing spontaneously.

And more. The optical system not only manages to correct for the defects by restoring what the image should be; it actually goes farther and compensates for systematic errors (ones that are not confined to isolated spots but which bias the result as a whole) by managing to see what it "knows" it "ought" to, somehow manufacturing information that never originated in the outside scene at all. For example, two identical fields of color can be seen as different when viewed against different background contexts, indicating that the eye responds not to absolutes, possessing meaning only in terms of their own narrow, innate properties, but to differences and contrasts—meanings interpreted in a broader framework of associations and relationships. Again, we perceive colors as true, even under enormous variations of intensity, direction, and composition of the illuminating light. Even though isolating an area of a scene might show its color to be undeniably, say, pink, nevertheless the eye takes account of the pink lighting, compensates for it, and in context registers the area as white.

Yet this is all before we've even started assembling the various fields in the image into representations of things we can recognize. We still have to find the boundaries, texture changes, and alterations in shading and lighting that denote major discontinuities where the world breaks up into regions and objects, and separate them from secondary detail—the outline of a head from the pattern of the hair, for example. And then, the visual system has to perform the inverse operation of that accomplished by the retina—which compressed a three-dimensional world into a flat representation—and reconstruct an impression of depth and distances, at the same time resolving all the ambiguities which that necessarily involves.

Take the leaf again. From a flat, two-dimensional image, it could be the end of a leaf-section bar pointing directly away. There's nothing that shows it to be at the same distance as the twig alongside it, which could be merely coincidentally aligned, but we instantly see them as connected, yet not as connected to the rock seen against a hillside, which appears equally aligned with the other fork of the twig. How? Because we "know" that rocks don't grow on twigs; that the rock is part of the hillside, which is farther away, and therefore the rock only looks the same size as the leaf because of distance, and so on. Or rather, something down in that unconscious vision-processing engine "knows" all these things and delivers to consciousness an account that has already been made sense of to an overwhelming degree. We can now use our conscious faculties to search for movement, human figures, a trail through the trees—things that are meaningful in the world of people, places, events, and things that we live in and think in terms of. Suddenly, the problems of identifying basic geometric shapes in a toyland somehow don't feel the same anymore, do they?

A COMPUTER'S-EYE VIEW OF THE WORLD

A computer doesn't have anything comparable to a retina, on which an image of the world imprints itself as a pattern. It can represent information internally only as numbers that it stores in addressable cells like the pigeonhole rack behind a hotel desk. An image in the form of a drawing, a photograph, or a frame from a TV sequence must be *digitized* before it can be input, which means encoded as a stream of numbers that are fed in as electrical pulses on a wire. To generate such a stream, the image is broken up into *pixels*—a mosaic of dots like the ones that form a TV picture—and each pixel is converted into a number corresponding to its brightness. Typically, there are 255 possible levels from darkest to brightest for each one. A color image is represented by three monochrome images, one each for red, green, and blue, and the mixing of relative intensities at each point produces the shades seen. TV images are coarse compared to typical computer images, however, comprising in the United States five hundred pixels across and a little over four hundred down. A moderately high resolution computer image might contain a thousand pixels along each side, giving a million of them.[3]

Consider, then, a million numbers sitting in a block of computer memory. That's all they are—numbers. The physical locations of the memory cells have nothing to do with the positions that the pixels occupied in the image. Indeed, the cell contents could lie in a single line as a Turing Machine tape. The task of an image recognition program is somehow to deduce by manipulating this array of numbers what the image they were derived from represents. Stacking them into lines like those on a TV screen to reveal any regularities isn't allowed since the regularities would require an eye and a visual system to detect them, and these the computer doesn't have. The aim, remember, is not simply to construct a corresponding pattern but full "end-to-end" image *recognition*. From a stream of raw numbers going in on a wire at one end, we want the computer to plunge, at the other end, into its reservoir of world knowledge and announce, "a truck on an interstate highway," "an elephant among trees," or whatever.

This is the task that our visual system performs. The apparent ease with which we accomplish it is deceptive because we do it unconsciously. Clearly, some enormously complex processes are involved, and for a realistic chance of duplicating them a comprehensive theory of the kind of way these unconscious mechanisms work is needed. David Marr thought so too, and that's what we'll take a look at next.

David Marr's Theory of Vision[4]

Marvin Minsky hadn't wanted to get involved in low-level vision, which he considered peripheral to understanding the workings of cognitive intelligence, but he was saddled with a commitment to it by ARPA. The priorities then reversed themselves, with low-level work elbowing aside the higher-level interpretive vision projects that Minsky and Papert had envisaged. A major factor in this was the arrival, in 1973, of twenty-eight-year-old David Marr from England, who insisted that vision was something to be studied not as a collection of computing projects but as a *science* in its own right, and that meant starting at the bottom.

A mathematical neurophysiologist by specialization, Marr moved to MIT at the invitation of Minsky and Papert following work he had done on the modeling of the brain's neural structures. Marr's own reason for accepting was the opportunity of testing his ideas through practical, hands-on experiments, and, as had proved irresistible for many others at around that time, MIT offered accessible computing power that was second to none. He was, by all accounts, one of those forceful and flamboyant yet charismatic personalities that people either follow after fervently or disagree with vehemently, but either way find impossible to ignore. His gift—or failing, depending on whether one views him from among the ranks of the inspired or the infuriated—was in making huge leaps of insight, leaving the gaps to be filled in later . . . or, alternatively, reckless flights of fantasy that others had to steer back to earth. Although many of the details turned out later to be wrong, his proposals provided the first coherent framework of a theory of vision, which has stimulated much imaginative thinking since. The nomenclature that he adopted in his 1982 book *Vision* became ubiquitous. The book was published posthumously. David Marr's career was cut short in 1980 by his death from leukemia at age thirty-five.

Marr's treatment of the visual system can perhaps be described in terms of two basic propositions. The first was in essence a restatement of the principle, already a cornerstone of AI thinking, that separated what a system or program is trying to *do* from the means that happen to be employed in the particular case to accomplish it. In other words, it reaffirmed the symbolic paradigm whereby two systems that perform the same function at the higher representational level are equivalent and their physical natures, biological or electronic, naturally evolved or synthetic, are secondary. The second proposition pertained to the visual system itself and held that there could be no direct transformation from the raw image level captured by the retina and the interpretation of three-dimensional objects and scenes. The process takes place in distinct stages, each with its own special mechanisms and representations. It was the need to understand the intricacies of these discrete levels and how they interacted with one another that elevated vision from the straightforward conversion that had been assumed to a complex problem that needed to be dealt with as a whole. Experimental evidence suggests that humans and other mammals process visual information in at least three such stages. The scheme proposed by David Marr is shown in Figure 13.1.

FIRST, FIND THE LANDMARKS

The main function of the Primal Sketch is to make manageable the first problem that any visual system confronts: coping with the vast quantity of raw data involved. We don't deal with images by trying to encode and process every picture element in an identical manner to render all parts of the visual field with equal precision. In fact, as a moment's attention on what one actually sees

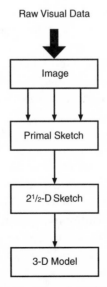

Figure 13.1 The Stages in David Marr's Theory

reveals, the only part resolved in any detail is the comparatively small region that we're focusing on at any instant, which we can move around at will to sharpen up any items of interest. The remaining part exists as vague outlines and shapes that we tend not even to notice unless they move. In short, we apply data-reduction procedures that enable us to deal with the significant landmarks and features as coherent units, without getting lost in masses of detail. We identify a tree instantly as a tree, without having to recognize every leaf, but a hillside registers as a hillside, not a construction from trees.

The way in which Marr and a student of his, Ellen Hildreth, accomplished this was to subject the image to a type of mathematical transformation (its technical name, for those who have always wondered, is the Laplacian of a Gaussian), which belongs to a class of operations known as "filtering," which has the effect of blurring everything.[5] The idea is to make the smaller details dissolve, leaving the coarser features that can generally be expected to indicate important things that should be noticed first.

It turns out that this transformation is very similar to the way in which the human visual system does indeed seem to process images. From such coarse-grained information, the brain constructs a first approximation, a "small-scale map," as it were, of what's out there, using specialized neural detectors that respond only to edges, bars, or blobs of shade, and then sometimes only when they occur in certain specific locations or orientations. In some animals this is taken to amazing levels of specialization. The retinas of rabbits, for example, contain neural configurations specifically tailored to detect the outline of a hovering hawk.

The Primal Sketch is assembled by grouping these map features into larger structures such as continuous lines and connected regions. We achieve this so effortlessly that the expectation of finding little difficulty in doing similar things via computer programs becomes understandable. But the task turns out to be far from trivial, as it involves applying all kinds of rules of thumb that we know from experience of the world and that computers don't know unless we tell them. Like the problem of telling a machine how to play chess the way Kasparov does, we first need to know what the rules are ourselves, which isn't easy when they operate unconsciously.

Consider the two patterns shown in Figure 13.2, for instance. We have no difficulty discerning a branching structure in one case and a rounded form in the other. But the continuity that we see is manufactured. Both are simply collections of dashes; how to specify to a program the rules for extracting the same meaning that we attach is far from obvious or straightforward.

The brain, it seems, seeks continuity, even to the degree of supplying it when it isn't there, where built-in knowledge of the world says it should be. Our vision systems thus make reasonable hypotheses for us about what to expect.

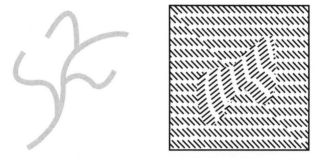

Figure 13.2 Manufacturing Continuity

CONSTRUCTION OF FORM

Marr criticized approaches that jumped straight from the determination of edges and blobs in an image to trying to identify three-dimensional objects. The problem is that the sharpest boundaries can be caused by secondary factors like shadows or reflections, while some of the most important real edges might easily blend into invisibility. The leaves and petals in a floral arrangement would be a good example. Marr's answer was the "$2^1/_2$-D Sketch," based to a large degree on work done by Thomas Binford and others. The key idea here, further extending the principle of finding continuity, was that the identification of *surfaces* and fixing their orientation in space forms an essential intermediate step between the grouping of two-dimensional features and full object recognition.

Finding surfaces could be said to be the primary function of the human visual system, which assembles its world from them. Indeed, so eagerly does it apply itself to the task that it easily finds surfaces that aren't there. Consider the well-known optical illusion reproduced in Figure 13.3. The actual reality is no more than a scattering of *V*s and notched disks, but the eye constructs a continuous figure with a solid white triangle overlaying it. Some people even manage to sustain their conviction by seeing an edge created by a subtle difference in shade between the triangle and the background and can be convinced of its nonexistence only by obscuring the rest of the figure.

PARALLEL MECHANISMS AND ROBUSTNESS

One of the most important principles that evolution uses to facilitate survival in challenging and changing environments is that of *robustness*. Robustness here doesn't mean physically strong or solid but is meant in a sense more akin to "resilient"—conveying resistance to breakdown or to becoming nonfunctional in operating conditions that are less than perfect or in a partially failed state. "Abuse tolerance" might be a good way to describe it.

Once dumped in a survival-oriented environment, a natural organism can't

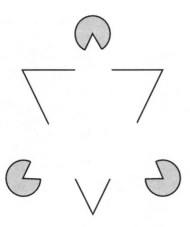

Figure 13.3 Creating Surfaces

be returned to a service center or taken out of the field for an upgrade if it turns out to be substandard. It's on its own. One of nature's principal means of affording robustness, widely used in critical engineering designs, is *redundancy*. Briefly put, this means that you don't put systems together in such a way that the failure of one sensitive component will mean total failure of everything. Instead, you duplicate failure-prone elements and provide alternate control paths, manual backup systems, and so on. In our own bodies, if an infection or injury impairs the normal breathing channel of the nose, the mouth acts as a standby, as well as a supplementary reserve for situations requiring high exertion; we can take the loss of one eye, ear, arm, lung, or kidney with impairment, not death.

In the case of vision, a variety of mechanisms provides independent identifications of surfaces by exploiting clues of widely differing natures. The most well known is probably the stereoscopic capability that arises from having a visual field composed of the overlapping images from two forward-facing eyes. (This is not universal, of course. Most fish and birds have their eyes on the sides of their heads, and recent research suggests that this might be a more efficient arrangement for navigation.) A sophisticated geometry transformation performed in the brain identifies matching parts of the two images and estimates relative distance from their differential movements against a fixed, faraway background. Seeing features move in rigid formation often provides vital information that they form a surface, for example, glistening patches of reflection on a roof or raindrops on an invisible windowpane. Variations in shading are usually interpreted under the assumption of a uniform source of illumination and taken to indicate changes in the orientation of a surface from point to point, such as the contours of a boulder, sculpture, or hillside. Changes in apparent texture combine information relating both to orientation and dis-

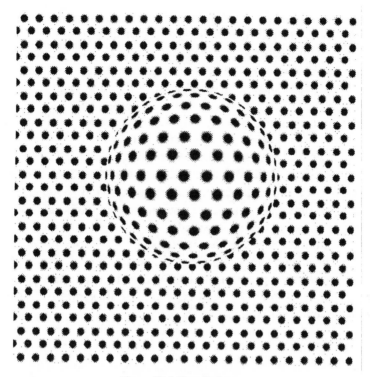

Figure 13.4 More Surfaces

tance. In Figure 13.4, a solid surface in the form of a plane with a hemispherical protrusion emerges from disconnected ellipses of varying size, eccentricity, and orientation.

An area in which opinions today generally differ from Marr's original contention is in the operation of these parallel mechanisms, which Marr called "modules," early in the visual processing system. Marr believed that they functioned independently, their separate conclusions being brought together only at the relatively late stage of the $2^1/_2$-D Sketch. In this way nature would have anticipated the modern practice of modular programming (doubtless a large factor in Marr's choice of term), whereby the effects of errors in one piece of code remain localized and don't make the correcting task impossibly difficult by affecting everything else. Once again, however, nature's solution turns out to be more complex than was supposed. The mechanisms all interact with each other, exchanging information in subtle and not fully understood ways. The processing of stereo vision, to take one instance, appears to be not the result of a single mechanism but of several, achieving overall robustness of vision at multiple levels. In effect, the vision system applies heuristics tried and selected by nature over hundreds of millions of years. It applies them automatically, even when the results are contrary to common sense or logic, which is why we see optical illusions. We have no control or choice in the matter and continue to see the illusions even when, at the intellectual level, we know them for what they are.

A number of projects through the seventies and eighties sought to incorporate these mechanisms into computer programs.[6] In general, these yielded effective methods for making low-level sense of the clutter and confusion that typifies raw images of the real world. The theory would be expected to be more reliable in the early stages of vision since a lot more is known from experimental results and animal visual-cortex studies than at the level of later, more abstract representations in which brain functions are not well understood. The program by Tomaso Poggio and Eric Grimson at MIT used the primal-sketch techniques developed by Hildreth to match parts of aerial photographic stereo images and determine the contours and surfaces of mountain ranges. The program performed at about the same speed as an experienced human analyst and was as good at feature matching, but it tended to be less accurate in estimating depths. An encouraging indication that the approach might be on the right track was that when the program was subjected to standard tests that psychologists use in studies of stereo vision, it exhibited a similar pattern of success and failure to that found with humans.

WHAT, IF ANYTHING, IS AN ELEPHANT?

Where the biggest gap remains between what happens in brains and what can be accomplished artificially is at the final stage: synthesis and recognition of 3–D objects. It's one thing to get a program to sort out blobs and lines and form them into clues that can be interpreted as surfaces, but supplying the wherewithal to assemble a collection of surfaces together and recognize a school bus, a railroad car, or an elephant is something else. Once again, the difficulty of being able to tell a computer how to do it is that we don't really know how we do it ourselves.

One thing that's certain, however, is that whatever we do doesn't operate on any principle resembling template matching. It simply wouldn't be possible to store enough templates sufficiently close together to record all the scenes and objects that we are able to recognize from any angle, with varying lighting and quality. Nor would it be possible to process such a collection at the kind of speed that enables us to identify virtually instantly a person we haven't seen for years. And we are still able to do it successfully when the image we see is unlike any we have actually experienced before—the person may have aged, grown a mustache, lost some hair; we can even recognize from behind a person we have seen only from the front. Just about everything visible has changed, so exactly what *is* it that's being recognized? Take the elephant again. We have no hesitation in recognizing it whether it is real, big, gray, rough, and wrinkly, walking around in a zoo; a pink and white Disney caricature; a battered fluffy toy with its trunk and an ear missing; a part of the design of a brass table leg; or a porcelain pepper pot painted with a few lines. Somehow, from all of these and an inexhaustible store of other examples, we manage to extract the common characteristic of "elephantness"—eerily reminiscent, in a way, of the Scholastics' forms. But how do you spell it out to a computer, which requires specific, step-by-step rules? Simply supplying a list of attributes for the program to check through, such as "An elephant has four legs, a trunk, . . . ," doesn't work. We have no difficulty recognizing the mutilated fluffy toy as an elephant; a three-legged elephant is still an elephant, and so on. It's the business of world knowledge again—knowing what makes sense in a given context and what doesn't—that crops up in every facet of AI.

Our eyes fill in far more than we're aware of consciously of what they expect to see. Sometimes they are mistaken, as when a figure in the shadows near a distant lamppost turns out to be an odd superposition of a mailbox and some shrubbery or when a patch of moonlight becomes a curve in the road ahead. Occasionally, actions taken on the strength of such mistakes can be fatal. But as we saw when talking about choosing from proliferating alternatives, the heuristics that seem to give the best compromise have evolved to be nearly right most of the time, not absolutely right all the time. While unlucky for some, the strategy that results gives better survival odds for the species as a whole.

Visual recognition remains one of the most challenging areas of AI work. As we shall see later, it seems to depend on mechanisms very close to those that enable us to perceive metaphor and analogy in using and comprehending language. Vision and language involve what are perhaps our most complex and abstract representations of the external and internal realities we experience. Comprehending how they operate would get close to the core of what true intelligence is all about.

"Object-Centered" Vision at Stanford

TOM BINFORD'S GENERALIZED CYLINDERS

Tom Binford worked on vision with the MIT AI lab until 1971 and then moved westward to join the robotics group that had grown with the AI activity at Stanford. His approach of identifying surfaces and grouping them into objects before attempting recognition of what the objects are anticipated the principle that Marr incorporated into his theory as the $2^1/_2$-D Sketch.[7] Now a professor at Stanford, Binford heads development of the "object-centered" approach to image understanding that his earlier work has grown into. Currently, it is achieving significant results in such areas as recognizing military vehicles, weaponry, and installations against complex background clutter in radar and infrared imagery, with the eventual aim of automated target identification and acquisition.

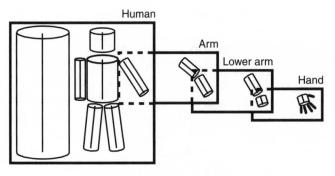

Figure 13.5 Hierarchy of Cylinders

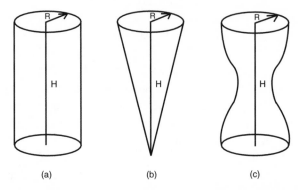

**Figure 13.6 (*a*) The basic cylinder, generated by two parameters: rotation of radius R
generates a circle, which sweeps along the axis *h*. Allowing R to vary instead of
remaining constant as the circle moves along *h* produces such forms as
the cone (*b*), or the vase (*c*).**

The starting point was to approximate objects by hierarchical structures
of cylinders arranged around a stick skeleton. Figure 13.5 illustrates the general idea.

The concept of generalizing cylinders gives this basically simple notion an
amazing degree of versatility. Figures 13.6 through 13.9 show a progression in
which a few elementary variations of the basic cylindrical form lead to a generalized form capable of representing just about anything.

It is tempting to seek variations in similarly simple generating parameters—
chemical gradients or pressure or temperature variations, for example—as
underlying causes for many of the seemingly complex forms found in nature.

The advantage of representing things in this way is that the underlying
functions responsible for generating these forms—a line curving in space, a
radius varying with rotation angle—are relatively straightforward to represent

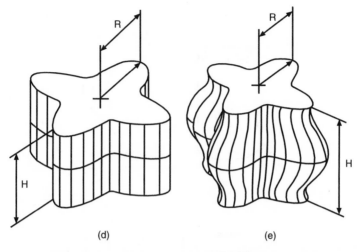

(d)   (e)

Figure 13.7 Alternatively, R might vary as it rotates, which when repeated along *h* generates the constant-section pillar, (*d*). Combining both, i.e., letting R vary as it rotates and as it proceeds along *h* gives rise to the plinth (*e*).

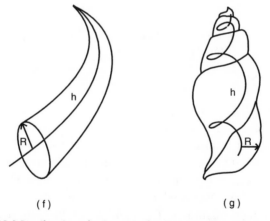

(f)   (g)

Figure 13.8 Bending the axis, *h*, and letting R vary leads to the horn (*f*), while turning *h* through a spiral results in the seashell (*g*).

mathematically. This permits the application of geometric transformations that can extract features of an object that remain unchanged ("invariants") regardless of the angle from which the object is viewed—the ratio between the lengths of two sections of a straight line is an example. Hence, the object can be classified according to its basic form and generation parameters, rather than having to be identified from an enormous range of possible 2–D image variations.

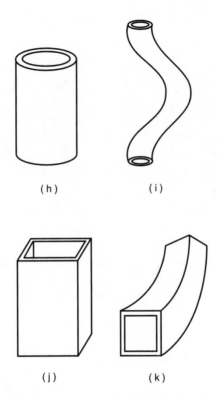

Figure 13.9 Making the generating surface hollow rather than solid produces tubes (*h*) and (*i*), a box (*j*), or a duct (*k*).

BUILDING CYLINDERS INTO OBJECTS

A combination of geometric constraints (commonsense restrictions on what is and is not possible), probabilities derived from experience, and inferential reasoning rules are applied to construct a graphical representation of how the component shapes fit together to form more complex structures. This information can then be compared against a catalog of "object image" descriptions to see if it conforms to anything recognizable. The significant thing with such an "object-centered" approach is that the structure is hypothesized first and recognition attempted afterward. Hence, the comparison made is of structural relationships that remain constant irrespective of viewing angle or lighting conditions and that are unaffected by different "poses" the object might assume. A fire engine, for example, is put together in the same way whether the ladder is extended or lying flat; similar aircraft can have widely differing surface markings.

With the perhaps more commonly encountered "view-centered" approach, by contrast, image matching takes place first, and a 3–D shape is deduced from the identification. This involves a much higher computational load since it requires processing and matching all the image's features with an enormous number of reference profiles. For example, processing a radar image consisting of 10,000 picture elements grouped into local regions taken five elements at a time would involve a billion billion combinations. At a billion per second, that's still thirty-one years. Figure 13.10 summarizes the two approaches.

If Seeing Is Believing, Doing Is Proving: Mobility and Robotics

Hans Moravec is a lively and charismatic six-footer, originally from Austria, who moved to Canada in 1953 and arrived at Stanford in 1971 to become one of John McCarthy's graduate students. He left Stanford in 1980 and is now director of the Mobile Robotics Laboratory of Carnegie Mellon's Robotics Institute. Moravec built his first robot, constructed from tin cans, batteries, lights, and a motor, at age ten. I talked with him for an afternoon in his office and laboratory, surrounded by several wheeled robots that wander around the corridors and occasionally make sorties out onto the campus. Conversation with Moravec is an entertainment, if for no other reason than the enthusiasm with which he expounds a diversity of ideas that range from transferring human consciousnesses from protein-based brains into purpose-designed machines, which he believes would have many advantages, to a fusion of human, nonhuman, and eventually alien minds that will one day transform the universe into a single conscious totality. In the meantime, he spends much of his time designing and studying robots.

Robotics is probably the ideal medium for bringing together and integrating all the mechanisms of general problem solving, planning, world knowledge, vision, and world representation that we have talked about so far. In fact, Moravec takes an extreme position among those who hold that the surest way of building a general intelligence is through an entity that is mobile and responsive. Mobility means that the system is constantly encountering fresh situations that cannot be anticipated. Hence, a generalized ability for dealing with the unexpected and muddling through in spite of less-than-perfect information and actions that fail to achieve expected results—surely a major defining human trait if ever there was one—becomes crucial. Working within formal domains such as games or mathematics, by contrast, tends to produce excellent but very specialized abilities. Responsiveness means that the system's world model and problem solutions are constantly checked against reality. What the Wright brothers learned about flying in a week was worth more than centuries of theorizing. It particularly impresses Moravec that all animals that have evolved perceptual and behavioral competence comparable to that of humans first adopted a mobile way of life. This is not so obvious from the vertebrates, whose universal mobility debars useful comparisons, but it is dramatically confirmed among invertebrates. Most mollusks are sessile shellfish exhibiting primitive behavior governed by a nervous system of a few hundred neurons. The octopus

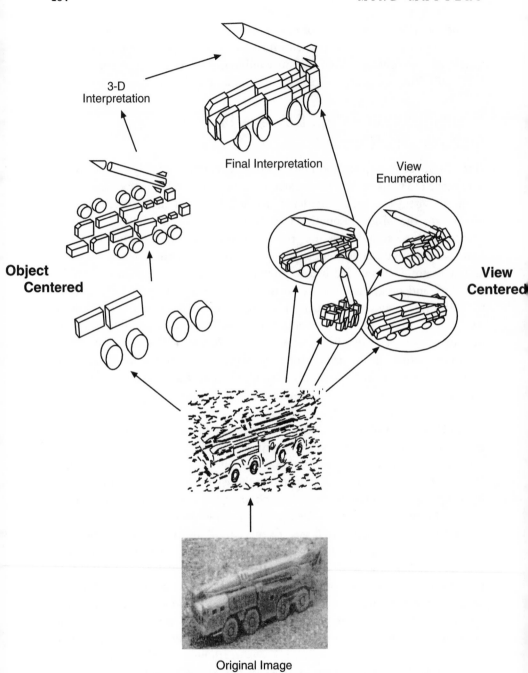

Original Image

Figure 13.10 Object-Centered versus View-Centered Vision

and the squid abandoned life in a shell for one of mobility and, as a consequence, developed imaging eyes, a large brain, and dexterous manipulators. No sessile animal or any plant comes anywhere near exhibiting their level of behavioral complexity.[8]

EARLY DAYS OF ROBOTICS

An act as seemingly simple as running a comb through one's hair requires the coordinated action of somewhere around forty muscles. Getting each one to contribute exactly its correct share to producing the composite movement requires monitoring the degree of contraction of each one, along with positional feedback from the shoulder, elbow, wrist, and finger joints, as well as adjusting from instant to instant to compensate for the resistance encountered, the changes of balance brought about by raising the arm, and so on. The reason we are able to carry on a conversation while we do all this is that like vision—which our brains are also processing at the same time—the routines laboriously learned through our baby and toddler-hood stages have been encoded as unconscious microprograms that we invoke through a single voluntary decision. Were it not so, we would be so swamped by maintenance tasks that our minds would have no time for any purposeful, higher-level activities at all. To duplicate such feats artificially, however, every detail of every function has to be spelled out explicitly somewhere as an instruction in a computer program. Once written and cleaned up, it's true that the routine might subsequently be called by a single command from a higher-level executive procedure. But it all has to be developed in step-by-step detail in the first place.

By the mid-sixties, hand-eye coordination projects were under way at Stanford and MIT in the United States and in Scotland under Donald Michie's group at Edinburgh. These all followed a similar pattern of using a TV camera and computer to guide a mechanical manipulator in the form of a claw or rudimentary hand in such tasks as stacking blocks on a tabletop, solving elementary puzzles, and identifying and connecting parts. One favorite demonstration of the Stanford device was its ability to assemble an automobile water pump from randomly scattered components. Some observers have commented on the difficulty of staying awake while watching even four-minute tapes of these contrivances painstakingly panning around the scene to assess the options and hauling together the elements of a solution. Perhaps they have forgotten what it was like to be two years old. The combinations of techniques brought to bear in these demonstrations—turning an image array into symbols of something meaningful, relating those symbols to a task to be performed, and constructing an appropriate plan and sequence of instructions for performing it—untangled knots of interrelated problems that had never been attempted before. Their purpose was to find out where the obstacles to further development lay, and the one they all uncovered was the same one that was being learned from pure vision and other lines of AI research: the absolute importance of world knowledge. "Seeing" is not possible without some understanding of that which is seen; meaning can only be assigned in terms of a context within which to assign it.

The fourth notable center of robotics work that began in the sixties and lasted into the seventies was at Stanford Research Institute, today unconnected with the university and known simply as SRI International. The team here was headed by Charles Rosen and included Bertram Raphael, who had moved there via UC Berkeley after receiving one of the first Ph.D.'s awarded by MIT for artificial intelligence. Niels Nilsson, also a member of the original group, later became head of the robotics group at Stanford University. Instead of equipping their computer with hands, they put it on wheels. This was at the instigation of the government funding agency ARPA, which was interested in an automated battlefield unit that would gather intelligence information, deliver supplies, and possibly even provide fire control for weapons.

"Shakey,"[9] as the robot was eventually named—the mountings and suspension didn't come up to Detroit standards—was implemented in two major versions, the first completed in 1969, both outwardly the same, consisting of a boxlike cabinet containing the on-board processor set atop a wheeled motor unit and adorned with a TV camera, range finder, and radio-link antenna to a larger control computer. Shakey lived in a life-size Blocks World of seven interconnected rooms containing cubes, wedges, and other geometric shapes. Responding to instructions typed in at a console, it would do things like negotiate its way around obstacles to find an object located in one room, then move it to stack on top of a box in another room. One of its star performances was to move a ramp from the far side of a room and use it to get to a target block sitting on a raised platform. This was quite an achievement for the times, and, like the hand-eye projects, brought a number of hitherto separate strategies together into a comprehensive solution not attempted before. Still, it was a long way away from a mechanical SEAL commando capable of crawling around and hiding itself on battlefields to search out hostile positions. This didn't prevent an overenthusiastic, or perhaps simply fanciful, journalist from writing in *Life*[10] that the robot was made up of "five major systems of circuitry that correspond quite closely to basic human faculties—sensation, reason, language, memory, ego." According to the article, the computer "sees," "understands," "learns," and in general has "demonstrated that machines can think." Hardly. No wonder the public sometimes gets confused.

Perhaps it wasn't only the press that got a bit carried away. DARPA (the D, for Defense, having been added since the project's inception) realized that the robot's performance was not going to meet the ambitious schedule that had been projected, and the program was terminated. In her book *Machines Who Think*,[11] Pamela McCorduck describes it standing forlorn and dilapidated in a corner when she interviewed Bert Raphael in his office. Charles Rosen says he was told later by the DARPA people that Shakey was canceled because there were too many people raising questions about its being a dangerous thing to have around. This from people whose stock-in-trade is explosives, napalm, and nuclear missiles. Life can be strange.

HANS MORAVEC'S STANFORD CART[12]

Shakey's world consisted of clean geometric shapes and brightly lit rooms, with dark, painted lines defining the boundaries between the walls and the floor. As in the Micro Worlds project at MIT, the intention was to discover the basic principles of object and spatial recognition by reducing the problem to its basic elements and then progressively adding in refinements to deal with the complications found in the real world.

It turned out that the simple solutions were not readily generalizable in this way. Methods that would find a cube among a restricted number of well-defined shapes could not practicably be expanded to deal with the enormous variety of objects that make up real environments. The certainty of outcome from a sequence of operations followed in the precisely defined domain of a chess game couldn't be assumed where sensor and interpretation errors produced accumulating discrepancies between internally maintained maps and the actual state of things outside. Moravec decided that the problem was not one that could be deferred and tackled later. The only way to produce systems rugged and robust enough to operate in the real world was the way nature had: by treating the handling of uncertainties, dirt, and clutter as inherent to the problem from the beginning, not something that could be added in later.

Moravec's Stanford Cart project was supported by DARPA, NSF, and NASA over the years 1973–1980, the vehicle itself dating from 1969, when it had been built under a NASA contract to study remote-controlled robots for lunar exploration. The Defense Department was still intrigued by the prospect of an autonomous vehicle capable of navigating over rugged terrains and had come around to the view that experiments in pastel-colored rooms were not going to get anywhere.

Essentially, the cart was a mobile camera platform controlled via radio link from a DEC KL–10 computer running a program that gained its knowledge of the world solely by information transmitted from the cart's on-board TV system. The aim was to study visually directed navigation in both indoor and outdoor real-world environments. After rolling forward a distance of a meter or so, the cart would stop and move its camera along a slide to snap nine stereo images. By identifying and tracking salient features from these images, the program applied stereoscopic methods to locate objects around it and deduce its own position relative to them and hence plan an obstacle-avoiding path to a destination.

In general, the system was reliable for short runs but agonizingly slow, requiring ten to fifteen minutes to process the information between meter-long lurches. A typical twenty-meter course would thus take somewhere around five hours to complete. Even so, the cart had difficulty with bland, featureless objects such as whimsical polygonal trees and rocks constructed from cardboard, which it saw from a distance and would then sometimes lose in close-up to the point of colliding with them, but it did well with such feature-rich objects as chairs. Another source of error resulted from the long processing time between moves, which in outdoor tests meant that shadows could move significantly between successive position fixings, causing a growing difference between the cart's actual location and where it thought it was. This sometimes caused the same object to be mistaken for two—the one discerned currently and its "ghost" from the preceding view—and the pair was interpreted as blocking a path that was actually open.

While much was learned in these years, such performances clearly fall far short of that of any human or animal infant. Until we try to emulate living systems artificially, we don't appreciate the stupefying excellence of biological nervous systems that can coordinate the movements of a cheetah cornering at speed or of a hawk coming in to land. Moravec's comment on this is illuminating. In all probability, he says, the big processors we're so proud of, which can compute astronomic calculations or sort encyclopedic volumes of information in seconds, are probably every bit as primitive, if the truth were known, as our robots. We just think they're good because nothing in nature ever had any reason to specialize in such tasks, so we have no living system to compare them to. Imagine a brain whose ancestral line had been selecting for chess playing, say, for half a billion years.

PLUTO, NEPTUNE, AND URANUS AT CARNEGIE MELLON

In 1980, Moravec moved to Carnegie Mellon and obtained a contract from the Office of Naval Research to extend the Stanford work to a more capable robot and explore further capabilities. His group's first design, named Pluto, had a roughly cylindrical body about a meter high and ran on three independently steerable wheel assemblies. The main problem causing the cart's slowness at Stanford had been limited processing power. Pluto carried a dozen on-board processors for faster local decision making, while the other end of the link was served by a thirty-two-bit VAX 11/780 and a Star ST–100 array processor capable of 100 million floating point operations (mathematical operations on numbers that can vary over many orders of magnitude) per second. In addition to its visual sensor, Polaroid sonar ranging devices provided all-around local surveillance, and infrared proximity detectors provided a secondary means of collision avoidance.

The main object was to continue work on computer vision, with design aims of reducing raw-image digitization from half a minute to one second per picture, speeding up low-level vision processing by a factor of one hundred, and developing faster routines for higher-level world modeling and planning. Construction was substantially complete by 1983. Early experiments, however, soon showed severe problems and failures with the wheel assemblies and drive systems. Its six motors and six servoloops allowed it too many degrees of freedom, permitting unexpected interactions that defied analysis. In addition to moving the robot forward, sideways, and spinning it about its axis, the individually drivable wheels were able to attempt twisting, compressing, and stretching in ways that shuddered and rattled, broke encoding disks, and burned out drive transistors.

Pluto became a dedicated platform for a separate line of studies of complex motion-control phenomena. The original vision project was transferred to a simpler robot called Neptune, based on a three-motor design from Stanford, which was operational by 1984. Neptune could locate itself with ten times the accuracy of the Stanford Cart and at ten times the speed, but it still failed one task in four. In 1985 work on what had begun as a wide-angle range measuring system using cheap sonar sensors resulted in a new approach to spatial mapping that virtually never fails. The method, dubbed "Evidence Grids," was subsequently extended to stereo data from TV cameras, also with good results. Uranus, the latest of the lab's line, designed as a mobile laboratory capable of deploying a variety of sensor combinations rather than any fixed configuration, began operating in 1988. Work that has continued to the present on combined vision-and-sonar using the new principle shows good prospects for a totally dependable navigation system for taking robots into complex, unprepared environments.

EVIDENCE GRIDS

Traditional approaches to computer vision had attempted to identify lines and vertices in images and infer the boundaries of objects early in the processing sequence. Stereoscopic methods tended to concentrate on identifying and matching small, distinctive patches in multiple views of a scene. A characteristic drawback of such systems is their tendency to brittleness—the opposite of robustness. The existence of an object is deduced quickly, in a snap decision as it were, from small, error-prone parcels of data. Chance properties of a signal can produce mistaken matches that lead to wildly incorrect conclusions. A noisy signal and a reflection are obvious examples; a more subtle example would occur if the camera's movement caused a previously tracked feature to be obscured and the program latched onto a spurious substitute that it took to be the same thing. When this happens, the entire chain of inferences that follows from the interpretation is invalidated, usually with catastrophic results. After ten years of development, the Stanford Cart had not solved this problem, failing one time in four, on average, to navigate a thirty-meter obstacle course successfully.

In 1983, Denning, a company specializing in mobile robotics, let a contract to investigate inexpensive sonar mapping methods, forcing Moravec's group at Carnegie Mellon to seek an alternative to locating object features as an initial step in sensory processing. The Polaroid range finders used send out an ultrasonic beam, and from the echo delay measure the distance to the nearest sound reflector within a 30-degree arc. Such a reading provides a general indication of whether or not a large area of space is occupied by something, without distinguishing or localizing any features. The question posed was, Could information of this kind somehow be used to derive a usable map of a robot's surroundings?

As far as one reading is concerned, the answer is clearly no. But how about combining the information collected in many readings from varying angles and distances as the robot changes position? The initial configuration to try out this idea used twenty-four sensors equally spaced around the robot. The space surrounding the robot was represented by a grid of cells, each six inches square, and the diffuse information from multiple readings was combined to build up a cumulative measure of each cell's probability of being occupied. This generated a map that increased in accuracy and reliability as new readings were integrated into it. The result was surprisingly detailed, given the coarseness of the sensors, and highly robust. Real features tended to produce readings that reinforced strongly; occasional sensor errors and transient noise had little effect. Figure 13.11 shows Uranus's impressions from a (st)roll along a tree-lined path outside the lab building. The trees are clearly visible. Whereas the cart, after ten years, was still unreliable at crossing a cluttered room, the very first program to be written using the grid worked every time.

Each cell in the map can vary from black, which indicates virtual certainty that the cell is occupied, to white, indicating virtual certainty that the cell is empty. The robot's perceptions are clear and unambiguous along the vicinity of its travel, and the features fade into the equivalent of a fog farther back.

The Sonar Evidence Grid is so named because each cell keeps a tally of the evidence of its being occupied. A given sensor makes its contribution by increasing the occupancy probability for the cells near the reflection it has registered ("there's something located about there") and decreasing the probability for the cells that lie in between ("there can't be anything in between"). The

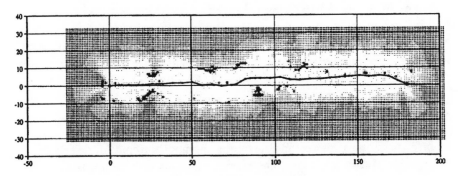

Figure 13.11 Sonar Evidence Grid

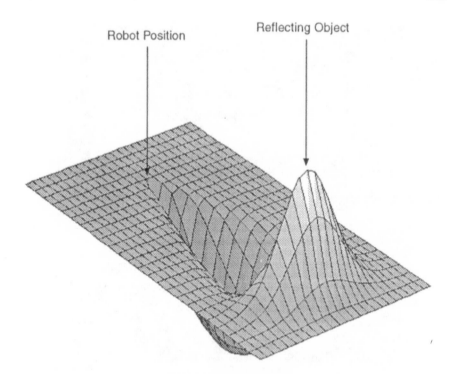

Figure 13.12 A Sensor Model

exact amount of the increase or decrease to be applied to each cell is given by a function termed the "sensor model." Figure 13.12 shows an example. The crest indicates the vicinity of an object, the highest probability of occupancy being at the central cells. The depression leading along the line of sight to the robot indicates negative probabilities to be added to the values of intervening cells.

Figure 13.13 shows an idealized representation of a section of an L-shaped corridor outside Hans Moravec's office, along with what Uranus was able to make of it from sonar. The result was easily good enough for most navigational purposes. Note that the robot ("robat"?) located numerous objects seemingly buried inside the walls. These were produced by outgoing signals reflecting away, off the walls, and eventually being echoed from features such as door edges via long paths. The extended delays were interpreted as being due to objects located correspondingly far off along the line of sight of the returned signal. Current work is addressing the reflection problem by having each cell measure not just the probability of being occupied but the probability of being occupied by an element of surface oriented in a particular direction in space.

Evidence does not have to come from just one type of sensor or even from a single program concerned with one kind of spatial representation. A strength of the grid method is the ease with which hypotheses formed in different ways—

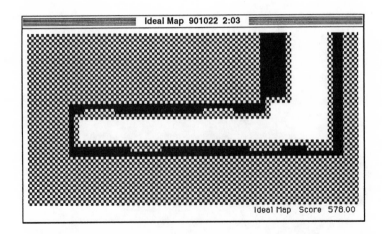

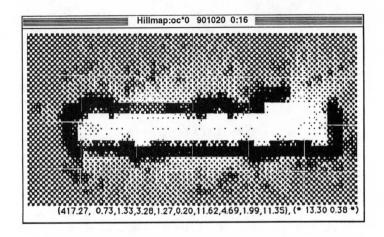

Figure 13.13 Corridor with Ghost Images

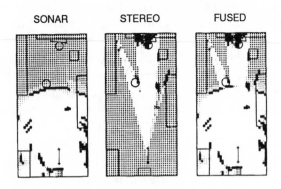

Figure 13.14 Fusion of Sonar and Stereo
The crosses mark the robot's travel.

sonar, stereo, infrared, surface recognition, say—can be fused into a consensus, with each contribution weighted according to its own measure of relative importance and confidence level. This is beginning to sound closer to the kind of thing that goes on in the brain. Figure 13.14 shows a fusion of sonar mapping and stereo vision. Note that the sensors can complement each other, each providing information about areas inaccessible to the other. Also, they can correct one another. Thus, a region that sonar sees as occupied is correctly cleared by stereo.

The latest extension of the project has been to go to a 3–D grid composed of smaller, cubical cells, 2.5 inches on a side. Preliminary results have been encouraging. With 1990s processing capability, programs to handle 3–D stereo images generate one hundred to one thousand times more good map data than the earlier 2–D system. Whereas the 1974 program used with the cart was able to find fewer than fifty features per stereo picture set, the 1996 program extracts on the order of 2,500.

One of the problems yet to be worked out is a convenient way of representing 3–D grids of cubical cells for visualization by humans. How do you depict a scene formed by surfaces embedded inside a solid assembly of Lego blocks? One method that appears promising is to make the unoccupied cells transparent and group assemblies of occupied cells into objects that can be differentiated by color.

It seems that evidence grids might be a major direction for the future. Since the late eighties, scientific papers dealing with various aspects and extensions of the concept have proliferated from academic, private, and public organizations worldwide.[13]

Robot Road Vehicles

The Mobile Robot Laboratory at CMU also houses an odd collection of vehicles that includes a Toyota van with a processor box in the space where the passenger seat should be and a former army ambulance, crammed with hardware and three TV cameras mounted over the driver's cab, that ventures out for excursions on the interstates. With potential applications ranging from self-driving trucks to safer passenger transportation systems, the prospect of automatic road vehicles has attracted interest for many years.

In 1977, Japan's Mechanical Engineering Laboratory demonstrated a stereo-vision-guided car that could follow well-defined roads for distances of about fifty yards at moderate speed. In the United States, DARPA, ever the optimist, initiated a program in 1984 called "Autonomous Land Vehicles" (ALV) aimed at producing stealthy robot crawlers for battlefield reconnaissance, supply, and sabotage. True to form, DARPA abandoned it five years later, but during that time ALV brought forth a number of experimental vision-guided vehicles that included a large, rough-terrain rover by Martin Marietta Corp., equipped with color TV cameras and a scanning laser range finder, and a similar project called

"Nav Lab" at Carnegie Mellon. Both were able to follow dirt roads, again at moderate speeds, tracking the road boundaries and stopping for obstacles, but they were easily fooled by discontinuities and seldom stayed on course for a kilometer. A project begun in Germany in 1984 produced a van, guided by a single monochrome camera, that has driven itself on the autobahns at speeds of up to eighty miles per hour.

All these systems work by keeping a small image window centered on a feature in the view—the principle employed by self-steering TV-guided bombs and missiles. A feature might be the highway edge or lane marking, a license plate, or other marking on traffic ahead. In none of these kinds of systems is it advisable for the human supervisor to let his or her attention wander far from the manual override button. The earlier versions of these systems were easily confused by such common occurrences as shadows, stains on the road, stopped vehicles, or sudden curves. Improvement has been steady in recent years, but we're still a long way from the intelligent automatic chauffeur depicted in the opening chapter. Some current approaches are investigating the use of satellite positioning signals for primary navigation, with sensing demoted to reaction to immediately local conditions and emergencies.

Doing Away with Representation

THE WORLD AS ITS OWN BEST MODEL

Whether top-down or bottom-up, all the approaches to AI that we have considered so far presume the manipulation of an internal world of symbols representing the objects and relationships that make up the world outside. The difference lay in the viewpoint as to whether this internal world was to be imposed from above as ready-made descriptions or built up from below out of accumulated experience.

A more radical appraisal of the work of the past twenty-five years concludes that human intelligence is too complex and too little understood to be represented in terms of the correct subpieces at present. The only way to acquire such understanding, according to this more fundamental bottom-up view, will be by forgetting about higher-level cognitive faculties and starting off with simple intelligences aimed at no more than managing to get by in their environment, the way nature did.

The most vigorous proponent of this philosophy is the Australian Rodney Brooks,[14] a former student of Tom Binford and his assistant in the development of a vision system called Acronym for monitoring airport traffic from satellite images. Originally from Adelaide, Brooks studied mathematics at Flinders University of South Australia and went on to obtain a Ph.D. in computer science from Stanford in 1981. After holding a research associate position at CMU

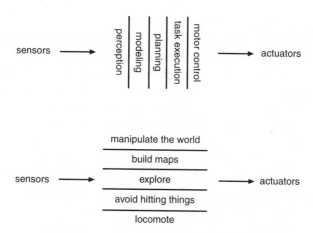

Figure 13.15 Traditional versus Layered Architecture

he moved to MIT, where he is currently assistant director of the AI lab under Patrick Winston.

The way in which biological evolution divided its time in the process of eventually producing intelligence tells us something important, Brooks says. A billion years were needed to produce photosynthetic plants from single-cell entities, another billion and a half to get from there to fish and the first vertebrates. After that came insects, reptiles, birds, and mammals, all in a space measured in hundreds of millions of years—which was actually starting to move at quite a fair clip on the scale at which these things happen. Finally, there came us, and pretty much all the things we make a song and dance about as setting us so much apart from the rest all took place in a few hundred thousand years. What this suggests, Brooks contends, is that such abilities as abstraction, problem solving, language, and all the things that AI has been trying to build, as it were, in midair are all relatively simple to add once the foundation—i.e., being able to exist in an environment and interact competently with it—is solidly in place. This is the truly hard part, where evolution has been forced to concentrate so much of its time and attention; AI's thinking it can get around the issue is the delusion that has caused all its problems.[15]

Like Moravec, the answer that Brooks advocates is mobility, acute vision, and the ability to carry out purposeful tasks in a dynamic environment as the unavoidable precursor to developing true intelligence. However, whereas Moravec sees robotics as a means of building a representation of the world from sensory-level perceptions, Brooks wants to throw out representation entirely. "Explicit representations and models of the world simply get in the way," he says. "The world is its own best model."

INCREMENTAL INTELLIGENCE

For the past ten years, Brooks and his group at MIT have been conducting a program aimed at producing a series of autonomous mobile agents to test these convictions, ranging from foot-long insects that clamber over artificial landscapes to wheeled robots wandering around among the building's laboratories and corridors.[16] This kind of thing is also a fairly common sight at places like CMU and Stanford. What distinguishes Brooks's designs is their departure from the traditional concept of a central information processor that receives a symbolic input from perceptual modules of some kind and exercises control via outputs to some system of action modules. This chain of modules linking perception to action, Brooks maintains, has brought about a retreat of AI work into specialized subproblems that reflect the conveniences of researchers rather than realities implicit in the task at hand. The symbolic descriptions are chosen more to the degree that they circumscribe the domains being worked in than define any natural divisions of the processes that make up intelligence. On the contrary, if anything, they obscure such divisions and make the likelihood of reproducing intelligence more remote.

Brooks's approach doesn't differentiate between peripheral and central. Division of the system is "horizontal," connecting sensing to action on the basis of a defined *level of activity*, which could be thought of as a "skill" level. The idea is that a basic "reflexive" behavior is implemented first, then thoroughly tested and debugged in real-world performance before a second level is grafted on, perhaps accessing the same sensors but running a different program to afford an added dimension of activity. The activity of the original level continues autonomously, unaware of the existence of the higher mode running parallel with it. The result is what Brooks calls "layered architecture." The first layer might be, for example, a simple collision-avoidance mechanism, while the second might instill an element of "curiosity" to visit visible places. The two layers interact to produce a more complex behavior in which "wandering" combines with local obstacle-avoidance maneuvering whenever the more primitive activity level is triggered. A third layer might then add a "purposeful" role of attempting to get to distant places when active but on other occasions give way to the general inclination to explore.

There is no central control or representation and no identifiable place where the "output" of a perception subsystem can be found. Totally different kinds of processing of the sensor data proceed independently, each layer of the system extracting those aspects of the world it finds relevant to its purpose. The macroscopic behavior emerges as the result of a collection of sometimes competing, sometimes cooperating activities, each essentially simple in itself.

Physically, the concept was implemented as networks of finite-state machines (microprocessors) communicating via messages that might or might not have effect at their destinations due to the overriding influence of other layers or which could even be lost at the expiration of an assigned time period.

Thus, there is no determinate behavior of a form defined by any resident control program. What emerges from the interactions is dynamic, dependent on the situation of the moment.

ROBOTS IN ALL SHAPES AND SIZES

The first robot to embody these techniques was "Allen," which contained, essentially, three layers as outlined above. With the first layer activated, Allen would sit in the middle of the room until approached and then scurry away, while at the same time avoiding collisions with other obstacles. This behavior was produced by interpreting sonar echoes as repulsive forces, each decreasing as an inverse square of distance, and using the resultant vector sum to decide which way to move. An additional reflex made the robot halt when there was something directly in front of it, when it would turn in place to seek a different direction. The second layer made it wander off in a random direction every ten seconds, but the obstacle avoidance layer still operated, its effects being subsumed into the operation of the higher layer (hence the alternative name "subsumption architecture"). Finally, the third layer impressed a compulsion to head for distant landmarks. This overrode the wandering instinct, but because the obstacle-avoidance reflex was still active, the actual path followed did not always keep to the course that the third layer had indicated. Hence, the robot constantly had to track progress and compute course corrections as the situation changed.

"Tom and Jerry" were toy cars fitted out to demonstrate how little computation power was needed to realize the subsumption principle. Again, this was a three-layer system, yet all data paths were just one bit wide, and the whole program fit into a single 256-gate programmable array logic chip clocked at a few hundred hertz. The wandering and avoidance mechanisms were combined with a moving-object detector that caused the robots to roam around looking for anything in motion, which they would then chase, although they would hang back a little if their quarry slowed down.

Then there was "Genghis," a one-kilogram, six-legged giant insect that walked over rough terrain under the combined influence of twelve motors, twelve force sensors, six pyroelectric (heat) sensors, and two whiskers. It has been recently superseded by a ruggedized version called "Attila," which stands, walks, and clambers over rocks using no central direction or control, each leg simply doing its own thing in response to the local forces and inclinations that it senses in conjunction with signals communicated from other parts of the network. When I talked to him, Brooks was involved in discussions with NASA on the idea of planetary surface exploration using swarms of autonomous, low-cost, expendable devices of this kind.[17]

"Herbert" was a more ambitious creation that had twenty-four distributed microprocessors forming a loosely coupled on-board computer, thirty infrared proximity sensors, a manipulator arm and simple grasping hand, also equipped with sensors, and a laser optical system that collected depth information over a sixty-degree forward field to a range of twelve feet. Herbert would wander about the office area, go into people's offices, and steal empty soda cans from their desks. (When I visited MIT, I noticed that some of the workers had laid strips of black adhesive tape on the floor across their doorways, which itinerant robots that were becoming a nuisance would interpret as a barrier and avoid.) Remarkably, there was no communication between any of Herbert's modules. Each was connected to the sensors, and behavior resulted completely from an arbitration network resolving the competing demands on the actuators.

"Toto" uses sonar navigation and has the added feature of a compass to enable it to construct a neighborhood map as it becomes familiar with its physical environment. At first sight the notion of a map may sound contrary to the subsumption principle we've been talking about. This map doesn't take the form of a static data structure as would conventionally be thought of, however, but of activity patterns in the processing nodes that the system has associated with particular landmarks. Thus, as the robot moves around the environment, nodes will become more active if they believe they are at "their" location. This activity spreads to "neighboring" nodes as the robot moves, enabling it to keep track of its whereabouts in terms of a distributed computational model rather than a centrally maintained symbolic representation. The concept of place maps of this kind is strikingly similar in some ways to what has been observed in the hippocampus of the rat.

"Seymour" added vision, using outputs from nine low-resolution cameras at roughly ten frames per second feeding into different layers, none of which exhibits particularly striking or reliable visual performance individually but which, operating together, can do things like track objects and find doorways successfully, switching back and forth between visual routines as one or another fails.

The current project, incorporating all of these principles developed on various prototype forms, is the development of "Cog," a fixed humanoid torso with a mobile head containing a vision system and, so far, a single movable and grasping arm. The vision system consists of two pairs of cameras carried in high-performance mechanical eyeballs that reproduce the human motions of panning and tilting, converging the sight lines, and making saccades, the rapid eye motions that take place continuously though unconsciously, avoiding overload of the retina through the persistence impinging of the image in one place. In Cog, this facility gives peripheral blurring, as we mentioned earlier, causing moving or otherwise significant features to stand out in a constantly perceived 115-degree background field. The other pair of cameras, with a 20-degree field, is then able to fixate on an area of interest and examine it at higher resolution, mimicking the foveal activity of natural biological optical systems. Further enhancements such as the incorporation of a second arm, more sophisticated tactile sensors, and perhaps sound and speech capabilities are tentatively planned for the future.

Marvin Minsky and Brooks's former tutor Tom Binford are highly skeptical that Brooks's predictions will ever be met from these kinds of beginnings. But as Brooks himself says, "Only experiments with real Creatures in real worlds can answer the natural doubts about our approach. Time will tell."

So What Happened to Intelligence?

We started this chapter on the note that direct interaction with the environment would accumulate the world knowledge needed for a true intelligence to function. Somehow along the way, both artificial vision and robotics seem, once more, to have skewed off that original path to find specialized niches of their own.

Text recognition and document scanning are already huge markets, and technology is beginning to provide a significant new input medium for computer systems. Automated stereo interpretation of aerial photographs for military intelligence gathering, mapmaking, and surveying has made considerable progress in the last decade, and enormous potential—for example, in robotic space exploration—awaits the development of truly reliable, all-around methods. Simple inspection and assembly-line robots are now standard in many industries where controlled environments and lighting permit basic template-matching methods and low-cost hardware, while much potential for more sophisticated varieties exists for employment in hazardous environments such as nuclear and chemical facilities, mines, construction, heavy industry, and underwater. And, of course, the Defense Department will no doubt always be there, ready to risk another few million on the promise of a mechanized Rambo superspy.

Industries have recently come into being that we already take for granted, and yesterday's research is opening up new market possibilities today. But the original vision of creating a true, humanlike intelligence that started so much of this research off remains as unrealized as ever. One reason could be that the commercial pressures of our form of society immediately drive anything promising into specialization. Or might it be that the capability we're looking for is proving difficult to find because it doesn't exist in the generalized form that we imagine? Perhaps we ourselves exist not as all-around problem solvers who can apply our ideas to anything but as collections of highly trained specialists living together under one name. If so, then before we can reproduce the collective, maybe we first have to create the specialists.

If there's one specialty that distinguishes humans from all other life on this planet, it has to be our use of language. What is the story of attempts to produce an artificial specialist in that area? We'll move on now to the next chapter and see.

1. Hebb.
2. Minsky and Papert.
3. For a more detailed discussion, see Kanade and Reddy.
4. Marr.
5. Marr and Hildreth (1984).
6. Marr and Poggio (1976), (1979); Grimson and Marr; Poggio.
7. Binford; Sato and Binford.
8. Moravec (1983).
9. Raphael (1976); also McCorduck, pp. 232–34.
10. Darrach.
11. McCorduck, p. 230.
12. Moravec (1983).
13. Martin and Moravec; Moravec (1996).
14. Brooks (1987), (1991a).
15. Brooks (1990), (1991b).
16. Brooks (1986); Brooks and Stein.
17. Brooks and Flynn.

14

Seeing What You Mean

COMPREHENDING NATURAL LANGUAGE

"Time flies like an arrow; fruit flies like a banana."—old AI adage

Language as the Reservoir of Knowledge

Among the life-forms on this planet, humans are unique in their powers of imagination, creativity, and reasoning; we are also unique in our use of language to represent and communicate the ideas that we imagine and create, and about which we reason. This is surely not coincidental. Just as animal behavior is an outward expression of reactions to the physical aspects of existence, language expresses the more abstract, inner workings and creations of more complex nervous systems.

The ability to use language is an innate quality associated with a specialized area of the human brain that has coevolved along with the concept-forming and connecting capability that we call intelligence. The two could be viewed as external and internal manifestations of the same phenomenon, reflecting the need for emerging consciousness to express itself. Constructing language seems to be as basic and universal a trait as walking or using our hands. As with those skills, the underlying instinct comes naturally, but the specific ways of applying it have to be practiced and learned (else we would all speak the same language). What we gain in return for the hours of labor, repeated generation after generation, is adaptability. Having to relearn means that a new generation's learning can be modified to incorporate new knowledge and, if necessary, to delete things that turned out to be not such a good idea.

The effort still takes a tiny fraction of the time that gene modifications would need to propagate through a population. Thus, we can change from burning wood to coal to oil to harnessing the internal energy densities of atoms as new discoveries become available and send missions to the moon less than three quarters of a century after the Wright brothers' first flight. Language thus fosters its own form of Lamarckian evolution in which, unlike the genetically driven variety, what is learned through the efforts of one generation can indeed be inherited by the next. In short, it is the possession of language that has enabled humans alone to accumulate knowledge.

Communication of knowledge, however, is not the only function that language serves. Less obviously, it also facilitates and shapes the way we perceive the world. Without language, thought could not attain anything like the complexity and level of abstraction found in humans. A picture might be worth a thousand words for some purposes, but what picture could capture the concepts contained in, say, the works of Plato or Shakespeare? We perceive most readily, and divide the world up in terms of, those things for which we have verbal expressions. A person observing a Gothic cathedral who is familiar with such concepts as "flying buttress," "pointed arch," and "fan vaulting" will see and understand more than somebody unfamiliar with those ideas. Speakers of different languages divide up the color spectrum differently. For example, when asked to sort color cards into piles, people who have no words corresponding exactly to our perception of "blue" will put part of what we see as blue and part of what we see as green together. Whether one argues that what they've learned to see is conditioned by the words they've been taught or, conversely, that they literally see differently (but why should that be, if we all have the same visual genetics?) and hence have invented different labels, the intimate connection between the language we use and the reality we live in is clear.

So it's not unreasonable to say that the first measure we'd expect of a truly intelligent entity is an ability to understand what we're talking about—at least as well as a normally developed child, one would think. And this, of course, was precisely what Turing had in mind when he proposed his test. Coherent, insightful responses and evidence of a listener's being reasonably quick on the uptake is the way we assess each other's intelligence.

(I am aware that I'm slipping into using "intelligence" here in a more specific sense than simply denoting purposeful, goal-directed activity, as proposed earlier. It would probably be more consistent to invoke a word like "consciousness" to describe the kind of ability touched on in this chapter, as this comes closer to describing what's required for the fluent handling of unrestricted natural human language. But the precedent of using "intelligence" in this connection is so firmly established that deviating from it would probably be jarringly distracting.)

However dazzling its performance in other specialized areas, then, a machine unable to compete in this respect, in failing to demonstrate real evidence of understanding, would be a poor candidate for convincing us that anything resembling true intelligence was taking place.

The Indispensability of "Understanding"

AN EARLY FAILURE: AUTOMATIC TRANSLATION

The idea that the new computers might provide a means of translating automatically from one language to another took shape well before the emergence of AI as a recognizable discipline in the mid-fifties. The success of Allied code-breaking efforts during World War II, using machines like the ones devised by Alan Turing at Bletchley, inspired thoughts that human languages were really nothing more than ways of representing the same meanings in different coding systems and application of the appropriate transformational rules would convert one into the other. In 1949 the mathematician Warren Weaver, at that time director for natural science at the Rockefeller Foundation, distributed a memorandum proposing a project to tackle the problem, in which he wrote, "When I look at an article in Russian I say, *This is really written in English, but it has been coded in some strange symbols. I will now proceed to decode.*"[1] The military and the intelligence agencies naturally relished such a prospect, and a program was launched under NRC auspices in a mood of heady optimism that anticipated full fluency within five years.

The method relied on automatic dictionary lookup and the application of grammar rules to rearrange the word equivalents thus obtained into the correct structure for the target language. But nobody actually believed it would be quite that simple. Some words have different meanings, depending on how and where they're used, and all languages have their own figures of speech and idioms that make no sense when translated literally into something else, but it was assumed that manual intervention and editing would take care of such exceptions. Weaver thought it might prove necessary to translate first into an intermediate language—a hypothetical interlingua that some believed underlay all human languages, or perhaps one that would have to be contrived—but somehow anything of the kind refused obstinately to emerge. As time went by, a certain unease began to be felt. Translation efforts produced a stream of examples that have become classics of hilarity but never seemed to get any better. Or they produced results that were questionably an improvement over no translation at all. An example from Harvard in the mid-fifties gave the following output from one sample.[2] Where the program was uncertain as to how to interpret a word, it listed alternatives in parentheses.

(In, At, Into, For, On) (last, latter, new, latest, lowest, worst) (time, tense) for analysis and synthesis relay-contact electrical (circuit, diagram, scheme) parallel-(series, successive,

consecutive, consistent) (connections, junction, combination) (with, from) (success, luck) (to be utilized, to be taken advantage of) apparatus Boolean algebra.

Whereas the original read:

In recent times, Boolean algebra has been successfully employed in the analysis of relay networks of the series-parallel type.

A decade later this was still much the state of the art and the early optimism had been replaced by a pervading sense of futility and acceptance that a solution was not even in sight. In 1966, after an outlay of $20 million, the National Research Council's Automated Language Processing Advisory Committee recommended that further funding for the project be terminated. Whatever the processes were that resulted in meanings being conveyed via language, they involved far more than a vocabulary of words and their definitions and rules for putting them in the right order.

Noam Chomsky's Transformational Grammar

The first attempt at machine translation thus ended in rout. The AI centers that had come into being during this period were not involved in the project and so escaped any share of the recriminations. Their approach to language was being shaped by a theory of formal representation amenable to rigorous mathematical treatment, which, not altogether surprisingly, had appeal for a community already engaged in the development of highly structured artificial languages for use with computers.

Noam Chomsky had studied linguistics, mathematics, and philosophy at Harvard and obtained a Ph.D. from the University of Pennsylvania in 1955. That same year he joined MIT, and in 1957 he published a book called *Syntactic Structures*, which, together with his somewhat direct and confrontational manner, stirred up the entire field of linguistics—until then leading a rather sedate existence of cataloging disconnected facts and observations somewhat in the fashion of biology prior to Linnaeus. Hence, he was in the right place at the right time to influence the leading figures of the new AI community who convened at Dartmouth in 1956.

In a way that paralleled David Marr's later approach to vision, Chomsky sought a systematic, testable theory that would tie all the empirical facts and ad hoc speculations together into a science. Like the dedicated vision system that operates unconsciously to give us no choice about what we see, Chomsky postulated the existence of a "language organ" within the brain, wired with a "deep-structured" universal grammar that is transmitted genetically and underlies the superficial structures of all human languages. He was impressed, for example, by the way in which children between the ages of about two and eleven take, almost compulsively, to the awesomely complex task of mastering language as spontaneously as they earlier learn to interpret vision, manipulate objects, and get up and walk. And they do it seemingly without effort, quite unlike the halting, stumbling ways in which as adults they might later rote-learn a foreign language, which almost invariably is accomplished imperfectly, with a strong imprint of accent. Even more remarkably, young children raised bilingually— an immigrant speaking one language at home and another at school, say—are able to learn both and keep them distinct. The basic rules had to be innate, Chomsky argued. The number of different ways for structuring grammar were too vast for anyone, let alone a preschooler, to figure out.

Chomsky asserted that underlying meaning was carried in the universal grammar of deep structures and transformed by a series of operations that he termed "transformation rules" into the less abstract "surface structures" that were the various natural languages. Moreover, these rules, once understood, could be applied with the rigor of a formal mathematical system, which the ears of those already eager for more fields of challenge to test the new computers equated to "mechanizable." The implication was that knowing the transformation rules would enable a sentence to be interpreted purely from the way it is structured according to its grammar rules. Having to understand the meaning in surface-language terms would be unnecessary if the sentence could be transformed to the deeper structure where the universal meaning underlying all languages resides. In a way comparable to the high-level computer languages that we talked about in chapter nine, natural languages were strings of symbols constructed to different conventions, which needed to be converted to a universal human "machine code." And, as machine code is what the computer actually responds to, the deeper representational language is what human minds actually interact with and "understand."

Such concepts were, in fact, applied with considerable effectiveness to writing compilers and designing formal, artificial languages. But somehow they never quite seemed to work for the natural languages that humans invent spontaneously, and the sought-after underlying structure with its transformation rules failed to appear. It should, for example, have yielded a ready means for developing an automatic translation capability—a natural agent to act as Warren Weaver's interlingua—but the results of translation attempts persisted in being as ludicrous as those being obtained by the British National Research Council-backed effort. Gradually, it was acknowledged that language could no more be decoded through the blind application of mathematical rules than by looking up words in thesauruses and matches in dictionaries. Understanding what was relevant and the situation that made it relevant was essential for grammatical inferences to be confidently applied.

This early work focused attention on the need for a more studied and systematic approach to the problem. The same 1966 report that killed the first, hopeful automatic translation project recognized computational linguistics as an endeavor still worth pursuing and concluded that funding should be continued for the study of language understanding.[3]

Understanding versus Recognition

Language understanding is not the same thing as language recognition. Recognition means simply identifying the characters and words that make up a piece of text and converting it into a coded form suitable for input to, say, a computer. Many systems that are familiar or under development already offer this kind of ability at varying levels of sophistication. The alphabets of special magnetic characters used on bank checks, for example, have been standard for many years and are read routinely with accuracies approaching 100 percent. Use of OCR (Optical Character Recognition) systems and text scanners is growing rapidly at the present time as prices fall and performance improves in the manner typical of a new line of products suddenly proving viable and drawing competitors.

Understanding of content is not the issue in this market. The key measure of performance is reliability; what level of reliability is acceptable depends on the application. The direction for improvement lies in being able to accept a wider range and variety of source inputs, for example, of cursive handwriting, which is still a major hurdle.

RECOGNITION OF SPEECH

In the mid-seventies DARPA funded a program known as SUR, for Speech Understanding Research, for which Carnegie Mellon acted as the main contractor. The end goal was primarily military, to enable voice-only, hands-off interaction with equipment in combat situations. The three experimental systems that developed resulted in HEARSAY and HARPY at CMU and a third known as HWIM (Hear What I Mean) from the firm of Bolt Beraneck and Newman in Cambridge, Massachusetts. HEARSAY is probably the best known—and perhaps the most notorious. The design centered around a feature termed a "blackboard," which pooled inputs from five subsystems using different clues such as analysis of phonemes (sound elements), word identification, and predictions of the next word to arrive at a consensus decision of what was being said. If one channel was unable to make a meaningful contribution, the others would work around it to come up with the best possible stab anyway, capturing the spirit of natural redundancy and robustness in a manner comparable to Hans Moravec's evidence grids.

According to Raj Reddy, the project leader at CMU,[4] HEARSAY more than met the benchmarks called for in the DARPA specification and was able to handle connected speech, a distinct improvement over previous systems, which could only accept separated words. But there were indications of sponsor disgruntlement, and the program was not continued after running its initial term. Apparently, there was some misunderstanding over what was expected. The system was designed to accommodate a vocabulary of one thousand words and handled it tolerably well provided the speech was limited to a constrained grammar. Although the specification hadn't explicitly called for full, human-range, grammar capability, DARPA found the constraints unacceptable.[5]

The drawback with restricted grammar is that it gives users a harder time than simply having to stick to a menu of choices. Learning a small menu is fairly straightforward, and using it soon becomes familiar. With widened but still not completely free versatility, however, getting to know what will and won't work can be an onerous and frustrating business. When some natural-sounding commands are accepted and others rejected for no obvious reason, the typical response is to quit trying to make sense of it and just make do with a few basic options that by trial and error have been found to work—in other words, going back to a menu list anyway but at ten times the price. Surveys have shown that most people react to overcomplicated software, electronics, and appliances in much the same way, never bothering to use more than a fraction of the options they've paid for. (I'm very much inclined that way myself, but, then, everything invented since I turned fifty is probably unnecessary anyway.)

Commercial speech recognition systems are continuing to improve steadily, although as a rule they still require restricted vocabularies and careful diction for acceptable performance. An enormous market awaits a genuinely high-reliability, high-tolerance system able to handle unbroken speech over its full range of expression and variation. The original military requirement addressed by the SUR program is still there, and this would undoubtedly open up all kinds of applications for voice-controlled devices in industrial, commercial, and possibly recreational situations where hands and eyes are occupied to capacity but the speech faculty isn't being used at all.

And, of course, there's the science-fiction standby of direct voice-to-screen transcription. But maybe only just science fiction. At least three commercial products are readily available now. Maybe so, but after recounting the story of earlier optimism concerning translation, I'll keep my money in my pocket for a while longer.

Illusions and Delusions

Nothing achieved to date involves understanding of what the symbols that are being recognized mean in any real sense. At the most, the system is able to discriminate a word or word group sufficiently to generate a unique associated output from a selection of possible outputs, for example, to activate programs or switches to carry out voiced commands. Some people would maintain that this constitutes "understanding" of a sort, and it's true that there are no hard rules to say that the word can't be used in this way. But if so, the level involved is trivial. "Understanding" as treated in this chapter is of a different order.

This is the reason why programs that relied on template matching to generate responses to simple sentences were covered in an earlier chapter. Despite being called Semantic Information Retrieval, the SIR program, for example, operated by using highly restrictive sentence formats as a guide to setting up algebraic equations, into which the computer inserted the supplied variables and then solved. All the same, some observers found the illusion of understanding that these demonstrations produced compelling enough to conclude that thinking machines had arrived, and excited media commentators did nothing to dispel the notion. Even some AI professionals seemed to subscribe to the view that what was going on bore a primitive resemblance to the way humans process language and declared that the first step toward machine comprehension had been taken.

JOSEPH WEIZENBAUM AND ELIZA

Originally from Germany, Joseph Weizenbaum was, by the early sixties, a computer engineer with General Electric. He played a leading part in implementing the Bank of America's ERMA project, one of the first large-scale data-processing systems to be used in banking. At about the same time, he was introduced to Stanford psychiatrist Kenneth Colby, who was dissatisfied with conventional theories and methods of psychotherapy and interested in computers' potential to provide new insights to behavior and even, perhaps, as a means of treatment.

Also, Weizenbaum had always been something of a trickster, describing himself humorously as "a kind of confidence man" who enjoyed playing upon human credulity. Some years previously, he had published a paper in the magazine *Datamation* entitled "How to Make a Computer *Appear* Intelligent."[6] It described a program that he had written to play the game "five in a row," which is like ticktacktoe but requires five *O*s or *X*s in a row to win and is played on an unbounded grid such as regular graph paper. The program was ridiculously simple, with no look-ahead or planning—nothing like the philosophical approaches talked about earlier in this book—but it managed to beat almost all comers since most people were new to the game and unfamiliar with the basic winning tactics that Weizenbaum had written into it. What impressed him was the ease with which people could be persuaded by the illusion that something intelligent was happening. The experience evidently aroused interest and some concerns he would later pursue.

In 1963 he joined MIT and became involved with some of the groups that were working on language recognition and question-answering programs, which were hot at the time. What struck Weizenbaum was the degree of mystification and awe of computers that could be produced by a few fairly basic sleights of hand behind the scenes. Could such tricks be contrived to produce an illusion of more complex behavior? Weizenbaum wondered. If so, what kind of reception might that have?

The subject matter of his dealings with Colby provided an ideal vehicle for examining these questions. Weizenbaum took the inspiration of a psychotherapeutic setting to produce a program he called ELIZA, which assumed the part of a nondirective therapist, interacting with a subject via a terminal. "Nondirective" meant excluding the analyst's own biases and presumptions by not steering the exchange in any definitive direction; specifically, the program's response style was modeled on the precepts of the "Rogerian" school of psychoanalyst Carl Rogers, who advocated letting patients talk their problems out in whatever way their inclinations led them, injecting little but drawing them out, Socrates-like, with questions.

Casting the program in the role of psychoanalyst was a shrewd choice in that it exploited human nature to overcome the inherent limitations that would otherwise have toppled the illusion. First, the conversational nature of the setting made it possible for the machine to camouflage total ignorance by imitating the kind of social politeness that humans use at cocktail parties. Thus, when someone informs us haughtily that he is a neuropathologist, we can reply, "Ah yes, synapses and that kind of thing," thereby exhausting our knowledge of the subject but allowing the speaker to nod and plunge on happily. Or we can attempt a diversion with "Tell me what it's like, working in Vermont," clutching at something someone said a minute earlier. Second, it provided a context in which the oddly disjointed exchanges that the machine's underlying simplemindedness made unavoidable would be accepted uncritically. If a neuropathologist asked us to tell him about synapses, we'd think it extremely odd. But if a psychiatrist tells us to talk about psychiatry, or just about anything else, it's okay. He isn't asking to be informed about the subject. He's doing it to get at our perspectives and feelings and why we hold them.

And it worked far better than Weizenbaum had ever dreamed possible. Very soon, people—including computer experts, who, one would think, should have known better—were pouring out intimate details of their lives and in some cases becoming emotionally involved with the machine. On one occasion, Weizenbaum recalls, his secretary, who had watched him working on the program for months and surely knew exactly what it was, asked him to leave the office before she continued a conversation that she was having with it. At other times, people would call frantically, asking for a few minutes with ELIZA to resolve some personal problem they were having. Below is a sample from a dialogue with a young woman. ELIZA's responses are in capitals.

Men are all alike.
    IN WHAT WAY?
They're always bugging us about something or other.
    CAN YOU THINK OF A SPECIFIC EXAMPLE?
Well, my boyfriend made me come here.
    YOUR BOYFRIEND MADE YOU COME HERE.

He says I'm depressed much of the time.
    I'M SORRY TO HEAR YOU ARE DEPRESSED.
It's true. I am unhappy.
    DO YOU THINK THAT COMING HERE WILL HELP YOU NOT
    TO BE UNHAPPY?
I need some help, that much seems certain.
    WHAT WOULD IT MEAN TO YOU IF YOU GOT SOME HELP?
Perhaps I could learn to get along with my mother.
    TELL ME MORE ABOUT YOUR FAMILY.
My mother takes care of me.
    WHO ELSE IN YOUR FAMILY TAKES CARE OF YOU?
My father.
    YOUR FATHER.
You are like my father in some ways.
    WHAT RESEMBLANCE DO YOU SEE?
You are not very aggressive, but I think you don't want me to notice that.
    WHAT MAKES YOU THINK I AM NOT VERY AGGRESSIVE?
You don't argue with me.
    WHY DO YOU THINK I DON'T ARGUE WITH YOU?
You are afraid of me.
    DOES IT PLEASE YOU TO THINK I AM AFRAID OF YOU?
My father is afraid of everybody.
    WHAT ELSE COMES TO MIND WHEN YOU THINK OF YOUR
    FATHER?
Bullies.
    DOES THAT HAVE ANYTHING TO DO WITH THE FACT THAT
    YOUR BOYFRIEND MADE YOU COME HERE?[7]

Yet the program had no more understanding of what it was doing than an
alarm clock. Through clever pattern matching and substitutions of "me" and
"you" where appropriate, sometimes with a leading phrase like "Tell me more
about that" or "Why do you think so" tagged on at the beginning, it simply
mirrored back the information that the subject had typed in. And for that
reason it probably referred to things seen by the subject as important in the
subject's life right now, which was the whole rationale of the Rogerian method.
Sometimes the program would make a transformation of some kind to draw out
new information, such as substituting "family" for the girl's mother, "family"
being the larger set that "mother" belonged to. At random intervals it would
dredge up something supplied earlier and return it with some general embel-
lishment such as the final sentence, which was a pure lucky shot. When all else
failed, ELIZA would fall back on the human practice of throwing in comments
like "That's interesting," "I see," and "Go on" to fill the gaps.

Colby in California, in the meantime, had used a version of ELIZA as the basis for developing a program called PARRY,[8] which simulated a paranoid patient with delusions of being pursued by the Mafia (one wonders what the outcome of the two programs talking to each other would have been). Weizenbaum was appalled at the serious attention ELIZA was drawing and in particular at Colby's unrestrained enthusiasm for promoting it as an instrument of genuine therapeutic benefit and extolling automated psychiatry as the way of the future.[9] The break between the two became complete over disagreements about the ethics of putting machines into such relationships with people and conferring respectability upon what Weizenbaum considered tantamount to fraud. Weizenbaum also contended that Colby had appropriated the work without giving him due credit as the originator, a serious breach of protocol in scientific circles. In 1976, Weizenbaum published *Computer Power and Human Reason*, in which he expressed strong reservations about the philosophy of AI and condemned the machine metaphor that we have constructed of ourselves and the dehumanizing effects of allowing machines to govern aspects of our lives that should be the preserve of human expression and values.

At Last—Getting Down to Meaning

SYNTAX AND SEMANTICS

Many nonlinguistic ways of communicating meaning exist, for example, insignia, icons, diagrams, expressions, gestures, traffic lights, and apparel. The most striking feature about language is that it enables an unlimited number of messages—sentences—to be generated from a finite collection of elements—words, which in turn are assembled from a tiny set of characters. Yet unlike the Boy Scout earning merit badges or a driver education pupil studying highway signs, we don't have to learn the sentences of a language one by one. We learn a general procedure for inferring the meaning of any sentence expressed in the language. What makes this possible is the existence of systematic rules that dictate how words are combined to form sentences. The rules fall into two broad categories.

The first determines which combinations are permissible, i.e., they define valid sentences within the language. Thus, for English, the combination (article + noun + intransitive verb) produces a permissible sentence, such as "A wind was howling." The combination (verb + noun + article + preposition), however, as in "Howled wind a from," does not. These are known as rules of *syntax*. Syntactic rules are concerned purely with the structuring of the elements that make up sentences. They have nothing to say about what the sentence is supposed to mean. A sentence can be syntactically correct but meaningless, as in "Oval sighs incline distractedly."

Semantic rules govern the way in which the meaning of the larger structure—phrase or sentence—is derived from the meanings and syntax of the constituent words. The semantic structure of language is enormously complicated and could probably be described as its least understood aspect. Trivial alterations in syntax can completely alter a sentence's meaning. For example, English is tyrannical about word order, which carries the greatest part of the burden of defining the role of each word. Most other languages make use of a greater variety of inflection (e.g., word endings) and grammatical gender to denote which parts of a sentence go with which. Consider, for instance, the effect of inverting "Dog bites man" to "Man bites dog" or the convention of inverting to turn a statement into a question: "You were there" versus "Were you there?"

Another source of complication occurs when the components of outwardly similar phrases interact differently, giving rise to different semantic implications: compare "driving hazard," "driving rain," "driving force," and "driving error."

There is no general consensus on exactly how the structure of language should be represented. But however the details are worked out, nobody disputes its amazing efficiency in enabling an infinity of thoughts and concepts to be expressed through the mastering of a manageable set of rules and elements. This flexibility gives language its preeminence among methods of communication.

Early attempts at mechanical translation, and Chomsky's quest for a transformational grammar, expressed the hope of capturing a sentence's uniqueness from precisely expressed syntax alone. And had it worked, the payoff would have been high indeed because it would have meant that the more complex task of working out how to determine semantic content would need to be tackled only once: for the deep-structure level where the meaning common to all languages is represented. But the results showed there was no such easy shortcut to universality. The semantic problem could not be put off as something separate to be dealt with postsyntactically. Once again, as with vision and robots, all the messiness, uncertainties, and ambiguities of the real world had to be faced and resolved up front. So how and where was a computer program to begin?

Language on the Dissecting Table

SENTENCE PARSING[10]

The first step in analyzing a sentence is to establish its anatomy—the way it's put together from its parts. This means relating the words and phrases to roles we identify as the subject, verb, object, subordinate clauses, and the other elements that most of us harbor vague recollections of from school as a process called "parsing." Let's resurrect some of those basics and consider an elementary language, styled on English, to remind ourselves of sentence structures. Our basic tenets are:

$$S \rightarrow NP + VP$$

A Sentence can comprise a Noun Phrase and a Verb Phrase.

$$NP \rightarrow (Article) + N + (PP)$$

A Noun Phrase can include an optional Article, a Noun, and an optional Prepositional Phrase. (Articles: *a, an, the, one.* Nouns: *cat, dog, boy, house.*)

$$VP \rightarrow V + NP + (PP)$$

A Verb Phrase can consist of a Verb, a Noun Phrase, and an optional Prepositional Phrase. (Verbs: *run, sleep, like, throw.*)

$$PP \rightarrow P + NP$$

A Prepositional Phrase can consist of a Preposition and a Noun Phrase. (Prepositions: *with, in, by, from.*)

The general structure for this elementary form thus looks like:

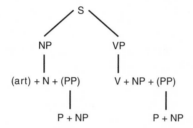

Figure 14.1

The elements making up the major Noun Phrase and Verb Phrase don't have to be in the order shown. The Prepositional Phrase might come first, for example: *"In the beginning . . ."*

A parser—human or program—has to try to figure out which parts go with what, taking the pieces in the order they're encountered as units of a word string. Let's take as an input *The cat likes fresh fish.* The first word to come in is *The,* which the parser can identify as the definite article. Since an article commences a Noun Phrase, the parser knows this isn't a Prepositional Phrase and expects a Noun—maybe followed by a Prepositional Phrase modifying it. The expected Noun follows as *cat,* and the parser can construct a Noun Phrase that may or may not be complete, hanging in midair thus:

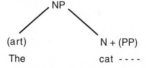

Figure 14.2

From the general structure of Figure 14.1 we see that an NP can be a part of S, a part of the VP, or part of either of the PPs. However, our rules require that a Sentence start with a Noun Phrase, so we can forget the last two cases and wait for either a P as the start of a PP continuing the opening NP or a verb indicating that we have moved on to the VP. Notice that at this point the parser has two incomplete branches to keep track of:

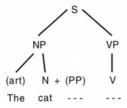

Figure 14.3

The arrival of the Verb *likes*, a transitive verb needing an object, resolves the matter, allowing the NP to be closed (i.e., no PP to follow *cat*) and setting anticipation for an NP to complete the VP:

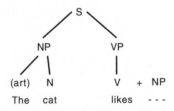

Figure 14.4

Finally, *fresh fish*, a Noun modified by an adjective, supplies the expected NP, and the period indicates the sentence is complete. All hanging slots are filled, and the parts have snapped neatly together:

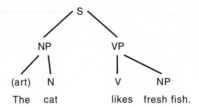

Figure 14.5

Well, that was fairly straightforward. Why should there be that much of a problem encoding these kinds of rules into computer programs?

The procedure above shows that we need to deal with two basic kinds of situations. One is a memorizing requirement—keeping track of the dangling branches waiting to be completed. The other is a decision-making requirement, which was kept trivial in the example considered—making the correct choice when a type of word or phrase can validly be fitted into more than one place in the partly completed tree. As seems to be the case more often than not in the AI field, what's hard for humans turns out to be easy for machines, and what we do without thinking (when dealing with well-written sentences, that is), machines quickly get into trouble over. Let's first take a look at the side of parsing with which humans have difficulties.

TYING OFF ENDS

Computers have, effectively, an unlimited number of memory slots that they can set aside for tagging tasks waiting to be completed. This is what makes them superb at keeping track of those gigantic calculations that number-theory specialists and galaxy-colliding cosmologists dream up, which can keep a supercomputer churning away for hours, days, or even longer. It is generally held that the number of items that people can hold in their short-term memory at one time is seven, which is why we are able to remember a telephone number just about long enough to dial it. The tendency for these temporary markers to fade quickly makes itself felt as a rising sense of insecurity as we progress into a sentence in which unfilled slots are having to be held open for too long. Consider:

The cat that we got from the farmer we stayed with on vacation in Montana last summer before we drove south likes fresh fish.

The enormous prepositional phrase that keeps *cat* waiting for its verb is a bridge that we can feel sagging.

Or, again:

He returned the book that he had inadvertently picked up in the apartment of the student involved with the program to the librarian.

Obviously, these constructions could be improved and still say the same thing. Many linguists believe that the reason natural languages allow choices among more or less synonymous alternative constructions (in contrast with the rigidity of artificial computer languages, for example) is to afford ways of avoiding overburdening the listener's memory. Hence, we have freedom to find ways of grouping words immediately into complete phrases without leaving dangling branches, giving an easy understanding of even quite complex sentences:

This is the cow with the crumpled horn that tossed the dog that worried the cat that killed the rat that ate the malt that lay in the house that Jack built.

After a one-word Noun Phrase, *This*, the rest of the sentence is the verb phrase, commencing with *is* and completing as a Noun Phrase formed by the noun *cow* and a series of modifying clauses. The bulk of the sentence consists of a succession of branches descending on the right to build the Verb Phrase. This type of structure is referred to, accordingly, as "right branching."

Sentences can also be left-branching, and on the following page an elabo-
rately developed NP terminates in a VP tagged on like an appendix:

The first-year student's parsing program's versatility is astonishing.

We should be comfortable with both these forms, and we can use them
effectively in stories for children: *In a castle on a hill, near a town by a river, in a
valley beneath the mountains, a prince was born.* The reason the sentence reads
easily is that each phrase is closed off before the next one begins and the parser
never has to retain more than one loose end at a time.

Suppose now we take the same information contained in the above sentence but assemble it with a different geometry.

Jack built the house that the malt lay in.

Jack built the house that the malt that the rat ate lay in.

We've embedded the clause *that the rat ate* inside *that the malt lay in* to
qualify *malt.* The result is a bit strained, but we can stay with it. But qualifying
rat by a further embedding brings on a groan of bending bridge girders again:

Jack built the house that the malt that the rat that the cat killed ate lay in.

And carrying the process through to completion results in total collapse.
Our mental parser falls apart into a ruin of intelligibility:

*Jack built the house that the malt that the rat that the cat that the dog that the cow
with the crumpled horn tossed worried killed ate lay in.*

What causes the trouble is the multiple dangling ends to the left of the final

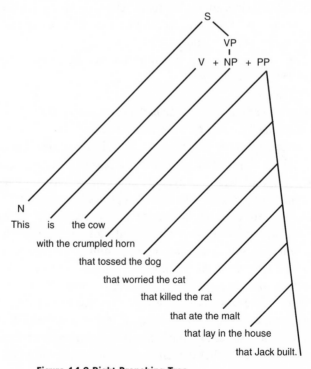

Figure 14.6 Right-Branching Tree

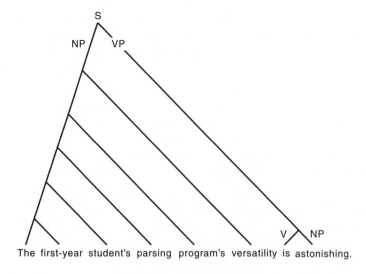

The first-year student's parsing program's versatility is astonishing.

Figure 14.7 Left-Branching Tree

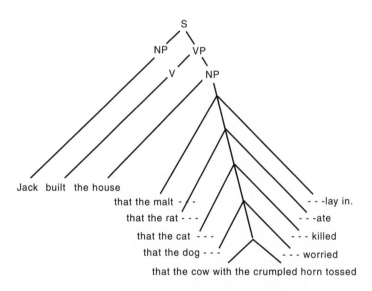

Figure 14.8 Multiply Embedded Tree

NP, all waiting for their respective completions. When the completions arrive in a torrent, we've lost track of where to attach them.

The problem appears to be more subtle than simply tying off the number of ends. Compare

The fish that the cat from the farm wouldn't eat turned out not to be fresh
with

The sensitivity that the retina that the eye that a frog has has has is remarkable.

Both sentences involve three layers of embedding, yet we take in the first unhesitatingly but choke on the second (which untangles easily when rearranged to the left-branching *The frog's eye's retina's sensitivity is remarkable*). It's the three *has*'s in a row that bewilder us. Not only is the number of phrases to be completed important but the "kinds of" phrase as well, as if the parser has only one marker for each type and gets flummoxed when it finds three of the same kind in a holding pattern, all looking for a landing ground. The second version of Jack's house falls down for the same reason: the string of *that* clauses all waiting for a verb to complete them.

Computers, however, have no trouble with this kind of bookkeeping and can keep track of an effectively unlimited forest of branches indefinitely. Complex industrial control and communications systems, for example, excel in their ability to let a running task be interrupted by a higher-priority task, then for that to be interrupted by something of higher priority still, and so on, nesting interrupts within interrupts sometimes for hundreds of levels. Each hanging end will be picked up again when everything above it on the priority schedule has been serviced, its operating context restored to precisely the condition that it was left in—the same principle used in the time-sharing systems first developed by John McCarthy.

To we of long-chain-carbon chemistry, this all sounds pretty impressive. Where, then, in silicon does such eidetic ability fail? The answer is in the second kind of requirement that parsing poses, which people are extraordinarily good at and machines are not: exercising judgment in making decisions.

DINERS CLUB PARTY. AMBIGUITY TESTS MATTER.

As we've seen before with things we do unconsciously, the impression of simplicity we get from the effortlessness we experience can be deceptive. The complexity of what actually goes on often becomes apparent when we attempt to make these inner workings explicit as precise instructions to a computer. Take something like *The man in the hat on the hill was happy.* Are we talking about a man who's wearing a hat being on a hill? Or a man being in a hat that a hill is wearing? If the answer seems "obvious," how do you explain *why* to a computer? Just telling it that hills don't wear hats doesn't work because having dutifully noted that fact it would be none the wiser when confronted by a man (or hill) wearing a coat; yet surely we don't operate by having a separate rule to cover every possible eventuality. We're up against world knowledge again, and that's exactly where computers start to flounder.

The difficulty isn't so much that so many words have multiple definitions, as can be seen in any dictionary, and happily take on roles as noun, verb, adjective, or whatever else suits the speaker's fancy. For example, "log" can mean a piece of tree, a device for measuring a ship's speed, a type of record, to cut down or harvest trees, an abbreviation for logarithm, or a Hebrew measure of liquids;

"turn" in my dictionary has thirty-two senses listed. If it were just a question of keeping track of the temporary ambiguities of such phrases as *the Chinese puzzle solver* or *a talk about books by Mr. Rider* until later information ruled out the incorrect possibilities, a computer would have no problem coping, although the programming would be a lot more complex. Computers perform perfectly well with convoluted but unambiguous constructions in artificial languages, but when precision is relaxed to a degree typical of natural language, the results can be unresolvable by any rules. Very often, they are equally ambiguous to people:

Her son has grown another foot.

I shot the woman with the Polaroid.

Humans, however, zoom in so quickly on the meaning that makes sense in the given context that they're rarely even aware that any alternative is possible. This ability to home in on the obvious sometimes blinds us to meanings perfectly legitimate within the grammar of the language, which the computer, meticulously applying its rules in the way it was told to, doesn't see anything "obviously" odd about at all. A classic example is from a parser at Harvard in the 1960s that was presented with the sentence *Time flies like an arrow.* Just five words, the one meaning pretty plain, yes? But to the surprise of the programmers, the computer found five:

Time proceeds speedily, in the way that an arrow proceeds.

Measure the speed of flies in the way you measure the speed of an arrow.

Measure the speed of flies in the way an arrow measures the speed of flies.

Measure the speed of flies that are like an arrow.

Time flies—a kind of fly—are fond of an arrow.

So how do humans jump straight to the intended meaning without bogging down over the impossibly implausible (interestingly reminiscent of the way our visual systems don't waste time trying to construct logically consistent but physically impossible objects)? One possibility is that our brains do, in fact, work somewhat like computers do, but unconsciously, i.e., storing large numbers of possible meanings all awaiting corroborating evidence and delivering only the final, confirmed one to consciousness. The other is that we make some kind of snap judgment based on experience and just go with it until we're either vindicated or run into a wall. If these strategies have a vaguely familiar ring about them, they should. They're called breadth-first and depth-first searches.

For individual-word ambiguities, it seems we use something close to breadth-first. It is an experimentally established fact that immediately after we hear a word, words closely related to it are identified more quickly than neutral ones. If *sky* is flashed on a screen, for example, words like *blue* and *cloud* evoke faster responses than, say, *peg.* It's as if the mental dictionary were stored in the form of a network in which related meanings are clustered together and activating a particular item leaves that area "primed" to expect further accesses. When a word has, say, two possible meanings, one of which makes no sense at all in the context being dealt with, both possibilities are nevertheless unconsciously recognized and memory is primed, ready to deliver close associations of both. Take the sentence *He found several spiders, roaches, and other bugs in a corner of the room.* As would be expected from what we have just discussed, a person listening to this retrieves words like "ant" and "insect" more rapidly immediately after hearing "bug." And it turns out that words like "spy" are also primed, as they are related to "bug" when it is used in the sense of a surveillance device but has no connection with the above context. This effect lasts only for milliseconds and leaves no awareness that it was ever there, but it has been confirmed from psychological experiments. What this gives us is a word lookup that is fast but not very selective, producing a lot of nonsense candidates that are then rapidly erased.

At the more complex level of phrases and sentences, however, we don't compute every possible branch of the parsing tree. A reason for this is that we simply don't see the quite sensible ambiguities because we've already rejected them as irrelevant. Newspaper headlines provide a rich source for collectors: KILLER SENTENCED TO DIE FOR SECOND TIME.

And bureaucratese: *The report gives totals of the number of students broken down by sex, marital status, and age.*

In fact, it sometimes happens that we are so insistent to see meaning that makes sense that we fail to find the *only* tree that is consistent with the grammatical structure, for instance:

The man who hunts ducks out on weekends.

Our first tendency is to blink, back up and look again, and then dismiss the sentence as an error. But, in fact, it is perfectly grammatical, as:

The man who fishes is available all week. The man who hunts ducks out on weekends.

What happened the first time was that following a depth-first approach our parser took *duck* to be (most plausibly) the object of *hunts* and plunged on with that assumption, only to come to a perplexed halt later when the pieces wouldn't fit. Another example:

Glass windows are made of has blemishes.

Makes perfect sense when seen as:

The glass that crystal goblets are made of is perfect, but glass windows are made of has blemishes.

What we see and hear is determined by our expectations as shaped by a lifetime of living in the world and getting to know how the parts of it typically relate to each other. One wonders what kind of an edifice the Blocks World stacking program would attempt to build, given the statements:

The ball is on the table.
John is on the ball.
The boss is on John's back.

The detective is on the boss's tail.
The commissioner is on the detective's side.

All in all, comprehending language comes through as a daunting prospect. As with anything else, you have to start somewhere.

Exploring Semantics

ASSOCIATIVE NETS

In 1966, Ross Quillian, a sociologist-turned-computer-scientist studying under Herbert Simon at CMU, delivered his doctoral dissertation on trying to program the associative nature of human memory.[11] This is the faculty, referred to above, that primes words that are in some sense semantically "close to" whatever our attention is focused on at the moment—a web of connections extending in the equivalent of many dimensions.

Quillian's idea was to represent each word as a point of intersection between the lattice lines of a grid—conveniently pictured flat, like a sheet of graph paper, although the actual interconnections represented multidimensional chains of relationships in a way more akin to the human scheme. The concept was inspired by the arrays of tiny magnetic doughnuts (known as "cores") used at that time to store binary digits before the semiconductor RAM came along. The doughnuts were strung on a grid of wires in the manner shown schematically in Figure 14.9. A 1 or 0 was written by magnetizing a core clockwise or counterclockwise which was achieved by appropriate pulses of electric current sent through the row and column wires. Two pulses applied simultaneously were

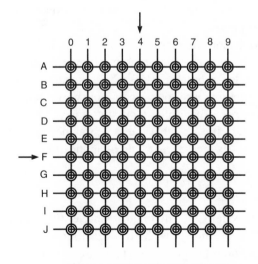

Figure 14.9 Magnetic Core Memory

needed to change a core's state. Thus, any core could be written individually by pulsing the two wires intersecting at its location.

Quillian's scheme used a similar concept to give a measure of the "closeness" between two words. Take the two sentences:

After the strike, the president sent him away.

After the strike, the umpire sent him away.

They are identical except for a single word, yet one immediately conjures up mental pictures of companies, unions, and labor disputes, while the other calls forth green diamonds, stadiums, and baseball caps. It was this association of "relatednesses" that Quillian was trying to mimic—or at least understand a little better.

Imagine the word "president" threaded in a grid like one of the magnetic cores in Figure 14.9. Now assume that the words forming a cluster around it are words strongly related to it in different contexts; those farther away are less strongly related, and so on. When *president* is activated, it sends out an "activation wave" that the words around it react to—you can imagine them lighting up in a succession that reflects their relatedness. Now set up a similar activation wave from the word "strike." Words in the grid that are activated by both waves indicate that they are related to both initiating words. *Union* and *labor*, for example, would likely be highlighted in this way. The number of such intersections and their distribution give a measure of how strongly *president* is related to the "labor" kind of strike as opposed to the "baseball" kind of strike. Hence, from other words appearing in the sentence and context, the program would be guided to the appropriate interpretation.

Quillian's initial work was hampered by the limited memory size of the machines then available. After obtaining his Ph.D., he continued his work at Bolt Beraneck and Newman in Cambridge. The approach aroused much interest at MIT and elsewhere, becoming known generally as "semantic networks." One of the most ambitious projects that this work inspired was by the cognitive psychologists John R. Anderson and Gordon H. Bower at CMU in the early seventies, which they implemented as the program Human Associative Memory.[12] Later, HAM was extended to become ACT, which, in addition to incorporating fixed, long-term information, also took account of shorter-term considerations that change in importance depending on circumstances. This enabled ACT to shift its focus of attention in somewhat the same way people do, depending on its interests at the time. Its most recent field of application has been to human learning processes.[13]

"DEEP CASES" AND ATNS

A 1968 paper, "The Case for Case" by linguist Charles Fillimore, evoked a vestige of Chomsky's concept, though without the call for a formal mathematical system, by proposing going below the "surface cases" of words as determined by their grammatical function in a sentence and seeking the roles performed by the things they stood for. Superficial rules of grammar can provide no clue for distinguishing *The cake is baking* from *The cook is baking.* Knowledge that cooks are animate and bake things, whereas cakes are inanimate and get baked, however, unravels such situations.

The paper's aim was to identify such "deep case" attributes as the *agent* instigating an action, the *instrument* by which it was carried out, the *object* receiving the action, and so on. This was a basically simple idea, but it provided a ready means of recognizing sentences as conceptually the same, although outwardly very different, as in:

John gave Mary the ball.

The ball was given to Mary by John.

Everything on the surface changes, but underneath it all the roles remain constant.

Case analysis can also get to the bottom of sentences in which the same surface structure means very different things:

John broke the window with his fist.

John broke the window with his friend.

(Not being a computer parser, we ignore the grammatically valid possibility that John threw the friend through the window.)

And, of course, the roles are the same whatever language the sentence is in, so this kind of analysis could form the basis of—or at least be a contributor to—the much-sought-after translator.

Nobody seems to agree on exactly how many cases need to be identified to represent a reasonable range of meaning. Fillimore originally proposed six; later workers have introduced as many as thirty.[14] The case analysis approach appeals to AI researchers because it deals with language structure and meaning in an integrated way. The idea of deep cases has continued to underlie much of subsequent language research, notable instances being at CMU and at Xerox Research in Palo Alto, California.

A conceptually similar approach of combining grammatical acceptability with some kind of knowledge base of what makes sense was Augmented Transition Network, developed by William Woods, another Bolt Beraneck and Newman language researcher. As with case analysis, ATN techniques form the basis of many contemporary natural-language systems that have proved useful in specialized domains.[15] An example is the BB&N system LUNAR, which was developed in the seventies as the access medium for a NASA database on moon-rock studies from the *Apollo* missions.

ROGER SCHANK AND "CONCEPTUAL DEPENDENCY"

We can describe the gist of a conversation we had a week ago but are unlikely to recall more than a few of the actual words spoken. We use words as codes to activate mental structures that we assume exist in the mind of another person and presume are similar to the ones we possess ourselves. Failure to appreciate this was what brought grief to the early attempts at mechanical natural-language translation. The meaning that is understood exists in the mind of the receiver, not in the word stream. Therefore, no amount of programming or analysis of syntax can get it out.

Take the utterance *Robin's bowstring broke halfway through the forest*. What context are you already mentally constructing? Men in green suits carrying arrows, riding through trees? But not a word gave a clue to anything like that. In fact, Robin is my cousin, a violinist, whose bowstring snapped while he and his orchestra were playing "A Walk in the Black Forest" (a popular tune in Europe in the 1960s, written by Kal Mann and Horst Jankowski). The picture in your mind didn't come from anything contained in the words that were said. It came from mental constructions formed in the process of growing up in a particular culture with shared notions of history and geography, a certain tradition of legend, ethical notions about the rich and the poor, movies, games, and children's books.

Roger Schank represented the full swing of the pendulum to the opposite of Chomsky's position. While agreeing that getting to the underlying meaning is what matters, he argued that no amount of formal operations with word structures was going to achieve it. He is quoted as saying, "There is no such thing as syntax,"[16] though given his assertive style of speaking this was perhaps an exaggeration to emphasize a point. His book *The Cognitive Computer*[17] expresses his view in more moderate terms:

> We used whatever grammatical rules were necessary in our quest to extract meanings from sentences, but to our surprise, little grammar turned out to be relevant.[18]

And elsewhere:

> Remembering stories and paraphrasing them requires that we *forget* the words originally used and that we invent our own ways of saying the stories to ourselves. . . . One task in AI, strangely enough, is to get the computer to *forget the words*.[19]

Originally from Brooklyn, New York, Schank received a bachelor's degree in mathematics at CMU, switched to linguistics, and earned a Ph.D. at the University of Texas in 1969. He moved to Stanford and worked with Kenneth Colby, the automated-psychiatry advocate mentioned earlier in this chapter, and carried out his founding work there in the early seventies. Language as it comes naturally, he decided, is too variable in structure and connotation to provide a reliable guide of what was intended. Was it possible to create some framework of underlying permanent relationships that could be activated by making the correct logical inferences from language, similar to the way in which language cues common mental structures in humans? The system he developed became known as "Conceptual Dependency" and was first implemented in his Stanford program MARGIE, standing for Meaning Analysis, Response Generation, and Inference on English.

The basic idea was to make explicit the implied information of a sentence. Take, for instance, the sentence *John sold an apple to Mary for twenty-five cents. We* know that Mary now has the apple, but the sentence doesn't say so. It's an understood implication of *sold*. MARGIE treated *sold* as just one instance of a general "semantic primitive" that Schank called ATRANS, meaning Abstract Transfer, any action involving the transfer of some abstract relationship, in this case "ownership."

ATRANS was one of eleven such semantic primitives, to which Schank claimed to have reduced all English verbs. Another was PTRANS, standing for Physical Transfer, which covers any change of location and hence handles the implication of all such verbs as *move, walk, climb,* and *enter,* and *carry, throw, put,* and *send,* depending on who or what does the changing, who or what gets changed (they could be the same), and so on. Reduction of all meanings to this primitive form also enabled MARGIE to make plausible inferences about further implications, for example, if Joe punched Mike in the mouth Joe was probably angry about something, Mike probably got hurt and might have punched back, or perhaps he was scared—all pretty basic stuff to us but a universe of revelations to a computer.

The intention was to use these inferences to make better sense of the information coming later, getting some sort of measure of the right probabilities again. However, that side of things didn't work out too well. The problem was that too many possible and plausible inferences could be drawn from one sentence for the program to have a clue which were important to subsequent developments and which were not. Once again, the uncanny human ability to home in instantly on what's relevant and ignore what isn't—Kasparov finding the right move, the eye spotting a fractional change of facial expression, the ear discerning a misplaced note in a melody—was too elusive to capture. Take as an example the very simple situation conveyed by the following four sentences:

John went to a restaurant. He ordered a hamburger. The hamburger was cold when the waitress brought it. He left a small tip.

Let's assume that the program has made the connections that a person who goes to a restaurant is probably hungry, hungry humans want food, a hamburger is food, waitresses bring food to customers in restaurants. Where is the link to connect the hamburger's being cold with John's leaving a small tip? From its database of inferences, the program could have noted that to bring the hamburger to John, the waitress came to the table; she was carrying a plate, the hamburger was on the plate; she put the plate on the table; the hamburger probably included lettuce, tomato, pickle, and mustard; there was probably ketchup on the table; she probably brought cutlery wrapped in a napkin; John probably already had a beverage, and so on, and so on, and so on for as far as you want to go and to whatever level of detail you want to go down to. Let's imagine that somewhere in that blizzard of facts there is a statement to the effect that cold food (when it's supposed to be hot) can make people unhappy. How is the computer supposed to fish this out and recognize it as the explanation for the final sentence?

SETTING EXPECTATIONS: "SCRIPTS"

In 1977, Schank moved to Yale University and continued his work in collaboration with psychology professor Robert Abelson. Together they extended the idea of conceptual dependency from situations presented piecemeal a sentence at a time to chains of events reflecting better the kinds of scenario settings that humans get to know and base their expectations on. Thus, inferences could be made across broader, more organized and connected bodies of information. They called these scenarios "Scripts."[20] A restaurant scene such as the one above, for example, would be treated not as isolated statements to be connected but interpreted in terms of the "Restaurant Script":

> EAT-AT-RESTAURANT Script
> > PROPS: (Restaurant, Money, Food, Menu, Chairs, Tables)
> > ROLES: (Hungry-persons, Wait-persons, Chef-persons, Manager-person, Customer-persons)
> > VIEWPOINT: Hungry-persons
> > TIME: (Times of operation of Restaurant)
> > PLACE: (Location of Restaurant)
> EVENT SEQUENCE:
> Enter-Restaurant script
> > IF: (Wait-to-be-Seated Sign or Reservation)
> > THEN: (Get Maître-d's Attention script)
> > ELSE: (Please-Be-Seated script)

And so on through a repertoire of situations and alternatives (including a possible "Exit-Restaurant-Angry" script) to cover the complete experience. Note that scripts point to subscripts so that information already formulated can be incorporated into larger contexts—the whole Restaurant Script could be one of a selection available for a more general "Where-to-Take-a-Date" script, for example. The idea was to set certain expectations in place of the undigested masses of facts that had swamped MARGIE and allow a manageable set of realistic inferences to be made accordingly.

The scripts were implemented by a program called Script Applier Mechanism, or SAM. From the threads it constructed, SAM was able to make reasonable sense of things like a newspaper report of an automobile accident and answer basic questions about things implicit but not actually stated. Moreover, since SAM's internal representations were in a form independent of any particular language or grammar, it was able to paraphrase its accounts not only back into English but also Chinese, Russian, Dutch, and Spanish. Thus, it did provide a limited but real translation capability.

But the world that SAM lived in was still a collection of logical implications and disconnected properties of the physical world, a bit like the vaguely perceived sonar image from Hans Moravec's robot compared to a view of real trees. Yes, it was possible for the program to construct a representation of the sentence *Will you come to dinner with me this evening?* But as Joseph Weizenbaum observed, "It is hard to see . . . how Schank-like schemes could possibly understand that same sentence to mean a shy young man's desperate longing for love."[21]

GETTING A PERSPECTIVE:
CARICATURES OF ATTITUDES

Weizenbaum's point was that systems like SAM functioned purely as neutral reporters of events and actions that didn't involve them. Having no subjective views or aims to advance, they had no way of attaching any of the significance that leads humans to find some things in the world crucially important while others are ignored—in a word, to feel a sense of *relevance*.

Abelson had already seen one ingredient of such a motivator in the goals that people seek and the plans they make for achieving them. This stemmed from a program he had developed in the sixties called Cold War Ideologue, which modeled the worldview of a stereotyped right-wing conservative.[22] Basically, the program carried a set of very simplistic underlying convictions that biased it to interpret everything from a particular, predetermined slant if it could. One of its precepts, for instance, was that Communists were committed to taking over the world and would do so unless opposed by force. Anything bad that happened was automatically attributed to the Communists and anything good to the free world. In fact, its ideas of reality were pretty erratic. When told that leftists in South America had thrown eggs at Richard Nixon it concluded that throwing eggs was "bad" (leftists did it; Nixon was an American) and therefore Castro (who by definition did bad things) would be likely to throw eggs at West Berlin. However, the work did demonstrate, as was Abelson's purpose, that a relatively simple set of rules could explain a fanatic's rigid perception of reality, where every event is interpreted as confirming evidence, no matter how many facts have to be ignored to make it fit.

Now this is starting to sound more like real people. And that, of course, was the point. All people have their own set of beliefs and preconceptions that cause them to see reality in a different way. Abelson codified a series of such attitude profiles, which reflected not set-piece situations but the biases in belief and perception that might be induced by the effects of *love, betrayal, alienation, antago-*

nism, and so on. If "Scripts" described what undifferentiated "persons" in set-piece situations "do," Abelson's "Themes" provided what "this kind" of person would be prone to do when confronting situations in general.[23]

In the late seventies, by which time Abelson was working with Schank and Robert Wilensky at Yale, Scripts evolved into PAM, or Plan Applier Mechanism, which took SAMesque stories further by being able to relate itself to one of the participants and frame its account accordingly. When told a story of John robbing a liquor store, for example, it was able to recount the event from the viewpoint of either John or the storekeeper and construct different motivations and interpretations for each case. Again, when told that *Sir Gallant loves the princess. The princess was stolen away by a dragon*, PAM could pick up the *love* theme and infer a goal for Sir Gallant to rescue the princess. As the story developed, PAM would interpret and explain the knight's actions in terms of that goal and subgoals that might help attain it.

The end of the seventies saw a number of projects by Schank and Abelson's students that extended PAM's ideas. One, called FRUMP, developed in 1980, was connected to UPI's wire service and summarized news stories in several languages, although still with the computer's penchant for getting things massively wrong if it got them wrong at all: it reported a political assassination described as having "shaken America" as an earthquake.[24]

HAVING GOALS AND MOTIVATIONS

Another researcher at Yale in the early eighties was Jaime Carbonell, who set out to apply Schank-Abelson techniques to producing an improved version of Abelson's 1960s cold warrior. The result, which he called POLITICS, turned out to be much broader in scope, modeling not just ideology but the effects of goals and personality traits on guiding behavior in various social and political conflict situations.[25]

To capture more of the complexity of human behavior, Carbonell set up not just a single set of rules corresponding to a fixed goal, as if we spend every moment obsessively pursuing a single end, but rules to elicit behavior that reflected varying goals as circumstances and priorities altered. Thus, he was able to build up patterns of motivations that reflected hierarchies of goals, which he termed "goal trees." By using goal trees to guide its reasoning, POLITICS could interpret an account of events not just from an all-or-nothing perspective of their effect on one objective that never changed but as subgoals helpful or hindering in their own right when considered against the background of a wider strategy. Thus, the foremost goal was assumed to be "Communist Containment"; however, subgoals not immediately material but generally supportive of achieving the main goal would be "Encourage Unrestricted Capitalism" and "Reduce Government Spending." With its insights shaped in this way, POLITICS was able to comment on the Panama Canal Treaty from either a conservative or a liberal perspective:

Conservative: *The treaty is bad for the United States. The United States would lose the canal to Panama, and the United States will be weaker.*

Liberal: *The Panama Canal Treaty improves relations with Latin American countries.*

Carbonell's next step was to consider a more general model of human personality by defining a hierarchy of goals applicable to the social context. For a typical Western society, he took the following to be first: preservation of self and family, followed by preservation of property, self-esteem, and so on. He then defined a personality trait as a deviation from this pattern by representing one or more of the elements to a greater or lesser degree. Thus, for instance, an *ambitious* personality would be one in which goals like Acquire Wealth and Control Others were elevated.

Carbonell is now continuing this line of work at CMU, where another group under Joe Bates is exploring the creation of artificial personalities and characters for interactive forms of drama.

In Conclusion

This chapter has covered a lot of ground, from simple template-matching programs to the first, ill-fated attempt at mechanizing translation. Despite everything that has been explored and achieved, nothing approaching the versatility that we carry around in our heads looks as if it will be demonstrated for many years—and some argue strongly that, in principle, it never can be. Speaking personally, I see history littered with the corpses of too many pronouncements that this or that would always be impossible "in principle" to be seriously perturbed.

One of the first wide applications of general language-understanding ability would be communication with computers. Imagine being able to simply tell a database, "Draw me up a list of everything you can find written in the last five years on the Many Worlds Interpretation of Quantum Mechanics." Automatic translation is still a natural, of course. And finally, the main theme of this chapter, *understanding* natural language, would be a necessary prerequisite to *generating* natural language, which we would look for before anything else as an indication of cognizant intelligence in action.

As seems to have happened repeatedly in this book, we started out examining one thing but have veered off along the way and ended up somewhere else. In this case, beginning with what some people anticipated would be a straightforward exercise in mechanically translating languages got us entangled with our innermost representations of reality. How we use language mirrors the way we perceive and understand the world, and instilling any degree of language understanding in machines seems inseparable from administering them progressively larger doses of a "humanlike" perspective. This suggests that the realization of general-language competence will be contingent upon, perhaps necessarily coevolutionary with, imparting a measure of that most elusive quality of all, which we call human common sense. Trying to convey even a glimmer of it is the most intractable problem being grappled with in the whole field of AI.

But before a machine can be expected to learn common sense about the world, it must first be able to learn.

1. Weaver.
2. Waldrop, p. 64.
3. Pierce.
4. Crevier, p. 116.
5. For opposing viewpoints, see Firebaugh and Jacky.
6. Crevier, p. 133.
7. Weizenbaum (1965).
8. Colby et al. (1972), (1973).
9. Colby's version of the program was called DOCTOR. See Colby, Watt, and Gilbert.
10. I'm indebted to Steven Pinker's wonderful *The Language Instinct* (1994) for much of the information in this section.
11. Quillian.
12. Anderson and Bower.
13. Anderson (1976), (1985).
14. Waldrop, pp. 71 *ff*.
15. Bobrow and Fraser; Woods.
16. Crevier, p. 165.
17. Schank.
18. Ibid., pp. 137–38
19. Ibid., pp. 95–96.
20. Schank and Abelson.
21. Weizenbaum (1976), p. 200.
22. Abelson and Carroll; Abelson and Reich.
23. Waldrop, pp. 78 *ff*., provides a good general summary.
24. Crevier, p. 171.
25. Carbonell.

15

Learning:
The Indispensable
Prerequisite

"Nature might already have become as good at programming in the last billion years as we have in the last forty. DNA might have already evolved from random generate and test into an expert program. What I conjecture is that beginning with primitive organisms and random generation, the first heuristics for improvement came into being. They then overshadowed the less efficient random-mutation mechanism, much as oxidation dominated fermentation once it evolved."
—Douglas Lenat[1]

What Teachers Don't Have to Teach

We've already seen how some things that don't come naturally at all to humans are fairly straightforward to program as procedures for machines: calculating, cracking codes, memorizing masses of detail—anything that involves systems of unnatural symbols and manipulations and is governed by precise rules. Since these processes characterize the intellectual tasks confidently held to represent human mental activity at its highest, an early optimism prevailed that extending these successes to cover the more "primitive" functions too would present no great problem. Computers were not just unimaginably fast; the effectively limitless number of states they could assume represented a vastness of complexity that had never been conceived of before. Matching and then surpassing the human mind were just initial steps toward a world that would be revolutionized within a few decades, hence the climate of heady predictions that natural-language translation would be a cinch in five years—at the outside.

The reality was the other way around. It was the things we do with such apparent ease—"mindlessly"—that not only proved difficult but have remained unreproduced to anything greater than a rudimentary degree to this day. Surpassing the feats of intellectual giants was child's play; the competence and coordination exhibited in the play of even young children was baffling. Minds were far more subtle and complex than Descartesian cuckoo clocks, Freudian sewer systems, Boolean telephone exchanges, Wienerian feedback loops, and logical Russellian problem solvers mounted on bundles of Skinnerian reflexes.

An obvious thing that children do that sets them apart from all of the above models is learn from their experiences. It was recognized early on that this would be essential for machines too if they were to make any real progress toward humanlike abilities. Alan Turing in his 1950 paper talks about giving a computer rules that would enable it to bootstrap its way to all-around intelligence, although along with most such advocates back then, he seems to have underestimated the task colossally. Estimating that a billion bits of memory should be sufficient for a program capable of producing an all-around behavior sufficiently close to human to pass the imitation game, he goes breezily on to suggest that instead of going through the tedium of having to write from scratch a program to simulate the entire adult mind, "why not rather try to produce one which simulates the child's? If this were then subjected to an appropriate course of education one would obtain the adult brain."

True to the general pattern, duplicating what children do instinctively turned out to be an enormously complicated thing to attempt artificially.

THE BOOTSTRAP PROBLEM:
HOW CAN SOMETHING LEARN HOW TO LEARN?

From the beginnings of the computer era, the enormous flexibility of the new machines compared to anything dreamed of previously raised the question of possibly programming them with the equivalent of the "ground rules" with which human learning machines arrive in the world ready-equipped. Machines able to create new associations and conclusions for themselves, instead of having to have everything supplied explicitly, would clearly be an advantage in regular application areas such as scientific and engineering calculation, accounting, and business. When it came to endowing machines with all-around intelligence, where the problem domain might encompass anything and everything connected with the real world, such ability became indispensable.

One of the standard ways humans learn is through repetition and practice. This applies both to physical skills such as typing and juggling and intellectual feats like learning the lines of a play or memorizing a phone number. The prime function of rhythm and rhyme was to facilitate the preservation of epic tales, rituals, and other large bodies of information by committing them to memory before a written language was established.

Another way we learn is by association, which works especially well for labeling circumstances that we seem wired to deem important. Events of high emotional impact, such as news of the death of somebody significant or a particularly perilous experience, are stamped with details of other things going on at the same place and time that we can recall years later. Very often these details have to do with place, especially if the experience was a negative one, as if the survival kit provided by nature included a mechanism for tagging risky places to be avoided in the future. Marvin Minsky tells of a dog he once owned that chased cars compulsively and was eventually hit by one; thereafter, it took care to avoid that particular street but continued happily chasing cars everywhere else.[2] Scents and sounds—everybody has his or her own private collection of favorite tunes with special meanings—are particularly effective in evoking emotionally laden memories. Exploring the psychological underpinnings of memory associations is another of the early tasks taken up by AI.

Creating Links

ED FEIGENBAUM AND EPAM

Alan Turing's ACE computer at the National Physical Laboratory in Britain in the early fifties was a magnet for people bitten by fascination for the new machines, many of whom would later figure prominently in AI and related fields. Edward Feigenbaum started out in January 1956 in the business school at Carnegie Tech, where he was an undergraduate trying out "unusual" courses, so he happened to be in the class to which Herbert Simon casually announced having developed, in conjunction with Allen Newell, a thinking machine over the Christmas holiday. To Feigenbaum, the idea that business strategy could be modeled on a computer was revolutionary and utterly captivating. He got involved with the project, helping to write some of the versions of the IPL language, coauthored a paper on computerized decision making (turned down by *American Economic Review* as too extreme),[3] and went to Rand in the summer of 1957 to work on the IBM 704. The year he spent in England was as a Fulbright fellow, and while there he became a close friend of Seymour Papert, who was visiting from Switzerland. In the course of their dealings, Feigenbaum developed an interest in the human learning process. On returning to the United States he went to the University of California at Berkeley to join another of Simon's former students, Julian Feldman, who was doing psychological research at the business school into how people go about making choices in the face of uncertainty.

Feigenbaum's main work, for which he received a Ph.D. in cognitive psychology, was a program called EPAM, which stands for Elementary Perceiver And Memorizer, and was developed to model the way people rote-memorize nonsense syllables.[4] The object was to design a mechanism that would reproduce certain characteristics of human learning that had long been known but that lacked an explanation; if the program showed the same tendencies, Feigenbaum's reasoning went, there would be grounds for supposing that minds work in a similar way.

The kinds of tests involved had long been standard for studies of memory. A subject would be presented with one from a series of syllables like JUK, TEG, ZOT, and WIB, which had no inherent meanings, and be asked to return an associated syllable that he had memorized to correspond with it. Current theories were unable to account for some of the patterns that seemed to be nearly universal, for example, why a series of associations would suddenly be forgotten and have to be learned all over again, often repeatedly, or why adding new associations to the list caused earlier, apparently solidly assimilated ones, to be disrupted.

Feigenbaum developed an associative structure he called "discrimination nets," which closely imitated what had been observed. The basic idea was quite simple. Let's suppose, Feigenbaum suggested, that the memory system doesn't load itself down with unnecessary detail but takes only those salient features needed to make a memorized item unique and distinguish it from others; such a structure would grow if further learning took place, extending itself only if it had to. Thus, to associate JIR with DAX, for instance, it would only bother remembering "if the stimulus starts with J, respond with DAX." If later, however, a new pair, JUK-PIB, is introduced, the association formed will no longer work and the system will thrash ineffectively until it has formed two new connections.

This way of economizing by bothering to note only salient distinguishing features fits with the way adult reading ability develops. Whereas children at the learning stage laboriously assemble words syllable by syllable, an adult recognizes familiar words by a few key indicators, such as the initial letter, length, and general shape. Note how much more difficult it is to identify a word when the upper part is hidden than when the lower part is hidden.

But working at Berkeley presented problems of a more political nature. For one thing, the two young newcomers from back east had managed to secure some extremely generous funding from the Carnegie Foundation in New York, and this raised some hackles and disgruntlement among the more established faculty members. Then there was an ongoing dispute over whether computer science should be a part of electrical engineering or a department in its own right. And finally, Feigenbaum found it impossible to develop a meaningful dialogue about the new information-processing methods with psychologists from the classical school, whom he described as "impenetrable."[5] They'd listen, nod politely, say how nice, and go back to their own work, he related. In the end, Feigenbaum moved south to join the AI lab that John McCarthy was setting up at Stanford and Feldman went to the University of California at Irvine. As materials for a course they put together at Berkeley on computer modeling of thought, they brought together papers describing such work from an assortment of scattered sources. In 1963 this was published as the collected work

Computers and Thought,[6] which became extremely popular for a scientific work and is still cited regularly as a standard reference to "classical" AI.

As a footnote, the abrupt departures of Feigenbaum and Feldman left one bemused figure, in the person of Bert Raphael. Having received his doctorate from MIT for the SIR program (see chapter twelve), totally unknown and unexpected, Raphael arrived at Berkeley, where Feigenbaum had invited him to join their work. He too finally fled, south, to find refuge at SRI, where he helped create the Shakey robot.

Learning by Discovering

DOUG LENAT'S "AUTOMATED MATHEMATICIAN"

The learning abilities exhibited by early AI programs were impressive achievements compared to anything computers had done previously, and, accordingly, they received considerable publicity. Samuel's Checkers Player improved its game until it could beat its creator; Patrick Winston's program learned to distinguish arches and similar concepts by being given examples; the program that controlled Shakey combined sequences it devised to build new block patterns it could recall under a single name if it encountered the same problem later. All these approaches, however, suffered from the same kind of limitation that prevented Micro Worlds' solutions in general from being expanded to deal with situations more representative of the real world, which was that the task domain was carefully predefined as a restricted collection of objects, relationships, and operations and the goals specified in terms of these. The context that made up everything relevant to what the program was supposed to do had been supplied by the programmer. While such a program could meticulously apply specific rules within the given context, it had no way of modifying the rules or devising new ones to operate in a wider context that it might construct or discover for itself. A program such as Winston's, for example, would search its domain for combinations of elements (blocks) that satisfied a set of criteria ("archness" or "tableness," for example) that the programmer had decided were interesting, but it couldn't go from there to find, in a more complex domain, combinations that satisfied the more general criteria of what makes something "interesting." Samuel's program learned by twiddling the coefficients of the terms in its polynomial and finding by trial and error which combinations yielded better results. But the programmer had specified the problem as one to be solved by application of a polynomial and supplied the rules giving which terms to use at different stages of the game. As is probably still true of most of the "learning programs" that we hear about today, the program could be taught as many tricks in its category as the programmer cared to teach it, but, unlike a human child, it would never "get the idea" of tricks in general and start inventing new ones of its own.

Doug Lenat, one of Ed Feigenbaum's students at Stanford, had taught himself programming on weekends while he was a high school student in Philadelphia. For his doctoral thesis at the Stanford AI lab, he developed a program called Automated Mathematician.[7] The idea was to get around the limitations of the kind of learning produced by saying, in effect, "*Here* are the elements; *these* are the rules; now find out how to build *that*" and, instead, let a curious program, with no directed rules or particular goals, loose in a playpen filled with numbers.

How do you make a program curious? Lenat's way was to endow it with a sense of what he called "esthetic sensitivity" by rating on a scale of 0 to 1,000, calculated by means of a set of fifty-nine heuristics, things that it stumbled on as being worth playing with further to see where they led—in a word, "interesting" things. The numbers in AM's playpen came as pieces of an unlimited Tinkertoy kit with the basic rules for combining them into sets, unions, intersections, equalities, and the other fundamental subassemblies of mathematics. An instinct to play with them was injected in the form of 184 LISP statements offering suggestions along such lines as "If you find that a process produces something interesting, try its inverse." Hence, after coming across multiplication and finding it "interesting," AM discovered division. Another was "Try to find extreme cases." On investigating division, the program established a class of numbers having minimum divisors, thus identifying the primes (numbers that have just two divisors: themselves and one).

So what kinds of things did AM find "interesting"? Regularities and similarities—the distinction that characterizes "odd" and "even," frequencies and distributions of types of number, and the equivalence of applying different procedures, such as repeated addition and multiplication. You could think of the program's search as comparable to the inquisitiveness that makes a toddler find that "things with parallel faces, prongs, and holes stack or link to form bigger structures and are therefore interesting. Things that are floppy and shapeless can't be made to do very much and aren't."

In this way, AM rediscovered something like two hundred concepts of standard number theory, none of which had been explicitly given. An instance is the rule known as the Unique Factorization Theorem, which states that a number can be broken down into prime factors in only one way—for example, no set of prime factors other than 2, 2, 2, 2, 3 gives (when multiplied together) the number 48. It also speculated that all even numbers above 2 can be expressed as a sum of primes. This is known as Goldbach's Conjecture, still unproved.

One of AM's most intriguing excursions occurred when it followed its curiosity about extremes in a direction opposite to that which had led it to primes. Whereas a prime is a number with a minimum of divisors, AM decided also to look at numbers having a maximum—that is to say, the smallest number with seven divisors, the smallest number with eight, and so on. Such "highly composite" numbers were not immediately recognizable as an established field of number-theory study, and at first Lenat thought that AM had come up with something truly original. It turned out, however, that the subject had been investigated by the Indian mathematician Srinivasa Ramanujan. In a way, this was wonderfully apt because Ramanujan was a completely self-taught genius who followed none of the set paths laid down by others, but instead investigated areas of mathematics that he personally found interesting. A better personification of the kind of spirit that Lenat had tried to capture in AM would be difficult to imagine.

LEARNING TO PLAY WITH THE RULES: EURISKO

After this promising start, however, AM's creativity dropped off and its meanderings took it into areas that made no sense, even though there remained well-traveled areas of number theory that it hadn't ventured into. It had never recognized the concept of remainders left after division as something worth investigating, for example, or the idea of a lowest common denominator (the smallest number of which all the "denominators"—numbers underneath—of a set of fractions as are divisors, thus, the LCD of $1/2$, $1/3$, and $1/4$ is 12) that we're introduced to in school. All the same, Lenat's work was greeted as a breakthrough, and after receiving a Ph.D. he moved from Stanford to Carnegie Mellon in 1976 to take a faculty position and pursue further the question of what had caused AM to reach a limit when so much remained to be discovered.

The problem, Lenat found, lay in the heuristics. You could think of them as the wheels of a child's Spirograph set that draws a pattern of loops and whirls that eventually connect, causing the same design to be traced over again on the paper. In a similar way, AM's heuristics were eventually repeating the same paths, leaving areas of reality that the program was never able to find a way into. As a solution, then, why not make the heuristics part of the Tinkertoy kit too, and let the program play with variations on them as well, instead of just with mathematical ideas?

The result was a program called EURISKO. And for a while the trouble that it brought seemed insurmountable. Like AM, EURISKO was written in LISP, which had been designed with the representation and manipulation of mathematical and logical structures in mind but not with structures representing heuristics. As a consequence, whereas even complex logical relationships would typically be expressed compactly in a single LISP sentence, a heuristic devised for the kind of discovery process that Lenat wanted to stimulate might require pages of densely written code. And this was the only means available to the program for expressing itself when it created a new heuristic.

In true Murphy's Law tradition, everything that could go wrong did go wrong. In ways probably as subtly unfathomable as why a group of Norbert Wiener's feedback loops, each stable in itself, could become unstable when acting together, or how the subsystems of Hans Moravec's robot drives found modes of interaction that defied analysis, the interactions operating through layers of complexity persistently found new ways of breaking down. The only way out was to do for heuristics what John McCarthy had done for logical expressions, namely, develop a language specifically suited to the task, and this Lenat proceeded to do in a labor that was to last five years. The outcome was called Representation Language Language, or RLL, which represented heuristics in forms as compact as those of standard LISP. EURISKO was now able to create new heuristics that worked. Not only did it do that, it monitored the performance of the variations in terms of their productivity of new concepts and weeded out the inefficient ones in order to concentrate on playing further with the ones that worked best. EURISKO's improvement was immediate and dramatic.[8]

Descending from its tower of mathematical academia, the program proved its practical worth by developing new rules for designing circuit chips. Chip designers were moving from the two-dimensional arrays of earlier circuits to stacking the layers into 3–D configurations whose complexity of interconnection required fresh insights that depended on mathematical ingenuity rather than intuition. EURISKO, it turned out, was remarkably good at providing them. But like Ada Lovelace and Charles Babbage the century before, and Arthur Samuel with his checkers program, Lenat was looking for a spectacular way of getting the attention of a wider audience. His choice was Traveler, a popular space-war game that involved designing battle fleets from a hundred-page book of rules for specifying fifty-odd parameters such as size, speed, armament, and armor for each ship. The fleets then battled against each other on a galactic board, and the results were determined by consulting complex tables in ways determined by rolls of dice.

Lenat prepared for the 1981 annual Traveler championship by giving EURISKO the rules and concepts of the game and getting it to design fleets that were evaluated by allowing them to battle each other in a Darwinian competition of selection and improvement that progressed through ten thousand contests requiring two thousand hours of computer time. The result was a fleet that went against all the principles that had come to be accepted as gospel by the aficionados—available resources spread over many small, heavily armored vessels as opposed to being concentrated in a few, gargantuan ones—and drew laughs when first presented . . . until it went on to take the championship easily. This caused some discontentment among the other entrants, and the following year, the game organizers announced modified rules just a week before the contest in an effort to thwart a similar ploy of preparing EURISKO ahead of time by extended simulation. But the program proved capable of working within the new rules quite adequately as it stood, and Lenat walked away with the title once more. The next year the organizers threatened to cancel the whole thing if he ran, and he let things go at that without pressing the point. The exercise had attracted the kind of notice that Lenat had sought, however, and the techniques developed for EURISKO were subsequently absorbed by the military into computer war-gaming simulations.

Like its predecessor, however, EURISKO eventually reached its own limit when it started arriving at strange conclusions, such as that it could never fail to achieve something interesting if it redefined as interesting anything it happened to do, or that one way of ensuring the impossibility of failure was simply to do nothing at all. "Strange" to us, that is—creatures embedded in a well-defined world with established ways of looking at things. But EURISKO lived in a world devoid of human notions, and looking purely from the point of view that it had been given, such aims in life were perfectly reasonable.

So, since the mid-eighties, Doug Lenat has relegated further EURISKO-like learning to the back burner in order to focus instead on finding ways of providing the framework of world knowledge. (We always seem to come back to this.) This has become known as the "Cyc" project, and we'll come back to it later in this chapter.

A SPECULATION FOR
NONRANDOM BIOLOGICAL EVOLUTION[9]

DNA can also be viewed as a "program" for constructing and maintaining an organism. Conventional accounts of evolution assume a process of random mutation of the DNA program, followed by natural selection. Early attempts, known as "automatic programming," to apply this process to the production of computer programs failed dismally. The reason was that while random mutation proved a viable mechanism for improving small programs—on the order of a few lines of code—as the programs grew in size, the number of variations to be explored grew explosively in the way we have already encountered. Not only did this result in search spaces too vast to be explored to any meaningful degree, but the "islands" of useful functionality were too thinly scattered across an immense ocean of nonviable variations that didn't work or made no sense to give any plausible expectation of finding bridges connecting them. Many biologists have come to the conclusion that for the same reasons there must be more to natural evolution too.

AM and EURISKO marked the beginnings of a more sophisticated approach to self-modifying programs that has shown significant success by incorporating the crucial element that the earlier programs based purely on random mutation lacked: knowledge about the particular task domains that the programs were to operate in. By employing this knowledge to constrain and guide the search process, even large programs have proved able to extend and modify themselves successfully.

Consider as a simple example a self-generating program for testing an input number to see if it's a prime. One general piece of programming knowledge is that a program should begin with some initializing functions, enter a computational loop, and ultimately output some value. Any program structure not exhibiting such features can immediately be eliminated. The definition of a prime number specifies "having only the divisors 1 and n," where n is the input, which constrains the form of the loop. The loop should terminate early, sometimes with a "not prime" output and, if the loop runs to completion, with "is prime." By making use of a collection of such pieces of knowledge about the problem domain, the space of allowable program structures shrinks and the chances of success rise, equally dramatically.

Such considerations led Lenat to speculate that since the same problems would apply, but to an enormously greater degree, to producing our 3-billion-line genetic "program," it may well be that their successful solution results from nature having discovered a similar principle. In other words, while the process might have begun as random mutations operating among primitive organisms, steady accumulation of knowledge about what kinds of mutation led to favorable results ("plausibility heuristics") led to the predominance of methods for guiding the development of higher organisms in which the generation of mutations is highly nonrandom.

The way this might work, Lenat suggests, is that some of the organism's DNA encode the history of the genome in earlier generations. From patterns in this record, future mutations could be guided in such a way as to encourage related groupings of mutations that need to work together for any benefit to accrue—the improbabilities of which, from isolated random coincidences, have long been a source of bafflement. The result of such genetic heuristics would be for mutation patterns that have proved successful in the past to be preserved and passed on as a group, which, of course, is what is observed universally. In the case of humans, for example, the correlation between increasing skull size at birth and wider maternal pelvic opening that contributed to the viability of the species would be conserved rather than left as a chance association that could as easily disappear.

Species whose evolution was guided by heuristics compiled from the line's genetic history would evolve at an accelerated rate and show a greatly enlarged propensity for producing offspring with favorably co-occurring genes. A large portion of their DNA, containing much information that is historical and used for inferring evolutionary patterns but not needed for maintenance of the adult organism, would be unexpressed. (About 10 percent of human DNA is actually expressed.) The incorporation of such guiding heuristics into the genome would provide the kind of long-term species stability that we see. Random mutation would still be present but its effects largely reduced to background noise.

"Chunking" with Soar

We left the Soar system at the end of chapter nine. Allen Newell, working principally with John Laird and Paul Rosenbloom at CMU, had produced the first version in 1982. Bringing together into one architecture the methods of

problem spaces,
means-ends analysis, and
automatic subgoaling

all bequeathed by Newell and Simon's General Problem Solver, along with

the provision of specific task knowledge via "production rules" as attempted
with the ill-fated Instructible Production System

and in addition employing:

fallback procedures in the form of "weak methods" to give a behavioral
continuum that could vary from novice to expert depending on the
familiarity of what it was doing,

Soar had emerged as a leading research tool for building general cognitive
systems.

But there was still an area it needed to fill in before it could become a true
competitive candidate. Whereas by being fed additional production rules, Soar
could always absorb more of the experience that others had gained, it couldn't
make new connections from its own. No matter how many times it arrived at
the airport without money to buy a ticket, until somebody gave it a specific rule
along the lines of "IF leaving to catch a plane, and don't already have ticket,
THEN check wallet for cash and credit cards," it would arrive without money
the next time.

Throughout the seventies, Allen Newell had been working with people
at the Xerox Palo Alto Research Center (PARC) on the psychology of human-
computer interaction, continuing the line that he had been pursuing in his
studies for the air force in the fifties at Rand, where he met Herbert Simon. The
continuing interest was in discovering quantitative laws underlying human
cognitive processes in order to use them as foundations for engineering models.
One of the laws they investigated, known to psychologists since the 1920s, is
called the "Power Law of Practice," which states that the time taken to accomplish a repetitive task decreases as a power.[10]

Using computers is something that improves with practice, and the law was
as relevant as to any other learned skill. A common explanation as to why
people never seem able to agree on whether one programming language is
better than another is that sufficient practice with any language makes it seem
superior to the user with experience of it. It turned out that the same law
applied to any deliberate task, perceptual, motor, or cognitive. It was unlikely
that something like that would come about through coincidence. Generally
speaking, a ubiquitous phenomenon does not arise out of aspects specific to
each occurrence but results from something elementary that pervades all of

them. This suggested that some extremely general, underlying structural feature of cognition was at work.

The result was a paper Newell and Rosenbloom published in 1981 in which they identified this as the known psychological phenomenon of *chunking*, whereby memory is organized by building up collections of information describing part of a situation into "chunks" that can be treated as units, those chunks into larger chunks, and so on. The paper invoked chunking as the basis of a general theory of learning that could explain how performance improves with practice, the shape of the power law, and why it would be ubiquitous. And the dual-strategy approach that was inherent in Soar suggested a ready way of incorporating chunking into the architecture.

Soar had two ways of arriving at solutions, and essentially they complemented each other:

1. finding subgoals and constructing a chain of solutions that would eventually get to the main goal (means-ends analysis)
2. using production rules directly wherever suitable ones were available

So, having gone through all the searchings and computations of (1) to figure out the subgoals of a situation it hadn't encountered before, why shouldn't it chunk the results together as a ready-made specification of what to do if it finds itself in the same situation again? This would enable it to create new IF . . . THEN . . . rules of its own from experience, in addition to the ones supplied externally, a close approximation of what humans seem to do.

Once the idea was conceived, implementation went remarkably smoothly—in a matter of days—and "Soar 3" became operational in 1984. From then on, Newell asserted, there was no separate consideration of problem solving and learning. The two were integrated into the same set of functions. Soar was a problem solver that learned whenever it solved problems, and how it solved them changed according to what it had learned. Later versions of Soar have become the subject of intense activity involving over one hundred researchers on both sides of the Atlantic. The sixteenth annual Soar Workshop, held at the University of California's Information Sciences Institute in 1996, featured thirty speakers covering topics that ranged from an overview of "Soar 7" to psychological modeling to simulations of the behavior of soccer players and air traffic controllers to various aspects of Soar technicalities, instruction, and training aids. A version called TacAir-Soar simulates a jet pilot and has performed competently in simulated combats—with some constraints—against human experts.[11]

Certainly, systems like these bring goal orientation, rational problem solving, task learning, and other qualities that would once have been viewed purely as the province of humans within the realm of machine reproducibility. And for application needs intensive in those areas, the effects promise to be significant.

There are, however, those like Douglas Hofstadter of Indiana University who point out that there's surely a lot more to what humans can do than can be cast in terms of rational problem solving in problem spaces.[12] Or, as Doug Lenat put it when I talked to him, the problem space is defined in terms of the constructs provided by the programmer. What seems to be missing from machine cognition is the ability of humans to extract what's *relevant* to the task at hand from the infinity of raw, inherently meaningless facts surrounding them and from this *create* a domain appropriate to their situation. Recognizing relevance is one of those things we unconsciously do all the time, which ought to be a hint that for machines it won't be easy.

But while different ideas were being traded and debated, an alternate, more immediately pragmatic line of AI was taking shape. There were still many useful things that machines able to perform in specialized-knowledge domains could do without needing general cognitive skills or anything resembling human common sense. It wasn't necessary to wait for an answer on how to get a machine to learn because there was another way: just hand-feed into it as much as it needed to know to perform in its own narrow area. So what emerged became known as "Expert Systems," which led to a huge market boom in the eighties.

Education by Brain Surgery: Expert Systems

DENDRAL: ORGANIC CHEMIST

By the time Ed Feigenbaum moved south from Berkeley to Stanford, he had decided he had spent enough time on EPAM, which Herbert Simon was taking further at CMU, and cast around for other challenges. This was the point where he found himself being drawn more in the direction of AI, from what would be better described as applied psychology. He was particularly interested in the possibility of modeling empirical induction.[13] This is the process by which, given a set of observations that could be, for example, the motions of planets in the sky, the past record of promises and excuses of somebody wanting to borrow money, or the different ways a bicycle wobbles, a person forms a general hypothesis about a part of the world and uses it to make guesses about the future. It's also the main business of science, so that was where Feigenbaum turned to have the procedures involved made more explicit.

He also sought an emphasis on the engineering side of AI as opposed to the academic, i.e., in the domain of difficult real-world problems where effectiveness could be assessed in practical terms, not as solutions to games and puzzles. This was in 1965, and a major reason for this focus, besides Feigenbaum's personal inclinations, was no doubt that DARPA, still the principal funding agency for this kind of work, was being influenced by critical reports from both sides of the Atlantic that AI so far had produced little in the way of usable results, and by the abandoning of the natural-language translation effort.

The problem that Feigenbaum eventually took up, along with Robert K. Lindsay, who joined him from CMU, was one being tackled by Joshua Lederberg, a Nobel laureate in genetics whom Feigenbaum had met before moving to Stanford. Lederberg was looking for help with the intricacies involved in determining the structures of complex organic molecules from the data produced by an analytical instrument known as a mass spectrometer.

Basically, a mass spectrometer works by vaporizing a sample of the substance to break the molecules up into their constituent fragments and sending a beam of the fragment particles through a magnetic field that separates them in a somewhat similar way to that in which a glass prism separates a beam of light into colors. Instead of showing the light intensity at different wavelengths, the "spectrum" produced in this way consists of a series of peaks indicating the relative proportions of fragments of differing mass. The job of the spectroscopist is to infer from the clues contained in the distribution and sizes of the peaks— and there can be dozens of them—the structure of the original molecule.

The logic involved is similar to that needed to solve puzzles presented as a series of statements along such lines as:

"Andy, Bob, Charlie through, say, George have three mustaches between them."

"Two who have hats don't have mustaches."

"Eddie or Charlie has a green hat."

"George has the same color hat as Dave."

And so on for a set of rules so related that between them they admit only one solution to a question like "Which one has a red hat and no mustache?"

However, for the compound Di-n-decyl $C_{20}H_{22}$, for example, the number of possible ways the fragments could be combined is over 11 million.

Needless to say, a chemist doesn't blindly start trying possibilities at random. An enormous amount of chemical knowledge, skill in judgment, and plain knack born of experience is involved. At the same time, nobody can bring to mind every obscure example and lesson encountered over the years. Mistakes were all too easy, and laborious searches of catalogs and standard references had become part of the accepted routine. Could computers automate, speed up, and regularize the procedure?

This problem combined exactly all the characteristics of empirical induction that Feigenbaum had been looking for. At the same time, it was typically AI: an enormous problem space of possible hypotheses impossible to search exhaustively, out of which it was necessary to select a few lines of promising conjecture. In some ways the problem resembled the same kind of branching structure as that of determining the few continuations worth considering in a chess game. Accordingly, Feigenbaum and Lindsay named their program DENDRAL, from the Greek for "tree."[14]

Its development was to last ten years. The big realization that the process brought home was the degree to which skilled human analysts did what they did not by applying some generalized form of reasoning but through the tremendous amount of specialized knowledge they carried in their heads. There was no way that a program could even approach such a task without incorporating that knowledge, so a huge part of the project became sitting down with the experts, watching them work, asking them questions, and trying to turn their answers into something unambiguous and definite enough to be expressed as computer code. This turned out to be far from easy, not for lack of cooperation but because in so many instances the experts were simply unable to say what they did. No more than a chess master muddles over his options a move at a time like a novice or an adult reader haltingly assembles syllables, the expert doesn't proceed in tidy, reasoned steps that can be picked apart and analyzed; he just *knows*. Coaxing this information out of the unconscious and into an explicit form emerged as the task of what was to become a new class of specialist: the "knowledge engineer." The resulting program represented the antithesis of typical AI thinking up to that time. Unlike GPS, for example, which looked to a general problem-solving methodology that could be applied irrespective of the nature of the problem, DENDRAL deemphasized reasoning and made specialized knowledge all-important. This made it the prototype of what would later be designated "knowledge-based systems."

At first the AI community reacted with reservations, tending to regard DENDRAL as a collection of lots of specialized facts about chemistry and little in the way of intelligence. But interest grew as the system eventually came to give a quite commendable performance, with one class of compounds actually managing to do better than experienced chemists. When DENDRAL moved out of the research environment to become a working tool for chemists at Stanford and other universities, and in industrial laboratories, suddenly all kinds of commercial possibilities were being talked about. Everybody was beating a path to the DENDRAL door.

DENDRAL was essentially a big LISP program with embedded conditional rules. The limitation it eventually encountered was that the initially flexible structure became so tangled and convoluted as it grew and sprouted new connections that beyond a certain size it became virtually impossible to add or modify rules without altering unpredictably—and often drastically—the behavior of the whole system. With hindsight the solution was to separate the general-reasoning heuristics from the domain knowledge into modularized systems that could be maintained independently of each other. This became the thesis work of a doctoral student, Donald Waterman, in 1972. The other part of the answer came with a new CMU addition to the team, Bruce Buchanan, who brought from CMU the method of IF ... THEN ... production rules that Newell and Simon were studying for application in what would become Soar.

These design philosophies formed the basis for the Stanford team's next major undertaking, which took shape in the mid-seventies: MYCIN.

MYCIN: CONSULTANT PHYSICIAN

Developed in collaboration with the Infectious Diseases Group at Stanford Medical School, MYCIN began as the Ph.D. project of Edward H. Shortliffe, under Buchanan's direction.[15] Its purpose was to advise physicians on the diagnosis of blood and meningitis (inflammation of the membranes surrounding the brain and spinal cord, often caused by bacteria) infections and on the selection of antibiotics for treatment. This revised architecture, with its incorporation of production rules, proved highly effective, as was readily acknowledged by the experts themselves. In one formal test, a judging panel rated MYCIN's prescriptions as correct 65 percent of the time compared to 42.5 percent to 62.5 percent for human specialists presented with the same cases.[16]

MYCIN's organization became the basis for the variety of knowledge-based systems that have emerged since. Known as "expert systems," these range from multimillion-dollar projects for dispensing information to oil-company geologists to interactive "Help" resources supplied as part of software to run on personal computers. Figure 15.1 summarizes the basic design structure.

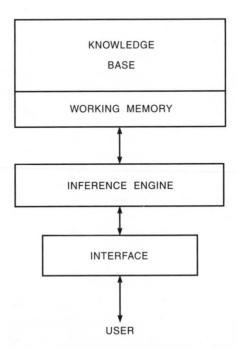

Figure 15.1 Basic Organization of an Expert System

The rules embodying the specialized knowledge are separated from the logical inference processes necessary to apply them. The Knowledge Base corresponds to the experience a doctor carries around in his head. Working Memory is the data specific to the case being considered—think of it as the patient's records on the doctor's desk screen or the clipboard in his hand. The knowledge base of MYCIN contained around five hundred production rules of the general form:

Rule 578

IF
    (i)   the infection is meningitis, and
   (ii)   organisms were not seen in the stain of the culture, and
  (iii)   the type of infection may be bacterial, and
  (iv)   the patient has been seriously burned,

THEN
there is suggestive evidence that *Pseudonomas aeruginosa* might be one of the organisms causing the infection.[17]

The advantage of separating the rules out in this way is that it makes them modular. Rules can be modified or deleted, or new ones added, without the whole system being affected and disrupted. The system provides weightings of the evidence it has used in arriving at a given conclusion. When, as often happens, it is unable to rule out all but a single diagnosis, it sets out the alternatives with an assessment of their relative probabilities.

The Inference Engine is the part of the program that tries to reason its way to a conclusion by combining facts from the Working Memory with rules from the Knowledge Base. The name was coined by another member of the team, Randall Davis, during a visit to Washington when he was faced with having to explain the concept to DARPA people who weren't physicians but who knew FORTRAN and had heard of Babbage.[18] If MYCIN needed further information, it would compose a question asking for it, e.g., "Has the patient ever been to an area that is endemic for coccidioidomycosis?"

At a time when most researchers were looking to complex systems of control logic, the secondary role played by the inference logic was significant in demonstrating that high performance could depend heavily on accumulated knowledge. This perhaps says much about how human thinking works and why we find it so difficult to analyze processes we have become expert at. Where effective action requires speed, being able to recall instantly the stored results of previous experience has a clear advantage over having to work things out from basics every time. Another resemblance between expert systems and the way humans think is their resilience. They can still function on incomplete information or if a rule is removed.

The Interface supports interaction with the user. Unlike DENDRAL, which simply provided a result, MYCIN allowed the user to query and evaluate the advice given by the system, a crucial feature for establishing user confidence or enabling a source of error to be pinpointed. For example, if the system asked if the patient in question had been seriously burned, the physician could type WHY to establish why the system considers it important. In response, the system might provide a trace of its reasoning procedure leading to the conclusion, perhaps, that Rule 578 is pertinent.

In a later development, the Inference Engine and Interface were implemented as a separate package that could be combined with different knowledge bases specific to other task domains. In this way, further expert systems were created to offer advice on such subjects as pulmonary dysfunction and psychiatric disorders. This again became a part of standard design practice, giving rise in later years to a string of companies specializing in producing expert-system "shells."

THE EIGHTIES BANDWAGON

MYCIN marked the debut of AI into the real world, where information is never complete, what exists is messy and often contradictory, and time is never sufficient. No longer a province of toy problems and robots stacking colored blocks, AI had shown that it could significantly improve the performance of scientists and physicians, indeed, professionals of every kind—in short, people whose knowledge and effectiveness made money. Suddenly, corporate executives, investors, and venture capitalists started taking notice. By 1980, funds were being lavished on a host of new projects at the universities, larger corporations were scrambling to set up their own in-house operations, and leading names in AI research from the three big centers at MIT, CMU, and Stanford were founding specialized companies. AI had gone commercial.

In January 1980, John McDermott of CMU turned over to the Digital Equipment Corporation in Maynard, Massachusetts,[19] the initial version of XCON ("eXpert CONfigurer"), work on which had been begun in 1978 as a configuration aid for DEC's new line of thirty-two-bit word VAX computers. Those who have gotten involved in ports, expansion slots, modules, and cables know that even desk-size machines can end up in as many variations as a new car with all its options. For computers that come in locker-room-size cabinets, the problem is a thousand times worse, and companies like DEC have entire factory floors devoted to preshipment assembly and test of the various customer configurations, no two of which are ever identical. Following the rules and conditions for putting it all together is a major time consumer, and the errors that inevitably happen anyway represent a significant overhead expense that has to be absorbed. The 1980 version of XCON contained about 850 rules and descriptions of 450 components and handled one computer model only, the VAX-11/780. By 1984 these figures had grown to over 3,000 and 5,000 and applied to ten models. In the same period, DEC's Intelligent Systems Technology Group had grown from five people to over seventy, and they were responsible for seven other knowledge-based systems in addition to XCON and achieving an estimated $40 million per year in reduced testing and manufacturing costs.

Meanwhile, other success stories continued to be chalked up and were enthusiastically plugged by the media. Nineteen eighty-three saw PROSPECTOR, developed at SRI, a few miles from the Stanford campus, helping geologists by successfully locating ore-grade molybdenum deposits in Washington state. CADUCEUS, developed by Harry E. Pople and Jack D. Myers at the University of Pittsburgh, took on the ambitious goal of a decision-support system to cover all internal medicine, including, for example, the effects of possible interactions between different diseases in the same patient.[20] By 1984, General Electric was using its DELTA system to diagnose trouble and breakdowns in diesel-electric locomotives and provide repair instructions. The Campbell Soup Company was reheating computer-condensed expertise to fix rotary cookers at its various plants across the country. General Motors came up with an automatic model of troubleshooting know-how pertaining to factory-floor lathes and grinders. In 1986 three major insurance companies opted for knowledge-based systems to assist underwriters with claim and risk assessment.

Expert systems arrived on the scene as part of a convergence of events that put computers in the spotlight of public attention. Vietnam was fading, the children of the flower children of the sixties swung with the pendulum into yuppies, and technology started to be respectable again; the Carter administration's capital-gains cuts made investment attractive; and the biotechnology revolution of the late seventies had focused interest on advanced sectors of research. A vigorously competitive market was causing the price of electronics to plummet, and the founding of the Apple Computer Company by Steve Jobs and Steve Wozniak in a Silicon Valley garage in 1976 brought computing out of the temples and into the price range and lives of thousands who until then had viewed it as something arcane, remote, and only for the initiated, like heart surgery or nuclear reactors.

When I was leaving DEC at the end of 1979 to write full-time, somebody in the company suggested I ought to look into "word processing," and I had to ask around to find out what it was. A minimal system—processor, disk drive, screen, printer, software—of the kind then available came out at around $10,000, and, faced by the uncertainties of a new, self-sufficient career with never again a guaranteed paycheck, I decided to wait things out a little longer. Three years and four manual-typewriter-crafted novels later, I felt that life had reached a point where I could spare such an amount and decided it was time to check the options again. On listing the same requirements, I was informed that the current price for a TRS-80–based system (with two disk drives, not one; there was no PC then, and hard drives on personal machines were unheard of) would be $4,000. So I bought two of them (who knows better than an Irish engineer that anything that *can* go wrong . . . ?) and still came out $2,000 ahead of budget.

ARTIFICIAL INTELLIGENCE the cover of *Business Week*, July 9, 1984, proclaimed. IT'S HERE! "Discovered" primarily as a result of the attention that expert systems had attracted from the commercial world, AI was one of the hottest items in publishing. Attendance for the American Association for Artificial Intelligence meeting at UCLA in August 1985 was over six thousand, up from one thousand at the first meeting in Stanford in 1980. Interest and funding from the Pentagon soared, and AI became a top research priority in Europe. The Japanese Ministry of Information and Technology announced a coordinated $850 million program that became known as the Fifth Generation to shape the next wave of information-intensive technology that would carry through to the end of the century. It centered heavily on fast, high-density hardware supporting advanced AI techniques. One AI laboratory director was getting calls from venture capitalists at the rate of at least one a month. "Just start a company and put 'Artificial Intelligence' in the name somewhere," they would say, "and we'll give you a blank check."

The figures who had been existing in low visibility for three decades decided that if all kinds of new names were in line to reap the harvest, those who had created the field should be there too. Feigenbaum and his Stanford colleagues had founded two AI consultancy companies in 1980, Teknowledge and Intelligenetics (changed to Intellicorp in 1983). At about the same time, groups from MIT formed Thinking Machines Corporation, which included Marvin Minsky as a founder, and Symbolics and Lisp Machines Inc., both also in Cambridge. Raj Reddy and others at CMU incorporated the Carnegie Group to market expertise in expert systems, language recognition, and robotics. Roger Schank at Yale set up Cognitive Systems Inc., and Larry Harris left Dartmouth to form Artificial Intelligence Corporation. Much of the business of these companies was in the design and creation of expert-system shells. Another strongly represented line, also covered by larger manufacturers such as Texas Instruments and Xerox, was the supply of "Lisp Machines," workstations resembling scaled-up PCs but containing hardware and software specialized for running LISP programs fast and selling in the rarified $50,000 to $100,000 range.

And yet . . .

Inevitably, an ominous feeling of something eventually coming unglued starts to creep over one when watching an expanding orb of self-feeding optimism shed ballast and float gently away from solid ground. Artificial intelligence, it was being proclaimed, was finally "here." Expert systems were the solution to everything. As with every promise of a panacea, the uneasiness grows. Many people in the field thought so too. Marvin Minsky and Roger Schank warned in 1984 that the answers-to-everything being hyped as the wonders of the age were based on programming techniques that were fifteen to twenty years old and were simply taking advantage of cheaper, faster hardware.[21] The newer systems were no smarter, but memories able to hold thousands of rules hadn't been available before. But to most people without the experience to judge such things, the sight of a computer apparently conversing with professionals in their own jargon was totally compelling. It was Joseph Weizenbaum's fears come true: the ELIZA illusion getting out of hand. Eventually, reality has a way of intervening to calm things down in such situations.

Sure enough, by the end of the eighties the balloon had not so much burst but found its level and hissed to ground downwind. Today, the Fifth Generation project idles in second gear, and much of Cambridge's AI Alley is up for rent. We had talking automobiles so irritating that the feature was discontinued, and there are devices around of one kind or another that can be trained to respond to simple sentences. But no one yet discusses philosophy with a laptop or goes out while the electronic butler straightens up the house and takes care of the chores. Worse still, what was a thriving AI research community in the late seventies still hasn't recovered from being gutted of talent and people drawn away by the financial lures of the eighties. Software being peddled as "state of the art" doesn't come close to the development tools that were being used ten years ago: incremental compilation and linking, object-oriented programming, programmable microcode, automatic memory management. One would be hard-pressed today to find many groups working seriously on commonsense reasoning or high-level vision.

Once again, what was going to be that final answer ended up carving itself a niche to the side—and let's be clear, expert systems in general continue to earn their keep and perform the tasks for which they were devised. American Express uses one for credit approval, the post office for address reading, every auto manufacturer for design, and every airline for logistics. They have certainly earned a permanent and important place in the overall future scheme of things.

But, like feedback and control, logical reasoning, heuristic searching, and pattern matching, knowledge turns out to be just another essential component that starts out with impressive early successes, only to run into its own kind of limiting factor that prevents its being pushed indefinitely. What were the limits in this case?

FRAGMENTS OF THE WORLD

There is one part of the eighties AI balloon that did burst spectacularly, and that is the specialized Lisp machine market. Since LISP was virtually unknown outside of AI work, production volume had always been low, and manufacturers were unable to benefit from the mass-market economies of scale being realized by Apple and IBM machines. By 1987 these machines were available at comparable power and a fraction of the cost, and there was no longer any reason to stick with a nonstandard product, especially since Lisp machines

were stand-alone and unable to integrate into the networks that were also proliferating by then. Finally, software became available to transport AI systems
over to the conventional machines and the Lisp machine business folded, to
massive hemorrhaging among the companies that had been set up to specialize
in the manufacture and sales of the specialized machines and the engineering of
software shells specifically for them. But that's the typical pattern of a market
shakedown in any business after a rush of heavy speculation on a bet that didn't
work out. If that had been all there was to it, the burgeoning knowledge
industry would have moved over to conventional machines and the race would
have continued much as before but with a changed mix of runners.

Whatever hardware or architecture they were implemented on, expert systems were running into a more fundamental limitation by virtue of their nature.
It had to do with the same impediment we keep coming back to, which seems to
stand in the way of every approach to instilling learning ability: a lack of that
elusive human quality, common sense.

By 1987, Digital Equipment Corporation's XCON configurer had grown to
ten thousand rules to keep up with changes and additions to the product
range—but it wasn't growing in efficiency and by that time was costing $2 mil-
lion per year just to maintain. Other companies who had invested in large
expert systems, for example, General Electric with its locomotive doctor
DELTA, were finding the same thing. The trouble was that such systems had
no innate knowledge structure of their own comparable to that of a human
mind, which is able to accommodate new information automatically, making
all the connections and associations to just where they need to go. Instead,
every new fact had to be inserted by hand, as it were, and integrated as it best
made intuitive sense. But in complex systems like these, such changes could
have effects that were far from intuitively obvious. Much as a seemingly minor
fluctuation in a stock market at a critical moment can trigger modes of
upheaval that resonate through the world's financial networks, altering or
adding to production rules could have results that were unpredictable, and
debugging costs rose accordingly.

Furthermore, the difficulty of getting knowledge out of experts' heads and
into a form that could be stated as precise rules still remained. A big reason for
this, the knowledge engineers were beginning to suspect, was that very often,
human experts don't think in rules at all—try explaining to someone exactly
how you recognize a face or form a sentence. As we noted earlier, much human
thinking seems to take the form of recalling the *results* of previously stored
experience intact, not working them through again. When we recognize a
family resemblance, or when a doctor spots a case as being "like" one that he
came across several years ago, or when a Kasparov gets a hunch based upon a
hundred board positions that were "similar," it's all but impossible to put into
words what processes lead to these conclusions. We think, very much of the
time, in analogies, not logical statements. And if natural language with all its

elasticity and flexibility is unable to describe them, what chance has a formal programming language?

The most serious limitation, however, is that at heart these systems are really automated card indexes, with no understanding of the things they reason about. MYCIN, for example, could provide information on—"know" about if you will—diagnosing disease, but it understood nothing of physiology, anatomy, or chemistry, let alone that the symbols stored in the "Name" slot represented a human being. With no concept of the consequences of treatment as opposed to no treatment, it had no capacity for going against the rules in the way a doctor might when judging the comparative risks, say, in deciding to go with a drug that wouldn't be the normal choice when nothing else is available. "Expert" was really a misnomer. Acting as a reminder and retriever of obscure facts, a computer could help a true expert do a better job, but it couldn't substitute for one.

In short, the reality that expert systems live in is narrow. They operate within their own tiny slice of the world with its own rules, treating it much the same as a puzzle or game that relates to nothing else and has no broader consequences or implications. In contrast, a genuine expert system ought to know enough about related fields and the essentials of reality to be able to approximate some kind of answer when its rules don't help, even if the answer is no more than to recommend another appropriate expert system. A structural engineer, for example, might have seen enough frames bend in a certain way to know how the forces are distributed within the members; if he comes across an instance that's new, however, he can ask for a few measurements, pull out a calculator, and figure out from basic principles what's going on.

In the same way, a true medical expert system needs to know that it doesn't know, and how to shift down to, say, physiology or chemistry to work out a solution. But that in turn could require knowing when to ask about personal habits, troubles on the home front, or work pressures. Very soon, the whole of human knowledge gets involved.

So does that mean you end up needing a machine that knows nearly as much about the world as a human? A lot of AI people had been saying for a long time that yes, eventually you'd hit a point where you found you couldn't get any farther until you had just that. And we seem to have hit this point several times already in this book. But one of the big unsolved problems was how to get a machine to learn as much as a human. Very well, Doug Lenat of AM and EURISKO fame decided. If nobody knew how to make a machine acquire general world knowledge for itself, the only alternative would be to put the knowledge there. And this he set out to do.

MCC and the CYC Project

In February 1982, four months after the Japanese announced their Fifth Generation program, representatives from eighteen major U.S. computer companies met in Orlando, Florida, at the invitation of William C. Norris, then chairman of the Control Data Corporation, to discuss forming a research consortium to pool their efforts in response. Almost a year of task forces, meetings, and discussions with the Justice Department over antitrust considerations followed, but in January 1983 the Microelectronics and Computer Technology Corporation (MCC) was formed in Austin, Texas, with the former deputy director of the CIA, Admiral Bobby Inman, as CEO. The initial ten-year agenda covered a broad cross section of computing and related technologies that included parallel processing, database management, human-factors engineering, AI, semiconductor packaging, software productivity, and computer-aided design. One aspect of policy that Inman was particularly insistent on was the hiring of top-rank personnel, and thus it came about that Doug Lenat, whose quest for years had been to find out how to make computers learn, was invited to head one of the AI groups. The project that he initiated is known as CYC, from "encyclopedia," and he continues to head it today as president of Cycorp, recently located in new premises a short distance from the original MCC buildings. Its aim is the realization of something Lenat had long been convinced would be necessary if AI was ever to make any real progress and which there was no easy way around: a database of general knowledge comparable in size and scope to that carried by humans.

Lenat's definition of CYC is "an expert system with a domain that spans all everyday objects and actions."[22] In 1984, when what he described as the AI "mania" was at its peak, Lenat had been one of the few who dared express pessimism about the coming decade. Ironically, eleven years later, when the rest of the world had realized that the dazzling scenarios were not about to happen *now* and turned elsewhere for sensation, he wrote in *Scientific American* that he believed AI stood close to the brink of success.[23]

His pessimism had stemmed from the idiot savant nature of the systems on which all hopes were being piled. As we've noted, existing expert systems were "brittle" in that while competent within their own specialized area, they failed totally when taken the slightest bit beyond it, with no concept that their knowledge was inapplicable. Given facts about a rusty car, a medical program could in all seriousness diagnose measles. They couldn't share their knowledge with each other, and they had no way of learning more for themselves. No amount of fiddling, Lenat finally decided and convinced his sponsors, was going to tell a machine how to discover for itself the framework of accumulated facts and observations that enables a child beginning grade school to organize and relate new information. Therefore, it would all have to be manually encoded and spelled out one assertion at a time. The big problem the whole AI world kept confronting in different guises was that nobody had faced up to the fact and done it.

The project was launched in 1984, and over the next ten years it involved the encoding of somewhere around 100,000 discrete concepts and a million pieces of commonsense knowledge about the real, everyday world of places and things, people and their affairs, time, space, causality, and contradiction into a gigantic database of over a billion bytes of information.

In the typical pragmatic Lenat style of doing it while everyone else is talking about how to do it, the group began by going through snippets of news articles, advertisements, novels, and the like and asking for each item they picked out, *What did the writer of this assume that the reader already knew?* It was the prerequisite knowledge that they wanted to capture and codify, not the content itself. And it turns out that in our dealings with each other we assume a colossal amount that seems so obvious that nobody would dream of wasting space with it in dictionaries or encyclopedias, even ones intended for children. Consider, to take a few samples, how much of our understanding depends on knowing without having to be told such things as:

You have to be awake to eat.
You can usually see people's noses but not their hearts.
You cannot remember events that haven't happened yet.
A piece of peanut butter cut in half is two pieces of peanut butter, but a table cut in half is not two tables.

Two of the first sentences used were "Napoleon died on St. Helena. Wellington was saddened." To anybody with even a smattering of European history, the meaning of this is pretty clear. Coding the prerequisite knowledge that a machine would need in order to make sense of it took the CYC team three months. They had to impart, for example, that Napoleon was a person and the import of what that meant, leading among other things to the notion that people die. Dying is an event in time, which brings in a whole net of further concepts. Tying it in with the implications of emotions affecting other persons is a whole further story that hinges, in this case, on knowing something about human ambition, politics, war, battles, and the notion of a respected enemy. And being told that St. Helena is an island doesn't say much unless you also know what an island is, which requires a basic course in land, sea, topology, and geography.

Slowly, the size of the task the team had taken on unfolded in all its ghastly enormity, and for a while they feared that the philosophers who had been criticizing the whole notion of AI on principle could be right: that once you set foot in the real world with all its ramifications and connections, there isn't anything you say that doesn't eventually lead everywhere, so that, in the spirit of the Buddhist worldview, every mustard seed contains everything, and there's no end to it. By late 1987, however, things had reached a point that Lenat terms "semantic convergence," where it became possible to define new concepts in terms of existing ones, easing the load considerably. Lenat believes that this stringing together of concepts and forming associations will lead to the development of language comprehension in the same way a human infant acquires it—simple connections, with a more sophisticated grammar capability coming later—at which point the whole process will accelerate enormously with new information being supplied as natural text—in short, when CYC learns to read.

As an illustration of its progress, a demonstration put together in 1994 retrieved stored picture images with descriptions meeting criteria that the user types in. Asked to find pictures with "seated people," for example, CYC included one with a description of a New York City street with cars and trees. Although no people were mentioned, the program knew that cars in motion have people inside called drivers and that drivers sit in driver's seats and inferred accordingly that the picture contained seated people. Big deal for a three-year-old. For a computer, a towering accomplishment. And indications are that CYC is continuing to progress well. In February 1997, while I was in the process of editing the final manuscript—for this chapter, as coincidence would have it—Doug Lenat told me over the phone that the project has just been approved further funding to the tune of $5 million.

What would CYC be used for? Think of it as the "commonsense" chip that would reside in your computer, household manager, or advise the "software robot" that filters your mail and takes care of web searches. If it works, the market could be truly enormous—nobody, for instance, would dream of buying or marketing a computer without common sense any more than today they would consider one without a graphics driver. Imagine your word processor reminding you that in an early sentence of the document you promised to elaborate on an item later but failed to do so, or querying an input to a document that is technically permissible but doesn't make sense—say, a résumé by a twenty-year-old that claims ten years of work experience, or simply being able to ask, "How many bytes are there in a typical volume of an encyclopedia?" without having to tell it where to look.

Will it work? Marvin Minsky is enthusiastic and considers it exactly the right way to be heading, as does John McCarthy. Hans Moravec, who was a fellow graduate student of Lenat's at Stanford, rates it at fifty-fifty. Allen Newell was pessimistic on the grounds of its ad hoc, messily unstructured nature. But as a vast, empirical experiment, it seems to hold a fascination for everybody, and if Lenat's estimates are accurate, interesting results should begin emerging in the next year or two.

The whole issue of common sense as the crux of developing a true artificial intelligence was identified by John McCarthy back in 1958, and it remains today just about where it stood then. A problem that has proved so formidable deserves a chapter of its own. And so, without further ado . . .

1. Lenat (1983), p. 293.
2. Minsky (1985), p. 203.
3. McCorduck, p. 274.
4. Feigenbaum (1963).
5. McCorduck, p. 276.
6. Feigenbaum and Feldman.
7. Lenat (1981).
8. For more background, see Lenat and Brown.
9. This is developed more comprehensively in Lenat (1983), p. 286.
10. X^n represents the number X "raised to the power" n—for example, 3^2, which equals 9. The "power" can be a fraction, such as $1/2$, in which case X^n means the nth root of X, which for $n = 1/2$ is the square root.
11. For more on Soar, see Tambe et al.; Laird and Rosenbloom (1996); and Lehman, Laird, and Rosenbloom.
12. Hofstadter (1995), pp. 372–73.
13. McCorduck, p. 281.
14. Lindsay, R., et al.
15. Shortliffe; Buchanan and Shortliffe.
16. Waldrop, p. 39.
17. Ibid., p. 41.
18. Crevier, p. 157.
19. Ibid., p. 161.
20. Pople.
21. Crevier, p. 203.
22. Lenat (1995a).
23. Lenat (1995b).

16

In Pursuit of
Common Sense

"What permits a writer to depict such seemingly real personalities? It is because we all agree on so many things that are left unsaid." —Marvin Minsky

"Everybody Knows": The Unsaid Obvious

BACKGROUNDS WE ALL SHARE

A well-known two-liner found in AI and psychological literature runs:

MAN: "I'm leaving you."
WOMAN (after pause): "Who is she?"

Most of us will nod, perhaps knowingly or with a show of sympathy, and not think too much about these lines beyond that. But reflect for a moment on what it takes in terms of understanding about the world and its ways, social customs and institutions, human relationships and their implications, to be able to follow just that simple exchange.

Language is necessary to communicate what isn't obvious. In typical human-world situations this could almost be described as dealing with the exceptions. Think of a couple of men who know their job and have worked together for a long time, say, putting up a fence or painting a house. What's voiced will be things like "Maybe we'll make the hole there to avoid the rock" or "How much white is left in the can?" Any sustained conversation is more likely to do with boating or a ball game—nothing to do with the task at hand.

We state things explicitly only when there's some reason for not assuming that the other person doesn't already know them.

This is in complete contrast to the way we use formal languages to define mathematical tasks or instruct computers. In these cases, everything needed in the way of knowledge is supplied explicitly or pointed to and anything not referenced in some way is assumed irrelevant. That's fine for the kind of narrow-domain applications in which computers find most of their work—it makes for speed and efficient use of resources such as memory, and systems like Soar are able to increase their flexibility by switching between different problem spaces as appropriate to the different aspects of a problem. "Get to San Francisco," for example, might invoke a "book seat" subproblem, in which the goal is to change the present ticketless state to one in which a paid-for reservation exists, involving a problem space that has nothing to do with getting to the airport. That in turn might find that the program has to solve a "contact travel agent" sub-subproblem, which in turn involves using the phone. But while such methods can produce astonishingly versatile performances, the problem spaces involved are still constructed out of elements and operators supplied by the programmer. Thus, the system might apply various strategies to search a space that contains cash, credit cards, or checkbook as things to consider because the supplied rules incorporated them into the program's sphere of "awareness," but it would never, on its own, come up with the possibility of tapping a friend for a loan, panhandling on the street, or mugging somebody.

It could be argued that all this information has to be put into people too, either genetically or by instruction or experience. While this is true, we've seen already, when looking at vision, the stupefying rate at which information pours into the human neural concept-forming system, literally from the moment one first opens one's eyes. Having to somehow supply the kind of background knowledge that we presume humans bring to a situation is a pretty daunting prospect, to put it mildly.

A program arrives at a solution by using the same methods it applies to a theorem, i.e., rigorously "proving" to itself that a particular sequence of actions will transform a logical expression representing the problem state into the goal state. Such formal systems are absolutely literal-minded, in that any consequences of an action not expressly stated don't exist. To contact a travel agent, we take it for granted that we can get the phone number from Information if we don't have it, that having the number means we can dial it, that dialing it will establish contact. A program has to be told all these things. It takes nothing for granted. (This is what makes computers so invaluable as an analytical tool in science and mathematics, because we *want* the system to be fragile so that any error will immediately reveal itself—just the opposite of natural-world robustness.) In programming a similar telephone situation, John McCarthy and Patrick Hayes found they had to state specifically that a person still has the phone after looking up the number—a necessary condition for rigorously proving a solution viable but not obvious to a computer.

This need to specify all the possible and relevant consequences of any action occurs throughout AI work. A robot stacking blocks might contain rules for keeping track of the situation by methodically updating its representation as it steps through its problem space: "I've released the blue cube and therefore no longer have it, which puts me *here*. The blue cube is now on top of the red cube, so the state of the tower is *that* . . ." But what happens when an unstable tower collapses into a state that the representation no longer models, or someone coming into the room knocks it over by opening the door, or a sibling in a ratty mood throws a block at it? A child would go into a state of exasperation or annoyance and promptly create a new problem domain (if that is indeed a valid description of what we do) appropriate to the changed situation. The program goes into catatonia.

McCarthy and Hayes recognized this as far back as 1969, when Hayes was with Donald Michie's AI lab in Edinburgh, in a joint paper that referred to it as the "frame problem" since it involves finding and managing the correct frame of reference. It is still far from being resolved today.

GENERAL PRINCIPLES APPLY—
EXCEPT WHEN THEY DON'T

Here's another situation presented by John McCarthy. Suppose I hire you to build a birdcage for me. When it's done and you present your bill, I refuse to pay because you haven't put a top on the cage. We go to court, and the judge rules in my favor even though you point out that I never said my bird could fly.

On the other hand, now suppose that you did put a top on, but this time I won't pay because my bird is a penguin and you're wasting my money on a top I don't need. This time the judge sides with you, even though, with nothing different said, you fulfilled the condition that I complained about as not having been met in the first case.

This is an example of what McCarthy calls the "qualification problem," similar in spirit to the frame problem but having to do with exceptions. The point, of course, is that given the preponderance of birds that fly over birds that don't, and the general contexts in which birds are thought of, we consider it reasonable to assume that an unqualified "bird" can fly. It follows in the second case that if my particular bird couldn't fly, it was up to me to say so.

Humans know thousands of things like this without having to be told. Computer programs don't, which means that some way has to be devised for telling them. Doing so turns out to be a far from straightforward matter.

Given some initial conditions and a set of rules for operating upon them, computers are good at deducing consequences—*all* possible consequences if you're prepared to wait long enough. In traditional logic, which is devised to deal with deductively structured situations, a conclusion follows necessarily and unconditionally from a given set of premises—a property known as being "monotonic." This is exactly what's wanted for things like theorem proving, as it makes it possible to state that *those* assumptions carry *these* implications and nothing else that happens can change it. But it's also another way of saying that new information can't reverse a conclusion once it's arrived at.

This goes back to deduction being based on sets and subsets. If D is defined as a subset of F, and we start distinguishing different kinds of D, the Ds are still contained within F and keep the characteristics that define "F-type" objects. But this doesn't square with our everyday kind of decision making at all, where we're constantly chopping and changing our minds.

Thus, if (premise):

Charlie is a Duck,

and (premise):

Ducks are a subset of Flying Birds,

Then (conclusion):

Charlie can fly.

But (additional information):

Charlie is dead.

All that conventional monotonic logic can make of this—since the second premise must stand—is to create a new subset of Dead Ducks That Fly.

This creates complications in trying to define general rules, since it requires any exceptions that need to be taken into account to be specified explicitly. Depicting real-world situations with any degree of authenticity soon becomes unmanageable. Take our example, once again, of wanting to get to San Francisco. General rule: "You can use the phone to call a friend there to have him meet you when you arrive." Now try to think of all the exceptions that would make it not true and thus call for some other action:

Your phone or his phone isn't working.

You don't have his number.

The phone book is missing.

The page is torn out of the book.

Somebody inked over the number.

His phone is newly installed, and Information doesn't have the number.

Information does have a number, but it's wrong.

His number is unlisted.

He's out of town.

His house is on fire, and he isn't taking calls right now.

And so on indefinitely.

Humans incorporate such "nonmonotonic" provisos all the time into our way of dealing with the world, which holds that things generally work unless there's a good reason why they don't. But trying to tell a program how to deal with every conceivable eventuality through the journey would obviously soon get out of hand—and would be futile in the end anyway since something else could always be added that the modified rules didn't cover.

Some workers have tried using numerical probabilities to weight the likely outcomes of situations, but it isn't really the basis for a suitable method. For one thing, the numbers may be unobtainable or little better than somebody's guess, or they may be inconvenient to apply. And for another, knowing some general probability is irrelevant when the matter that concerns us is a particular instance of a particular situation. Thus, while it might be true, statistically, that the average bird has a high probability of being able to fly, the information wouldn't be any help for making bets in Charlie's case.

The method that John McCarthy has developed is known as *circumscription*, which he describes as a rule of conjecture for jumping to certain conclusions. Basically, it states that the only factors that can prevent a general rule from being applied are those whose existence follows from the facts at hand. Circumscription can be especially useful in situations where detailed weighting evidence of relevant factors is not available and snap decisions are called for. The correctness of its conclusions do depend on all the factors of relevance being taken into account when the conditions are defined. Hence, it doesn't match humans' flexibility for adapting to sudden changes of perspectives and circumstances. But nobody claims that it does. Formal systems of nonmonotonic reasoning remain the subject of much of McCarthy's ongoing work today.

MARVIN MINSKY'S FRAMES OF MIND

Trying to create intelligent programs brings home just how much information is required in even such apparently straightforward tasks as making a phone call or deciding what a bird is. The reason we don't need to saturate each other with detail to convey a simple fact or make a request is that we presume that most of the information necessary to complete what we mean will be filled in by the listener. We just supply what doesn't fit the shared pattern—the parts that deviate from the other person's expectations.

In the early seventies, Marvin Minsky, at that time involved in a seeing-robot project among other things, hypothesized that this could be how we go about abstracting information from the world in general—visually, for example, as well as via personal communication. The suggestion was that a lot of what we think we see is actually supplied by preexisting expectations and what the perceptual system concerns itself with to a large degree is finding and interpreting the parts that are novel. Certainly, that would help account for the way we avoid the impossibly high processing loads that would be implied if all the raw data constantly assailing us from the outside had to be analyzed and reintegrated from the bottom up. Minsky's theory was published in a 1975 essay, "A Framework for Representing Knowledge." The concept quickly caught on among AI researchers and stimulated ideas that in various evolved forms and guises underlie much of the experimental work continuing today.

The associative character of memory, whereby whole strings of related scenes, events, and other concepts can be triggered by a few key words, was receiving much attention at that time. Consider again the complexities of scenery and background situation evoked by something as simple as "Robin rode through the forest." Clearly, a lot of memory and inferential reasoning is involved in constructing the pictures that spring to mind. Traditional psychological theories seemed to be based on memory retrieval in increments that were either too small or too large. Having to reassemble meaningful impressions from primitive data elements would be too rule-intensive and slow; yet it would be impractical to store entire scenes and attempt to match them in real time against our experiences. Minsky's answer was to propose an intermediate structure that he termed a "frame," large enough to constitute a conceptual unit yet small enough to number millions and yield virtually unlimited complexity through combination.

A frame is a kind of skeleton concept, like an application form with a lot of blank spaces needing to be filled in. Minsky referred to these as *terminals*. A terminal is a connection point for attaching further information. So the "chair" frame would consist of a basic notion of something for sitting on that falls between "couch/settee/sofa" and "stool," with terminals to be filled in as appropriate for "legs," "back," "arms," and so forth. "Person" would have terminals for "body," "arms," "size," "hair," and so on. To complete the picture for a particular chair or person, we fill in the slots with details specific for that case. The information to attach to a terminal can come from all kinds of sources; particularly noteworthy, it could be another frame that comes complete with its own set of terminals, such as an "arm" frame with terminals for "hand," "fingers," "watch," or "sleeve." Thus the whole system is hierarchical.

A terminal doesn't have to have any information to complete it at all—a chair might not have arms, or it might have a center post instead of legs. Normally, though—and this is what makes frames attractive—they come with "default" assignments already filled in with what our experiences lead us to consider "typical." So we assume that shoes appearing beneath trousers have feet inside even though we can't see them, that obscured legs of a chair are nevertheless there, and so on. Hence, we automatically make "reasonable" assumptions involving enormous amounts of information that would otherwise have to be supplied explicitly. However, where the actuality doesn't bear out the assumption, the default is replaced by whatever specific information applies. When told that Charlie is a duck, we likely conjure up a generic picture of a green-headed bird with a white band around the neck, flying over marshes or waddling up out of a pond. When it's added that "Charlie is dead," we have no difficulty changing the image to one of a less fortunate avian plucked and hanging in a meat-and-poultry store.

By bringing our previous experiences to bear on every situation, default assignments have an enormous impact on all facets of our lives, affecting how we reason, recognize things, generalize, make predictions, and act when what we expect doesn't materialize. Learning, Minsky contends, consists to a large degree of creating new frames by modifying existing ones and adding them to our collection. When meeting a stranger we seem able to react almost instantly, but, to a far greater degree than we're conscious of, what we react to lies not so much in what we see as in what the sight "reminds" us of. As soon as we perceive "person," superficial similarities of appearance and behavior start activating defaults that we've associated with individuals we've met previously, biasing us toward a constellation of presumptions that we're more likely than not unaware of. When this results in opinions and attitudes that we disapprove of we call it "stereotyping"; otherwise, it's praised as displaying "sensitivity" and "empathy."

Framelike structures could also be involved with the way we comprehend ordinary language. Consider, for example, the consequences of hearing or reading the two simple sentences:

Mary was invited to Jack's party. She wondered if he would like a kite.

Ask a child what the kite was for, and you'd probably get a strange look and the answer that it was "obviously" something to take to the party as Jack's birthday present. Why? "Birthday" was never mentioned, and neither was "present." And, we didn't specifically say that "she" is Mary and "he" is Jack or that either or both of them are children. But a picture of that general kind would be clear enough in most people's minds—*unless something specifically told them differently.*

That's what we call common sense, which involves a whole chain of knowing that a kite is a toy, toys are typical presents for children, children get presents on birthdays, birthdays are occasions for parties, parties involve inviting other friends, and hence a reasonable assumption is that Mary and Jack are children. How is all this scattered information brought together into a mental picture that we're able to create vividly—complete with notions of gaily colored wrappings, balloons, games, ice cream, and other things similarly never mentioned—even before the sentence is finished? In Minsky's submission, an entire "party-invitation" frame that comes complete with default attachments already in place, which we put together in the course of growing up in our culture, is activated.

Frames as a means of setting expectations could also say a lot about our grammatical sense as discussed previously and why we are comfortable with some structures but not others. To take an example from Minsky, *Round squares steal honestly* strikes us as correct, even though we can form no clear idea of what it's supposed to mean. The structure fits with a well-established sentence frame in which the words naturally fall into slots where the adjective, noun, verb, and adverb slots say they ought to be.

But while grammar becomes necessary to convey more finely graded shades of meaning, elaborate chains of meaning can be conveyed without any grammatical form at all. For example, the disconnected sequence *thief . . . careless . . . prison* bypasses grammar frames completely, yet it takes on a clearly discerned meaning in terms of a moral tale about crime and just reward by calling up a familiar story frame. Imagine the amount of explicit explanation that would be needed in programming a computer to understand pidgin.

A final interesting example from Minsky is that we appear to use framelike structures for setting expectations as to the order in which adjectives should arrive, so we know what to do with them.

The wooden three heavy brown big first boxes . . .

leaves our mental decoder choking in perplexity. Yet the same words re-arranged to:

The first three big brown heavy wooden boxes . . .

are processed without effort.

Expectations seem to form a large part of the mechanism by which we perceive patterns and likenesses. Much of our esthetic sense, for example, in hearing music as structures stems from the satisfaction of creating expectations and having them satisfied. Much humor is based on deliberately building up expectations and switching to an unanticipated completion.

(It shouldn't be surprising if some of this sounds somewhat reminiscent of Ross Quillian's semantic nets and Schanks and Abelson's "Scripts." Different attempts at mapping the same territory should, after all, show resemblances.)

Not everybody was excited by Minsky's formulation into a general theory of frames, however. The most common complaint was that its explanations were too vague, offering little guidance as to what researchers interested in pursuing the notion further were actually supposed to *do*. Minsky defends it as being "at just the right level-band in detail." While agreeing that the theory would have been ignored had it been any vaguer, he believes that describing it in more detail would have consigned others to just testing it instead of getting involved creatively and contributing their own ideas. Instead, he contends, many versions were suggested by others, which was what caused "frame-based" programming to become popular. Herbert Simon was among those not especially dazzled. One of the main things he and Allen Newell needed for the IPL languages they used with GPS, Simon told Daniel Crevier, was a way of representing more general relations than list structures. To meet it, they came up with "description lists" of "attribute pairs" that plugged into "slots" contained in what were described as "themas." Clearly, he didn't see what all the fuss was about. "As far as I'm concerned," Simon grumbled, "I've been using frames since 1956."

Induction and Inference

GENERALIZING

Parties are great. We get to play games and eat ice cream.
Einstein liked cowboy movies.
All crows are black.
Planetary orbits follow an inverse-square law of gravitation.

We hear statements like this all the time and rarely, if ever—unless we're philosophers, programmers, or somebody trying to write about such people— think twice about them. Nearly our whole conceptual world-model is built out of pieces of information of this kind and the ways we connect them together.

"Connect together" are the operative words here. They describe the kinds of observations that children are already expert at making long before they learn to articulate them. Yet, as perhaps we're coming to anticipate by now, what's easy for children to do turns out to be extraordinarily difficult to get computers to do. The difficulty isn't so much one of communicating the concept—a computer program can obviously apply something like the inverse-square law to calculating orbits once it's been given it; it's more a case of getting a program to arrive at the concept for itself in the first place. (And while we're at it, why did it seem reasonable to me to guess that the reader might be "coming to anticipate" anything a few lines above? You see, we do it all the time.)

The everyday reasoning—arriving at conclusions from the information available—of humans is different from the rigorous logic embodied in computer programs. Humans reflect traits that were handed down as a result of being part of the makeup of ancestors who were better at surviving long enough to hand them down. Our strengths lie in an ability not only to make plausible snap decisions in a highly complex environment but to do so in such a way as to be capable of modifying them or, if necessary, changing them completely in the light of further experience. That kind of logic doesn't require that the answer be right every time; in fact, it would be less effective if it were. When survival is at stake, settling for a good-enough answer sooner is a better strategy than waiting any longer for a perfect answer that might never get applied at all. Hence, we trade guaranteed accuracy for speed and hope that the answers we get wrong don't include any of the really important ones (which tends, over time, to be a self-correcting problem).

Computers, on the other hand, are suited to just the opposite kind of domain—which shouldn't be surprising since we devised them specifically to be good at things that we're not—where the environment is very constrained and predictable and precise, irreversible solutions are required. After all, who'd want to set up an elaborate marketing campaign, or have all the designs complete and subcontractors selected for building a jet airliner, only to be told "the computer has changed its mind again"? Such machines would be useless for the purposes we use them for, and creating systems with the complexity of a modern commercial airliner would probably be impossible.

WHAT'S INDUCTION?
LET ME GIVE YOU A FEW EXAMPLES

Computers are powerful engines for *deducing* consequences from premises. Give them the general rules, Newton's gravitational law, for example, and they can apply it to determining the outcome of any particular instance, such as predicting where and when the next lunar eclipse will take place or how to aim a gun to land an artillery shell on a target.

But as any parent, teacher, or speaker knows, rather than reciting general rules or principles, a better way of getting a point across to humans is often to give examples. Compare the effectiveness of intoning "A solid of revolution is generated by rotating a surface about an axis" with "Rotating a rectangle about one of its edges makes a cylinder; rotating a semicircle about the diameter makes a sphere. Get the idea?"

"Getting the idea"—inferring the general rule from a limited number of instances—is something humans do amazingly well (very often too well; we're also very good at seeing causes and connections that don't exist). Called *induction*, it represents the inverse process of deduction, in which particular cases are derived from the general. Induction is what enables us to get the message after one or two painful experiences that hot things burn or that big animals with black and yellow stripes should be treated with respect and caution. Those with built-in deficiencies for such reasoning are unlikely to produce descendants.

Induction can follow from premises that are certain and still be wrong: "The last three times we planned on going to the beach, it rained" might be true, but to infer "Whenever we want to go to the beach, it rains" is an overstatement. Deduction arrives at conclusions that are incontestably valid but only as true as the premises "Whenever we want to go to the beach, it rains. We're planning to go to the beach next Sunday. Next Sunday, it will rain." Whatever you do, it seems you can't win.

Philosophers, for the most part, exist in conditions that have progressed considerably toward being stable and secure as opposed to life-threatening and hence attach greater value to rigor and predictability than timeliness of results. Since inductive conclusions, however many times they are reinforced by confirming instances, and despite the absence of a single observed exception, can never be shown, rigorously, to be true (how do you *prove* that the sun will come up tomorrow?), philosophers have never been comfortable about admitting the respectability of inductive reasoning. David Hume, in the early nineteenth century, was one of the first to make it a serious issue, much of Immanuel Kant's work was an attempt to refute him, and the debate has carried on ever since without ever really being settled. Fortunately, the human race and other biological organisms continue to place their bets and survive regardless.

What causes the discomfort is that inductive conclusions go beyond the premises, and so the former cannot be a logical consequence of the latter. But this is another way of saying that inductive reasoning leads from what is known to the unknown, which is the only way to discover anything new. Hence, induction plays a leading role in science; indeed, it has been described as the essence of the scientific method. However, merely making conjectures and guessing at general laws on the basis of apparent regularities and coincidences would be arbitrary and useless—the word for it is "superstition"—without testing them against actuality.

All crows are black illustrates the fundamental asymmetry of inductive theories, first appreciated by Francis Bacon in the sixteenth century. No amount of confirming instances will suffice to "prove" this true since every crow in existence would have to be checked, and it could never be said with certainty that that had been done. Only a single, verified instance of a nonblack crow would be enough to disprove the statement. We insist on such *falsifiability* as a condition of a theory's being validly "scientific." If there's no way of showing a theory to be false, then not a lot more about it can usefully be said.

Predicting results that ought to be observed in particular instances—called experiments—if the induced rules are correct, is where the rigor of deduction plays its part. Indeed, the aim of science is often said to be the making of successful predictions. Thus, a series of observations of how the moon and the planets move, coupled with an intuitive leap of putting the sun in the center, leads to a general gravitation law expressible as an inverse-square relationship. Deduction from that law enables predictions of future astronomic observations, which, when confirmed, add confidence to the theory. In dress regalia the complete process is known as the *hypothetico-deductive experimental method*. Biological organisms, with their necks (maybe metaphoric ones) on the line serving in the role of predictive experiment call it having the smarts to get by.

EXAGGERATION AND UNDERSTATEMENT—
WE DO IT *ALL THE TIME*

The best that can be said about an inductive conclusion is that it's very probably true, which is a politically tactful way of saying that sometimes one won't be. When a scientific theory turns out to be wrong and has to be revised, the error is often a result of overgeneralizing or undergeneralizing. To a computer program diligently trying to get the hang of this generalizing business, it wouldn't be so bad if the statements that it was supposed to base its guesses on could always be relied upon to mean what they said, i.e., were expressed in a precise and consistent language. This is the way science tries to work, and programs written to make inductive inferences in areas where precise representations are available, such as fitting curves to experimental data points or inferring geometric patterns, have met with considerable success. This doesn't, however, get them very far toward reasoning the way humans do because humans don't generalize in the same precise, consistent way.

Take, for example, the elastic way in which we interpret the continuum *none . . . some . . . many . . . most . . . all* in casual conversation. No sane person would take the statement *Parties are great. We get to play games and eat ice cream* at the beginning of this section as meaning *all* parties, although that's what a literal-minded computer would hear. And in the statement *Einstein liked cowboy movies*, a human sees at once that what's meant is this: as a fraction of the cowboy movies that Einstein watched, compared to a similar figure for other kinds of movies that Einstein watched, he found the cowboy ones enjoyable to a degree that the speaker assumes most people would find significant.

Oh, so does whoever is saying this have the actual numbers?

No.

Is the speaker saying that Einstein saw all cowboy movies?

Of course not.

So did he enjoy every one that he did see?

Probably not.

The computer mind boggles at what it's supposed to make of the statement.

Schemes have been tried for using probabilities and statistics to produce programs that will get a measure of things like this, but such approaches miss the point. When we say things like *Everybody in town showed up; the line stretched around the block* or *Nobody showed up; the place was empty,* whether the words are literally true or not and what the exact numbers were is irrelevant; what we're talking about is the quality of a movie.

In principle, yes, you could write rules telling the program when to alter its number weightings, how to interpret "some" and "most," when to take extremes literally. But covering all the conceivable instances and exceptions quickly becomes a combinatorial explosion and turns into another version of John McCarthy's qualification problem again.

So, our computer program trying to get a human's-eye view of the world might well ask bemusedly, if we don't use numbers or formal logic, and even the sloppy language that we do use can mean different things at different times, then what's left that a computer can trust and rely on? After all, if we're blathering about activating similar "structures" residing somewhere in what we assume to be a similarly formed mind, isn't that saying that there must be something at the bottom of it all that remains constant from one individual to another? Yes, there is, and it's at the root of this shared—"common"—sense that we find it so difficult to convey to anything that doesn't naturally share it: our uncanny ability to find the same patterns and similarities—between objects and feelings, situations and people, ideas and things—in the unlikeliest of places. It underlies just about everything that we perceive, say, and do. Probably the most visible expression is in our use of analogy and metaphor.

An Analogy Is Like a Lens:
Focusing Attention in the Right Place

FINDING "LIKENESS"

At the beginning of the seventies, R. E. Kling of Stanford developed a program called ZORBA, which he described as using reasoning by analogy to reduce the massive search-spaces associated with proving theorems of abstract algebra.[2] The principle was to select from the total axiom set available a subset that had already been shown as sufficient to prove theorems determined to be "analogous to" the current theorem. Here, however, we're concerned with analogy more as used in the everyday sense—by humans as opposed to theorem provers.

The principle of analogy is straightforward enough: a concept that is new or complex is made clearer by comparing it with something similar that's already understood. Some people, for example, aren't sure what a turbine is.

"It's like a fan, only it gets driven by the air or whatever, instead of doing the driving."

"Oh, okay. I get it."

Such direct analogy, based on immediate physical similarities, is the simplest and most obvious kind. Describing the workings and parts of the eye in terms of a camera is another, familiar example. Recognizing the correspondence of identifiable parts generalizes easily into analogies between physical systems in general—electricity is often explained in terms of fluid flow, where voltage plays the part of hydraulic pressure, resistance is the counterpart of the constrictiveness of pipes, and so on. In fact, "analog computers" work by setting up electrical circuits in such a way that the mathematical equations relating the voltages and currents are analogies of the ones the computer is required to solve.

Less direct are cases where the similarity that's meant is present among others, which it's assumed any listener above the imbecile level will ignore as being beside the point. When somebody says, *That car of his is built like a tank,* he doesn't mean it's assembled from engineered components and driven by an internal combustion engine, although all of that is true. The same could be said of a lawn mower, helicopter, or power sled. What we're supposed to home in on are the qualities for which "tank" was singled out that make it *different* from other things like it. When we hear *Henry runs his company the way he used to run his ship,* we know the point isn't that his company has a "captain" heading a team of "officers" who oversee a workforce "crew." All companies do. What we understand is that the management style is more authoritarian and rule-driven than is normally considered appropriate in civilian environments. Again, the aspect of running ships that we're supposed to pick out is selected precisely for being *not* like the running of companies. So already analogies are becoming tricky things, and uncertainty is starting to creep in as to exactly what the rules are. We can sense our computer program's rising apprehension that this is going to get worse.

Which, of course, it promptly does, when the humans that it's trying to follow start comparing things that have nothing readily discernible in common at all:

Janet got the promotion and was thrown straight in at the deep end.

Order is an exotic in Ireland. It has been imported from England but it will not grow. It is suited neither to the climate nor the soil. (J. A. Froude)

At times, the meaning to be understood is just the opposite of what's stated:

Ain't had so much fun since my draft physical.

The assault troops slipped through the night with the stealth of a combine harvester.

And sometimes our ingenuity permits us to construct analogies that are purely verbal, and you can take your pick among interpretations. A classic has to be the remark attributed to the British orchestra conductor Sir Thomas Beecham to a lady cellist:

Madam, you have between your legs an instrument capable of giving pleasure to thousands—and all you can do is scratch it.[3]

TWO PARTS TO AN ANALOGY:
REPRESENTATION AND MAPPING

We mentioned early AI programs that recognized the analogous roles of things like the geometric shapes used in some IQ tests and the parts of similar structures such as arches and pedestals. Though these were fine as far as they went, there are two fundamental sides to constructing analogies, and programs like these really only addressed one of them. The first is forming a representation of an object or situation; the second consists of mapping features of the representation against corresponding features of whatever it is being compared to. Although T. G. Evans's ANALOGY program (the one that compared IQ test patterns) did go some way toward deciding how to build its representations, most applications focused on the mapping function. The main reason was no doubt that exactly how to go about constructing high-level conceptual representations from low-level data was a difficult problem—nor does it have a clear solution today, for that matter; this was the point of David Marr's insistence on going right down to basics to make artificial vision work.

In the meantime, until a system exists that is able to construct representations for itself, the representations used have to be supplied by the programmers. There is an implication here that at some later time it will be possible to add a low-level "front-end" to the system that will deliver the same representations. This carries the assumption that high-level cognitive concepts can be modeled as unique sets of properties and relationships independent of perception. It's not clear, however, that this is valid. What we see in a situation—in other words, the characteristics that need to be presented to an analogy mapping system for comparison—is intimately tied in with the circumstances, our beliefs and purpose, and what we're looking for.

Philosophers and psychologists recognized this a long time ago. William James wrote in 1890: *There is no property that is ABSOLUTELY essential to one thing. The same property which figures as the essence of a thing on one occasion becomes a very inessential feature upon another.* I see very different aspects of even something as basic as a piece of paper, depending on whether I want to write a letter, kindle a fire, wedge the leg of a table, cover a carpet against spills, make an origami pattern, or any number of countless uses—to which one could always add more. So what properties would a front-end perception system provide as its representation? To pick out the right ones to suit the purpose of the moment, it would have to know what the purpose of the moment is, which means it would have to interact with the cognitive system and couldn't simply be added afterward, independently. If, on the other hand, the front-end tries to deliver *every* conceivable interpretation for the cognitive system to select what it wants, the possibilities multiply without limit and we run into the frame problem again.

This—finding the right representation—is surely the significant issue that has to be addressed as far as progress in the AI sense is concerned, after which the mapping aspect becomes fairly straightforward. Yet it's not always apparent from some of the enthusiastic claims that have been made for what are essentially representation mapping programs that this adequately acknowledged.

An example that's widely cited is a program called Structural Mapping Engine, or SME, originally developed at Bolt Beraneck and Newman in 1990, continued at the University of Illinois, and which now resides at Northwestern University. In one of its demonstrations it is said to have discovered the analogy between the solar system and atomic structure that most people are familiar with from schoolroom physics. Figure 16.1 shows schematically the representational structures of the two situations that the program is given in the form of statements in the predicate calculus. It then evaluates various possible correspondences between elements as to how well they preserve the high-level structures of these representations, and selects the one with the highest score as the best analogical mapping.

Selecting the representations and deciding which data are relevant has already been done, pretty much setting the program up. The only relationships provided are "attracts," "revolves around," "gravity," "opposite sign," and "greater," precisely those required to make the analogy intended. But suppose we had comprehensive representations that were independent of the context provided by a particular problem, giving information, say, on the systems of moons as well as the planets, axial rotations and inclinations, the compositions and surface features of the various bodies, which ones had atmospheres, ring systems, magnetic fields; and, of an atom, its electronic quantum states, its energy levels, and their transitions. I wonder what the program would make of that.

Another program, called BACON, dating from its beginnings at CMU around the mid-eighties, is said to have discovered, among other things, Boyle's law of ideal gases, Kepler's third law of planetary motion, Galileo's law of uniform acceleration, and Ohm's law of electrical resistance, starting with the same initial conditions and using the same original data as the human discoverers. Heady stuff, indeed. On the face of it, surely a breakthrough.

But again it turns out that what was accomplished was a mapping between representations that had been preselected to fit the problem—in this case, between data pertaining to a physical system and mathematical equations describing its behavior. Taking Kepler's third law as an example, the program was given only data on the planets' mean distance from the sun and their orbital periods and told to find an equation relating them. From all the things that could be said about the motions of planets, these are precisely the data required to yield the third law as we, with hindsight, know it.

Using "the original data" evidently does not mean *all* the original data, which in Kepler's case were for the most part irrelevant, misleading, or plain wrong. The situation confronting Kepler was that at the turn of the seventeenth century, when Copernicus's work was new and far from being universally accepted, there was no notion of forces to produce planetary motion and the sun was regarded purely as a source of light—and, in any case, the idea of the cause of motion lying ninety degrees to the side of the motion observed would have been thought strange by most people, to say the least. Even the concept of using mathematical equations to describe natural relationships was still

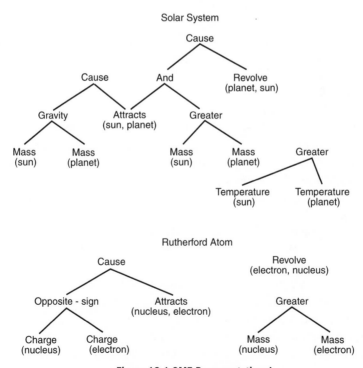

Figure 16.1 SME Representations[4]

rare. And a strong influence on Kepler's thought was the observation that planets' distances from the sun happen to be such that the five regular poly-hedral solids of classical geometry fit into the five planetary "spheres," a seductive but misleading coincidence that pressed for a geometric rather than an algebraic solution. Not only this, but a whole host of conceptual frameworks such as religious symbolism and Christian cosmology were in competition, any of which, for all Kepler knew, might have been the correct one for explaining the regularities of planetary motion.

Within this context, it becomes understandable why it took Kepler thirteen years to unscramble that conic sections, not Platonic solids; ellipses, not Aristotle's "perfect" circles; and distances, not the polyhedra that they fit into, were the *relevant* factors. It's difficult to believe that he would have taken this much time had he been supplied with a table of mean distances and periods and asked to find a polynomial to fit them. A study conducted in 1990 found that university students starting with the data that BACON was given could make the same derivation within an hour (compared to BACON's minutes). So either Kepler was spending a lot of time on things they didn't have to trouble themselves with, or natural intelligence is evolving at a faster pace than we realize. Given some of humanity's other performances during the same interim period, it's difficult to give the second alternative much credence.

DOUGLAS HOFSTADTER'S NUMBER SEQUENCES

Douglas Hofstadter is an atypical figure in the AI world in not having graduated into the field through the major centers that we have met repeatedly through this book. His Ph.D. was in physics, which he obtained in 1975 at the University of Oregon. After a two-year, privately funded stay at the Institute of Mathematical Studies and Social Sciences at Stanford, he moved to Indiana University, where he continues his work today as a professor of cognitive science. There, he and a dedicated group of graduates and students, explore and endeavor to model the aspects of cognition by which we find "likenesses" in number and letter patterns, and to perceive constancy of underlying alphabetic form through wildly varying ranges of character designs and typefaces.

The amazing human capacity to find analogies in everything from number sequences and landscapes to why the vice president is the spare tire on the automobile of government has always fascinated Hofstadter. His 1979 classic, *Gödel, Escher, Bach,* was a seven-hundred-page exposition of the philosophy of AI set against an ongoing three-way structural analogy drawn between mathematical logic, geometric depiction, and musical construction. Like his writing, Hofstadter's work tends to follow his own whims and fancies with little regard to what the current fads are or what's getting public attention. "I suppose I'm a bit of an outsider because I don't attract DARPA money into the right departments," he told me wryly when I talked to him. "And then when I write a book that does well, it's 'Oh, he's just a popularizer.' "

Hofstadter has long had a fascination for number series, and for one of his projects he set his students challenges to produce programs capable of divining the underlying patterns governing sequences such as:

2,1,2,2,2,2,2,3,2,2,4,2,2,5,2, . . .

or:

1,1,2,1,1,1,2,3,2,2,1,1,2,3,4,3,3,2,1,1,2,3,4,5,4,4,3,2,1, . . .

To give a feel for the kind of thing to expect, Hofstadter's project was more concerned with pattern and analogy of structure than arithmetic relationships. As an example of what this means, consider the two sequences:

A: 1,2,3,4,5,5,4,3,2,1

B: 1,2,3,4,4,3,2,1

Now ask, what plays the role in B that 4 plays in A? (Note, this leaves it to the solver to decide what the role of 4 actually is in A—the idea being that this is for the program to figure out.) Most people would say 3, on the basis that both sequences have a central pair of equal digits; 4 precedes the central pair in A, and the digit that plays the same role in B is 3.

Then how about the same question asked of C?

C: 1,2,3,4,5,6,6,6,6,5,4,3,2,1

The central pair in this case is 66, which is flanked on either side by 6s. Although there could be no *logical* objection to 6 as the answer, most people prefer 5. Human instinct seems to see pattern and structure before logic. Our tendency is to generalize the "central pair" notion to "central entity"—in this case a "plateau" of 6666—and see 5 as the element that precedes it. Let's play with the theme a little more:

D: 1,1,2,2,3,3,4,4,5,4,4,3,3,2,2,1,1,

Now we've retained the original structure but reversed the roles of the elements from which it's formed. Instead of a "hill" (which is what many people quickly perceive) consisting of slopes rising from both sides in single-digit steps toward a multidigit plateau, we now have slopes of double-digit steps rising to a single digit at the center. Again, a perfectly "logical" choice might be 4 since it's next to the center. But wouldn't it be truer to the spirit of the structural interpretation to generalize the notion of "element" further and say 44, on the basis of its being the element preceding the central one, namely 5? This might be easier to see by grouping the digits:

D: (1,1,)(2,2,)(3,3,)(4,4,)5(4,4)(3,3)(2,2,)(1,1,)

Very well, now what happens when we try it with:

E: 1,2,3,4,6,5,5,6,4,3,2,1

Now we've added a crater. There seem to be three ways to go in answering what plays the role of the original 4: 6, conforming rigidly to the previous notion of flanking the central plateau; 5, for those who remain unimpressed by central elements and seek the number second to the highest; and 4, which results from generalizing the "central entity" notion further to take in the crater and see 4 as preceding it. There's no "right" answer. It's more a question of what "feels right," and even before we get to this point not everyone agrees. So how do you program it as a set of rules?

And now that we've said a little more about the principles, the pattern of the first sequence given originally becomes clear on rewriting it as:

$(2,1,2,)(2,2,2,)(2,3,2,)(2,4,2,)(2,5,2,)$ . . .

which can be expressed as the general "template" $(2,n,2)$, where $n = 1, 2, 3$ . . .

Without the parentheses, the burst of five 2s in a row is confusing, especially for anyone looking for an arithmetical law to continue the terms. It results from their being a mixture of two "kinds" of 2s: the two 2s constant in every group and the value of n enumerating the second group.

The second sequence is understood readily by charting it as another landscape:

1,   1,2,1,1,   1,2,3,2,2,1,   1,2,3,4,3,3,2,1,   1,2,3,4,5,4,4,3,2,1,

Figure 16.2 Variation on a Theme: Expanding Hill with Plateau

Hofstadter's programs don't make any claims about understanding or perceiving complex relationships in the real world. But in their own tiny domains, they are extracting for themselves the features they find relevant and using them to construct representations appropriate to a particular context. This is getting down to the crux of what recognizing context-relevance is all about. My own guess is that true inference and generalizing ability spring from modest beginnings like these.

This instinctive sense of what "matters" is what enables us to pick out from a complex environment what things to think about when invited to a birthday party or when organizing a flight to San Francisco, how to know when *everybody in town saw that movie* doesn't mean "everybody in town saw that movie," and so on. The rules are fluid, which is what makes them so difficult to formalize. What doesn't matter in one setting can become crucially important in another.

A program with no basis for connecting together and extracting one aspect of reality in preference to any other is confronted by a virtual infinity of undigested facts, any of which may or may not be pertinent to what it's trying to accomplish at the time. To investigate the consequences and exceptions for everything is impossible, but trying to get the rules out of humans as to how they manage is like asking them what they have to "do" to see a duck. The only answer one can give is, "I just open my eyes and it's there." Actually, like walking and talking, it probably took us a long time to learn to see things like ducks. We've simply forgotten how much work was involved.

The knack that we possess for instantly zeroing in on things, or people, or situations that are "like" one another in some subtle but relevant way is absorbed deep into our unconscious. It reveals itself, however, in the way that we've already said represents not just a way of communicating but is an outward expression of all the processes that make us cognitive, thinking beings: our use of language. It is revealed particularly in the verbal analogies we make all the time that show how we perceive and think: the universal human use of metaphor.

Metaphor: Recycled Experience

Analogies are comparisons that we make deliberately and use language to describe. Sometimes they are constructed consciously and carefully; at other times, a familiar form may come to mind so naturally that its analogous nature fails to register. But we also build conceptual connections of a deeper nature from the world of direct experience in which we are constantly immersed. These are the metaphors that reflect what and how we perceive; rather than being something that language describes, they shape the very language we use. Metaphor pervades every aspect of the conceptual system that determines how we think and act. Analogies say something about a part of the world as we see it; the way we use metaphors perhaps says more about us.

Metaphor is the understanding and experiencing of one thing—revealed in the way we speak of it—as if it were another. Frequently, the result is to render an abstract concept more tangible by treating it as if it were an object that we can think of in the way we do concrete things. Thus, we might talk quite easily about, say, a theory "collapsing" or an idea "evaporating." Towers collapse. A puddle can evaporate. But of theories and ideas? The words are hijacked from a physical realm where theories and ideas don't exist. But the words we borrow say much about how we conceive the abstraction to which we apply them.

In giving theories and ideas the attributes of physical structures and substance, they become objects of an extended vocabulary in which theories can be "well-grounded," "rickety," "demolished," or "besieged." Having permitted ideas to evaporate, we are now free to "swallow," "digest," "chew over," or "choke on" them. Notice also that assigning to intellectual invention the qualities of tangible property also means that it can be bought, sold, stolen, transferred—notions that, for all we know, might be literally inconceivable in a different culture.

In their book *Metaphors We Live By*, George Lakoff and Mark Johnson give an illuminating example (suns and lamps illuminate, but examples?) of a concept's being metaphorical and how such a concept can influence everyday attitudes and activity. The conceptual metaphor ARGUMENT IS WAR is reflected in many familiar expressions:

He attacked *every point in my argument.*
They'll shoot you down *if you try that* strategy.
The criticisms were right on target.

Yet in their essentials warfare and argument are very different. One consists of armed conflict, where the purpose is to crush and destroy; the other is verbal discourse, with the aim . . . of what? How much of the way we "engage" those of different beliefs or opinions will presume an adversarial confrontation with an outcome unconsciously conditioned by the way we regard war? What purpose can this serve in science, say, where whatever is true will remain so with complete indifference to how passionately some would prefer things to be otherwise, or how many they persuade to share their convictions? Lakoff and Johnson invite us to imagine a culture where argument is not viewed as war, where no one wins or loses or defends or gains ground. The metaphor they offer as an alternative is argument as a dance, but I prefer the picture of a team of climbers scaling a metaphoric mountain of ignorance. What differences might such a conceptual shift make to our personal relationships and collective enterprises such as science?

One of our most basic qualities is that we exist as physical entities bounded from the rest of the world by an enclosing surface. This makes each of us a container with an orientation that distinguishes "inside" and "outside." Having developed an ability to apply this faculty easily and deftly, we use it to a remarkable degree as a way of conceptualizing as "containers" areas of abstraction that have no correspondence with physical space. Here are a few sample everyday container metaphors:

Occupations: How did you get *into* computer programming?
Duty/obligation: It was his round, but he wriggled *out of* it.
Visual field: The plane is *in* sight now.
Circumstances: Every year he was *in* some kind of trouble.
Condition: Another month and I'll be *out of* debt.
Linguistic expression: It's an *open and closed* case.
Life: Her life was *full* of opportunity.

In a related vein, hundreds of expressions exist "in"(!) English that apply the metaphor of a "conduit" transferring objects of some kind (which might be "containers") from one place to another. Over 70 percent of them involve some form of communication:

I can't *get* the idea *across* to him.
He put it *in* the report, which *went through* yesterday.
The point was lost *along the way.*
I couldn't fault the *delivery.* I just wish it had more *content.*

Container and conduit metaphors are just two examples of the ubiquitous use we make of metaphors that invoke extent in, or motion through, physical space. We naturally extend and project the conceptual grounding derived from our real, experiential world:

> *Try* looking at *the problem from a different* angle *and you might* get somewhere.
> *The argument just* wanders *all over the* place.
> In *one week, they've* covered *quite a lot of* ground.

And last, consider how many desirable, positive things (health, optimism, wealth, success) are "up" and how many negative, undesirable things (sickness, dejection, bad times, poor luck) are "down."

Marvin Minsky doesn't think it's any accident that we frame so many of our thoughts in spatial terms. Much of the way we think in later life is based on what we learned at the beginning of life in our first explorations of space. Treating our more abstract and complex thoughts as if they were things enables us to economize by pressing our existing mental machinery into service and reusing it for new tasks. Processes that have been refined over millions of years to facilitate orientating, moving around, and interacting in a complex physical environment shape the way we see the world today and represent it in the forms the processes have always used. Although they function for the most part invisibly, buried in the unconscious parts of our thinking, the processes reveal themselves in the ways we use language.

Rediscovering "Mind"

A SCIENCE OF GENERAL COGNITION

Finally, then, we seem to be getting close to the roots of that all-around general-purposiveness Alan Turing sought that makes us "human." Our elusive common sense is the result of taking the result of several hundred million years of cumulative genetic experience expressed as a sensory and neural package and running it through several decades of the intensive learning process called life. Now that we've looked a little more closely into some of the things that it involves, what can we say about the prospects for reproducing it artificially?

Apart from the fact that it's a far more involved business than some apparently perceived it to be forty years ago, the only honest answer is, not a lot. But the changed light we can view the question in today is itself a result of the work done during that time. Putting together a comprehensive account of human mental activity involves not only the reasoning and problem-solving processes investigated by traditional AI but findings from, among other things, communications and information processing, computation, the various neural and behavioral sciences, philosophy, psychology, linguistics, child development, and interpersonal relations. Since the eighties, a discipline consolidating elements drawn from all these areas has emerged under the name "cognitive science." It's devoted to the study of cognition in all its aspects, in particular to those general principles common to human and machine—and, for all one knows, one day, perhaps, alien—forms of intelligence. Indeed, some researchers in what would almost certainly have been referred to as "AI" fifteen years ago, wary of the commercialization and instances of media hype that have lent the term something of a false image in more recent times, prefer to be referred to as "cognitive scientists."

The common ground upon which these disparate forces come together into their sometimes uneasy alliance is the central role played by computing, both as a subject of study in its own right and as an investigative tool. The computer program continues to be viewed as one of the prime candidates with the potential to capture and reproduce the activities that constitute thought. Computers also bring methods of greater precision and repeatability into the experimental psychology lab—with the additional advantage observed by Patrick Winston that they require little care and feeding compared to the traditional rat and they don't bite. In view of the ubiquitousness that computing has attained in every field of research, such an observation might risk blurring the dividing lines between cognitive science and its contributory disciplines in all directions, but then, that would describe the situation pretty closely anyway. Cognitive science can be said to be recapitulating cybernetics' attempt to unify the various theoretical and experimental insights to cognition under a common roof but with computation replacing feedback and control as the central paradigm.

The Soar system we met earlier is an example of an integrated approach to a Unified Theory of Cognition based on the traditional top-down, highly structured concept of AI implementation. The outcome of coupling such a general reasoning capability to a knowledge base of the kind that Cyc is intended to become is interesting to speculate on.

It could be, however, that such highly organized structures are not the way to represent this befuddling phenomenon that we call "mind" at all. Alternative proposals have been made that the integrated, coherently functioning "selves" that we are conscious of being in fact arise from a chaos of disorganized "subminds," endlessly negotiating, competing, and jostling for attention.

Mind as a Consensus

PROGRAM POLITICS

In the late fifties, Oliver Selfridge of MIT's Lincoln Lab—the same man who had visited Rand and converted Allen Newell to computers with his talk on pattern recognition—developed a program called Pandemonium to demonstrate the principle of a complex process arising as a result of the interactions of many simpler subprocesses. Instead of a single, orderly procedure working out all the components of an answer to a problem—say, to recognize a written character—a collection of highly specialized routines would each watch only for its own set of conditions, signaling according to the degree that they were satisfied. Selfridge called these "demons." The idea was that all the demons would shout at a level that indicated how sure they were that the characteristic they were looking for was present in the object, and from the cacophony of voices a "master demon" would decide what the object was. Thus, for an *L*, the vertical-stroke demon would be more insistent than for an *i*, say, while for a *T* the horizontal-stroke demon would contribute twice as much as it had before. The technique could be applied to a wide variety of inputs, not just character shapes: chess moves, geometric patterns, anything for which correlation statistics could be provided. Its drawback was that the program could never be persuaded to create new demons for itself, which limited it to recognizing only things about which it had been told. The principle contributed to Frank Rosenblatt's Perceptron, developed through the sixties, but that line too reached a plateau because of an inherent absence of originality, as we saw earlier.

Raj Reddy's "blackboard," used for weighing competing interpretations of speech units in the HEARSAY system, and the "evidence grids" in which Hans Moravec's robots accumulate descriptions of their surroundings from different sensor arrays, both apply the principle of consensus decisions made by combining the contributions of several independent processes.

Highly modularized programming caught on in the seventies, characterized by asynchronous interaction between many independent units with no definable overall supervisory function or central control. A major impetus in this direction came from the growth of distributed systems and communications networking, which replaced many of an earlier generation of room-size "mainframes" with webs of home or office desktop and portable units interacting worldwide. Could minds too work more in this way?

MARVIN MINSKY'S HIGH SOCIETY
In 1986, Marvin Minsky published *The Society of Mind*, which described a theory that he and Seymour Papert had conceived around 1970 and which Minsky in particular had been developing extensively since. The contention is, basically, that mind arises out of the ongoing interactions and transactions of countless mental entities that Minsky terms "agents." Each agent in itself is very simple and totally specialized, with the result that, through cooperation, exploitation, trickery, or by whatever other means work, the help of other agents must be enlisted to accomplish any but the absolute simplest of tasks. The tactics employed to secure such aid resemble those resorted to in any family or community of individuals with mixed goals and interests, some in accord and others in conflict, hence the name of the theory.

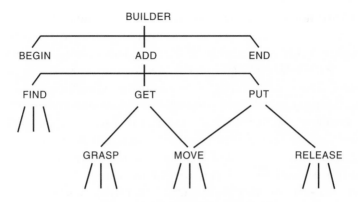

Figure 16.3 A Minsky Agent Workforce

As an example that traces its origin back to the unstructured tangles of pieces of code calling up other pieces of code seen in Terry Winograd's SHRDLU Blocks World, Minsky asks us to imagine a child wanting to build a tower, so that just at this moment, an agent BUILDER is in control. The job is too complicated for a single agent, however, and BUILDER functions as an administrator who doesn't actually do anything but calls in three subcontractors: BEGIN, who can find a site; ADD, who places new blocks; and END, who decides when the tower is high enough. But even adding a block has to be broken down into FIND block, GET block, and PUT. GET in turn has to call upon GRASP block and MOVE hand. And PUT engages MOVE hand again and RELEASE. This delegation continues downward until eventually we reach a level where the task is simple enough for an agent to actually carry out— maybe the contracting of a single muscle in a finger.

Note that just knowing the names of the subsidiary agents involved is insufficient to tell what BUILDER does. It's also necessary to know how the parts are related. MOVE, for example, is under the control of GET and PUT at different times.

Why break tasks down into such small parts? Because that's the way Minsky believes minds are made, and every one of those tiny component skills had to be learned at some time. But we've forgotten how much fumbling and practice it took. Years later, as adults, we initiate such chains automatically, and each agent in its turn knows its job so well that it all seems like ... well, common sense.

It is all a bit fanciful in that no neural structures have been identified as corresponding to any of the agents that Minsky proposes. The model, however, does offer plausible mechanisms for a surprisingly wide range of observed mental phenomena. Some examples:

Perceiving an object, a small white rubber ball, for instance, simultaneously activates appropriate agents associated in different attribute divisions such as SHAPE, round; SUBSTANCE, rubber; COLOR, white; SIZE, fist. At the same time, what Minsky calls a "Knowledge Line," or K-line, is created to interconnect those concepts. Recalling the ball later involves reactivating that K-line, which turns on all the agents to which it was connected at the time it was formed. This is consistent with the associative character of memory, which enables all kinds of scattered, diffuse aspects of a situation to be linked into a single percept that we can reexperience. K-line connections can be strong or weak, the weaker representing "typical" default values easily replaced by other connections when they clash with experience—the "frame" idea again.

Storing and subsequently recalling complex perceptual experiences, say, attending a concert—which surely doesn't involve storing every detail—can be explained by the far more economical procedure of taking the same process to a higher level by creating a "K-line K-Line," i.e., a new K-Line that activates all the K-lines that were active at the time, which in turn reactivate their associated agents. This can be taken to further levels to construct a hierarchy of memories, reusing existing mental machinery again, which as we suspected accounts for much of our use of metaphor. Such a hierarchical memory would tend not to reactivate every sight and sound that took place, just those associated with what we recognized or focused on at the time—vague impressions punctuated by isolated instances of greater clarity but with most of the details lost. And, indeed, this is how human memory does seem to work.

The theory goes on to account for phenomena as diverse as consciousness, emotions, reasoning, humor, learning, what gives us our sense of continuity in a constantly changing world, and why younger children's drawings of people look like heads with arms and legs sticking out. All the same, the theory of agents did not create the same stir within the AI community as had the earlier theory of frames, from which it was clearly descended. Part of the reason could be that this time it went too far in leaving details for the experimental researchers to fill in. Sweepingly general and metaphoric in its descriptions, it left would-be followers with little to go on as to what, exactly, they were supposed to do.

Allen Newell's criticism was that the communication between agents couldn't achieve the rates it would need to for the level of coherence that our behavior and our thinking displays. "A community of scientists with telephones in their hands," he says, "cannot produce an integrated intelligence."[5]

Both approaches—a highly ordered architecture like Soar's, or a distributed, chattering society—remain true to the "top-downer" faith that, with time and perseverance, the rules governing human cognition can be comprehended and encoded. The "bottom-uppers" continue to believe that they can only form through direct experience of the real world, in the way that has produced the only cognitive intelligence we know. Neither side is saying that anything sensational is going to happen soon.

And, hardly surprisingly, there is a strong body of skepticism that says both sides are wasting their time because the whole thing is impossible on principle. It's about time we gave them a voice too. So we turn to the skeptics next.

1. Crevier, p. 174.
2. Jackson, p. 241.
3. Metcalf, p. 169.
4. Hofstadter (1995), p. 183.
5. Crevier, p. 277

17

Critics and Skeptics

"Computability is not at all the same thing as being mathematically precise. There is as much mystery and beauty as one might wish in the precise Platonic mathematical world, and most of it resides with concepts that lie outside the comparatively limited part of it where algorithms and computation reside."
—Roger Penrose, *The Emperor's New Mind*

Aliens Approaching

Fascination with the idea of artificial humans or artificial beings with human-like qualities runs through the mythologies and technical crafts of just about all cultures. Sometimes they are envisioned as helpers, such as the cast of mechanical assistants created by the divine blacksmith Hephaestus to work in his forge. Others get out of hand in the style of Mary Shelley's invention or the robots in Karel Capek's 1920 play *R.U.R.*, perhaps the first depiction of man-made intelligences getting rid of their makers and taking over the world. A preoccupation that manifests itself universally is usually tapping into emotional currents that run deep in the human psyche, and it should come as no great surprise that reactions to the suggestion of AI tend to be strong and polarized. In our own eyes, our thinking ability is what defines our uniqueness as the species *sapiens*. Such a distinction is not one to be shared lightly, and it probably tells us something about our inner image of ourselves that while our mythical productions may rampage around freely as testimony to the hazards of human ambition and pride, they never rival us in intellectual skill or knowledge. Where beings of equivalent or better qualifications in this department are needed to dispense wisdom and justice, we never create them without calling them gods. Any talk about moving the servants out of the kitchen to eat at our table is asking for trouble.

Arguments against AI can be grouped into three broad, frequently overlapping categories:

AI is impossible because the very notion violates some tenet deemed to be unquestionable, and that's the end of it.

AI is possible in principle, but the prospects for achieving it are unlikely or, at best, remote.

Even if AI is technically feasible, there are reasons why it shouldn't be pursued at the present time, and even then with a lot more deliberation and caution than has been exhibited so far.

The third kind of objection is really of a different nature in that it questions what we ought to do rather than what we can do. It's treated separately, in the final chapter of the book.

OUR UNIQUENESS UNDER SIEGE

The suggestion that intelligent machines might even be possible touches a nerve that lies close to the roots of our most cherished notions about the exclusivity of being human, and this alone is frequently a sufficient cause for its rejection. Such arguments typically base themselves on a premise of intelligence as an exclusively human property by assertion or definition, which, if the premise is incontestable, leaves very little to say. This category includes objections made on the religious grounds that thinking is a function bestowed only upon humans because only they have a soul. Alan Turing, referring to this as "The Theological Objection" in his 1950 paper, said he would find it more convincing if animals were classed along with humans, for he saw a far vaster difference between the animate and the inanimate than between humans and animals. For the sapients who were still getting over being told by Darwin that they were not as far removed from apes as they would like to think, this now smacked of being asked to accept that they were little better than bicycles or wheelbarrows. The results were predictable, and the righteous took to their pens in indignation. For those who insist that mind equates to soul and that creating one usurps the power of the Creator, Turing hardly helped matters by denying that making machines capable of thought was any more of an irreverence than procreating children. "[R]ather we are, in either case," he wrote—I can't help feeling, somewhat tongue in cheek—"instruments of His will providing mansions for the souls that He creates."

Whether cloaked in religious pronouncements or not, Turing held that this kind of argument "is likely to be quite strong in intellectual people, since they value the power of thinking more highly than others, and are more inclined to base their belief in the superiority of Man on this power." Interestingly, Marvin Minsky made very much the same observation in a conversation noted by Pamela McCorduck:

The interesting thing is, according to my youthful stereotype, it would be musicians and artists who would be hostile to the idea of intelligent machines. But I never got over it, that musicians and artists weren't hostile at all. They'd say, well, oh gee, that's great, what's the idea? How would it do that? And it would be mathematicians and physicists who would get very angry.[1]

Minsky's conclusion, which came after he had pondered the apparent paradox for a long time, was that as in all walks of life, dealing with a subject on a day-to-day basis has a great demystifying effect, with the result that working artists are not superstitious about creativity. They readily admit to learning by looking at other people's work, discussing techniques, and asking questions and feel that they don't have much time for abstract theories of talent. Mathematicians, by contrast, never talk about how they think mathematics and worship their creativity as a God-given gift.

J. Clifford Shaw, the principal programmer of the Newell-Shaw-Simon team, kept a collection of contemporary diatribes against thinking machines. The ones belonging properly to the category we are considering here, as opposed to those calling for closer examination of where the real difficulties lay, tended to be characterized by copious outpourings of such words as "moron" and "idiot," as if they were seeking reassurance through repetition of the inviolability of the human difference that was being challenged. Stafford Beer, a British cyberneticist, declared that even "moron" is an overstatement for describing computers.[2]

A major contributor to Shaw's collection was an engineer named Mortimer Taube, whose tirades of derision, among other things scorning reputable scientific journals for even printing articles on computers, were brought together in his 1961 book, *Computers and Common Sense: The Myth of Thinking Machines.* Although ostensibly setting out to assess the claims being made at the time on their scientific and philosophical merit, Taube's selectivity in choosing the landmarks hints of a predetermined conclusion. And that's unfortunate because many of the predictions being made did indeed turn out to have been grossly exaggerated, for example, automatic language translation, one of Taube's major targets, which, as we have seen, ended up as a debacle. Taube's stance was that some things in science were difficult but possible according to natural law (e.g., putting up a space station); others were permanently impossible (e.g., a perpetual motion machine). AI, he thought, fell squarely into the second class. Although Taube made appeals to theoretical limits on what was computable in order to place mind in a territory that lay permanently beyond realizability, scientists reading his book were left with the impression that these were rationalizations after the event rather than reasons and that what was really bothering Taube went a lot deeper. Ultimately, it seemed to have to do with his perception of AI as symptomatic of all that was wrong with the way in which science had come to be conducted, compared to the higher standards of an idealized past in which rigor and integrity prevailed, personal rivalry and animosity did not exist, and premature speculation not based upon theory solidly grounded in fact and experiment was unknown. In short, a past that had never existed.

Ultimately, then, this line is founded on unshakable faith and really boils down to religion masquerading in secular trappings. For that reason, Turing considered attempts at refutation pointless and suggested instead that consolation might be more appropriate, appending as a note that "perhaps this should be sought in the transmigration of souls."

SKIRMISHING AROUND GÖDEL:
THE MATHEMATICAL OBJECTIONS

In a book called *The Modeling of Mind: Computers and Intelligence*, published in 1963, the philosopher John Lucas published a paper entitled "Minds, Machines, and Gödel," which held Kurt Gödel's Incompleteness Theorem (see chapter four) as proof that computing machines would never be able, on principle, to match human thinking.

To recapitulate, Gödel contrived an ingenious coding scheme that enabled him to construct the logical equivalent of a sentence that stated, "This statement cannot be proved using the formalism of this system." A few moments of reflection—perhaps interspersed with some frowns, mumbles, and backtracking to start again—shows that it *has* to be true. For were it not (in other words, the statement were provable), then the statement stating it not to be not provable would be false. Thus, a false statement would be provable, which by definition a consistent system of axioms cannot do. (Remember, Gödel's theorem proved that for any consistent system of axioms at least powerful enough to contain ordinary arithmetic, statements exist that are undecidable within that system.)

What Lucas latched onto was the intriguing fact that the truth of the above can be grasped by human reasoning, whereas from what we have just said it will be forever beyond the ability of any logical process conducted within the system to deduce. And no matter how much we expand the system, the same will apply. Hence, no machine programmed in any language consisting of sentences in such a system—in other words, any formal system—can or ever will do *everything* that a mind can do. The case rests.

When I put this to Marvin Minsky, he suggested that a more illuminating way of viewing Gödel's conclusion might be that any formal system operating under the constraint of being consistent would be too weak to support the familiar forms of commonsense human reasoning, particularly with regard to "reflexive" processes, in which thoughts are directed toward themselves. What this means is that to make machines appear reasonably smart in the ways we humans take pride in being smart, one must use logically defective shortcuts (i.e., "heuristics"). This isn't particularly difficult to program machines to do, but the results wouldn't be acceptable in any of the typical application roles we're accustomed to seeing for computers, where the whole point of using them

lies in their predictability and repeatability and anything short would be considered tantamount to worthlessness. It would mean that when interpreting what they were doing in commonsense terms, we would find the "logic" they were using inconsistent. This is another way of saying that sometimes they'd get things wrong and other times contradict themselves—just like people. And that's the point: machines are *capable* of the kind of reasoning humans do, but as Deep Thought warned in Douglas Adams's *Hitch-Hiker's Guide to the Galaxy*, "You won't like it."[3]

So in Minsky's opinion, the whole mathematical objection springs from the mistake of overlooking this possibility. Not only *can* we program machines to use inconsistent or defective logic, but we probably have no alternative if we want machines that are "smart." Since intuition by definition means being persuaded of the truth of a conjecture without proof, there can be no guarantee that the rules involved in generating it were any more consistent either. In short, there is no evidence that such intuitive understandings are based on anything more than very good rules of thumb, both innate and derived from experience, for making guesses about mathematics—guesses that may well turn out to be wrong.

Critical assessments citing Gödel's theorem have continued since Lucas's time nevertheless, one of the more notable in recent years being from the eminent Oxford mathematical physicist Roger Penrose.[4] With heavyweights like Minsky and Penrose drawing opposite conclusions from the same mathematical universe, I'm not about to take sides or pass judgments. I will say, though, that my guess is there's a shade of Mortimer Taube still at work in both camps. In other words, both sides are defending ostensibly reasoned positions that involve large emotional investment and deeply held convictions, and continuing debate is as unlikely to change things any more than it has in the last thirty-five years. But all of us would like to have the tanks fight their battles in the remote frontier deserts rather than the streets outside our door. Gödel, I suspect, provides a convenient skirmishing ground for token shots to be exchanged comfortably far removed from the home territories where the damage could really get serious. Penrose is unhesitating in admitting as much. On the concluding page of *The Emperor's New Mind*, for example, he writes:

> *Consciousness seems to me to be such an important phenomenon that I simply cannot believe that it is something "accidentally" conjured up by a complicated computation. It is the phenomenon by which the universe's very existence is made known. . . . Some [of the book's arguments] are admittedly speculative, whereas I believe there is no escape from others. Yet beneath all this technicality is the feeling that it is indeed "obvious" that the conscious mind cannot work like a computer, even though much of what is actually involved in mental activity might do so.*

This is a refreshingly candid affirmation of faith in intuition to come at the end of a work covering just about all aspects of knowledge of the physical world from mathematical proofs and the physics of mind, to quantum mechanics, to cosmology. Minsky cautions that such intuition could be wrong. From his general tone, I think Penrose would cheerfully agree.

Enter the Philosophers: Hubert Dreyfus

"ALCHEMY AND AI"

"The heart has its reasons that reason does not know."
—Blaise Pascal

After Newell, Shaw, and Simon's pioneering work using the JOHNNIAC computer, which had led to Logic Theorist and GPS, there was considerable interest at Rand in what was perceived as the emerging field of computer intelligence. Other companies, however, argued against risking significant investment of time and money without more solid grounds for accepting that such a revolutionary proposal was even feasible. Minds and intelligence were traditionally the business of philosophers. Accordingly, in 1964, Rand hired Hubert Dreyfus, whose brother, Stuart, was also one of the programmers working on the JOHNNIAC, as a consultant to evaluate the achievements and future prospects of what was then called Cognitive Simulation, or CS.

Dreyfus had started out as a physics student at Harvard and in graduate school transferred to philosophy, which he went on to teach at MIT. He had early parted company with the traditional line of Western philosophic thought epitomized by Socrates, Plato, Hobbes, and Descartes, which held that all cognitive processes could, given the requisite level of understanding, be reduced to definitions and rules capable of being stated explicitly. Indeed, Socrates could be thought of as the original knowledge engineer, touring Athens and interrogating the worthy for the rules that would identify such qualities as "piety" and "justice" so that he would recognize them when he saw them, as if he intended writing an expert system that would capture them.

Instead, Dreyfus was drawn to the humanist school, represented by mathematician Blaise Pascal and including such names as Martin Heidegger, Maurice Merleau-Ponty, and Ludwig Wittgenstein, which maintained that people have no access to the basic elements and first principles underlying their perceptions, actions, and use of everyday knowledge. Rather, understanding and competence are rooted in our direct experience of the world, and learning to deal with it successfully is more a matter of cultivating the right intuitions and behavior than knowing a lot of facts and rules for relating them. If this were so, then the rule-based endeavors that people down the street in the MIT buildings on Technology Square were talking about to make machines intelligent wouldn't work. Troubled by the claims, and initially somewhat apprehensive,

Dreyfus began attending the AI group's lectures, and in 1961 he and Stuart entered a one-page discussion note into the proceedings volume of a conference given by Herbert Simon on the EPAM model of short-term memory. The tone was scathing, ridiculing the entire AI enterprise and finding it as ill conceived as trying to reach the moon by climbing a mountain, definitely not the way to win the hearts and minds of what Dreyfus had openly dubbed the "artificial intelligentsia." His views today haven't changed.

The title of Dreyfus's report for RAND was "Alchemy and Artificial Intelligence," which pretty much sums up its tenor. Work on CS at Rand was then in what Dreyfus described as its manic phase, and, with the output of research papers proliferating, he confesses to approaching the task with feelings of trepidation that a prediction made by Newell and Simon in 1958 that "in the visible future . . . the range of problems [computers] can handle will be coextensive with the range to which the human mind has been applied"[5] might already be well on its way to being fulfilled. But as Dreyfus read the papers, he reports his excitement and fear turning to disappointment and relief. Some original and impressive work had been done in showing that machines could solve certain problems through symbol manipulation, he concluded, but the broader claim of casting general light on understanding, intuition, and learning was not supported by the actual results. Dreyfus disagreed with the optimism that it was fashionable to express, submitting instead that in spite of the impressive initial work, a general pattern had already emerged in which success with simple forms of information processing led to great expectations of a continuing trend, only to stagnate and eventually fail when confronted by more intuitive forms of intelligence. The reason this was so, Dreyfus contended, was that, as with the alchemists of old trying to turn lead into gold, the whole theory that the work rested on was simply wrong.

Naturally, this didn't do much to improve Dreyfus's standing in the AI popularity stakes. Paul Armer, the head of computer science at RAND and the person who had hired Dreyfus, was caught between two equally vociferous factions. Simon, Newell, and the AI advocates insisted that the report was nonsense and that Rand had no business condoning it, while others, like psychologist Robert Ryanstat and mathematician Richard Bellman, later to publish his own book critical of AI,[6] agreed with the report and reminded Armer that it was Rand's standing policy to let views be heard and allowed to stand on their merit, not be sat on because somebody didn't like the conclusions.[7]

The wrangling went on for almost a year, but eventually the paper was released in 1965 as a Rand memo, the lowest level of Rand publications, with a printed version following in 1967. "The fears of those who tried to prevent [its] distribution were justified," Dreyfus records with satisfaction. As the first detailed criticism of CS, it drew attention worldwide—for example, at Novosibirsk, the Soviet "science city," in Japan, and among scientists at such places as Bell Telephone.[8] But it was not discussed at the principal AI centers. In fact, at

MIT the rejection was so total that students and faculty working on the robotics and AI projects dared not be seen eating lunch with Dreyfus for risk of incurring wrath from their superiors. David Waltz (developer of the propagation-constraints method for vision-recognition—see chapter thirteen) recalls heated debates involving Dreyfus and Joseph Weizenbaum on one side—Weizenbaum was also having reservations on the way computers were being uncritically promoted as the answer to everything—and notably Marvin Minsky and Seymour Papert on the other.[9] Papert was particularly incensed by "Alchemy and Artificial Intelligence" and wrote a refutation entitled "The Artificial Intelligence of Hubert L. Dreyfus: A Budget of Fallacies."[10] The atmosphere didn't cool down, and all chance of its eventually doing so probably evaporated when excerpts from Dreyfus's report found their way into *The New Yorker* and made him "Talk of the Town."[11]

After spending a semester as a research associate in computer science at Harvard to continue his investigations, Dreyfus accepted a position in the philosophy faculty at Berkeley. Stuart continued at Rand running formal models of decision making on the JOHNNIAC, which he shared with Simon, the two of them barely on speaking terms. All in all, a long way from Mortimer Taube's dream world of nonpartisan objectivity and genteel scientific discourse.

A CRITIQUE OF IMPURE REASON

Dreyfus's book *What Computers Can't Do: A Critique of Artificial Reason*, published in 1972, expanded and developed the arguments presented in "Alchemy and Artificial Intelligence." It can only be described as unfortunate that relationships between the AI community and what in many ways turned out to be one of its most cogent critics should have degenerated into such acrimony. In some cases, Dreyfus was years in advance, not only anticipating many of the difficulties that AI was to run into but providing an explanation of why he considered it inevitable that they would happen. Both sides had points worth pondering, and one can only speculate what other, untried lines of research might have been opened to funding and investigation by a more constructive and sympathetically motivated dialogue.

The pattern of early dramatic successes with simple tasks, leading to diminishing returns and eventual disenchantment as attempts were made to extend the method to more complex domains, could be accounted for, Dreyfus submitted, by four characteristics of human cognitive ability that enabled them to get around difficulties that programming methods had no way to avoid.

The first of these is that marginal awareness we possess of the situation around us, outside our immediate concern but registering sufficiently to seize attention if a good-enough reason dictates—like the blurry area of peripheral vision that surrounds the highly resolved spot that our eyes are focused on but applying to all the senses. As an example, Dreyfus gave a situation in a chess game in which a player had begun a description of his conscious thought processes with "Again I notice that one of his pieces is not defended, the rook, and there must be ways of taking advantage of this." How, Dreyfus asked, did the subject notice that the rook was undefended? The conventional AI answer is by unconsciously applying heuristics of the kind that programmers were trying to extract from players' heads and build into their programs. But Dreyfus took this more as an assertion of faith, for no master-level heuristics had been found. The conscious process that the subject described of looking for various alternative ways to attack the rook—"counting out," as Dreyfus termed it, comparable to the tree-searching heuristics implemented in programs—began only *after* the player had "zeroed in" on that part of the board and that aspect of the position.

Analysis of the MacHack program we met earlier showed that at a tough point in a tournament game the program had calculated for fifteen minutes and weighed up 26,000 alternatives before choosing a move—and quite an excellent one, as it turned out. A human, by contrast, would consider perhaps one hundred alternatives in a similar situation, two hundred at most, with a good chance of spotting something brilliant that the machine had missed. If, as conventional AI theory maintained, the human unconsciously counted out thousands of alternatives in a similar fashion to the machine, applying astoundingly powerful heuristics to get to the point of focusing on the rook, why would he not simply carry the same process through to completion until the best move just popped into consciousness with no demand or effort at all? Why resort to the cumbersome process of having consciously to labor through the last few details?

FOUR PILLARS OF WISDOM

Dreyfus's answer was that the zeroing-in part didn't depend on programlike, heuristically guided searching at all. Rather, an ability to organize perceptions globally causes patterns recognized in the background suddenly to take on a significance that becomes instantly apparent, such as noticing the ticking of a clock when it stops or the face of a friend when scanning the vaguely perceived faces in a crowd. According to Dreyfus, the inability to give a program such *fringe awareness* accounted for the pattern of early success and later failure in cognitive simulation. In game playing and the kinds of puzzle problems solved by GPS, for example, the early successes were attained by working on those parts of the problem in which heuristic searching was feasible; failure set in when complexity reached the level that such global awareness would be necessary to avoid exponentially explosive growth of the search problem.

But how do you write the rules for "Notice the rook if it's important"? For a program to decide that a rook was important it would first have to "notice" it, which means that to give anything a chance to be deemed important everything would have to be examined—like constantly having to scan every element of the visual field—defeating utterly the purpose of the exercise. It's significant to note that the chess engines of recent years all owe their power to faster, more specialized hardware for extending the search-space, not to advances in more "humanlike" evaluation methods. In the second direction, Arthur Samuel's Checkers Player was about as far as it went. Dreyfus would perhaps say that was as far as it could go.

The second human faculty that Dreyfus held to be unprogrammable was our *ambiguity tolerance*, which he illustrated primarily with reference to the problems that the attempts at automatic language-translation had run into. As we saw earlier, the order of words in a sentence—its syntax—is not sufficient to decide through formal rules which of several possible parsings is the appropriate one, and neither can the written context—the words surrounding a given word or phrase—be relied on to indicate a writer or speaker's particular meaning. Yet people are generally able to get the intended point unequivocally—"zeroing in" again on what matters against a background of extraneity, which doesn't.

What makes the difference, and what computers can never share, Dreyfus says, is that when people use natural language they do so from the perspective of being *involved* in a particular situation and pursuing certain goals. It is this perspective, constantly changing, not precisely stated, and in general not statable, that provides the cues needed to reduce the ambiguity to a level tolerable for the task at hand. An instruction like "Stay near me" can mean anything from "Don't let go of my hand" addressed to a child in a jostling crowd to "Keep within a mile" in the case of a fellow astronaut exploring the moon. Such meanings are never unambiguous in all possible situations. But our shared *context awareness* makes them sufficiently unambiguous in any *particular* situation. And despite the chorus of protests from the AI citadels that Dreyfus didn't know what he was talking about, were not their later preoccupations with things like party frames and restaurant scripts an acknowledgment that only with a more humanlike, situational slant would programs have a chance of making sense of anything?

In making his third point, Dreyfus refers to a book on psychological theory by George Miller and Eugene Galanter, *Plans and the Structure of Behavior*,[12] which begins by quoting from Polya on the role of insight in problem solving:

> *First, we must understand the problem. We have to see clearly what the data are, what conditions are imposed and what the unknown thing is that we are searching for.*
>
> *Second, we must devise a plan that will guide the solution and connect the data to the unknown.*

The authors then minimize the importance of the first part or decide not to worry too much about it:

> *Obviously, the second part of these is most critical. The first . . . is indispensable, of course, but in the discussion of well-defined problems we assume that it has already been accomplished.*

But the whole crux of solving complex problems, Dreyfus points out, lies precisely in grasping the essentials and structuring a plan in such a way that a workable method of solution can be applied. Like GPS's monkey, once the need to get to the banana has been specified and a tool with the requisite properties (the chair) selected from the world of undifferentiated objects, the rest can be handed over to a mechanical procedure that will eventually stumble on the right way of connecting them together. The standard response to this criticism is to cite "learning" as the answer, but short of trying everything, this could only mean learning to apply what was identified as relevant, thereby presupposing what needed to be solved. The only learning project of note at that time was Ed Feigenbaum's EPAM program for studying the association of nonsense syllables—the significance being, in Dreyfus's submission, that mechanized methods had proved effective in the one situation where any *meaning*, by design, was rigorously excluded and no form of comprehension required. In short, what humans are able to bring to bear at the outset of tackling a problem is the insight necessary for *essential/inessential discrimination*, as opposed to being stuck with trial-and-error search. This is how they avoid bogging down as the dimensions of the problem grow beyond being well defined and restricted.

Finally, there was what Dreyfus called *perspicuous grouping*, that human ability we saw that takes place when we talk about metaphors, analogies, and family resemblances to recognize instantly "likenesses" in ways that are relevant to the purpose of the moment and that defy verbal description. We don't, Dreyfus contends, identify such patterns by extracting lists of features and matching them in the way a program must. Rather than assembling perceptions from primitive elements, we seem to go in the other direction, moving from the realm of globally identified *concepts* down to the level of consciously analyzing detail only when relevance has been established—as when looking for a way of attacking the rook or focusing on a visual feature that has already captured our attention. Our uncanny pattern-recognition ability requires a combination of fringe consciousness, ambiguity tolerance, and insight, all of which Dreyfus puts beyond the reach of digital machines. "It is no wonder, then," he comments dryly, "that work in pattern recognition has had a late start and an early stagnation."[13]

Dreyfus went on to ask how, in the light of these problems, AI researchers were able to persist in their belief that what digital computers do reveals anything about hidden information processes in humans and that there must be digital ways of performing human tasks. Noting that nobody in the field appeared to be reexamining such questions, he criticized AI as the least self-critical field on the scientific scene: "There must be a reason why these intelligent men almost unanimously minimize or fail to recognize their difficulties, and continue dogmatically to assert their faith in progress." Dreyfus's conclusion was that it had to lie in the force of their assumptions. He went on to identify them essentially as:

—The mind operates as a symbol manipulator operating according to formal rules.

—All knowledge can be formulated in terms expressible as logical relationships.

—The world—or, at least, enough of it to produce intelligent behavior—can be analyzed into situation-free determinate elements, i.e., a set of facts each logically independent of all the others.

Disputing each one of these, Dreyfus developed the case that it is our difference of situation as embodied beings, immersed from birth in *experiencing* a world of aims and purposes, that creates our perspective out of a potentially infinite reservoir of contexts. Without any comparable subjective views to guide it, a machine must be either confined within a limited domain where general processes remain tractable or lost in a hopeless maze of permanently trying to interpret and look for connections between everything.

GOING BY THE BOOK—UNTIL YOU KNOW BETTER

A later book, *Mind Over Machine* (1986), coauthored by Hubert and Stuart Dreyfus, invoked essentially the same arguments to express reservations about the claims then being made for the future of expert systems. In areas where mere competence as opposed to expertise is sufficient, and where the limitations are clearly understood, the Dreyfuses agree that expert systems can be appropriate. They give as an example a system called PUFF, which was assisting Dr. Robert Fallat at the Pacific Medical Center, San Francisco, in diagnosing lung disorders. PUFF's usefulness lay in taking over the large part of the job, including much of the thinking involved, that was mostly routine and didn't require any special human effort. When it came to pronouncing an actual diagnosis, PUFF agreed with Fallat only 75 percent of the time. In this instance that was of little importance, however, since the data on which the decisions depended were fully quantitative and could be represented graphically, and Fallat's interpretive skills approached 100 percent accuracy. The difficulties in promoting such a system to expert decision-making level would arise when the criteria were less clear-cut and the human component of expertise lower. In short, while such systems might help a human expert do even better, they wouldn't replace one or elevate to expert the performance of an amateur. The danger would arise from the false confidence likely to be generated when the amateur, or the organization employing him, didn't realize it.

And this would remain so because of the differences between the ways humans are able to process information and the way computers are forced to, a belief Dreyfus had been expounding since the sixties. Mechanically following step-by-step rules that have to be consciously deliberated, the Dreyfuses maintained, is the way a novice acquires a new skill—the new employee working from the procedure manual, the conscientious new nurse doing everything exactly as she has been taught, or anybody learning to type or play the piano. And how else could it be, for what else has the beginner to go on than memorized rules or the ability to reason new solutions from basic principles?

The transition from novice, through competent performer, to expert consists precisely of acquiring through *experience* the unconscious abilities we talked about earlier that involve processing information in a different way and make the spontaneous displays of judgment and excellence we call "expertise" possible. Flying instructors, for example, give students specific procedures to follow for scanning their instruments; it turns out, however, that the instructors don't observe those rules when piloting themselves. Their experience gives them an awareness of how priorities can change with circumstances and a sense of when to make exceptions that can't be expressed as IF-this-THEN-do-that rules for the simple reason that no such rules are being followed to begin with.

Hence, it becomes understandable why trying to put such rules into words is so difficult. When prevailed upon by the knowledge engineer to articulate procedures that can be written down and encoded, the best an expert can do is offer pretty much the same kind of advice the instructor gives to students. Far from being "expert," therefore, the resulting system is perforce constrained to the level, at best, of "advanced competent." The risk of giving human novices such systems as models is that the humans never progress beyond the rule-based procedures and become locked out from developing true expert-level performances of their own.

The Dreyfuses thus saw further evidence that the way toward true, human-like artificial intelligence—if, indeed, such a way existed at all—was not in the direction of formally manipulated systems of symbols.

John Searle's Chinese Turing Test

The suggestion that a machine might have conscious thoughts in the same sense as any human being is not what gets the philosophers seething. As John R. Searle, another professor of philosophy at U.C. Berkeley observes,[14] humans are machines of a special biological kind, and humans can think, so of course machines can think. And for all anyone knows, it might be possible to produce a machine in a different way, out of different materials, that can also think. What gets the ink and adrenaline flowing is the proposition that a machine could think just by virtue of implementing a computer program. This is the claim that Searle labels "strong" AI: that thinking is merely the formal manipulation of symbols, and since that is what a computer does, the mind is to the brain as the program is to the hardware. Searle doesn't agree with it, and to refute it he uses AI's own proclaimed measure of intelligence: the Turing test.[15]

Suppose, he says, he is put in a room containing baskets full of pieces of paper carrying symbols in Chinese, a language Searle doesn't speak. Also, he has a rule book in English for matching Chinese symbols with other Chinese symbols, identifying them solely by their shapes. Imagine now that people outside the "Chinese Room," who do speak the language, pass in through a slot in the door questions written in Chinese and in response Searle manipulates symbols according to the rule book, which is written so that it generates sentences indistinguishable from those of a native Chinese speaker. In answer to the question "What is your favorite color?" for instance, the answer might read, "My favorite is blue, but I also like green a lot," although the meaning would be quite unknown to Searle. Yet with the book functioning as "program," the people who wrote it the "programmers," and himself the "computer," he would have satisfied the Turing test for understanding Chinese, although he is totally ignorant of it and could never have come to understand it in the way described. Like a computer, he simply manipulated symbols to which he attached no meaning.

His point is that he does not understand Chinese solely on the basis of running a program, nor is he running a program sufficient to produce any other kind of cognition, regardless of what behavior might have been simulated. A program has syntax but no semantics. Thoughts, by contrast, are about such things as objects, feelings, and states of affairs in the world, meanings that we supply from our knowledge of the world. Such meaning cannot emerge from mere manipulations of innately meaningless symbols.

What, then, is the essential difference that makes outwardly identical behavior one thing for computers and another for brains? In Searle's view it lies in the fact that the computational processes that define a computer are independent of the specific type of hardware that the processes are implemented on.[16] A computer capable of carrying out a computation as specified by a particular Turing Machine could be made out of anything from electronic chips to contraptions built from beer cans and driven by windmills or pebbles manually manipulated on a roll of toilet paper. But for the phenomena that take place in brains—pain, thirst, vision, thought—the anatomy and physiology responsible are highly specific. The causation, in other words, is from the bottom up.

But beyond that, brains also *cause* mental activity by virtue of specific neurobiological processes. Computers might be programmed to simulate such processes, and this could be usefully informative, but such a simulation is no more capable of producing the effects of neurobiology than a computer simulation of the oxidization of hydrocarbons is capable of powering an automobile. In summary, the fundamental tenet of strong AI—that the physical features of the implementing medium are totally irrelevant—is what makes it untenable. Symbols don't have the power to cause anything; hardware does, and, in the case of thinking, the specific hardware that causes it is a brain. Mind is as biological as digestion.

The Chinese Room argument prompted a flood of objections that has continued to the present, ranging from things like "You really do understand Chinese, but you don't know it" and "You don't understand Chinese, but you have an unconscious subsystem that does" to "Semantics doesn't exist, only syntax. All else is a prescientific illusion." The most commonly encountered objection, according to Searle, runs something like "You don't understand Chinese, but the whole room does—the system comprising Searle, rule book, baskets, symbol papers, etc. You are like a single neuron in the brain, which by itself cannot understand anything but contributes to the understanding of the whole that does." Searle's reply is that symbol shuffling by itself does not give him access to the meaning of the symbols, and this is as true of the room as of the person inside. He makes the point by extending the idea to supposing that he memorized the contents of the rule book and baskets and did all the manipulating in his head. The whole system is then inside him, he says, and since he still doesn't understand Chinese, neither does the system.

Frank Tipler, professor of mathematical physics at Tulane University in New Orleans, told me the argument was invalid because he had calculated that for Searle to emulate a human rate of response, assuming something like a ten-story building to hold the baskets and the volumes of the rule book, he would have to work at a power output equivalent to six hundred one-gigawatt (i.e., large) power plants. I'm not sure I consider this fair to Searle, however. We don't take speed into account when declaring Turing Machines to be equivalent; all that's deemed to matter is the final computed output. Why, then, shouldn't the same apply to the argument of one's opponent.

In general, the exchanges I've looked at on the Chinese Room strike me a bit like the ones I alluded to concerning Gödel: more in the way of tokens waved to legitimize a position already held than to account for having adopted it, much less convey any expectation of inducing others to. In short, nobody was about to budge an inch on either side.

Two more philosophy professors, Paul M. Churchland and Patricia Smith Churchland, both at U.C. San Diego, take the position that while Searle may have a point about the way AI has been attempted to date, the shortcomings stem not from the underlying theory but from the nature of the computing architecture traditionally employed. Newer, massively parallel and revived neural-net approaches, they suggest, provide compelling prospects for the discernible future. The Dreyfuses, in their book, were more positive about the possibilities for such an approach too. Parallel processing, especially in distributed form, has become a strong center of attention in recent years. Accordingly, we'll move on to have a look at it next.

1. McCorduck, p. 174.
2. Ibid., p. 173.
3. See also Kugel (1979), (1986).
4. See Penrose for a book-length treatment.
5. Dreyfus and Dreyfus, p. 7.
6. Bellman.

7. McCorduck, pp. 194–95.
8. Dreyfus and Dreyfus, p. 9.
9. Crevier, pp. 122–23.
10. Papert.
11. "The Talk of the Town" *The New Yorker*, June 11, 1966.
12. Miller and Galanter.
13. Dreyfus (1972), p. 32.
14. Searle (1990).
15. Searle (1980).
16. Ironically, as we saw in chapter eight, the AI advocates had adopted pretty much an identical paradigm as the basis for their definition of "mind."

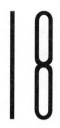

Getting Better Connected

PARALLELISM AND NEURAL NETS

"The work [on PDP processing] *in no way can be interpreted as growing from our metaphor of the modern computer. Here, we are talking about a new form of computation, one clearly based on principles that have heretofore not had any counterpart in computers."*
—Donald A. Norman

Parkinson's Law of Computing

"Work expands so as to fill the time available for its completion."
—C. Northcote Parkinson, *Parkinson's Law*

MORE ON EXPONENTIAL EXPLOSIONS

Time and again in this book we have run into situations where problems that are manageable on a limited scale or within a restricted domain escalate out of all proportion as the size of the problem gets bigger ("escalate" referring to the amount of computing required to produce a solution). The exhaustive game-tree searching that works for ticktacktoe couldn't be extended to chess; perceptions and manipulations of toy worlds didn't scale up to yield general visual recognition and competent mobile robots; the syntactical ways of decoding formal languages couldn't resolve the ambiguities and context dependencies of natural language.

The problem is not something that arises just in trying to extend AI to the real world, however. Even within the domains of regular computing application, problems exist whose solution rises beyond all conceivable limits of computability as the size of the problem increases. This has nothing to do with Gödel's theorem, which says that for any system of logic there will always be

301

unsolvable problems on principle. What we're talking about here are problems that have solutions, and procedures for computing them are perfectly well known; but it could take longer than the estimated life of the universe for the solution to be reached.

In chapter eight we found that scheduling a shopping trip—if one were to meticulously list every possible alternative—rapidly gets out of hand as the number of places to be visited grows beyond a few. This was an instance of a well-known problem known as "The Traveling Salesman's Tour": given an itinerary to visit a list of cities, say, worldwide, find the shortest route that passes through all of them and returns to the starting point. The solution is simple when the number of cities, let's call it n, is just a few, but it quickly becomes unmanageable as n rises. Note, we mean unmanageable when attempted by means of a rigorous search of all possibilities, which is what mathematicians mean when they say they've "proved" something. In practice, we manage to arrange a promotional tour of the Pacific Rim or a sightseeing vacation around Europe without too much difficulty. That's because we apply such commonsense "heuristics" as "Finish Japan first, then go to Indonesia." An exhaustive-search algorithm would test everything, including such options as San Francisco to Tokyo, back to Oakland, and then to Osaka.

The Salesman's Tour is more than an idle puzzle or curiosity; it represents a whole class of immensely important problems encountered in mathematics, science, and other fields. We saw in chapter eight that the size of this kind of problem increases as $n!$, or "n factorial"—the number obtained by multiplying together all the numbers from 1 to n. Hence, the time taken for a computer to solve the problem would increase at this rate.

Clearly, not all problems grow explosively in this way. Calculating the total of a groceries list increases linearly with the problem size: one extra addition to make for each extra item. Sometimes an intractable problem can be made manageable by looking at it in a different way. Figure 18.1 shows a famous example known as the "Königsberg Bridges," which has nothing to with AI but is still interesting, and we might as well stop to look at it now that we've gotten this close.

In the eighteenth-century German city of Königsberg (now the Russian city of Kaliningrad), there was a park that covered parts of the banks of the River Pregel and two of its islands. Seven bridges connected the banks and the islands as shown, and a popular puzzle of the time asked if there was a route by which one could walk through the park and cross each bridge only once.

The problem can be represented as a graph in which each location that can be visited (riverbanks or island) is shrunk to a point and the bridges become lines connecting them (Figure 18.2). The exhaustive-search way of tackling the problem would be by listing each possible path through the graph, continuing as far as possible without repeating a line. Even for a small graph such as this, there are many paths—the sample shows only the paths that begin with line a.

When the Swiss mathematician Leonhard Euler was shown the problem,

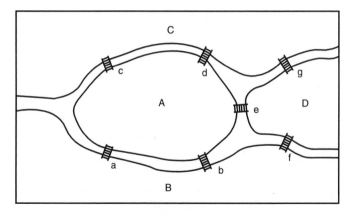

Figure 18.1 The Königsberg Bridges

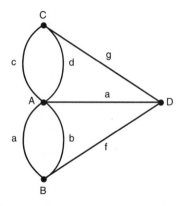

abcdef	abcdeg	abcged	abcgf	abdcef	abdceg	abdgec	abdgf	A: abcde	= 5
acdbfe	acdbfg	acdefb	acdeg	acgebf	acged	acgfbd	acgfbe	B: abf	= 3
adceg	adgebf	adgec	adgfbc	adgfbe	aefbcd	aefbcg	aefbdc	C: cdg	= 3
aegdbf	aegdc	abegcd	abegdc	abef		adcbfe	adcbfe	adcefb	D: efg	= 3
aefbdg	aegcbf	aegcd							

Figure 18.2 Graph of Euler's Problem

he realized that any such problem (i.e., involving a connected graph) could be solved if not more than two of the nodes had an odd number of lines terminating at them. His reasoning was that for a solution to exist, every event of arriving at a point (bank or island) must be accompanied by a corresponding event of departing from it; however, this condition can be relaxed in the case of the starting point and end point. In recognition of Euler's achievement, a path that traverses each line of a graph exactly once is known as a Eulerian path. (There is no Eulerian path for the bridge problem.)

The point as far as we're concerned is that the problem of deciding whether such a path exists reduces to the simple, grocery list–like one of having to check one more item only for each additional node instead of an explosively increasing number of lines. Another way of saying this is that the problem's size increases linearly with n, which makes it a particular type of the mathematical functions known as polynomials. Other examples would be $5n$, n^2, n^3, and the sums of such functions, as we discussed earlier. In the case of the exhaustive search, however, each time some fixed number of points and lines is added to the graph, the length of the list to be searched doubles. Growth of this kind is described by the function 2^n. The distinguishing feature is that n appears in the exponent ("power") of the function, which is what produces the runaway growth. These, along with functions that grow even faster, such as $n!$ or n^n, are termed "exponentially" increasing.

For sufficiently large values of n any exponential function will overtake and exceed any polynomial function. For small values of n a particular polynomial function may well exceed a particular exponential one, but there will always be a value beyond which the exponential function will eventually become greater. It is generally agreed that computing algorithms whose execution time increases exponentially as a function of the problem's size is not of practical value. Figure 18.3 shows this essential difference between polynomial and exponential growth.[1]

The most powerful computer could not be larger than the known universe (100 billion light-years diameter) or built from logic units smaller than the proton (10^{-13} centimeters diameter), which means that at the most it could consist of 10^{126} units of hardware. By currently held beliefs, the propagation of information could not be faster than the speed of light, which puts an upper limit of 3×10^{-24} seconds on the switching speed. Logicians have devised certain formalized languages for which Gödel's unsolvability problem can be circumvented by restricting the kinds of statements that are permitted. Within such languages, therefore, algorithms can be devised that are capable of deciding correctly the truth of any statement that can be formulated. One is known as the "second-order language of one successor," or S1S. In S1S there are considerably more than $10^{1,000}$ possible statement of length 675 symbols. In the late seventies, Albert R. Meyer of MIT and Larry J. Stockmeyer of IBM's Thomas J. Watson Research Center showed that the most powerful computer would take at least 20 billion years to determine the truth value of every 675-symbol S1S statement.[2] Hence, simply having an algorithm doesn't automatically get you home and dry if the algorithm is exponential. Problems of this kind, where no simpler approach—such as reducing the solution to a polynomial—is known, remain one of the big areas of ongoing computing research.

All of this is a roundabout way of saying that huge areas exist outside of AI where available computing power sets significant limits on what can be done. The engineering details of the universe-size, proton-switch computer might not

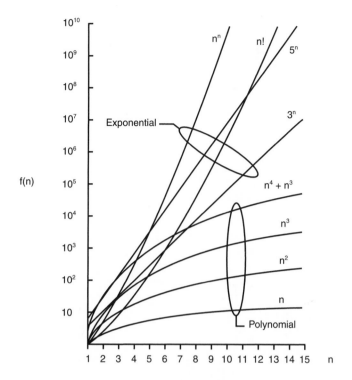

Figure 18.3 Algorithm Efficiency

be quite worked out yet, but that doesn't mean there's nothing that can be done to improve on the computer architecture that we use now. After all, it has remained essentially unchanged in concept for the best part of half a century.

RUNNING A ONE-DESK COMPANY:
SERIAL ARCHITECTURE

Before the advent of the machines that have become familiar to us, a "computer" was a person skilled in performing numerical calculations quickly and accurately. Imagine such a person at a desk, performing all the accounting and other computation for an entire company. The records are kept in banks of filing cabinets, and a harassed filing clerk scurries around continually, fetching and storing files in an effort to keep the computer busy by trying to have the file that will be needed next always ready and open on the desk. Our "computer" is every bit as simpleminded as his electronic namesake and has to follow step-by-step instructions from another file open on the desk. These can get quite elaborate and sometimes have to be supplemented or replaced by more files of instructions, which are also stored in the cabinets.

This is the kind of scheme, known as "von Neumann architecture," which was adopted for the earliest electronic computers, and it remains the standard

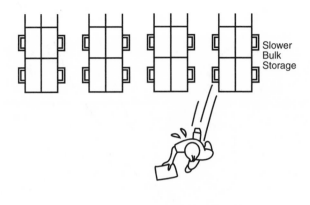

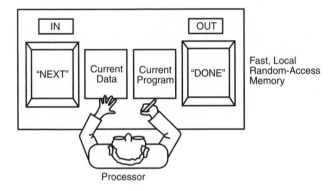

Figure 18.4 Von Neumann Computer

today. The "electronic computer" is literally that: data are brought to the processor for computations to be performed. The filing cabinets represent the libraries of cards, paper tape, magnetic drums, tapes, and later disks that the data and programs are stored in. The desktop is the fast, local memory—electronic circuits, then magnetic cores, today's RAM—carrying the open file or files that the processor is working with currently.

Office space was expensive in the early days, which meant that desks were small and there was room for only a few open files. A lot of skill went into creating compact files that would enable a useful amount of work to be accessible on the desktop at any time. With time, that became less of a restriction, and today we can provide a desktop as big as the company president's—one on either side too, if you want—with a troupe of Olympic runners to deliver files from the library. But everything still goes through that one processor. True, he's been in training and has gotten leaner and faster, but there are limits. And departments with huge files of data like those of astrophysicists and meteorologists or those with enormous programs to hack through like the AI people are coming up with more and more pressing needs that nobody would have thought of even twenty years ago.

The fastest supercomputers such as Crays, manufactured by Cray Research of Minneapolis, are already having to be designed with relativistic constraints in mind: electronic signals can't travel faster than light, which means that beyond a certain point the switching speed of a logic unit ceases to matter much since the limiting factor becomes transmitting the result to somewhere else. Specifically, for an electrical signal to travel a foot along a wire takes 1.76 nanoseconds, which limits the maximum "clock" frequency to 568 million "ticks" per second. (Recall that a computer is an immense finite-state machine—like a New York subway turnstile but a bit more complicated. Its transition from one state to the next is initiated by a timer that sends out a pulse for all the logic circuits that are waiting to switch to do so in synchronism, like galley slaves coordinated to a drum.) Making the circuits smaller helps up to a point, but as more circuits are put on a chip and the chips are jammed closer together, getting rid of the heat generated starts to impose limits of its own.

In the one-desk company, the obvious answer is to hire more computers and distribute the workload. In a computer this means having a number of processors working in parallel.

REGIONAL OFFICES OR A BRANCH ON
EVERY MAIN STREET? DEGREES OF PARALLELISM

There is only one basic way to build a von Neumann serial machine, but the number of ways to lay out a parallel machine is virtually unlimited.

First, how much parallelism do you want? A "coarse-grained" architecture would use fairly large processors, breaking the task down into a few well-defined modules, computational assembly lines performing the same operations repetitively on enormous throughputs of data. This would typify large scientific and engineering applications, which tend to be mathematically intensive and orderly in structure—modeling supersonic airflow over a wing or the collapse of matter into a black hole. The other extreme would be large numbers of smaller units performing simpler tasks, for example, a dedicated image-processing array with a separate processor for each pixel, able to generate a contour map from a stereo pair of aerial images in seconds rather than hours.

Should you sit all your new-hire computers in one big office or give them offices of their own? In other words, will the processors share a common memory or be equipped with their own local memories—or possibly use a bit of both? And what kind of communications paths should there be between the processors?

Finally, what about coordination and control? Does a "head computer" farm out the work to the rest, or are they all put in charge of their own sections and left to work to their own schedules? There is no one best answer, of course, and different formulas emerge to cater to different needs.

Parallel computing had, in fact, been discussed since the 1940s, but it wasn't really until the beginning of the eighties that a combination of factors came together to produce concerted action in that direction. The first, as noted above, was the pressure on the industry for faster processing and more memory to accommodate bigger programs and ever-larger mountains of data. Then there was the announcement of the Japanese Fifth Generation program, which prompted outpourings of funds from DARPA, DOE, NSF, and a number of major computer and semiconductor manufacturing corporations. And finally, the rapid advances in VLSI (Very Large-Scale Integration) technology in the seventies, which enabled thousands of integrated circuits to be etched onto a single silicon chip, provided a basis for design and fabrication highly suited to parallelism.

An example of a coarse-grained implementation conceived as a scientific number cruncher was the Cosmic Cube, developed at the California Institute of Technology, which used sixty-four processors each about equivalent to a PC. Capable of executing a hundred million instructions per second, it offered a tenth the power of a Cray 1 for around a hundredth of the price. In 1985 a commercial variant with up to 128 processors was announced by Scientific Computers of Oregon as the iPSC line. At the other extreme came "massive parallelism" in the form of the Connection Machine from Thinking Machines Corporation of Cambridge, Massachusetts, which was conceived by W. Daniel Hillis, a former MIT graduate who then went on to found the company. Configurable up to 64,000 processors, and with a combined capacity of a billion instructions per second, the design's potential challenged the best of the supercomputers.

The architecture that finally prevailed, however, was of a kind that none of the experts and analysts had anticipated. The same plummeting prices and staggering leaps in performance of the conventional, mass-market Apple-Macs and PCs that wiped out the special-purpose LISP machines also wreaked havoc in the marketplace that had been prophesied for parallelism—or, at least, parallelism of the kind described above that had been envisaged. What happened was that instead of being put in a crowded "computer pool" or a warren of offices around the building, the new hires moved south to work from the sunshine states or even their own homes. The communications and networking infrastructure, which had also expanded beyond all expectations, gave parallelism not in the form of chips on a board, or boards in a cabinet, but of tens of thousands of von Neumann machines linked via optical cables and satellites, dispersed enough not to melt down, totally asynchronous so that clock issues didn't come into it, and running standard software.

And of the huge market for the gamut of parallel designs being forecast only a dozen years ago? There's not much of it left. A few continue to find niches, and doubtless some always will, virtually as customized designs for a few users having highly specialized needs and who are willing to pay the price. Deep Blue is an example. And the Fifth Generation doesn't seem to be doing too well, largely because the programming turned out to be a lot more difficult than was anticipated.

Many AI workers—Roger Schank at Yale, for example—consider that the excitement over parallel architecture was all misplaced anyway.[3] In itself, it offered purely increased speed. Nothing new was brought to bear on such fundamental issues as representing world knowledge, learning, and commonsense reasoning that AI was up against. These were still programmed symbol processors, and any procedure executable on a parallel machine could be duplicated, even if more slowly, on a serial one. Skeptics such as the philosophers John Searle and Hubert Dreyfus, whom we met in the last chapter, had scoffed all along at the excitement within the AI community for this very reason, since their position had always been that humanlike intelligence couldn't be emulated through symbolic representation anyway.

But they had never said it couldn't be achieved by *any* artificial system. Along with the Churchlands (who were not hostile to the symbolic view), they saw better prospects in another form of parallelism that was undergoing a revival. The underlying concepts were immediately more evocative of such words as "brainlike." The architecture didn't involve any "von Neumannish" separating out of function into processing and memory, which generations of psychologists and neuroscientists had never been able to track down and isolate. And it wasn't based on formal representation by means of symbol systems at all.

The New Connectionism

DISTRIBUTED MIND: THE ARCHITECTURE OF BRAINS

Thought is our most celebrated achievement—at least it is by humans. Once in a while when we find ourselves doing something like conversing while driving on the freeway and at the same time planning whether to eat lunch before or after visiting the mall, we reflect for a moment on the complexity of it all, and we are impressed. Yet these activities are only ripples on the surface of all that is going on. The zebra and the whale might well grin derisively as they continue to munch and spout unperturbed, for by far the bulk of the organ that we revere as the quintessence of what makes us so different does pretty much the same things in our skulls as it does in theirs.

Brains are designed chiefly to run bodies. If you put your closed fists together, touching at the heels, the result is about the same size and shape as a human brain and suggests about the same symmetrical structure. By far the greatest amount of its volume is taken up with monitoring and regulating behavior that goes back to our most primitive origins: breathing, blood flow, temperature, digestion, eating, sleeping, balance, movement. The reason elephants and whales have bigger brains is to handle the higher input load associated with their greater number of body-surface sensors and to generate the corresponding control outputs. (The human brain is the largest when expressed as a percentage of body weight.) Everything we think of as making us distinctly human—thinking, creating, imagining, speaking—is performed in its most recently evolved outer layer, the cerebral cortex, which contains more neurons than any other brain structure.[4]

If spread out flat, the cortex would be about the size of a dinner napkin and an eighth of an inch thick; its conspicuous convoluted appearance results from the folds produced by wrapping it around an inner system of earlier structures about the size of a grapefruit—limited in size by the human birth canal. This, finally, even with neurons operating a million times slower, is what in many ways far outperforms a Super Cray in its cabinet the size of a refrigerator with liquid cooling. And the physical contrast is actually a lot greater than that, for much of the constituents of each neuron, as of any cell, are devoted to such functions as transporting messenger molecules, absorbing nutrients, and eliminating waste, which if taken into account when comparing man-made computers would call for the inclusion of chip fabrication and circuit assembly plants too! How is this possible? Through the use of parallelism on a scale that no human designer has ever dreamed of.

The cortex consists of six layers of "computing" neurons at a density of around 150,000 per square millimeter, which, when multiplied by the area of the cortex, gives a total in the order of 30 billion—the famous "gray matter." It is organized broadly into thousands of columnar groupings of neurons, each a tiny fraction of a millimeter in diameter, extending vertically though the layers of the cortex like the pile on a carpet. These seem to encode the basic units of concept and perception. Below the gray matter is the "white matter," a layer of connecting neurons that forms the cabling to connect remotely located neural structures within the cortex. As chip designers well know, routing the interconnections becomes a problem of major proportions as the number of components increases. Nature's approach was to separate the cabling rather than to mix it in with the processing, a solution that might well have been forced as a result of newly evolving structures having to work around older ones already firmly in place. The volume of white matter is actually greater than that of gray matter, which perhaps indicates the size of the problem.

Neurons are in many ways the most remarkable cells in biology. From jellyfish to humans, they all use the same basic electrochemical process to conduct information. Most of the neurons in the brain are tiny, with a diameter no larger than a few millionths of a meter; some in the body can be as long as three feet. Seven different kinds exist within the cortex. Figure 18.6 shows a typical one.

A nerve cell resembles the body's other cells in having a nucleus that contains the DNA program for internal protein manufacture, an enclosing membrane, mitochondria organelles to produce energy, and other common cellular

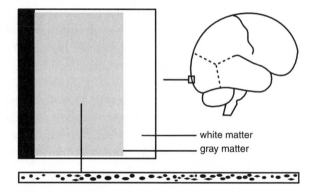

Figure 18.5 Columnar Structure of the Visual Cortex

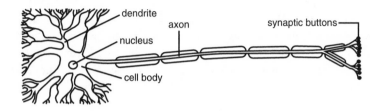

Figure 18.6 A Typical Neuron

components. What makes the neuron special is its elongated structure, which is adapted for communication.

Information from other neurons is collected through a treelike structure of filaments called *dendrites*. There can be as many as ten thousand of them—and this is just the input to one cell. Neurons are often likened to the switching elements of a computer, but this is not a very accurate analogy. In fact, a neuron is constantly processing information, some inhibitory, some excitatory, that it receives from all these other cells, as well as from chemical messengers arriving via the bloodstream. It would be truer to say that each neuron is closer to a computer in its own right. Whatever a cell makes of all these inputs, it communicates as a stream of variable-frequency ("FM" in radio parlance) pulses, typically at the rate of one hundred per second, sent down along the main body of the cell, or *axon*. At the far end, the axon divides into another branching structure that can again number thousands, each filament making contact with a dendrite of another cell via a termination called a *synapse*. The usual estimate for the number of neurons in the entire brain is 10^{11}—a hundred billion computers networked in parallel. With an average of several thousand synaptic connections for each cell, there will be at least 10^{14} synapses in total. It's worth noting, however—and reassuring for our pride in individuality—that the number of *possible* synaptic connections in a single human brain is probably greater than the number of atoms in the universe.

There is another major difference between neurons and other cells, and that is that after a certain point in development they stop reproducing. After multiplying at the astounding rate of 250,000 per minute through the months of fetal growth, the process has virtually ceased by the time of birth. The sobering implication of this is that for the rest of life the number can only diminish, although nature does seem to provide us with a generous excess to start with.

And there's probably good reason why this should be so. If, as is generally believed, acquired behaviors and learning are retained by stimulating new sets of connections between nerve cells, these patterns of connections would be lost if the cells were to divide and reproduce. The male canary is an exception to this general rule in that a part of its brain shrinks and regrows every year. This is the region associated with singing, and it grows in the spring as the bird learns its song to attract a mate. At the end of the mating season the area diminishes; when it regrows the following year the song has been forgotten and the canary has to learn a new one all over again. What use would schooling be if our entire brains worked like that?

It is through this extreme degree of parallelism that the brain achieves its amazing performance. It doesn't require highly purified crystals capable of switching at nanosecond speeds—indeed, the slower operating rate of its elements keeps heat generation down to a level that no electronic system could come close to for a comparable amount of processing—about twenty-five watts. And it's astoundingly robust. Minor damage has little effect on memory, which is somehow spread around and not localized in any one spot that would be vulnerable, and very often the functions of a dysfunctional area can be taken over by others, even if only to a sufficient degree to get by. Naturally, people became curious to find out if some of its astonishing properties can be understood and put to work artificially.

ARTIFICIAL NEURAL NETS

In 1943, McCulloch and Pitts experimented with artificial neurons and developed a theory showing that networks of such devices were computationally equivalent to conventional circuit elements. All the same, nobody was sure how such networks could be made to learn. Donald Hebb, in 1949, showed how this would arise from strengthening the signal transmission across a synaptic connection when the elements on either side of it were active simultaneously. (Reinforcing a signal that was contributing to the activity beyond the synapse would make that activity easier to evoke in the future.) The first attempt to test Hebb's ideas was probably Minsky and Edmonds's Rube Goldbergish Snarc, in 1951, mentioned in chapter eight. A line of work that included experiments like Oliver Selfridge's Pandemonium and its demons, demonstrating the dynamic interaction of separate computing processes, followed through the fifties.

Then, well into the sixties, Frank Rosenblatt developed his Perceptron, which we also talked about previously. The Perceptron consisted of detector cells and decision elements interconnected in the fashion of neurons, coupled up to retinalike arrays of pattern-input cells. The idea was to "train" the network to recognize patterns—alphabetic characters, say—by exposing it repeatedly to the stimulus and adjusting the strengths of the connection paths in such a way as to improve performance. Unlike conventional computing, no explicit procedure was spelled out for extracting specific features of the image. More in the manner of training a rat to run a maze, initially random behavior was either reinforced or discouraged until an acceptable level of performance was attained. At least that was the idea—and a good one, generalizable in principle to all kinds of problems beyond just recognizing spatially structured data such as the pattern of dots in a matrix. Instead of being simply an array of on-off signals, the inputs might, for example, be numbers representing statistical samples and the output a prediction based on them.

However, the systems being investigated used a single layer of adjustable connections, and it was eventually shown theoretically that there were certain types of computation that such an architecture was inherently incapable of performing without a prohibitively large number of cells.[5] Examples were "parity" (whether the number of "on" elements in the retina was even or odd) and the topological function of connectedness (whether all the "on" elements in the array connected to all the others). With the early successes that were being enjoyed by symbolic AI at about this time, general interest in parallelism waned for the next fifteen years, although significant work continued in several places on theoretical studies and simulations. (Even if the explicit function relating the input data pattern to the appropriate output is not given or not known, the operation of each node in the network is specified and can be expressed as a program run on a regular machine. Hence, a digital computer can simulate any neural net, albeit much more slowly, by mimicking each node in turn. But we already knew this from their Turing Machine equivalence.)

Marr and Poggio's work on vision at MIT and the HEARSAY project at CMU in the seventies marked something of a revival in the field. And then, in the early eighties, several independent studies showed that multilayer systems overcame the restrictions of single-layer architectures and were fully universal.[6] Since then, a vigorous industry has emerged for the development and marketing of neural-net simulation software, with a lot of active research effort being put into special hardware chips. Applications range from sales forecasting and stock market analysis to missile and fighter aircraft guidance, automatic road vehicles, failure prediction for machinery, speech recognition, and focusing of optical telescopes. The projected market worldwide for 1997 is over $1 billion.

Parallel Distributed Processing

A NEW MODEL FOR COGNITION

Distributed computational architecture seems more suited to dealing with the kinds of natural, real-world information-processing tasks that biological systems are good at. A major characteristic of such tasks is that performing them effectively requires the simultaneous consideration of many items of information that conspire to rule out whole categories of possible approaches that fail to meet all of them. Hence, the solution is constrained to a few viable alternatives, or perhaps only one. It is by operating within such multiple simultaneous constraints that we solve the problems of focusing on relevance and resolving ambiguities in real-world contexts.

Consider the simple (to us) example of reaching over and around objects on a cluttered desk to pick up a pen or push a button on a telephone answering machine. The workable solution might involve a highly unnatural combination of shoulder, elbow, and wrist movements, but taking account of the simultaneous constraints imposed by the need to clear the edge of the desk while also staying between the edge of the computer monitor and the coffee cup enables us to arrive at it instantly. A conventional computer program trying to compute it from the equations describing all possible motions of a triply jointed system, each able to move in three dimensions and rotate about three independent axes, would get lost in the bewilderment of possibilities.

Very often, the meaning of an item of information can only be inferred through the existence of other items present at the same time. We saw this with the role of words in a sentence, when we talked about language. In the examples

I saw the Grand Canyon flying to New York.

I saw the sheep grazing in the field.

syntactic rules alone cannot tell us what grammatical role the prepositional phrases will play. It is the other words in the sentence that fix the context and tell us that the sheep were doing the grazing and I the flying. Or to take another, famous example from Oliver Selfridge,[7] Figure 18.7 shows a character that cannot in itself be identified as a deformed *H* or an incomplete *A*. Place it in a context, however, and the constraints the other characters impose on what does and does not make sense resolves the ambiguity.

Figure 18.8 shows a striking example of how constraints can operate mutually. With the portions obscured, every one of the characters can be read ambiguously—*P* or *R*, *E* or *F*, *D* or *B*. Yet the constraints on combinations that are meaningful operate together and enable us to make a single interpretation without difficulty.

A

TAE CAT

Figure 18.7 Constraints Resolve Ambiguity

Figure 18.8 Mutual Ambiguity Resolution

We are able to make sense of the world by applying the knowledge of many relationships and situations that we have accumulated. The restaurant "script" and party "frame" were schemes to try and capture such knowledge in structures that programs could utilize. Most everyday happenings, however, cannot be adequately described by a single, scriptlike representation. More often they involve parts of several interacting situations, better exemplified by holding a children's party in a restaurant, or, more generally still, making use of the elements from many experiences to structure a completely new situation. It is problems like these, involving the bringing together of pieces of data scattered across many sources, that distributed representation and processing seem particularly suited to. (Once again, a regular serial computer *could* eventually produce the same result, just as a suitably programmed Turing Machine could, given thousands of years and a few million miles of tape, generate the same moves as Deep Blue. But since time is restricted in tournament chess, the Turing Machine couldn't sensibly be pitted against Kasparov.)

Such considerations have resulted in rapid growth over the last ten years of a different approach to AI from operating on symbolic data structures with rules of some kind stored as a program in memory. Known under the general term "Parallel Distributed Processing," it views cognitive processes as emergent phenomena produced by the interactions of large numbers of simple processing elements referred to as "units," each sending out excitatory signals to some units and inhibitory ones to others. Exactly what a "unit" comprises as a processing entity and what it represents is not fixed by the PDP concept. Units could stand for possible hypotheses about the letters in a sequence or the roles of words in a sentence, or they could stand for the goals of an action, with the connections representing subgoals and causes involved in attaining those goals. In other instances a unit might stand not for any particular concept such as a hypothesis or a word but for some aspect of them. Thus, the very concept itself could end up not being represented specifically in any one place but as a pattern of activations distributed among a large number of units. The PDP concept places no constraints on the kinds of processing performed by the nodes of a network or on how they are interconnected.

AN EXAMPLE OF A PDP MODEL

On a timescale of seconds or minutes, human thinking has a decidedly serial aspect. Ideas and thoughts come and go, are mulled over, and some are acted on while others are rejected. Actions unfold as sequences in time. Could such characteristics arise from a microstructure of many processes taking place in parallel? The following is an example of a distributed model constructed to examine such questions.

Skilled typing involves more than simply learning to perform a succession of keystrokes rapidly and accurately in the way that might at first be supposed. A part of the mind is constantly scanning ahead and priming the fingers to anticipate the keystrokes. When two successive keys are to be pressed with the fingers of the same hand, preparation results in different hand positioning depending on where the keys are located. Consider, for instance, the difference between typing *ev* as opposed to *er*, both of which involve the left hand only in the same section of the keyboard.

Q W E R . . .

A S D F . . .

Z X C V . . .

Both sequences involve the middle finger followed by the index finger. In the first case, however, the hand as a whole remains steady in a compromise position over the home row while the fingers extend first to reach the top row and then the lower one; in the second case, where both letters lie in the top row, the hand moves up to bring both fingers immediately over their target keys. As with recognition in the case of words, constraints arising from the presence of several letters simultaneously produce the behavior of finger and hand movement.

Rumelhart and Norman[8] describe a PDP mechanism that simulates the effect. In the model, a unit in the network was assigned the word to be typed, which in turn activated units corresponding to the various letters. Interactions between these units determined the positioning and movements of simulated hands and fingers. Figure 18.9 shows the activation pattern that arises in typing the word "very."

Each letter unit inhibits the activation of all letters following it in the word. The unit for *v* thus inhibits the second and later letters and as a result of the initial interactions is the most strongly active. The *v* wants to move the index finger down to the bottom row and the left hand with it, but the *e* and the *r*, which are both partially active, exert influences priming the middle and index finger for the top row and would like to move the hand up. Since they

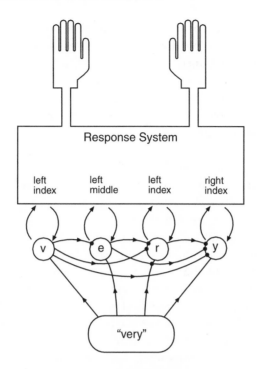

Figure 18.9 PDP Typist
Inhibitory connections are indicated by lines terminating in solid dots.

come later in the sequence, their individual effects are weaker, but together they combine to offset the strong downward pull and the *v* is typed primarily by moving the index finger without motion of the whole hand. The key press causes a strong inhibitory signal to be sent to the unit for the letter typed, which removes its influence. This allows the next letter in the sequence to become the most strongly activated and a new set of positioning weights to stabilize.

The model was successful in producing a keystroke pattern that resembled that of humans. Injecting some noise into the activation process also resulted in the same kinds of errors that occur in transcription typing. The model illustrates that serial behavior, such as a succession of keystrokes, need not be the result of a serial procedure but can emerge from processes interacting in parallel.

RUGGED TOO
Since the information involved in any decision is not localized in one place but comes from distributed sources, PDP systems are highly fault tolerant. Where the input information is incomplete or messy, or a part of the processing system is disabled, the system as a whole will still be able to produce an output,

although maybe a degraded one. In speech recognition over a noisy channel, for example, PDP systems are often able to fill in missing syllables in much the same way that people do unconsciously. Similarly, they are good at making plausible guesses for completing partially available words or other patterns. They don't even have to have seen the correct word before. Very often, they can come up with reasonable possibilities purely on the basis of having been exposed to a sufficient number of examples "like" it before.

REMEMBERING BY ASSOCIATION: CONTENT ADDRESSABILITY

"Can you remember the name of that guy we met in Europe?"

"I'm not sure. Didn't it began with a Z?"

"Oh, that's right! Wezernitski, it was."

A salient feature of human memory is its ability to retrieve information on the basis of just about any association with part of it. Some cues, of course, are better than others. An attribute that is common to many things is not very useful as a selection key since it tends not to make anything in particular stand out. Thus, getting a few Es in a crossword puzzle isn't as helpful as a W or a Z. Regular computer files such as personnel, customers, products, and suppliers can be indexed to be accessible by content, of course, like library cataloging, but their rigid classification schemes often mean that the categories available for searching are never quite what you want.

A distributed network, however, can represent a stored item not as a list of attributes but as a set of interactions between a unit standing for it and others denoting the properties it possesses. The interactions can be mutual, which means that not only will activating the item activate its properties but that activating any of its properties will affect the item. Thus, "content addressability" comes automatically as part of the architecture.

To make this more specific, consider the list of couples we've met in the course of the year:

Names	Age Range	Interests	Reside	Children	Impression
Fred and Nancy	20s	Movies	In city	No	Wild
John and Jean	30s	Books	Out of city	Yes	Interesting
Joe and Kay	30s	Outdoors	Out of city	No	Boring
Jack and Jill	40s	Dancing	In city	No	Interesting
Bob and Lucy	30s	Outdoors	Out of City	Yes	Okay

Figure 18.10 shows schematically a network that represents this information. Each couple is represented by an identity unit that is linked via mutual excitatory connections to all the attributes indicated, including their names.

Activating "John and Jean," say, will activate the corresponding identity unit, which in turn will give rise to the particular pattern of activation associated with those names. In effect, the system will have retrieved a representation

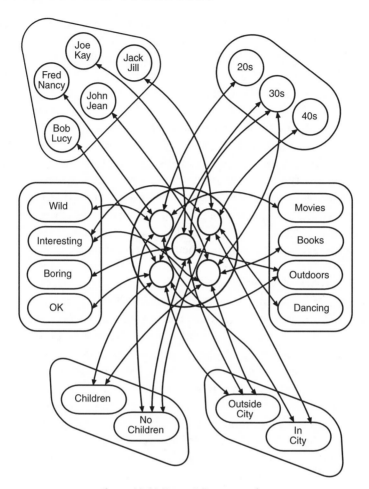

Figure 18.10 Network Representation

of John and Jean. But the process can work the other way around too. We may be unable to recall the names of a couple but remember that they live in the city and like dancing. Activating these two attributes will activate their identity unit, hence retrieving their names along with other information about them as well. In addition it will provide any other names that also happen to be connected to the same two attributes. Other names that share some of the attributes will be affected too: dancers who live outside the city, city dwellers who don't dance. But since the match is only partial, their activation level will be lower.

Naturally, such a network is not error-proof. If incorrect criteria are supplied, wrong sets of associations will eventually take precedence over those intended. However, with this kind of representation degradation from functional to useless tends to take place gradually rather than suddenly and catastrophically, which is more usual with formally structured systems when an error occurs in specifying the retrieval key. Again this is an example of robustness versus fragility.

One final feature of distributed memory is its ability to find what is common among items that become activated by a retrieval key too general to isolate any one of them. For example, we could activate just the unit corresponding to "Books" interest. This would partially activate all associated sets of attributes, yielding a typical description of the couples we know who have an interest in books, even though none of them fits the resulting profile precisely. Thus, the system is capable of producing the general characteristics of a set of instances that satisfy a given specification—just the kind of generalizing ability required to recognize broad likenesses and make context-specific analogies. Explicit procedures must be programmed to implement such things on conventional databases—when they can be implemented practicably at all. With PDP systems, it comes as a natural by-product of the retrieval process.

REPRESENTATION AND LEARNING
Knowledge in conventional systems is stored as static patterns of symbols usually separated into data and procedures for operating on them. In PDP models, by contrast, representation is achieved by an activity pattern existing at a particular time. What is stored permanently are the connection strengths between units, which can be thought of as the knowledge necessary to re-create these patterns. In the example above, activation of the identity unit assigned to a particular couple causes the characteristic pattern for that couple to be reestablished across the attribute units. Knowledge and processing are inextricably bound up together. The associations of an experience are not something that has to be found in a body of static descriptions but are automatically brought into existence through the process of reactivating it.

This has great implications for learning. If knowledge is stored as connection strengths between units, learning becomes the process of finding the right combination of connection strengths to generate the correct patterns of activation in the right circumstances. Such systems can therefore learn by tuning their connections to capture interdependencies between activation patterns without any requirement for formulating explicit rules. This seems to reflect a relationship between actuality and representation that is in greater accord with the real world. While we might devise formal systems, say, of differential equations that to an acceptable degree of accuracy describe the motions of planets, it is difficult to accept that planets actually go about solving anything resembling our representations as they trace their orbits. Planets simply do what they do, just like a child cornering on a bicycle, and we invent ways to describe it that enable us to make useful predictions. Likewise, networks of distributed units generate patterns that "do what they do" *as though* they knew the rules governing the formalizations by which we represent them.

Furthermore, such a learning mechanism requires no powerful computational ability. Connection strengths can be adjusted by simple processes responding purely to local conditions. (Note, however, that this does not mean the network can be left to do all the work. *Designing* a network to capture the right combination of interdependencies can be every bit as elaborate and demanding as programming.)

DISTRIBUTED KNOWLEDGE AND PATTERN ASSOCIATION

In Figure 18.10, an "identity unit" was assigned to each couple. These units held the connection strengths needed to re-create each particular pattern of associations, but it is not necessary to assign a discrete unit to each pattern in this way. The knowledge about any individual pattern may itself be distributed across many different units. When this happens, the units cease to stand for anything in particular that can be expressed in terms of meaningful concepts, and their function becomes purely one of exerting the appropriate connection strengths for the right activation patterns to appear. An example of a PDP model that makes use of distributed knowledge, while at the same time producing a performance strikingly suggestive of the way in which biological systems seem to function, is the *pattern associator*. Figure 18.11 illustrates the principle.

The network can associate a pattern produced in a set of "A" units with a pattern produced in a set of "B" units. The diamonds represent synaptic connections that cause either pattern to influence the units normally activated by the other. The precise way in which the network associates the patterns is given by the expressions:

$$B_1 = A_1.K_{1,1} + A_2.K_{2,1} + A_3.K_{3,1} + A_4.K_{4,1}$$
(where the dot in $A_1.K_{1,1}$ means A_1 "times" $K_{1,1}$ etc.)
$$B_2 = A_1.K_{1,2} + \ldots$$

and so on through B_4

and:
$$A_1 = B_1.K_{1,1} + B_2.K_{1,2} + B_3.K_{1,3} + B_4.K_{1,4}$$
$$A_2 = B_1.K_{2,1} \ldots$$

and so on through A_4.

Suppose now that the patterns generated by the activation of A units represent the sights of various objects and those of B units represent aromas. Figure 18.12, on the left, shows the values for the A's and B's that correspond respectively to viewing and smelling, say, a grilled steak. The connection weights shown couple the vision pattern to the aroma pattern in such a way that the sight of a steak, represented by the A pattern, will activate the B pattern for steak aroma even in the absence of any actual B inputs.

This can be verified by applying the above expressions for deriving the B values from the A values and the weightings shown. For example,

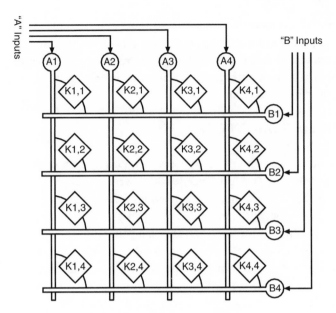

Figure 18.11 A Pattern Associator

"A" Units

+1	−1	−1	+1	
−.25	+.25	+.25	−.25	−1
−.25	+.25	+.25	−.25	−1
+.25	−.25	−.25	+.25	+1
+.25	−.25	−.25	+.25	+1

"B" Units

Steak

"A" Units

−1	+1	−1	+1	
+.25	−.25	+.25	−.25	−1
−.25	+.25	−.25	+.25	+1
−.25	+.25	−.25	+.25	+1
+.25	−.25	+.25	−.25	−1

"B" Units

Rose

Figure 18.12 Steak and Rose Association Matrices

$$B_1 = (+1) \times (-.25) + (-1) \times (+.25) + (-1) \times (+.25) + (+1) \times (-.25)$$
$$= -.25 - .25 - .25 - .25$$
$$= -1,$$

which is the value of B_1 when the B's are activated by a steak aroma input. The remaining B values are reproduced similarly.

And the scheme does indeed work in the other direction as well, as can be seen from:

$$A_1 = (-1) \times (-.25) + (-1) \times (-.25) + (+1) \times (+.25) + (+1) \times (+.25)$$
$$= +.25 + .25 + .25 + .25$$
$$= +1,$$

which is the value for A_1 when the A's are activated by a steak visual input. And again the remaining A's are also reproduced in the same way. Hence, the aroma of a steak conjures up an image of one—a not unfamiliar phenomenon.

The right-hand side of Figure 18.12 shows a similar setting for a different object, let's say a rose. The interesting thing is that if we create a new, compound matrix by summing together the corresponding elements of the two individual matrices it still works for either input. For example:

$$K_{1,1} \text{ (steak)} + K_{1,1} \text{ (rose)} = K_{1,1} \text{ (compound)}$$
$$= (-.25) + (+.25)$$
$$= 0$$

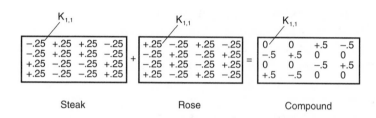

Figure 18.13

Give it a steak odor or picture and it will generate an image or odor pattern for a steak; give it the patterns for a rose, and it will generate the corresponding ones for a rose. So the associations between multiple sets of patterns can be stored in the same set of interconnections.

A number of methods for establishing desired connections and weightings have been developed, ranging from "hard wiring"—values inserted specifically by the system designer—to allowing the machine to learn and reinforce its own connections through repeated exposure to the patterns to be associated. Degradation is again graceful, not catastrophic. An input pattern that is incomplete or distorted will still produce the correct kind of association, but it will be somewhat weakened. The same applies if the model is damaged, for example, by the failure of processing units or connections.

GENERALIZING AND LEARNING

The same set of interconnections was able to associate the sight of a steak with the aroma of steak and the sight of a rose with the aroma of a rose because the two sets of patterns were uncorrelated. This means that rose-pattern inputs have no effect on the connection weightings that work for steak (the outputs in this condition are all zero) and steak-pattern inputs have no effect on the connection weightings that work for roses. The result is that the weightings can be added without interfering.

Patterns that do correlate to some degree—which is another way of saying that they show some similarity—will interact in the sense that the features they share in common will reinforce the same connections. When inputs are presented with a little random noise added to each element (analogous to blurring visual images to eliminate extraneous detail), the network will tend to associate the common trends and ignore the noise. Thus, distributed models are able to exhibit a kind of spontaneous generalizing ability for associating patterns to a greater or lesser degree according to some "similarity" that the network has extracted.

Interestingly, and perhaps significantly, distributed networks used in this way exhibit the same style of learning and make the same kinds of errors people do. An example of this is a model that learns how to construct tenses of verbs from their root forms by being presented with examples. Training initially consists of presenting a small number of the kinds of verbs that children typically learn early in the language-acquisition process. At first, the model can only produce appropriate outputs for the instances that it has been explicitly shown. But as learning continues, two notable behaviors emerge. First, at some point, the network begins generating the standard *ed* past-tense ending for verbs it hasn't seen before. Second, once it has grasped this generalizing principle, it will overapply it by incorrectly regularizing irregular verbs it had previously completed correctly, such as *goed* instead of *went*, and sometimes blending a correct irregular past tense with the regular ending, for example, *camed*. Such tendencies strikingly mirror the trial-and-error learning observed in young children. Once again, the behavior results from simple adjustments in connections made in response to repeated examples. No explicit rules are supplied specifying the nature of the associations to be made, but the network eventually operates *as if* it were following such rules.

PDP CRITICISMS AND LIMITATIONS
Although the parallel distributed approach offers some interesting alternatives in certain areas where traditional symbol processing encounters difficulties, it would be a mistake to get too carried away by the human proclivity to see an answer to everything. The high hopes of the particle physicists notwithstanding, in the real world there is never a single answer to everything.

A common criticism of the PDP approach is that it is too reductionist, reducing all psychology and the behavioral sciences to neural physiology and, ultimately, to physics. The objection is raised that the processes it deals with operate on too low a level to impact seriously the ultimate purposes of AI; there is too great a gap between fiddling to adjust synaptic weights and the level at which interesting things start to happen. Attempting to understand and implement intelligence on such a basis is likened to designing automobile engines using the statistical dynamics of molecules instead of the gas laws of thermodynamics, in which the average behavior of huge numbers of molecules becomes expressible and comprehensible at the macroscopic scale. What's the point in trying to assemble complex cognitive phenomena out of the equivalent of psychological microcode, the argument goes, when they could be expressed directly and more succinctly in an appropriate high-level language?

An immediate answer is that for better understanding of anything you need both top-down and bottom-up approaches to complement each other. It's true that the hardness of a diamond cannot be understood or predicted from the internal structure and properties of a single carbon atom; it derives from the regular lattice structure that arises when many carbon atoms link up under the right conditions. On the other hand, knowing the electron configurations and charge distributions of the different atomic quantum states helps explain why the atoms form lattices in the way they do.

Having said this, however, it is difficult to see immediately how the low-level properties manifest by distributed networks would come into the more abstract issues involved in the general study of cognition. An illustration of PDP limitations in this respect is the "type-token problem." While PDP systems are good at representing general properties, they have trouble where it is necessary to distinguish different instances of the same concept. Given the knowledge that "John is eating a sandwich" and "Mary is eating a sandwich," it is not easy to instill the realization that these are different sandwiches, which is easily represented in conventional programming statements.

Another shortcoming of PDP systems related to more abstract conceptualizing is their inability to represent variables. Higher-level processes seem inherently to demand some form of symbolic representation, which means interpreting symbols that can take on variable values. When we solve a problem mentally, we have to postulate hypothetical solutions, evaluate them, and make decisions. How do we plan our activities, understand science, or compose music? Don't these involve mental symbols that are somehow manipulated? Most people feel the answer has to be "yes," and the inability to represent them constitutes a fundamental limitation on the extendability of PDP systems as they presently stand. As so often turns out in cases with these apparent dichotomies, the eventual solution will almost certainly exploit and combine the advantages of both—just as we do.[9]

Emergence of the Dual-Mode Mind

The applicability of a parallel distributed approach is seen most readily in areas close to perception and motor control. Nobody questions its importance with regard to things like pattern recognition, vision, interpreting speech, and coordinating movement—the things that take place automatically and unconsciously. But something more, over and above it, further removed from the domain of direct experience, is required to describe the higher human faculties of reasoning, imagining, problem solving, and conscious introspection.

The PDP kind of system is highly adept in tasks related to the particular part of the picture for which it is specialized, but that specialization makes it unable to take account of the whole picture. An ensemble of such tasks can each work competently in its own field like the departments in a company or the units of a military command, but none is concerned with the problem of how the tasks all fit together. The sales department is specialized and motivated to maximize orders; however, continuing to do so beyond manufacturing's capacity to supply will result in more harm than good. Meticulously planning a beach landing is no good if the ships to execute it aren't available. In all such cases an additional evaluation capability is needed that can take stock of the global situation and needs of the organism as a whole. This is particularly true of learning processes, where some faculty of trainer and overseer, separate from the learning mechanism, is essential to monitor and assess the performance. Otherwise, how does the dedicated system know in which direction to steer itself?

This second evaluating system might well be another PDP structure, but if so, it needs to be separate from the specialists, monitoring and feeding back to them. In fact, it might comprise many modules of them all interacting because a PDP system is only able to adjust to one stable state at a time. (Any conceptual resemblance to Marvin Minsky's Society of Mind is probably far from coincidental.) The significant point that emerges is that while each specialist might be very fast in responding to a complex situation to find its closest matching state, the behavior of the system as a whole at the "higher" level of interpreting and analyzing the resulting state changes will be highly serial and comparatively slow.

Such a multiple organization (we could be talking about thousands of PDP-like systems) gives a promising model for the dual mode of cognitive behavior observed in humans: on the one hand, rapid, efficient, and unconscious; on the other, slow, serial, and conscious. Skilled performance involving the minimum of conscious intervention—the kind identified by Dreyfus, which experts find themselves unable to articulate—involves reaction to situations in ways that have become automated, and PDP structures seem the ideal candidates to account for it. But how do these finely tuned PDP structures come into existence in the first place? By practice, evaluation, correction, and learning. And this is where the conscious system, involving constant awareness and control of the task, termed "DCC" for Deliberate Conscious Control, comes into play.[10] In effect, the PDP system is trained—rather in the manner of an artificial neural network having its weights and connections adjusted—by the DCC system, which is able to determine when things are going well overall and when they are not, and perhaps make other judgments that affect the connection parameters.

But this is only one of the DCC system's roles. For if the PDP system's function still has to be performed in some way before its training is complete, or perhaps barely begun, it can only be performed by the slow, serial DCC system, which at least has the ability to figure out what's required to muddle through while the specialist is coming up to speed. Once the skill has been perfected, then, like any good manager or teacher, the best thing the DCC system can do is stay out of the way and let the newly established expert handle it. And again, this is just what we saw earlier.

Applying this to AI, a widely held belief is that symbolic representations of more "worldlike" concepts will emerge in similar fashion as an intermediate level between PDP activity and recognizably cognitive abilities. For this reason, the PDP approach is also known as "subsymbolic." However, the current state of the art is still a long way from seeing anything resembling higher cognitive functions emerge from ensembles of PDP modules operating in concert, which means that regular symbolic representations are needed to model them. And a strong school of thought is still of the opinion that waiting for such functions to emerge makes no sense anyway when we have ways of programming them directly. So either way, the future would appear to involve a combination of both approaches for a long time yet.

In this chapter our attention shifted from the symbolic representations that have characterized mainline AI work for most of the time since its inception to the subsymbolic level where the processes involved become more a business of statistics than programming. Such processes have assumed a rapidly growing importance with respect to AI in recent years. The next chapter takes a closer look at some of them.

1. For a general introduction, see Lewis and Papadimitriou.
2. Stockmeyer and Chandra.
3. Waldrop, p. 116.
4. I've taken a lot of this information from Ornstein and Thompson, which is worth a look for David Macaulay's illustrations alone. See also Restak; Hunt.
5. Minsky and Papert.
6. Hopfield; Rumelhart and Zipser; collected papers in Rumelhart; McClelland.
7. Selfridge.
8. Taken from Rumelhart and Norman.
9. Persuasively put in Minsky (1991).
10. Norman and Shallice.

19

Molecules of Mind

STATISTICAL EMERGENCE FROM THE WORLDS OF THE SUBSYMBOLIC

"Practice yourself in little things; and thence proceed to greater."
—Epictetus (A.D. c. 55–135)

The Halfway Level: "Copycat" at Indiana University

DOUG HOFSTADTER'S ANALOGIES—AGAIN

We met Douglas Hofstadter in chapter sixteen, when we were talking about analogies. There, he was using simple patterns of number sequences as a vehicle for developing programs that would not just find similarities but be able to infer and generalize the rule that made them similar. Here, we take a look at some of his work once more, not because its subject again happens to be analogy-making but because of the method it uses, in which symbolic structures emerge from competing processes taking place at a lower level. The structure-making activity resembles the assembly of proteins in an organic cell.

Symbolic systems manipulate explicitly defined data structures that represent concepts or objects—things that have meaning. In a subsymbolic system, undefined, elementary entities, such as weights in a connectionist network, give rise to symbolic properties as statistical effects. Hofstadter's work can be thought of as an intermediate between the two. On the one hand, there is a degree of distributed concept representation, which shares the spirit of connectionism; on the other, certain higher-level notions that could not realistically be expected to arise from a pure connectionist architecture of the kinds that currently exist are implanted explicitly. An example we touched on in the last chapter was that connectionist architecture has difficulty dealing with *token* instances—specific cases—of a concept as opposed to their Platonic *type*. Since the specific and the general tend to activate the same sets of connections, network systems have trouble making this distinction.

Although connectionist models might be more neurologically realistic, their distance from the cognitive level results in a gap that is too wide to bridge at the present time. A useful distributed model of cognition should show exactly how high-level, semantically meaningful structures arise as consequences of the operations taking place at the lower, subsymbolic level. This, however, is beyond pure connectionism as it currently stands. The Copycat project illustrates the intermediate range Hofstadter explored.[1]

Copycat came about in the mid-eighties as an approach to getting computer programs to spot analogies, similar in concept to the one we previously saw for extracting pattern similarities in number sequences, except that it worked on letters. For example, given the change of *efg* into *efw*, what is the result of "doing the same thing" to *ghi*? There are two answers, each having different appeal. One is literally to replace *g* with *w*, yielding *whi*, which, yes, is inarguably "the same thing" but with a certain crudeness and inelegance about it; it's the kind of mundane, mechanical answer we'd expect from mundane, not very imaginative people—or maybe from our idea of a computer program. The other answer is *ghw*, which is obtained from paying heed to the structure as well as the content and replacing the right-most letter. Although there's no definable "right" answer, most people find the second more insightful and satisfying. Here are two more examples so you can capture the spirit of Copycat more fully:

1. *abc* becomes *abd*. How does *ijk* change "in the same way"?
   Almost invariably the answer given is *ijl*, which is obtained by replacing the right-most letter with its alphabetic successor. Possible but far less frequently offered alternatives are *ijd* (rigidly replacing the right-most letter by *d*), *ijk* (rigidly replacing all *c*'s by *d*'s [there are none]), and even *abd* (blindly replacing everything with the supplied model).
2. *aabc* becomes *aabd*. How does *ijkk* change "in the same way"?
   Here, things get more subtle and interesting. Once again, the right-most letter is replaced by its alphabetic successor. But applying the same rule as before to get *ijkl* no longer seems adequate since it takes no account of the obvious fact that the *k* was doubled. The two *k*'s together seem to form a natural unit, and a solution that many prefer is to stretch the rule to "replace the right-most *group* by its alphabetic successor," which gives *ijll*. Hence the concept of "letter" has generalized into "group of letters."

This is not the end, however. Many people still feel dissatisfaction that the doubled *a* in *aabc* has been ignored. Focusing on this quickly leads to seeing the *kk* group as the counterpart to *aa*, which then raises the question of what corresponds to the *c* that changed? Having related "left-most object" (*aa*) to "right-most object" (*kk*), the rule could be adapted to replace the object at the opposite end with its alphabetic successor," giving *jjkk*. However, few people who arrive at this point are content to rest there. The two crosswise mappings that have been made exert a compulsion to read the complete string *ijkk* in reverse, which reverses the alphabetic flow. This has the effect of suggesting the notion of alphabetic "predecessorship" as an implied counterpart to "successorship," and taking it into account yields the answer *hjkk*. "The same thing" thus turns out to be quite a slippery notion. The aim of Copycat was to capture this subtlety by being able to recognize that a rule acceptable in one case doesn't "feel right" in another.

GENERALIZED ANALOGY-MAKING

It would be a mistake to dismiss the program as interesting but irrelevant to anything useful, good only within its tiny domain of simple letter sequences. The architecture was designed expressly with generality in mind and is intended to demonstrate features that transcend not only the specific micro-domain used in illustration but even the task of analogy-making itself. In short, Copycat is not about making analogies per se. Its design is such that the demonstration domain stands for any domain, and the particular relationships employed, such as "adjacency" or "successor," are treated as idealizations of what could be any relationship, such as "neighbor of," "employed by," "parent of," and so on. The groupings within which such relationships are expressed then play roles that could represent "neighborhood," "workplace," "family," and so forth. Thus, the alphabetic microworld is meant as a tool for exploring general aspects of cognition, not anything to do with letters in particular. Such properties as the shapes or the sounds associated with particular letters are irrelevant and therefore ignored. Similarly, arithmetic facts such as that *t* happens to follow eleven letters after *i* in our alphabet are not used. Copycat does, however, recognize *local* sequences to a few places, as well as pairs and trios of objects—the kinds of things that humans recognize with relative ease.

The main aim is to model the general human art of understanding a novel situation by summoning up from a vast repertoire of knowledge and prior experience just the items that are judged by their "likeness" to the present situation to be relevant to dealing with it. This bubbling up of the right concepts out of the subconscious when needed, extracted from a mass of irrelevancies, is what Copycat set out to achieve. A major inspiration for the project was Raj Reddy's HEARSAY at CMU, so it is no coincidence that the description reads like a model of perception. Indeed, one of the main ideas was that even the most abstract and sophisticated cognitive acts resemble perception. Here again is the notion of reusing existing mental machinery that we met when talking about language comprehension.

SOFTWARE ENZYMES: COPYCAT'S ARCHITECTURE

The analogy that Hofstadter offers—he can't get away from them—for the way in which Copycat constructs its hypotheses is the building of protein molecules in the cytoplasm of a biological cell. In the cell this takes place at sites called "ribosomes," which can be thought of as tiny assembly machines following instructions brought from the cell's master DNA for stringing together the components from which the long chains of protein are formed. The components—amino acid molecules—are brought to the assembly sites by enzymes, which are also proteins, each specialized to its particular task, busily scuttling about trying to get its particular product manufactured in competition with all the others. Which demands get serviced is determined by complex feedback processes signaling the needs and condition of the organism as a whole.

Imagine, then, a construction site littered with partly assembled letter sequences, each of which embodies a proposal for a "same as" rule derived from the supplied example. (The process is probably easiest to visualize as parallel, although it is actually simulated on a serial machine.) All the action of analyzing the initial letter-string and its transformation, identifying the various concepts and relationships that it contains (for example, "second letter is successor of first letter," "first two letters are the same," "group forms an alphabetic succession"), and turning those insights into a solution that follows the same rule is performed by a swarm of autonomous, enzymelike agents that are termed "codelets." At the beginning of a run, the "Workspace" contains an initial population of primitive codelets that is not affected by the situation presented since at that point they have no knowledge of it. Their action begins as a purely random process of scanning for basic similarities and building descriptions of what they discover. As new structures representing the program's accumulating knowledge appear in the Workspace, new codelets are created whose action becomes more directed and purposeful, aimed at realizing the concepts that are being awakened.

To illustrate, in Example 2, above, once the *aa* is recognized, the concept of "group" is activated and takes precedence over "letter" as we look for a counterpart. This was what created the "pressure" that made us look further for a satisfactory solution, beyond the rule that had worked fine for the first example. As construction in the Workspace proceeds, Copycat becomes more aware of the "deeper" concepts that are operating—those that are more general and abstract, farther removed from immediate perception. The concept of identity of the letter *a*, for example, is immediately apparent and trivial; the presence of a *successor* to it involves a bit more work to establish and is considered a "deeper" concept; its *opposite* in a comparable string is more subtle still, and so on.

These deeper correspondences are what people are more likely to have in mind as the things that matter when they make analogies, which was the reason we felt compelled to push the rule farther with Example 2. Copycat takes account of this by ensuring that deeper concepts, once activated, exert greater influence on forming the solution than shallow ones do.

The central idea is to allow many "pressures" shaped in this way to coexist simultaneously, competing and cooperating with one another to drive the system in certain directions. The codelets provide the agents through which these pressures make themselves felt. Thus, there exists at any one time a pool of codelets, each characterized by its own measure of "urgency," all waiting to run.

It's important to note that "urgency" is not the same thing as priority, which would imply a determinate order of running in which the highest priority is always attended to first. The rule for running codelets is "stochastic," or indeterminate but weighted. What this means is that a high-urgency codelet has a higher probability of being run, but the chance is always there that a lower-urgency one could get the nod instead. This is perhaps the most crucial difference that sets Copycat apart from other architectures. Its effect is to make the "obvious" solutions more likely; however, those rarer possibilities that people sometimes spot with deeper insight—or perhaps come up with as a smart-aleck response just to be different—will also occur, but with lesser frequency.

And this is good since it captures more faithfully just what is seen with humans. It provides an escape from the rigidity we found with heuristics for reducing search trees, where the same unpromising-looking branches will always be passed over. But occasionally it happens that the brilliant surprise win following the queen sacrifice lies in just that direction. With Copycat, the chance that an apparently unpromising path will be explored is always there.

Here are the results of one thousand runs of the program when presented with the analogy *aabc* → *aabd*; *ijkk* → ? (Example 2, above):

Solution	Number of times arrived at	Average final temperature
ijll	612	29
ijkl	198	49
jjkk	121	47
hjkk	47	19
jkkk	9	42
ijkd	6	57
ijdd	3	46
ijkk	3	69
djkk	1	58

The most frequent solution, *ijll,* reflects an understanding that the doubled *a* calls for the *kk* to be treated as a group, as we discussed earlier. The ploddingly mechanical *ijkl* comes next, perhaps, not inappropriately, suggestive of many people. The next group, *jjkk*, which Copycat arrived at 121 times, is where the concept of mapping crosswise took control, and in 47 instances the program went on from there and generalized to reverse the alphabetic flow. The remaining few answers resulted from other bizarre things that went on in Copycat's mind at other times. It might amuse the reader to try and figure out what they were.

A key variable for monitoring the stage that processing has reached and guiding its transition from initial, random, exploring to final, guided, purposeful is usefully conceived of as *temperature*. At the beginning of a run, it doesn't matter too much which codelets are run since the system has formed no hypotheses about the problem and has no guidance to offer based on the appeal of any particular concept rather than another. Hence, it's appropriate for many possibilities to be explored and decisions to be capricious. However, as the system acquires information and more coherent organizing themes begin to suggest themselves, decisions need to become more focused on the concepts that have been singled out as relevant. The guiding principle to control this shift is seen to be the *degree of perceived order* in the Workspace, which immediately evokes temperature as a metaphor.

As in biological organisms, temperature provides a ready measure of the general condition for all parts of the system. What it controls in Copycat is the *degree of randomness* used at all levels of decision making. At the outset, when activity is mainly random and exploratory, the system temperature is high. As the system homes in on definite organizing concepts, the temperature falls, reducing the random content of activity and thereby rendering the emerging structures less susceptible to change. As a corollary, a solution's quality (the "insightfulness" that went into producing it) relates closely to the strength and coherence of the structure produced, which is precisely what temperature attempts to measure. Thus, the final temperature can be taken as an indication of how "satisfied" the system feels with the answer it has come up with. Interestingly, in the problem considered above, the lowest temperature listed is the 19 corresponding to *hjkk*, which, as we noted earlier, grasps the notion of replacing "successor" with "predecessor" in keeping with the theme of reversing the alphabetic flow. The answer that almost got there, *jjkk*, might have occurred more often, but at a temperature of 47 the system knew that it still didn't "feel" right. The remaining excursions into strange pathways of perception are all distinctly feverish.

Copycat, and others of similar concept that Hofstadter and his students have devised, provides a striking demonstration of purposeful, serial decision making emerging from many microprocesses interacting in parallel. Randomness operates innovatively at the "unconscious" level, but the resulting macroscopic behavior is coherent and guided. Hofstadter doesn't talk about battlefield robots or controlling oil refineries, or catch the headlines with promises of automatic chauffeurs that you'll be conversing with tomorrow. But there have to be Galileos to figure out the basics of pulleys and pendulums before you can have flying machines and satellites. I have the feeling that much of our eventual understanding of how conscious minds come together out of many discordant voices clamoring for attention underneath will come from work like this.

On a closing note, how many ways can you translate a twenty-eight-line poem, each line consisting of just three syllables, rhyming in couplets, and then how much can you say about it? Hofstadter's next book, *Le Ton beau de Marot: In Praise of the Music of Language,* is a study of two hundred English-language versions of a poem "A une Damoyselle malade," written by the French poet Clément Marot in 1537 for a young girl who was ill. Somehow, Hofstadter has found over eight hundred pages' worth of things to say about the poem's translation and related topics, ranging from the fuzzy halos of word meanings to the nature of metaphor and its implications for AI. It will be a while yet before a computer program can find enough variations and shades of meaning to compare with that.

Thermodynamics of Thinking: Boltzmann Machines

Ludwig Boltzmann was an Austrian mathematical physicist who lived from 1844 to 1906. It has become an everyday phrase that "entropy increases," usually uttered despairingly in connection with desktops and children's bedrooms. Loosely, it expresses the principle that any physical system left to change of itself—a cooling cup of coffee, a crystal goblet dropped on a stone floor, a sand castle left on a beach—will pass from a more ordered to a less ordered state. This is intuitively obvious to just about everyone, but it wasn't until the nineteenth century that it became possible to describe precisely the underlying reasons why.

Basically, the reason is that ordered states are comparatively rare occurrences that come about through the operation of some organizing principle, such as the exercising of intelligence and energy to tidy up a room, the locking up of energy in a highly structured hydrocarbon molecule by living processes, or the formation of a uranium atom in the conditions of a supernova explosion. (It is generally believed that our sun and its planets are second-generation, formed from the debris of stars of an earlier epoch that exploded billions of years ago.) "Rare" means that there are vastly more states that the parts can be in that are less ordered. So when a highly ordered system changes to a different state, the chances are that the change will be to a less ordered one. When the number of objects involved is enormous, as with the molecules making up a gas or a liquid, the chances become so overwhelmingly probable that we treat them as laws. There are vastly more ways in which the energy of the violently vibrating coffee molecules can be shared out among the air molecules in the room than there are for it to be partitioned. So overwhelmingly probable is it that the heat will flow from the cup to the air and not the other way that we never observe an exception, although in theory such an infinitesimal probability does exist. Similarly, all the air molecules underneath the desk that I'm working at *could*, instead of rushing around randomly and colliding in all directions, suddenly assume the fantastically improbable minimum-entropy state of all traveling in the same direction at once and hurl it through the ceiling, but I'm not going to worry unduly about it. Boltzmann's contribution to statistical mechanics was a precise mathematical definition of entropy and the formula relating it to probability.

So what does all this have to do with artificial intelligence? Not a lot, except that in the last couple of chapters we've been shifting farther from "macroscopic" symbols and their representations to the world of statistical entities underlying them, and Boltzmann's name has been coopted as the generic name for a class of neural-net machines that make use of statistical properties.

Figure 19.1 shows the general form of part of a neural net as we discussed it in the last chapter. Patterns are presented to the network via the "input layer," which communicates to one or more "hidden layers," where the actual processing is done, via a system of weighted connections. The hidden layers connect to an "output layer," where the answer is presented.

Many different rules have been devised for enabling neural nets to learn. The most common class is known as "back propagation," in which the system is presented with the desired response to a training pattern (by "clamping" the outputs to the required levels) and the network begins by making a random selection of weights as a first guess at the transformation function necessary to produce it. This will invariably be wrong, and the ensuing error is propagated

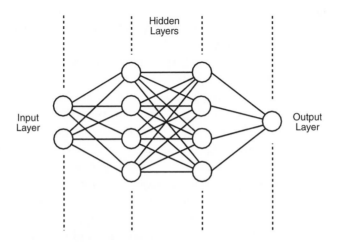

Figure 19.1 Scheme of a Typical Neural Net

back to the input, enabling a correction to be applied for a second try. Eventually, after many cycles, the network will be trained to a satisfactory performance level. It can then be used as an analytical tool on actual working data by running in forward propagation mode only and utilizing the resultant output for whatever the object of the application is. It is possible to overtrain a network, which means that it will respond exactly to only one type of input, making it incapable of further learning and too restricted in capability to be of much practical use. In neural network jargon a system in such a condition is said to be "grandmothered."

Boltzmann comes into it, both in the training and subsequent application phases, by way of ensuring that the system has, in fact, found the correct solution and not a counterfeit of it. When physical systems change from an improbable state to a more probable one, they move in a direction of lower energy. Hence, water flows downhill, lowering its gravitational potential energy; electricity flows from a higher electrical potential to a lower one—and each can be made to do useful work along the way.

The mathematical "space" formed by all the internal states that a neural net can assume in response to a given input can be represented as a landscape of hills and valleys. If the particular state that the network is in is thought of as a marble free to roll around the landscape, training consists of inducing the proclivity to roll downhill, where, since we're talking mathematical space and not physical space, "down" measures reduction in error rather than energy.

There is the risk that the marble could get stuck in a hollow somewhere up a mountain instead of finding the valley bottom where the correct solution lies. One answer to this is to repeat the problem through a large number of runs to find the best solution. Most learning rules come with built-in terms to optimize the settling process by controlling the "speed" and "momentum."

Another approach is to add in a disturbance function to induce a mathematical "earthquake" aimed at dislodging the marble from any local minimum it may have found. Designing such earthquakes can turn into a science of its own. Too violent a shake can be just as likely to send the marble uphill from the correct solution only to have it fall into an upland crater it had managed to avoid before. The most effective profile is usually a fairly hefty main quake followed by a series of diminishing aftershocks. An alternative, widely used mode is better represented by a reducing "vibration," at once again suggesting the analogue of temperature Hofstadter invoked. For this reason the method is usually referred to as "annealing," from the heating-followed-by-slow-cooling process employed to relieve stress in heavily worked metals.

How long, then, before we can expect to see intelligent Boltzmann machines? My answer for the present is, don't even think about it. Neural networks are universal approximators and work well at modeling systems with a high tolerance for error or discovering regularities within sets of patterns; they work well where the diversity of data is very great or relationships are only vaguely understood or difficult to describe with conventional methods. They wouldn't be the thing to use for balancing one's checkbook.

General statistical analysis and areas involving application of statistical techniques, however, is an area where they are coming into widespread use. Others are studies of nonsymbolic processing methods in computer science, signal processing and control engineering, interpretation of nucleic acid sequences in large biological molecules, and modeling of brain functions in cognitive and neurological science. Overall, their general appearance and acceptance seems to have followed a pattern somewhat similar to that of expert systems. After originating largely out of AI-related research, the technology quickly specialized into distinct application niches with visible shorter-term payoff potential. But at least this time the initial rush of overselling the newest tool as the answer to everything seems to have been avoided.

Grubbing About in Statistics:
Data Mining

DATA OVERLOAD: A SAHARA OF NUMBERS

One consequence of the general adoption of computers has been that humans are now able to gather more data than they can digest. Modern scientific instruments, for example, can collect data at rates that were unimaginable even a decade ago. A satellite engaged in Earth observation, a telescope conducting astronomic surveys, or a microscope scanning images of a cell, coupled with data-acquisition computers, can easily generate terabytes (10^{12}) and petabytes (10^{15}) of data at rates as high as gigabytes (10^9) per second. It is not unusual for databases maintained by commercial and financial institutions to reach perhaps 1 billion (10^9) records, each of which may contain a hundred or—in medical diagnostic applications, for example—even a thousand item fields. Within two years, multiterabyte databases are expected to become commonplace.[2]

We've tossed numbers like this around before in the course of this book, but just to be sure of not getting a little blasé about them, let's stop for a moment to be reminded of what this means. In the room that I'm working in as I type this, there happens to be a set of *Collier's Encyclopedia*. I estimate that an average volume contains 3.5 million characters, which would equate to about the same number of bytes. A data acquisition system capable of generating 10^9 bytes per second would produce the equivalent of over 17,000 such volumes every minute. The United States Bureau of Soils classifies sand as consisting of grains from 0.05mm to 1mm in diameter. Taking an intermediate value of 0.5mm, if every byte in the minute's worth of accumulation were represented by one such grain, the resulting pile would be four hundred meters in diameter and almost one hundred meters high. The problem faced by the scientist or other user at the receiving end is, of course, "What do I do with all this?"

To begin with, what we have is just mountains of numbers—what are called raw data. What we ultimately want is something that makes sense in a way that can influence decisions or actions. The cartographer doesn't deal in the streams of numbers pouring out of a radar scan digitizer but in images. The market researcher isn't interested in masses of detail about individual earning histories or buying habits as much as what they add up to in terms of group behavior forecasts and the likely effectiveness of a proposed advertising campaign. The traditional approach to providing information of this kind relied on specialized analysts, who became intimately familiar with the data pertinent to their field and served as interpreters. This is becoming impractical in many areas, and in response to a rapidly escalating demand for automating the work, a comparatively new computer discipline known as "data mining," which is concerned with applying primarily statistical analysis and learning methods to unearthing meaningful patterns and structures from massive volumes of data, has taken shape.

Data mining refers to the specific task of extracting patterns from data. It forms part of a more general process known as "Knowledge Discovery in Databases," or KDD, which, in addition, covers the preliminary stages of preparing and cleaning up the data, the subsequent incorporation of other relevant knowledge, and the final interpretation. As an indication of rapid growth in the field, what began in 1989 as a small workshop aimed at bringing together the few scattered researchers working on such matters became the First International Conference on KDD, held in Montreal, Canada, in 1995 and attracting 350 attendees. By the time of the Second International Conference, held in Portland, Oregon, in August 1996 in conjunction with the AAAI, 60 percent of the 215 papers submitted for review came from overseas.

Here are two specific applications to give a feel for the kind of work involved.

CATALOGING THE SKY[3]
The Palomar Observatory recently completed a survey of astronomic objects that took six years. The resulting three terabytes of image data contained an estimated 2 billion celestial objects captured on 3,000 photographic images, each encoded as $23,040 \times 23,040$ pixels with sixteen bits of resolution per pixel. The requirement was to turn this into a catalog classing each of the objects in the category of star or galaxy, along with forty other attributes. To meet it, the SKICAT system (Sky Imaging Cataloging and Analysis Tool) was developed by Usama Fayyad of Microsoft, Professor S. George Djorgovski of Caltech and Palomar Observatory, and Nick Weir, at the time a Ph.D. student at Caltech, now with Goldman Sachs on Wall Street.

One aim was to include objects a magnitude of brightness fainter than anything classified in previous surveys, which would increase the amount of useful information available to astronomers by 300 percent. This means *very* faint. Visual inspection of photographic plates or the classical computational methods used in astronomy would not suffice. (To give an idea of just how sensitive modern instruments are, it's estimated that the total energy captured by all of the world's radio telescopes since they began operating forty or so years ago—and from which our entire knowledge of the sky at radio wavelengths is constructed—is about equal to the amount of energy released by a cigarette ash falling one foot.) The approach adopted was to use a small number of ultra-high-quality images obtained with high-resolution equipment to establish a decision-tree learning procedure for predicting the classes of objects. This procedure was then used to extract classification rules by applying statistical optimization over multiple trees. The results were material in helping astronomers discover sixteen new high-red-shift quasars in an order of less observation time than would otherwise have been required. These are extremely difficult objects to find, being the farthest away, and hence oldest, in the observable universe.

At least eight of the forty features listed for each object were needed for an accurate classification to be made. For humans, deciding which eight from the forty to select would be hard enough, let alone finding out how they should be used, which is another way of saying that manual classification methods simply weren't feasible. Decision-tree methods involving blind, greedy search proved an effective tool in bringing automation to bear on the problem.

Currently, further learning is being incorporated to search for unexpected features in the data such as structures and clusterings of objects, which in a database of hundreds of millions of items would be all but impossible to spot by manual browsing through the survey's subsets. Given an idea of things that are "interesting," the system will be able to focus astronomers' attention in appropriate directions.

DETECTING CELLULAR PHONE FRAUD[4]

Fraud involving the use of cellular phones is estimated to cost the U.S. telecommunications industry hundreds of millions of dollars per year. A particular form of fraud, known as *cloning*, is particularly costly and widespread in major cities.

A cellular phone transmits two unique numbers, which are necessary to identify the unit for billing purposes, that can be picked up and decoded using special equipment: the *Mobile Identification Number*, MIN, and the *Electronic Serial Number*, ESN. Cloning consists of programming the MIN and ESN assigned to a legitimate customer into a different cellular phone, which can then be used to make unlimited calls, which will appear on the legitimate customer's bill. What usually happens then is that the bill is disputed, a credit applied and the carrier takes a corresponding loss. MIN-ESN pairs can be bought on the street in most major cities for prices varying from $5 to $50.

Tom Fawcett and Foster Provost of NYNEX Science and Technology, New York State, developed a system called DC–1 based on training a type of learning system known as a Linear Threshold Unit to dig into the database of call records and identify irregular patterns of usage that could indicate fraud. The advantage of such a system is that it works from the data being accumulated while the pirated numbers are still in use, before the legitimate customer is even aware of any problem. This makes it possible for a new number-pair to be assigned and the existing ones invalidated much sooner, with a corresponding reduction in the incurred losses.

It will occasionally happen that the legitimate customer and the illegal user each use their different instruments at the same time. Such "collisions" are a clear indication of fraud. Another occurs when two calls are made too close together in time from locations too far apart for the caller to be the same person. In addition to watching for such standard giveaways, the system was designed to determine a characteristic behavior profile for an account and report suspicious deviations from it. General criteria cannot usefully be applied here since a call that is unusual for one customer might be typical for another. The profiles have to be judged by their own pattern of indicator features that the system discovers. Also, since virtually everyone from time to time makes calls from odd places at various times of the day and night, an alert to possible fraud can't be based on a single call tagged as atypical.

The evaluation study used call data from a pool of 2,500 accounts in the New York City area for four months of use. The profilers were trained on randomly selected sets of data covering 5,000 account days for which the content of fraudulent calls had been determined; they were then run against different, similar-size sets of data, also with a known fraud content, to test the results.

DC–1 performed better than the standard checks normally employed to watch for basic signs of fraud like collision but not quite as well as the best "hand-crafted" profiling methods. Set against this, however, is the fact that a hand-crafted profiling system typically takes several person-months to build, whereas the training time for DC–1 is a few hours. This difference becomes more significant because fraud behavior changes constantly and adapts to new detection techniques, and a system like DC–1 is easy to retrain whenever a sufficiently altered environment so dictates. The Linear Threshold Unit was chosen for the experiment because it is simple and fast. Use of a neural net would certainly achieve higher accuracy, perhaps matching that of a tailored system in any case.

DIGGING AI FOUNDATIONS

Many of the techniques that contribute to data mining are recognizably derived from work that came out of AI: learning routines, pattern matching, tree search and decision making, trial-and-error adaptation. But the flow is really potentially two-way, for the very essence of what data mining is tackles one of the major obstacles that AI found itself running up against.

Isn't extracting significant patterns from vast agglomerations of data precisely the problem of finding relevance among the undifferentiated mass of experience that makes up the real world? So while the shorter term, perhaps inevitably, focuses on what is of more immediate benefit to those prepared to provide the backing, it could be that on a longer timescale the techniques developed in the process will play an important role in advancing AI. Once again it turns out that erecting a crucial part of the eventual edifice depends on digging deep foundations. In this particular case the metaphor is an apt one. And the foundations go very deep indeed.

Holographic Mind

There is an alternative model of mind that has been gaining currency over the last fifteen years or so that sees the focus on computers as misleading, responsible for directing attention in the wrong direction for nearly half a century. According to this view, the human brain doesn't arrive at precise conclusions, representable by the manipulation of mathematically certain symbol systems, which then have to be banished to the unconscious due to lack of any firm evidence that they exist; nor does it retrieve information by flipping through thousands of stored templates looking for matches. The delusion came about as a result of assumptions that anything capable of reproducing certain logical and intellectual operations that were supposedly the pinnacle of human mental accomplishment would automatically make short work of the more "primitive" tasks that were obviously simpler. In fact, the opposite turned out to be the case. Why should it be surprising that machines specifically designed to outperform us in areas that we're abysmally poor at should do exactly that? But by the same token, the design philosophy that makes this possible is exactly what makes them unsuitable for the things we *do* excel at.

On the other hand, there are physical processes in nature that seem to work in a way that's a lot closer to the way we do.

Throwing a couple of pebbles into a calm pond produces a complicated interplay of disturbances on the surface as the two expanding rings of wave systems overlap and start to interfere with one another. Logically enough (even mathematicians and scientists are capable of it sometimes), this is known as an *interference pattern*. Interference patterns are generated when two systems of wave motion—processions of "humps" of some kind moving past in a regularly spaced train—cross paths and come into collision.

Light can be represented as a wave motion (the humps being peak values of the two components—"electric" and "magnetic"—that make up the electromagnetic field). One way of generating an interference pattern from light waves is to split a laser beam into two separate rays, send the rays around two different paths via mirrors and lenses, and then bring them back together on a screen or sheet of photographic film for the pattern to be displayed or recorded.

If one of the rays is now diverted to reflect off an object—say, a porcelain figurine—on its way to the screen and the other, "reference ray" is left alone to get there directly as it did before, the resulting interference pattern will encode the information that the reflected ray carries defining the figurine's surface. Unlike a regular photograph that simply records reflected light, the pattern doesn't look like the figurine. In fact, it doesn't resemble anything recognizable at all. But all the information necessary to reconstruct an image is in there.

The way you do this is to shine an identical reference ray through the hologram, and, lo and behold, the pattern plus the ray interact to reverse the original process and generate a reproduction of the ray that came from the figurine. You can view it from the other side, capture it on film . . . whatever suits your purpose. Holograms, as most people know, actually regenerate the original wave front of light, not just the image seen in a particular direction, as regular photographs do. That's why you can move your head and see a changing perspective as if it really were solid.

An even more interesting difference from photography is that the information in the hologram isn't stored as points having a one-to-one correspondence with the points on the image—so if the part of the photograph that records the figurine's nose is cut out or smudged over, you've lost it. Rather, the information pertaining to every visual point in the image is spread out across the entire hologram: every point in the hologram contains some measure of every point in the image, and every point in the image is represented to some extent at every point in the hologram. The result is another example of "graceful degradation." Cutting out a piece of the image will not prevent the entire image from being reproduced, although its quality will gradually decline as the amount of damage increases.

Well, yes, all very neat, but what does this have to do with minds and brains?

It has to do with the fact that human vision works in a similar way. If part of the retina is impaired or lost, everything is still seen but less distinctly. So straightaway, the physics of holograms has a "mindlike" feel about it. Also, a hologram exhibits the same kind of associative ability that the mind does. If you use a single hologram to superpose the patterns of two scenes, illuminating the composite pattern with light encoding one of the scenes will cause the other to appear in the transmitted ray (reminiscent of steaks and roses again). But more striking still, perhaps, is the way holograms are able to detect similarity.

Suppose you make a hologram of this page and then make a separate hologram of the letter *h*. Now, if you superpose the rays shone through both holograms, the astonishing result is a black field in which a bright spot appears at every location where an *h* is located on the page. Moreover, the brightness of each spot will be a measure of the degree of similarity between the *h* occurring in that position and the one used as the model. If the letter on the page is rotated, deformed, or incomplete, the spot formed at its location will be correspondingly dimmer. The crucial point is that the process involves no "information processing" of the kind used to extract and compare lists of features. Similarity detection arises everywhere as an instantaneous result of the interference of the two wave systems. Once again, this has a distinct "feel" about it, like the way a face we're looking for in a crowd suddenly jumps out or, in a different situation, how a name that's close but not the right one comes to mind.

Though this is decidedly suggestive of the kinds of properties that we found are exhibited by neural nets, nothing approaching the complexity of human cognitive functions is yet in sight of the things that are being done artificially. It's perhaps significant to note, however, that the mathematical formulations that describe holographic processes do bear a similarity to certain statistical methods used for representing data and concepts in distributed form. At this stage, it would be premature to jump to the conclusion that the brain *must* work like a hologram. I've mentioned the possibility, though, to draw attention to the fact that other physical processes that many people feel offer more intuitively appealing and plausible models of mind than traditional assumptions take into account do exist.

Emulating Genetics:
Toward Programs That Write Themselves

It's not strictly true to say that animals evolve. A cat is every bit as much the same cat when it dies as it was the day it was born. Through life, its cells, as they divide, for the most part continue faithfully to pass on to the newly formed daughter cells the same genetic package that the cat received from its parents. What evolves is this *information* as it is passed on down the generations. The shape and form of an individual from any generation could be thought of as a "snapshot" capturing a stage of the process—a physical expression of the accumulating message as it stands at that particular time. The "message" is an elaborate list of instructions for producing proteins. The cat—or whatever—is what a kit of proteins assembled according to the instructions current for that particular line (species) will grow into.

This talking about sequences of instructions being executed to direct processes toward an end is beginning to sound like computer programs again, and, indeed, the program metaphor is commonly invoked to help describe the DNA→RNA→Protein transcription process. Now, writing a computer program of even moderate complexity is a taxing and tedious business, and at the end of it all the final product still tends to be highly fragile in the sense that tiny errors are liable to have grave consequences. (A Venus probe was once lost due to the omission of a comma from a crucial line of code.) Nobody had to sit down and hand-code, line by line, the genetic instructions for a self-assembling cat, and yet here we are surrounded by billions of existence-proofs of the successful operation every day of programs of a scale and complexity that no human programmer has ever contemplated. Furthermore, these naturally evolved programs excel in such qualities as ruggedness, graceful degradation, and other features that we would very much like to see incorporated as a more regular characteristic of our own creations. In short, the complexity and reliability of the genetic programs that evolutionary processes have shown themselves able to produce is awe-inspiring. It should be hardly surprising, therefore, to find that interest has been growing in seeing if the same processes can also be applied to producing computer programs.

The reason cats are not all the same is that their precise genetic makeup varies within a common framework of "catness" that has settled down to be highly stable. (It has been estimated that the number of possible human genetic endowments is $10^{2,400,000,000}$.[5] I have no idea even how to begin suggesting an analogy to indicate a number that size. Every number we've touched on in this book shrinks to invisibility in comparison with it.) This *genetic variation* comes about in three basic ways: (1) *Random assortment* of chromosomes into eggs or sperm. The immature cell contains two of every chromosome—one from each parent—which on division of the cell are distributed randomly to form the single set of chromosomes that goes into each egg or sperm cell. That's why, apart from identical twins, no two offspring of the same parents are exactly alike—and sometimes not even similar. (2) *Mutation* of individual genes in the sex cells. (3) *Recombination* by exchanges of genetic material between chromosomes, enabling favorable mutations in different chromosomes to be brought together.

Much of the terminology has carried over into the field of genetic computer programming. A *genetic algorithm* refers to a model of machine learning in which the role of chromosomes is played by arrays of bits or characters, which can be variable or fixed in length, that form an algorithm's components. The algorithm might, for example, be an optimizing routine to generate a set of values best suited to some stated purpose. Functions analogous to mutation and recombination ("crossover" in programmer parlance) upon an initial population of chromosomes is effected by bit manipulation operations, and the "fitness" of the resulting variants is evaluated by comparing their performance with that displayed by the parent generation. The variants that show improvement are selected for further experimentation ("mating"), the older population is discarded, and a new cycle of the process repeats. Generally, rearrangement rather than mutation is found to be the dominant factor. Since the testing to establish fitness can be as automated as the rest of the process, a well-implemented genetic algorithm can drive toward improvement with surprising rapidity.

Genetic programming is the extension of this concept to produce better programs (in other words, the output of the process is a new program, not a number or numbers as produced by an algorithm). Here, the entities being operated on are program segments and, therefore, necessarily variable in length. Generally, the structures are expressed in the form of "parse trees" rather than lines of code, since they are better able to show the kinds of recombination operations typically implemented. Thus, the simple program to compute A + B×C would be expressed as:

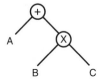

Figure 19.2

Evaluating fitness is probably the most difficult concept to convey to a genetic program. A program to set the time on a clock would have a very simple task of comparing the amounts by which the clock was wrong and selecting the program that produced the smallest error. In contrast, to fire a gun to hit a moving target, a genetic program would need to learn to take account of such variables as wind velocity, type of gun, target range and bearing, target speed and acceleration, even though the fitness would again be expressed as a single number, i.e., the distance by which the shot missed. This type of problem, involving a simple fitness function and a large number of variables, is where genetic programming tends to work best. As one would probably expect, it also seems to reflect the kind of situation that natural evolution deals with: number of variables, astronomic; fitness function, very simple—you either survive or you don't.

Crossover is one of the most important operations employed for modifying structures in genetic programming. Two parent programs, already selected for fitness according to whatever criteria apply, are combined "sexually" to create a pair of offspring. This is accomplished by deleting a fragment of the structure of one parent and inserting the crossover fragment from the other; the second offspring is produced reciprocally. Figure 19.3 illustrates the principle.

The child on the right may be recognized as representing the solution for the positive root of a general quadratic equation of the form $ax^2 + bx + c = 0$:

$$x = \frac{-b \pm \sqrt{b^2 - 4ac}}{2a}$$

Parents for a crossover operation can be different or identical. As with biological parents, they can have multiple progeny.

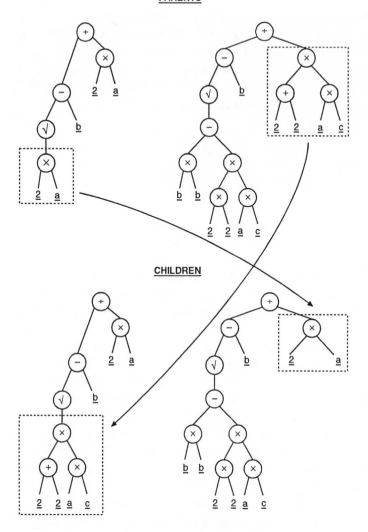

Figure 19.3 Crossover Recombination

Mutation is a process akin to budding, involving a single parent. One form simply entails the random replacement of one function (+, −, ×) or variable (a, b, c) by another; alternatively, entire subtrees can be switched or replaced as a unit.

Although genetic programming is in its infancy, some workers in the field already see it as the beginning of programs that will write themselves. The notion is attractive to AI researchers in that it seeks to apply the same principles that resulted in the successful—more or less—emergence of the only reasoning intelligence we know. Also, it promises ways of exploring avenues that conventional analytical programming, guided by assumptions and ways of looking at the problem that could be overly restricted, could fail to open up. As with other things we've seen such as neural nets and statistical, hologramlike representation, genetic programming represents a radical departure from the traditional logic-machines paradigm, tending more toward the kinds of processes observed to take place in real brains and the real world. Such techniques, used in conjunction, could perhaps form the basis for a whole new approach to AI that will characterize the next half century.

Quantum Mind— the Root of Originality?

At the beginning of the eighteenth century, Isaac Newton reduced all motion to a set of simple laws relating force, acceleration, and mass that could be applied equally to planets and moons orbiting in the heavens, an apple falling from a tree—indeed, every particle in the universe. The universe thus became a gigantic machine whose motions were completely determinate, every state following inexorably from what went before, its entire history, future and past, computable in principle even if the necessary computation were impractical. This naturally raised the question of whether we were also predictable machines, and for two centuries philosophers and clerics argued over the moral and other implications of whether human free will is what it appears to be or an illusion. After all, if I were a lawyer and my client had no choice but to rob the bank because of forces set in motion by the big bang, it would hardly be fair to hold him to blame. But then, I suppose, the judge could equally well argue that he has no choice but to pronounce a sentence of ten years.

Then, in the early part of the twentieth century, the new insights of quantum mechanics revealed that the seemingly regular, clockwork universe rests on underpinnings that operate in a very different fashion; bizarrely so, in fact. In a manner strangely reminiscent of the way the gas laws we regard as immanent and fundamental emerge from statistical averagings of innumerable chaotic micromotions of invisible particles, the solidity and apparent permanence of matter itself turns out to be illusory, arising from fleeting appearances of . . . we really don't know what—strange entities that resist all attempts to describe accurately in terms of anything we know. Nothing that's localizable actually moves in the quantum world but instead vanishes from one place and reappears in another without going through the points in between. And nothing happens with certainty. When an event has several possible outcomes, all that can be said is that each one has a certain probability of happening.

An example of the probabilistic basis to everything is provided by the electronic state transitions of an atom. If an atom absorbs energy and becomes "excited"—perhaps an atom of neon gas in a street lamp under the influence of the applied electric field—one of its outer electrons "jumps" to a higher-energy state. At some later time the electron will fall back to a less energetic state, releasing the energy difference as a photon (in the case of the street lamp, visible light). For most such transitions there are several lower-energy states that the electron could fall to. The probabilities of each can be calculated, and experiments to test them show these predictions to be among the most successful in any branch of physics. But *which* of the possible transitions will occur in a given instance, there is no way of telling.

Chance, then—pure indeterminism—rules the quantum realm. And this was no small discovery to scientists and thinkers wrestling desperately with the implications of seemingly having to concede to being simply parts of a huge machine. (Note, there is a difference between being deterministic and being predictable. A machine can be deterministic in that what it does has a fixed outcome and yet be so complex that there's no way to predict what that outcome will be. A flipped coin's fall is totally determined by the initial momentum, gravity, and momenta of air molecules acting on it; we just don't know what they are—and wouldn't know how to calculate the answer if we did. This was cold comfort to those who chose—or did they?—to insist that they did things because they *wanted* to and not because the working out of some vast mechanistic process made it inevitable. I readily admit to being one of them.)

With all processes operating at the macroscopic scale of existence having been found to be equally mechanical, it appeared, and still appears, that if the freedom of choice that we are conscious of is indeed real—which is another way of saying not determined—the indeterminacy must originate from the quantum level; it surely doesn't exist anywhere else. The question, then, is, how do indeterminate events of subatomic scale manage to play any part in the workings of a macroscopic brain and contribute to the form of the thoughts taking place in it? The only honest answer is, nobody knows.

Frank Tipler, who calculated that John Searle's Chinese Room would need six hundred large nuclear plants to operate, believes that some such mechanism provides the basis of those things we call "creativity" and "originality," where new ideas and inspirations seem to pop into our minds unbidden out of nowhere. Not out of nowhere, says Tipler, but "up" from below. Tipler's concept is suggestive in a way of Hofstadter's ideas with which we began this chapter, of part-formed entities bubbling around in a kind of subconscious froth until they take on enough form and coherence to get attention. He envisages a bottom level of brain activity sufficiently sensitive to be influenced by quantum events, generating nothing coherent or resembling thought but able to cause random activations and connections among the most primitive building blocks of which thoughts are made. Most of these make no sense and are screened out by layers of "plausibility checkers" that insulate us from the babble of inanity going on constantly down below, but every now and again a combination that isn't immediately nonsensical is allowed through and passed up to a higher level of scrutiny. Every once in a while, one of them makes it all the way to consciousness—and another brilliant flash of insight appears.

Tipler's point is that the source of true originality must lie in randomness. The mutations that give rise to evolution are random, even if the selection processes that operate on them subsequently aren't. (At least in the early epochs of molecular and primeval evolution, the mutations were random. We saw when talking about Doug Lenat's EURISKO that processes giving more direction may have taken over later.) And the randomness at the quantum level is the only true randomness we know.

Roger Penrose, whom we also met, speculates that there might be neural cells deep in the brain sensitive enough to be triggered by quantum events. Experiments with toads have shown that a *single photon* impinging on the dark-adapted retina can be enough to trigger a macroscopic nerve signal. Apparently, a similar sensitivity exists in humans, but an additional mechanism that filters out low-level noise from the visual system results in a need for a combined signal of about seven photons in order for anything to register.

Does all this mean, then, that a true all-around intelligence, one capable not just of reasoning, interacting competently with its environment, and using language but also able to match human creativity, will need to incorporate some kind of mechanism that makes use of quantum phenomena? Well, what else can one say but yes, quite possibly it does?

The Price of Versatility

This whole chapter has been a process of moving down through levels of activity below thought where the elements from which thought emerges become progressively more diffuse and probabilistic. We have no conscious awareness of these processes, and even our knowledge that they exist is derived indirectly through the use of highly sensitive instruments.

Every design engineer knows about trade-offs. Some of the requirements that a design has to meet always conflict with others, and improvement in one direction extracts penalties in the other. A Ford pickup is great for work around the farm, but you don't enter it in the Indianapolis 500; F–15s wouldn't be the right buy for TWA, and so on. "General-purpose" systems offer a compromise by fulfilling a number of roles moderately well without excelling at any of them—for example, the family car and the home computer. You could say the trade-off is excellence for versatility.

The human nervous system is probably the best example of versatility there is. It can do almost anything to a degree, but its performance in any given area is limited. So we supplement it with all kinds of specialized accessories such as microscopes, calculators, and long-range communications equipment, each of which outperforms it by orders of magnitude in its own area but is useless for anything else.

Conceivably, if we ever did produce a system of comparable versatility to the brain, we might find that one of nature's basic trade-offs is that thinking narrow and thinking wide are mutually exclusive. In the same way that our consciousness operates without any awareness of what our neurons are doing, or even that we have any, an artificial electronic (or photonic, or whatever) intelligence might find itself necessarily "shut off" from the levels at which its fast, mathematically precise operations are taking place. Perhaps, therefore, it wouldn't be able to perform astronomic calculations in seconds, recall word for word a conversation that it had a week ago, or make a decision without grappling with all kinds of imponderables. So what would it do if it wanted to know *pi* to a couple of thousand decimal places or prove a logic theorem? I suppose it would either have to build itself a computer or buy one. And that's a good reason to suppose that long before then we'd have started calling it something else.

In fact, having talked about genetic programming, it seems reasonable to guess that by that time we would have turned to similar methods to give it a supporting hardware system that could grow itself through applied genetic engineering. Maybe we could call it a *B*iologically *R*eproduced *A*rtificial *IN*telligence. It seems appropriate enough. And the acronym would be irresistible.

1. Described in Hofstadter (1995), and more comprehensively in Mitchell.
2. Fayyad, Piatetsky-Shapiro, and Smyth.
3. From Fayyad, Haussler, and Stolorz. In the same paper there is also a fascinating application involving finding volcanoes on Venus. For more on the sky-catalog project, see Fayyad, Djorgovski, and Weir.
4. From Fawcett and Provost.
5. Dobzhansky.

20

So Where Does
It All Leave Us?

"Within thirty years, we will have the technological means to create superhuman intelli-gence. Shortly after, the human era will be ended." —Vernor Vinge

"The computer arrived just in time to save—and save very nearly intact, indeed to entrench and stabilize—social and political structures that otherwise might have been radically reno-vated or allowed to totter under the demands that were sure to be made on them."
—Joseph Weizenbaum

All in all, we've covered a lot of ground since talking about automatic chauf-feurs and space-going robotic mining teams in chapter one. And yet, judged by the standards that such visions imply, we haven't really come a long way. Despite forty years of astounding technological advances that have exceeded all predictions, the early AI vision of reproducing all-around, humanlike rea-soning and perception remains as elusive as ever. Instead, we've seen the repeated pattern by which a new approach that is going to be the answer meets with early success, sometimes with overselling and wild media speculation, only to find its own niche of specialized application where it becomes another tool in the overall computing inventory. The result has been a quiet retreat into less ambitious goals, in which AI is now seen as a collection of general tech-niques for getting machines to do things that would normally be called intelli-gent if done by people. We thus have "smarter" cars that know how to optimize fuel-air mixtures and programs to find patterns in prospecting data—useful and profitable, to be sure, but not yet the stuff that makes for exciting science fic-tion. The more restrained language testifies to much that has been learned.

Perhaps most significant, and certainly one of the causes of greatest

351

surprise, was the discovery that the relative ease of programming machines to perform tasks that humans find hard was no indication that the things we don't even have to think about would prove easier still. On the contrary, it is precisely those things that even children accomplish effortlessly that turn out to be extraordinarily difficult to mimic. What this shows is the enormity of the gap that separates even the simplest of biological systems from the inanimate, and in so doing brings home the truly astonishing qualities that all humans share, compared to which such differences as who commands armies or wins Nobel Prizes are reduced to trivialities. This should say much about the imagined differences and ensuing social problems that have plagued so much of our history and perhaps better prepare us for the challenges of eventually expanding into the universe as a single, united species.

I haven't said too much about the ultimate characteristics that would make a machine truly humanlike in every respect and that form the staple fare of nearly all science-fiction treatment of the subject: the ability to share our capacity for self-awareness and to feel emotions. As to the possibility of such a development, I can merely point to the existing proof of 5 billion examples of electrochemical systems operating within the laws of physics that are aware and that feel emotions, and offer the conclusion that there's no obvious reason why some other form of system that happened to have originated in some different kind of way shouldn't be capable of doing likewise. This shouldn't be taken as a prediction that it will happen, or even that I think it's likely. Those like Joseph Weizenbaum and John Searle who insist that the ability to perceive the world in a humanlike way is deeply and inseparably rooted in the experience of being born into it as a human, of growing up in it as a human, and in forming the relationships of dependency and trust and all which that entails may well have a point. And besides, as Peter Kugel of Boston College asks, why go to enormous effort and expense trying to get robots to behave like humans when we're still educating and employing people to behave like robots? Or to cite Pat Hayes, now with the Institute for the Study of Human & Machine Cognition at the University of West Florida, if genuine humanlike capability is what you want, there's a much easier, cheaper, and proven way of going about it—it takes two people nine months, and it's more fun than bolting things together in factories.

The reason I haven't dwelt on this aspect is that at best it's a long way off, which means anything one says can be only speculative, and there's little I can add to the speculations already made. Marvin Minsky feels that awareness of some kind will be an inevitable outcome of systems becoming sufficiently complex, a consequence of the need for functions to supervise and evaluate overall performance and guard against such self-defeating behavior as going into infinitely repeating loops. Allen Newell disagrees, pointing out that such systems already exist, like the global communications networks that possess stupefying complexity and monitor their own operations but surely can't be credited with "knowing" much about anything. What's missing, he suggests, is the tightly coupled interaction of all parts of the nervous system that give it its sense of "I" and a perspective on the world. My own guess is that, in the same way as eggs produce flying things that chirp and have feathers but what engineering gets you is a 747, whatever awareness that might eventually emerge artificially will be utterly unlike our own. If this means that it comes complete with interests and goals that are also unlike our own, perhaps it's just as well that the prospect is a remote one, and we still have plenty of time to think about it. But not everyone agrees that we do. Vernor Vinge gives it not more than thirty years. At that point he sees what he describes as a "Singularity," beyond which the accelerating rate of changing machines brought about by machines makes all attempts at further forecasting meaningless. Our role as the dominant species will then be over, and what happens will no longer be up to us, he cheerfully predicts.[1] Just thought I'd throw this in to be upbeat.

Hans Moravec sums up emotions as internalized biases—"feelings"—that incline us to repeat behavior that is beneficial and survival-oriented and to avoid that which is destructive. In this sense he sees emotions as readily implementable in machines. The household robots and domestic nannies that sold best would be the ones that proved best at pleasing their owners, he gives as an illustration, which means they would be able to learn your tastes and preferences and feel "distressed" when they didn't meet them. Weizenbaum, the author of ELIZA, concurs, but, like many others, doesn't go along with accepting that outwardly indistinguishable behavior necessarily means being accompanied by similar subjective feelings inside. Moravec is solidly of the Alan Turing school, which holds that if you can discern no difference, there is no difference. He and I have discussed this, and I admit to being with the skeptics on this one. "But suppose the machine assured you that it felt all the same things as you do, and asked, 'What else can I do to convince you?'" Hans said. "When a human tells you exactly the same thing, you accept it. So why not when it's a machine?" The short answer is that extraordinary claims require extraordinary evidence. When I'm talking to a human, who I know is made like me, grew up like me, and has the same kind of accumulated cultural experience as me, I have little hesitation in accepting that the person probably feels things very much they way I do. I'm less easily persuaded when none of these things apply. And in any case, it doesn't always work, even with people. There are many occasions when the only honest answer to somebody looking at you pleadingly and saying, "How do I convince you I'm sincere?" is "You can't."

"But what if the machine could compose poetry and songs, write a moving novel, and do all the things that genuine emotional, feeling people do?" Hans persists. Well, we're getting closer. But you can see now my reason for saying the time to worry about it is a long way away yet. And if it's on the other side of Vernor's Singularity, there won't be any point in worrying at all.

John McCarthy agrees that instilling emotional qualities into machines would probably be easy enough, but doesn't think it would be a desirable thing to do. Making robots display visible signs that would be interpreted as being sad or bored, angry or anxious would be an invitation for humans, starting with children, to react to them as if they were persons, he maintains. Who wants to have to deal with a computer that loses its temper or a robot bank teller falling in love? And robots that started feeling sorry for themselves would start demanding rights and obligations, and we already have enough trouble figuring out our duties toward fellow humans and animals. The last thing we need, McCarthy says, is machines coming to acquire status in human society. Society is already complicated enough.

It is customary when concluding books on artificial intelligence to review the spectrum from pessimism to optimism about the impact of computerization in general, and the prospect of intelligent computers in particular, on the future and ourselves, especially on the quality of life that we can expect to result from it. Once again, there isn't a lot I can add to the volumes that have been written. The dark end deals with such specters as automating the control of weaponry, target selection, and battle management and the assaults on dignity and privacy that are threatened by intelligent eavesdropping machines, extensive personal databases, and an electronic totalitarianism in which bureaucratic intrusion pervades every facet of existence. The brighter visions see worlds of universal leisure and affluence, with automated subterranean and off-planet manufacturing complexes churning out unlimited quantities of everything and life filled with opportunities of every description, enriched by machines serving as intelligent tutors, mentors, and companions.

Personally, I see movement in either direction as possible, although neither is preordained. Technology in itself is neither good nor evil, but it does have the power to amplify the dispositions toward one or the other that exist in people, just as it amplifies the physical work they are able to accomplish. It does not have the power to make us other than what we are. Shaping who and what we are and determining how we direct our lives—which includes deciding the ends to which technology will be put—is the traditional role of morality, philosophy, and religion and the purpose of our social and political institutions. Perhaps the accelerating pace that is being forced on us by technology will encourage a reappraisal of the importance of such foundations as the basis of education and our culture as a whole. In any case, I can't see it slowing down. Too many commercial and international competitive pressures add up to a relentless logic that says the only victim of holding back will be you, because if you don't go for what's possible now, somebody else will. It's not an entirely daunting prospect to have to live with, because I suppose that if all those amoebalike things slithering around in the ooze billions of years ago hadn't thought the same way, we wouldn't be here to moralize that they were wrong.

Marvin Minsky sees no reason why machine intelligence has to stop at our level and goes on to suggest that far from being cold, alien, and impersonal, such a superintelligence could turn out to exceed us in emotional capacity too. Why, after all, would we wish to equip it with a reptilian brainlike set of reflexes that some people tell us are the cause of most of our problems just because we're stuck with them? The result could be a kind of electronic Buddha that manages the world's affairs wisely and efficiently not through any built-in optimizing heuristics but because it feels humanity's suffering and wants to end it. . . . And then Herbert Simon would ask, "What's the difference?"

Hans Moravec's solution to the Vingeian crisis of humanity being made obsolete by advanced machines is to make them the same. All that stands to become obsolete, says Moravec, are the biologically limited bodies we've inherited from a long line of trial-and-error-driven evolution whose solutions were not always for the best, to the degree that they've become hindrances. To eliminate this, he says that the codes that define human consciousness can be transferred out of their slow, accident-prone, relatively isolated brains into well-designed inorganic bodies that would confer unimaginable physical abilities and capacities to interact with the world and with each other in ways that transcend anything achievable through our five natural, limited, senses. Ultimately, we will become immortal, participating in a vast composite consciousness that continually grows and adapts itself so that nothing it learns is ever lost or forgotten, until it becomes the embodiment of the universe itself becoming conscious.[2]

Frank Tipler goes even further, envisioning not only everyone who has lived but every individual who might have, along with every conceivable reality that could exist, enacted as simulations created in a fantastically accelerated time frame by godlike machine intelligences in the far-distant future.[3] Tipler sees this as the ultimate demonstration of the benign nature of such intelligences, in effect bringing about for us the biblical promise of resurrection. When I asked what would happen if I wasn't sure I wanted to be resurrected, he was taken aback. After a moment's thought he assured me, "They'd ask you first." Well, I thought to myself, that's nice to know, anyway.

My own suspicion is that the reality won't be as bad as the worst the pessimists fear or as great as the pictures painted by the headiest of the optimists. Realities never are. In fact, realities have a habit of coming about in ways that the experts all miss that I find endearing. When the moon landing happened, none of the prognostications had foreseen that ordinary people throughout the world would be watching from living rooms. Computing power that would have awed the writers of a generation ago isn't dispensed by high-priest guardians out of columned municipal centers resembling Greek temples but comes from the store next to the supermarket and resides in the children's bedroom. An engineer around the turn of the century would probably have agreed that the electric motor was a great invention and every home should have one. He would then probably have gone on to install it on a pedestal in the basement and design systems of belts and shafts to transmit the power to parts of the house where it could be used.

What he couldn't have imagined was having scores of electric motors hidden about the place and involved in everything we do, from shavers and hair dryers, to computer fans and CD players, to the washing machine and the power tools in the workshop. (It would be interesting to count how many you have in your house. Don't forget things like the air pump on the fish tank and the battery-powered crawling doll in the children's toy box.)

Similarly, through smaller chips and cheaper RAM, artificial intelligence might seep into our lives in a highly distributed, invisible kind of way as everything around us gets "smarter." Your car will know where it is and where it's going, even if you're still driving, know your preferences for climate control and seat adjustment, maybe be able to take over in an emergency stop or skid situation, and warn you when it detects a variation in your driving pattern that could indicate fatigue. Your computer—no, your automated home secretary—takes care of the mail, puts your household and accounts in order, and selects items you'll be interested in from the news and worldwide information web. Meanwhile, factory-produced conformity becomes a thing of the past as custom-designed options enable you to specify at your local store your personal options for anything from a new automobile to a purse or a pair of shoes. Rooms alter their decor according to the mood and play any music required; a universal book can reconfigure its print into pages of any book ever written or become a means of communicating with anyone, anywhere; when the sight of the neighbor's yard gets boring, the windows can present, instead, anything from a view across the Amazon to a vista of the Himalayas. Magic will have become commonplace, and in all probability we won't even have noticed. Well, let's be honest—it already has, and we didn't.

The electronic revolution in information handling is often compared to the revolutions brought about by the invention of writing and the introduction of the printing press. It might be added that pessimistic prophecies greeted those developments too. Egyptian records from four thousand years ago deplore the effects that written records would have on the art of memorization and the verbal traditions of reciting epic and verse. Moral degeneracy and a decline of respect among the young was blamed on the laxness that resulted from not having to work hard at the old disciplines anymore. With the spread of literacy in fifteenth-century Europe, concern was expressed over people becoming passive and lackadaisical, withdrawing into silence to read their books and broadsheets instead of gathering to hear news and correct opinions broadcast in the town squares and at church services. On the other hand, there were those who prophesied a Golden Age of universal wisdom and enlightenment. Instead of having to travel across a continent to view a famous manuscript, any scholar could own his own copy. Indeed, every man would become a scholar; knowledge would replace ignorance everywhere, and the days of strife would end.

In reality, of course, literacy achieved neither of these things. Humanity did not sink into apathy and helplessness from the technological peak attained at the time of the pharaohs. Neither was there an end to ignorance, injustice, cruelty, and poverty. The same codes of writing that brought Homer and Shakespeare to the masses, that enabled scientific knowledge to accumulate, and that made possible written systems of law that afforded long-term economic security also recorded the edicts of the Inquisition, the treaties by which entire peoples were robbed of their lands, and the files of the Nazi and Stalinist police states. As we said above, technology cannot make us other than what we are.

It is probably true to say that literacy, through the technologies and political systems that it has made possible, has solved many of humanity's material problems. Although governments have inflicted incalculable havoc when they ran amuck, on balance the modern nation-state, in maintaining a stable social order within secure borders, brings about economic conditions that create more people than in their times of madness they destroy. The growing populations everywhere as more modern conditions take over surely testify to this. People in the past didn't have fewer children—in fact, for the most part, quite the opposite. They just died much younger and in greater numbers—Hamburg, Hiroshima, and the Gulag system notwithstanding. Given the will and the motivation, we know how to create enough wealth to support comfortably any number of human beings who might reasonably be imagined for the foreseeable future. The real problems that face us today are social and political—deciding who gets what share of the wealth and the political power that results from it. Another way of expressing it might be as the incompatibility of twenty-first-century technology with nineteenth-century ideas of education and economics.

The widespread introduction of computers to the commercial and industrial workplace in the fifties and sixties was commonly referred to as the "computer revolution." In many ways, ironically, it was just the reverse. By and large, the new machines were enlisted to do the same things in the same ways, only faster, i.e., by keeping going existing institutions and methods and the attitudes that came with them, which would otherwise have had to be replaced and rethought through sheer inability to cope. Workers displaced from one sector could, sometimes with a little government help through subsidies, assistance, and retraining programs, be reabsorbed into another, but the general principle of evaluating the worth of human beings on the same cost-accounting basis as any other item on the balance sheet and acquiring or discarding them accordingly didn't change.

With the spread of automated skills, judgment, and decision making into all levels of activity traditionally performed by service, managerial, and professional personnel, it could be that a change will finally be forced in this situation—indeed, there are signs of it already starting to happen. While one can only sympathize with the economic and psychological hardships experienced by a skilled person with years of experience being replaced by a fifty-dollar chip, at the same time I can't stop a part of my mind from asking why, if a fifty-dollar chip can do the job, was a human being spending a lifetime doing it in the first place? The answer, of course, is that that is what's demanded before you're allowed to have the sliver of the wealth you need to keep going and hold everything together. In the past, when only those like blue-collar machinists or laborers were affected, we could move them into white-collar departments or a retailing outlet and make them put in their forty hours there instead. But when everybody is affected and there's nowhere else to put them, what do you do then?

Norbert Wiener recognized the same thing in his introduction to *Cybernetics* when he observed:

> It [the possibility of coupling computers directly to machines] gives the human race a new and most effective collection of mechanical slaves to perform its labor. Such mechanical labor has most of the economic properties of slave labor, although, unlike slave labor, it does not involve the direct demoralizing effects of human cruelty. However, any labor that accepts the conditions of competition with slave labor accepts the conditions of slave labor.

The key word in Wiener's view was *competition*. He couldn't see it as an entirely good thing for the new potentialities to be assessed purely in terms of the money they saved. The answer, he felt, had to be a society based on human values other than buying and selling. I'm inclined to agree, although I don't have faith in any board of planners or committee of experts to know what form such a society would take.

But what I do have faith in is the combined ingenuity and ability of 5 billion people to come up with answers and solutions that are totally innovative and creative and that no amount of guessing is capable of forecasting or even imagining. But we've said several times in this book that there seems to be a level of creative, highly intuitive activity that the expert systems and theorem-proving programs can't reach. Wouldn't it be tremendous if different ways of valuing people and recognizing what they do were to come about, whereby more of them were able to spend greater parts of their lives learning to do and to be those things that are uniquely human. The really significant things never happen in straight, predictable lines or even curves that can be extrapolated, such as life adapting to a poison like oxygen or the consequences of learning to lay an egg out of water. That's what evolution is all about.

In summary, the big problem our ancestors faced was creating enough wealth to keep everyone alive and secure. The energy-intensive technologies and social institutions that grew as a result of the spread of literacy pretty much solved that, but they didn't offer any new insights as to how the wealth should be shared. The new intelligence-intensive technologies, and the attitudes that might be forced as a result of replacing human robots with electronic ones, could go a long way toward solving that problem too.

1. Vinge (1993b).
2. Moravec (1988). See also the forthcoming book *Mind Age*, not yet published, by the same author.
3. Tipler.

Bibliography

FICTION

Anderson, Poul. *Harvest of Stars*. New York: Tor, 1993.
———. *The Stars Are Also Fire*. New York: Tor, 1994.
Asimov, Isaac. *I Robot*. New York: Bantam/Spectra, 1991.
———, ed. *Machines That Think: The Best Science Fiction Stories About Robots and Computers*. New York: Holt, Rinehart & Winston, 1984.
Benford, Greg. *Ocean of Night*. New York: Bantam, 1987.
———. *Great Sky River*. New York: Bantam, 1987.
———. *Sailing Bright Eternity*. New York: Bantam, 1996.
Bierce, Ambrose. "Moxon's Master," in Asimov, Isaac, Patricia S. Warwick, and Martin H. Greenberg (Eds.), (1995), *Machines That Think*, Holt, Rinehart and Winston, New York, 1984, pp. 15–25.
Brown, Frederick. "Answer," in *The Best of Frederick Brown*. New York: Ballantine/Del Rey, 1977.
Butler, Samuel. *Erewhon*, first published in 1872. New York: Lancer Books, 1968.
Card, Orson Scott. "Homecoming" series: *The Memory of Earth* (1992), *The Call of Earth* (1994), *The Ships of Earth* (1995), *Earthfall* (1996), *Earthborn* (1996). New York: Tor.
Gerrold, David. *When Harlie Was One*. Garden City, N.Y.: Doubleday, 1972.
Gibson, William. *Neuromancer*. New York: Ace Books, 1984.
Heinlein, Robert. *The Moon Is a Harsh Mistress*. New York: Putnam, 1966.
Hogan, James P. *The Two Faces of Tomorrow*. New York: Ballantine/Del Rey, 1979.
———. *Code of the Lifemaker*. New York: Ballantine/Del Rey, 1983, and sequel, *The Immortality Option*. New York: Ballantine/Del Rey, 1995.
Ovellette, Pierre. *The Deus Machine*. New York: Villard Books, 1994.
Simmons, Dan. *Hyperion*. New York: Doubleday, 1989.
———. *Fall of Hyperion*. New York: Doubleday, 1990.
Swanwick, Mike. *Vacuum Flowers*. New York: Berkeley, 1988.
Taylor, Robert, and Burchenal Green, eds. *Tales of the Marvelous Machine: 35 Stories of Computing*. Morristown, N.J.: Creative Computing Press, 1980.
Vinge, Vernor. *True Names and Other Dangers*. New York: Pocket Books, 1987.
———. *Fire Upon the Deep*. New York: St. Martin's Press, 1993.

360

NONFICTION

Abelson, Robert P., and J. D. Carroll. "Computer Models of Individual Belief Systems." *American Behavioral Scientist* 8 (1965): 24–30.

Abelson, Robert P., and C. M. Reich. "Implicational Molecules: A Method for Extracting Meaning from Input Sentences." *Internat. Joint Conf. on Artificial Intelligence* 1 (1969): 647–748.

Albus, J. *Brains, Behavior, and Robotics.* New York: McGraw-Hill, 1981.

Anderson, John R. *Language, Memory, and Thought.* Hillsdale, N.J.: Lawrence Erlbaum, 1976.

———, et al. "Intelligent Tutoring Systems." *Science* 228 (1985), p. 456.

Anderson, John R., and Gordon H. Bower. *Human Associative Memory.* Washington, D.C.: V. H. Winston and Sons, 1973.

Barr, Aaron, Paul R. Cohen, and Edward A. Feigenbaum. *The Handbook of Artificial Intelligence.* 3 vols. Reading, Mass.: Addison-Wesley, 1982.

Bartley, William Warren, III, ed. *Lewis Carroll's Symbolic Logic.* New York: Clarkson N. Potter, 1977.

Beesley, Patrick. *Very Special Intelligence.* London: Hamish Hamilton, 1977.

Bellman, Richard. *Artificial Intelligence: Can Computers Think?* Boston: Boyd & Fraser, 1978.

Berliner, Hans. "Computer Backgammon." *Scientific American,* June 1980, p. 64.

Binford, Thomas O. "Visual Perception by Computer." Paper presented at IEEE Conference on Systems and Control, December 1971, Miami, Florida.

Bobrow, Daniel G. "Natural Language Input for a Computer Problem-Solving System." Report TR-1, Project MAC. Cambridge, Mass.: MIT Press, 1964; reprinted in Minsky, *Semantic Information Processing,* p. 189.

Bobrow, Daniel G., and J. B. Fraser. "An Augmented State Transition Network Analysis Procedure." *Proc. International Joint Conference on AI.* Washington, D.C. (1969) : 557–67.

Boole, George. *The Mathematical Analysis of Logic.* Cambridge, 1847; reprinted, Cambridge: Oxford University Press, 1948.

———. *An Investigation of the Laws of Thought.* London: Walton & Maberly, 1854; reprinted as *The Laws of Thought.* New York: Dover, 1951.

Brooks, Rodney A. "A Robust Layered Control System for a Mobile Robot. *IEEE Journal of Robotics and Automation,* vol. RA-2, no. 1 (March 1986).

———. "Intelligence Without Representation." In *Artificial Intelligence* 47 (1987): pp. 139–59; also in Luger, *Computation and Intelligence,* pp. 343–62.

———. "Elephants Don't Play Chess," *Robotics and Autonomous Systems* 6. North Holland: Elsevier Science Publishers B.V., 1990, pp. 3–14.

———. "Intelligence Without Reason." MIT AI Lab Memo 1293, April 1991(a).

———. "New Approaches to Robotics," *Science,* 253 (September 3, 1991[b]): 1227–32.

Brooks, Rodney A., and Anita M. Flynn. "Fast, Cheap, and Out of Control: A Robot Invasion of the Solar System." *Journal of the British Interplanetary Society,* 42 (1989): 478–85.

Brooks, Rodney A., and Lynn Andrea Stein. "Building Brains for Bodies." *Autonomous Robots* 1 Boston: Kluwer, 1994, pp. 7–25.

Buchanan, Bruce G., and Edward H. Shortliffe, eds. *Rule-based Expert Systems—The MYCIN Experiments of the Stanford Heuristic Programming Project.* Reading, Mass.: Addison-Wesley, 1984.

Burnham, David. *The Rise of the Computer State.* New York: Random House/Vintage, 1980.

Calvocoressi, Peter. *Top Secret Ultra.* New York: Pantheon, 1980.

Carbonell, Jaime G. *Subjective Understanding: Computer Models of Belief Systems.* Ann Arbor: UMI Research Press, 1979.

Cave Brown, Anthony. *Bodyguard of Lies.* New York: Harper & Row, 1975.

Charles Babbage Institute. *Reprint Series for the History of Computing.* Cambridge, Mass.: MIT Press, 1986.

Charniak, E. "Toward a Model of Children's Story Comprehension." AI-TR-266, Cambridge, Mass.: MIT AI Lab, 1972.

"Chess 4.7 v. Belle." *Scientific American,* September 1979, p. 80.

Chomsky, Noam. *Syntactic Structures.* The Hague, The Netherlands: Mouton, 1957.

Churchland, Patricia Smith. "From Descartes to Neural Networks." *Scientific American,* July 1989, p. 118.

Churchland, Paul M., and Patricia Smith Churchland. "Could a Machine Think?" *Scientific American,* January 1990, p. 32.

Clowes, M. B. "Picture Syntax." In *Picture Language Machines,* edited by S. Kaneff. New York: Academic Press, 1970, pp. 119–49.

Cody, Dan. "Your Move, Deep Thought." *SKY,* July 1991, p. 11.

Colby, K. M., J. B. Watt, and J. P. Gilbert. "A Computer Method of Psychotherapy." *Journal of Nervous and Mental Diseases* 142 (1966): 151.

Colby, K. M., et al. "Artificial Paranoia." *Artificial Intelligence* 2 (1972): 1–26.

———. "Turing-like Indistinguishability Tests for the Validation of a Computer Simulation of Paranoid Processes." *Artificial Intelligence* 3 (1973): 47–51.

Crevier, Daniel. *AI: The Tumultuous History of the Search for Artificial Intelligence.* New York: Basic Books, 1993.

Darrach, Brad. "Meet Shakey, the First Electronic Person." *Life,* November 1970, pp. 58–68.

Dewdney, A. K. "The King (a Chess Program) Is Dead, Long Live the King (a Chess Machine)," "Computer Recreations." *Scientific American,* February 1986, p. 13.

Dobzhansky, Theodosius. *Mankind Evolving.* New Haven, Conn.: Yale University Press, 1962.

Dreyfus, Hubert L. "Alchemy and Artificial Intelligence." Rand Corporation Paper P-3244, December 1965.

———. *What Computers Can't Do: A Critique of Artificial Reason.* New York: Harper & Row, 1972.

Dreyfus, Hubert L., and Stuart E. Dreyfus. *Mind Over Machine.* New York: The Free Press, 1986.

Dubbey, J. M. *The Mathematical Work of Charles Babbage.* Cambridge, Eng.: Cambridge University Press, 1978.

Evans, T. G. "A Program for the Solution of Geometric-Analogy Intelligence Test Questions." In Minsky, *Semantic Information Processing,* pp. 271–353.

Ewing, Alfred W. *The Man of Room 40.* London: Hutchinson, 1939.

Fawcett, Tom, and Foster Provost. "Combining Data Mining and Machine Learning for Effective User Profiling." AAAI, *Proc. of Second International Conference on Knowledge Discovery and Data Mining,* August 1996, pp. 8–13.

Fayyad, Usama, S. G. Djorgovski, and N. Weir. "Automating the Analysis and Cataloging of Sky Surveys." In *Advances in Knowledge Discovery and Data Mining,* edited by Usama Fayyad et al. Cambridge, Mass.: MIT Press, 1996.

Fayyad, Usama, David Haussler, and Paul Stolorz. "KDD for Science Data Analysis: Issues and Examples." AAAI, *Proc. of Second International Conference on Knowledge Discovery and Data Mining,* August 1996, pp. 51–52.

Fayyad, Usama, Gregory Piatetsky-Shapiro, and Padhraic Smyth. "From Data Mining to Knowledge Discovery in Databases." *AI Magazine* 7, no. 3 (Fall 1996): 37–54.

Feigenbaum, Edward A. "The Simulation of Verbal Learning Behavior." In *Computers and Thought,* edited by E. A. Feigenbaum and J. Feldman, pp. 297–309.

Feigenbaum, E. A., and J. Feldman. *Computers and Thought.* New York: McGraw-Hill, 1963.

Feigenbaum, E. A., and Herbert A. Simon. "EPAM-Like Models of Recognition and Learning." *Cognitive Science* 8 (1984): 305–36.

Fillimore, Charles. "The Case for Case." In *Universals in Linguistic Theory,* edited by E. Bach and R. Harms. New York: Holt, Rinehart and Winston, 1968, pp. 1–88.

Firebaugh, Morris W. *Artificial Intelligence: A Knowledge-Based Approach*. Boston: Boyd & Frazer, 1988.

Flanagan, Owen J., Jr. *The Science of the Mind*. Cambridge, Mass.: MIT Press/Bradford Books, 1984.

"Force v. Guile." *Scientific American*, February 1980, p. 76.

Franklin, Stanley P. *Artificial Minds*. Cambridge, Mass.: MIT Press/Bradford Books, 1995.

Friedman, William F. *The Zimmermann Telegram*. Santa Barbara, Calif.: Aegean Park Press, 1976.

———. *Solving German Codes in World War I*. Santa Barbara, Calif.: Aegean Park Press, 1977.

Galilei, Galileo. *Message from the Stars*. Originally *Siderius Nuncius*, 1610—astronomical observations.

Gelernter, H. "Realization of a Geometry-Theorem Proving Machine." Proceedings of an International Conference on Information Processing, Paris, UNESCO House 1959, pp. 273–82; reprinted in Feigenbaum and Feldman, *Computers and Thought*, pp. 34–52.

Gelernter, H., J. R. Hansen, and D. W. Loveland. "Empirical Explorations of the Geometry-Theorem Proving Machine." In *Computers and Thought*, edited by E. A. Feigenbaum and J. Feldman, p. 155.

Gödel, K. "On Formally Undecidable Propositions of *Principia Mathematica* and Related Systems I." *Monatshefte für Mathematik und Physik*, 38 (1931); reprinted in Martin Davis, ed., *The Undecidable*. Hewlett, N.Y.: Raven Press, 1965.

"Good Try." *Scientific American*, June 1997, p. 56.

Grimson, W. Eric L., and David Marr. "A Computer Implementation of a Theory of Human Stereo Vision." *Proceedings of the Royal Society of London* B292 (1980): 217–53.

Guzman, A. "Computer Recognition of Three-dimensional Objects in a Visual Scene." Ph.D. thesis no. AI-TR-228. Cambridge, Mass.: MIT AI Lab, 1968.

Hayes, Brian. "Computer Recreations," *Scientific American*, December 1983, p. 19.

Hayes, Patrick, and Kenneth Ford, "Turing Test Considered Harmful," *Proceedings of the International Journal Conference on Artificial Intelligence*, 1995, Vol. 1, pp. 972–77.

Hebb, D. O. *The Organization of Behavior*. New York: John Wiley, 1949.

Hillis, Daniel. *The Connection Machine*. Cambridge, Mass.: MIT Press, 1985.

Hodges, Andrew. *Alan Turing: The Enigma*. London: Hutchinson, 1983.

Hofstadter, Douglas. *Gödel, Escher, Bach: an Eternal Golden Braid*. New York: Basic Books, 1979.

———. "How Might Analogy, the Core of Human Thinking, Be Understood by Computers?" "Metamagical Themas." *Scientific American*, September 1981, pp. 18–30.

Hofstadter, Douglas. *Le Ton Beau de Marot: In Praise of the Music of Language*. Basic Books, New York, 1997.

Hofstadter, Douglas, and the Fluid Analogies Research Group. *Fluid Concepts and Creative Analogies*. New York: Basic Books, 1995.

Hopcroft, John E. "Turing Machines." *Scientific American*, May 1984, p. 86.

Hopfield, John J. "Neural Networks and Physical Systems with Emergent Collective Computational Abilities." *Proc. Nat. Academy of Sciences, USA* 79 (1982): 2554–58.

Huffman, D. A. "Impossible Objects as Nonsense Sentences." In *Machine Intelligence*, vol. 6, edited by B. Meltzer and D. Michie. Edinburgh, Edinburgh University Press, 1971, pp. 295–323.

Hunt, Morton. *The Universe Within: A New Science Explores the Human Mind*. London: Corgi, 1984.

Hyman, Anthony. *Charles Babbage: Pioneer of the Computer*. London: Oxford University Press, 1982.

Jackson, Philip C. *Introduction to Artificial Intelligence*. New York: Petrocelli Books, 1974.

Jacky, Jonathan. "The Strategic Computing Program." In *Computers in Battle: Will They Work?*, edited by D. Bellin and G. Chapman. New York: Harcourt Brace Jovanovich, 1987.

James, William. *The Principles of Psychology*. New York: Henry Holt, 1890.

Jones, R. V. *Most Secret War*. London: Hamish Hamilton, 1978; published as *The Wizard War*. New York: Putnam, 1978.

Kanade, Takeo, and Raj Reddy. "Computer Vision: The Challenge of Imperfect Inputs." *IEEE Spectrum* (November 1983): 88.

Kister, J., et al. "Experiments in Chess." *Journal of Computing Machinery* 4 (1957): 174–77.

Kling, R. E. "Reasoning by Analogy with Application to Heuristic Problem Solving: A Case Study." AIM-147, Stanford Artificial Intelligence Project (1971).

Knuth, Donald E. "Algorithms." *Scientific American*, April 1977, pp. 63–80.

Kolata, Gina. "Computer Math Proof Shows Reasoning Power." *New York Times*, December 10, 1996.

Kugel, Peter. "The Controversy Goes On": Can Computers Think?" *Creative Computing*, Pts. I-III: August, pp. 46–50; September, pp. 104–9; October, pp. 78–86 (1979).

———. "Thinking May Be More Than Computing." *Cognition* 22 (1986): 137–98.

Laird, John E., Paul S. Rosenbloom, and Allen Newell. "Chunking in Soar: The Anatomy of a General Learning System." *Machine Learning* 1 (1986): 11–46.

Laird, John E., and Paul S. Rosenbloom. "In Pursuit of Mind: The Research of Allen Newell." *AI Magazine* (Winter 1992): 18–45.

———. "The Evolution of the Soar Cognitive Architecture." In *Mind Matters*, edited by D. Steir and T. Mitchell. *LEA* (1996): 1–50.

Lakoff, George, and Mark Johnson. *Metaphors We Live By*. Chicago: University of Chicago Press, 1980.

Langley, Patrick, et al. *Scientific Discovery: Computational Explorations of the Creative Process*. Cambridge, Mass.: MIT Press, 1987.

Lehman, J. F., J. E. Laird, and P. S. Rosenbloom. "A Gentle Introduction to Soar, an Architecture for Human Cognition." In *Invitation to Cognitive Science*, vol. 4, *Methods, Models, and Conceptual Issues*, edited by S. Sternberg and D. Scarborough. Cambridge, Mass.: MIT Press, 1997.

Lenat, Douglas B. "AM: An Artificial Intelligence Approach to Discovery in Mathematics as Heuristic Search." In *Knowledge-Based Systems in Artificial Intelligence*, edited by R. Davis and D. Lenat. New York: McGraw-Hill, 1981.

———. "Computer Software for Intelligent Systems." *Scientific American*, September 1984, pp. 204–13.

———. "The Role of Heuristics in Learning by Discovery: Three Case Studies." In *Machine Learning*, edited by Ryzsard S. Michalski, Jaime G. Carbonell, and Tom M. Mitchell, pp. 243–306: Tioga Publishing, Palo Alto, CA, 1983.

———. "CYC: A Large-Scale Investment in Knowledge Infrastructure." *AI Magazine*, ACM 0002-0782 (1995a).

———. "Artificial Intelligence: A Crucial Storehouse of Commonsense Knowledge Is Now Taking Shape." *Scientific American*, September 1995(b), p. 80.

Lenat, Douglas B., and John Seely Brown. "Why AM and EURISKO Appear to Work." *Artificial Intelligence* 23. North Holland: Elsevier Science Publishers B.V., 1984, pp. 269–94.

Lenat, Douglas B., and R. Guha. *Building Large Knowledge-Based Systems*. Reading, Mass.: Addison-Wesley, 1990.

Lewis, Harry R., and Christos H. Papadimitriou. "The Efficiency of Algorithms." *Scientific American*, January 1978, pp. 95–109.

Lindsay, R., et al. *DENDRAL*. New York: McGraw-Hill, 1980.

Lucas, J. R. "Minds, Machines, and Gödel." *Philosophy* 36 (1961); reprinted in Alan Ross Anderson, *Minds and Machines*. Englewood Cliffs, N.J.: Prentice Hall, 1964.

Luger, George F., ed. *Computation and Intelligence*. Menlo Park, Calif.: AAAI Press, 1995.

McCarthy, John. "Programs with Common Sense." In Minsky, *Semantic Information Processing*.

———. "Ascribing Mental Qualities to Machines." In *Philosophical perspectives in artificial intelligence*, edited by M. Ringle. New York: Harvester, 1979.

———. "Circumscription, a Form of Nonmonotonic Reasoning." *Artificial Intelligence* 13, no. 1 (1980): 27–39.

McCarthy, J., and P. J. Hayes. "Some Philosophical Problems from the Standpoint of Artificial Intelligence." In *Machine Intelligence*, vol. 4, edited by B. Meltzer and D. Michie, Edinburgh, Edinburgh University Press, pp. 466–67.

McCorduck, Pamela. *Machines Who Think*. San Francisco: W. H. Freeman & Co., 1979.

McCulloch, W. S., and W. H. Pitts. "A Logical Calculus of the Ideas Immanent in Nervous Activity." *Bulletin of Mathematical Biophysics*, Chicago University Press, 5 (1943); reprinted in W. S. McCulloch, *Embodiments of Mind*. Cambridge, Mass.: MIT Press, 1970.

Macrae, Norman. *John von Neumann*. New York: Pantheon, 1992.

Marr, David. *Vision*. San Francisco: W. H. Freeman & Co., 1982.

Marr, David, and Ellen Hildreth. "Theory of Edge Detection." *Proceedings of the Royal Society of London*, B207 (1980): 187–217.

Marr, David, and Tomaso Poggio. "Cooperative Computation of Stereo Disparity." *Science* 194 (1976), pp. 283–87.

———. "A Computational Theory of Human Stereo Vision." *Proceedings of the Royal Society of London*, B204 (1979): 301–28.

Martin, Martin C., and Hans P. Moravec. "Robot Evidence Grids." CMU-RI-TR-96-06, Carnegie Mellon University, Pittsburgh, March 1996.

Menabrea, L. F. "Sketch of the Analytical Engine Invented by Charles Babbage." In *Charles Babbage and His Calculating Engines*, edited by P. and E. Morrison.

Metcalf, Fred. *The Penguin Dictionary of Modern Humorous Quotations*. London: Penguin, 1987.

Metropolis, N., J. Howlett, and G. C. Rota, eds. *A History of Computing in the Twentieth Century*. New York: Academic Press, 1980.

Michalski, Ryszard S., Jaime G. Carbonell, and Tom M. Mitchell, eds. *Machine Learning: An Artificial Intelligence Approach*. Palo Alto, Calif.: Tioga, 1983.

Miller, G. A. "The Magical Number Seven." *Psychological Review* (1956): 63–81.

Miller, George, and Eugene Galanter. *Plans and the Structure of Behavior*. New York: Holt, Rinehart, and Winston, 1960.

Minsky, Marvin. "Steps Toward Artificial Intelligence." *Proceedings of the Institute of Radio Engineers* (now IEEE) (January 1961); reprinted in Luger, *Computation and Intelligence*, pp. 47–90.

———. *Semantic Information Processing*. Cambridge, Mass.: MIT Press, 1968.

———. "A Framework for Representing Knowledge." In *The Psychology of Computer Vision*, edited by Patrick H. Winston. New York: McGraw-Hill, 1975, pp. 211–79.

———. *The Society of Mind*. New York: Touchstone, 1986.

———. "Will Robots Inherit the Earth?" *Scientific American*, October 1994, p. 87.

———. "Logical Versus Analogical, or Symbolic Versus Connectionist, or Neat Versus Scruffy." *AI Magazine* 12, no. 2 (Summer 1991), pp. 52–69; reprinted in Luger, *Computation and Intelligence*, pp. 647–74.

Minsky, Marvin, and Seymour Papert. *Perceptrons: An Introduction to Computational Geometry*. Cambridge, Mass.: MIT Press, 1968.

Mitchell, Melanie, *Analogy-Making as a Perception*. Cambridge, MA, MIT Press/Bradford Books, 1993.

Moore, O. K., and S. B. Anderson. "Modern Logic and Tasks for Experiments on Problem Solving Behavior." *Journal of Psychology* 38 (1954[a]): 151–60; and "Search Behavior in Individual and Group Problem Solving." *American Sociological Review* 19, no. 6 (1954[b]): 702–14.

Moravec, Hans. "The Stanford Cart and the CMU Rover." *Proc. IEE* 71, no. 7 (July 1983).

———. "Three Degrees for a Mobile Robot." Robotics Institute, Carnegie Mellon University, Pittsburgh, May 1984.

———. *Mind Children: The Future of Robot and Human Intelligence*. Cambridge, Mass.: Harvard University Press, 1988.

————. "Robot Spatial Perception by Stereoscopic Vision and 3D Evidence Grids." CMU-RI-TR-96-34, Carnegie Mellon University, Pittsburgh, September 1996.

Morgenstern, O., and J. von Neumann. *Theory of Games and Economic Behavior*. Princeton, N.J.: Princeton University Press, 1944.

Morrison, P., and E. Morrison, eds. *Charles Babbage and His Calculating Engines*. New York: Dover, 1961.

Murray, A. *Reason and Society in the Middle Ages*. Oxford: Clarendon, 1978.

Newell, Allen, and P. Rosenbloom. "Mechanism of Skill Acquisition and the Law of Practice." In *Learning and Cognition*, edited by J. R. Anderson. Hillsdale, N.J.: Lawrence Erlbaum, 1981, pp. 1–44.

Newell, Allen, and Herbert A. Simon. *Human Problem Solving*. Englewood Cliffs, N.J.: Prentice Hall, 1972.

Newell, Allen, J. C. Shaw, and H. Simon. "The Logic Theory Machine." In *IRE Transactions on Information Theory* (September 1956); reprinted as "Empirical Explorations with the Logic Theory Machine," in Feigenbaum and Feldman, *Computers and Thought;* also in Luger, *Computation and Intelligence*, pp. 365–90.

————. "Chess Playing Programs and the Problem of Complexity." *IBM Journal of Research and Development* 2, no. 4 (1958); reprinted in Feigenbaum and Feldman, *Computers and Thought*.

Nilsson, Niels J. *Principles of Artificial Intelligence*. Palo Alto, Calif.: Tioga, 1980.

Norman, D. A., and T. Shallice. "Attention to Action: Willed and Automatic Control of Behavior." In *Consciousness and Self-regulation: Advances in Research*, vol. 4, edited by R. J. Davidson, G. E. Schwartz, and D. Shapiro, New York: Plenum Press, 1986.

Ornstein, Robert, and Richard F. Thompson. *The Amazing Brain*. Illustrated by David Macaulay. Boston: Houghton Mifflin, 1984.

Papert, Seymour. "The Artificial Intelligence of Hubert L. Dreyfus: A Budget of Fallacies." MIT AI Lab Memo 154, 1968.

Penrose, Roger. *The Emperor's New Mind*. Cambridge, Mass.: Oxford University Press, 1989.

Pierce, John R. "Language and Machines: Computers in Translation and Linguistics." Publication 1416, National Academy of Sciences/National Research Council, Washington, D.C., 1966.

Pinker, Steven. *The Language Instinct*. New York: William Morrow, 1994.

Poggio, Tomaso. "Vision by Man and Machine." *Scientific American*, April 1984, pp. 106–16.

Polya, G. *How to Solve It*. Princeton, N.J.: Princeton University Press, 1945; reprinted in 1971.

Pople, Harry E. "CADUCEUS: An Experimental Expert System for Medical Diagnosis." In *The AI Business*, edited by Patrick H. Winston and Karen A. Prendergast. Cambridge, Mass.: MIT Press, 1984, chapter 5.

Popper, K., and J. Eccles. *The Self and Its Brain*. New York, Springer Verlag, 1977.

Post, E. L. "Formal Reductions of the General Combinatorial Decision Problem." *American Journal of Mathematics* 65 (1943): 197–215.

Pratt, Vernon. *Thinking Machines: The Evolution of Artificial Intelligence*. New York: Basil Blackwell, 1987.

Quillian, M. R. "Semantic Memory." Doctoral diss. no. AFCRL-66-189, Carnegie Mellon University, Pittsburgh, 1966; reprinted in part in Minsky, *Semantic Information Processing*, pp. 227–70.

Randell, Brian. *The Origins of Digital Computers*. Berlin: Springer-Verlag, 1975.

Raphael, Bertram. "SIR: A Computer Program for Semantic Information Retrieval." Report TR-2, Project MAC. Cambridge, Mass.: MIT Press, 1964; reprinted in Minsky, *Semantic Information Processing*, pp. 33–34.

————. *The Thinking Computer: Mind Inside Matter*. San Francisco: W. H. Freeman & Co., 1976.

Restak, Richard M. *The Brain: The Last Frontier*. New York: Warner, 1979.

Roberts, L. G. "Machine Perception of Three-Dimensional Solids." In *Optical and Electo-optical Information Processing*, edited by J. Tippett. Cambridge, Mass.: MIT Press, 1965.

Rosenblueth, A., N. Weiner, and J. Bigelow. "Behavior, Purpose, and Teleology." *Philosophy of Science* 10 (1943): 18–24.

Rumelhart, David E., and James L. McClelland. *Parallel Distributed Processing*. 2 vols. Cambridge, Mass.: MIT Press, 1986.

Rumelhart, D. E., and Norman, D. A. "Simulating a Skilled Typist: A Study of Skilled Cognitive-Motor Performance." *Cognitive Science* 6 (1982), pp. 1–36.

Rumelhart, D. E., and D. Zipser. "Feature Discovery by Competitive Learning." *Cognitive Science* 9 (1985), pp. 75–112; reprinted in Rumelhart and McClelland, *Parallel Distributed Processing*, vol. 1, pp. 151–93.

Samuel, Arthur. "Some Studies in Machine Learning Using the Game of Checkers." *IBM Journal of Research and Development* 3 (1959): 211–29; reprinted in Feigenbaum and Feldman, *Computers and Thought*, Section 2; also in Luger, *Computation and Intelligence*, pp. 391–414.

Sato, Hiroaki, and Thomas O. Binford. "On Finding and Recovering Straight Homogeneous Generalized Cylinder Objects on an Edge Image." *Image Understanding*, New York: Academic Press, 1993.

Sayre, K. M., and F. J. Cooson, eds. *The Modeling of Mind*. Notre Dame, Ind.: University of Notre Dame Press, 1963.

Schank, Roger C. *The Cognitive Computer: On Language, Learning and Artificial Intelligence*. Reading, Mass.: Addison-Wesley, 1985.

Schank, Roger C., and Robert P. Abelson. *Scripts, Plans, Goals, and Understanding*. Hillsdale, N.J.: Lawrence Erlbaum, 1977.

Searle, John R. "Minds, Brains, and Programs." *Behavior and Brain Sciences* 3, no. 3 (1980): 417–58.

———. "Is the Brain's Mind a Computer Program?" *Scientific American*, January 1990, pp. 26–31.

Selfridge, Oliver G. "Pattern Recognition in Modern Computers." *Proceedings of the Western Joint Computer Conference*, 1955; reprinted as "Pattern Recognition by Machine" in Feigenbaum and Feldman, *Computers and Thought*, pp. 237–50.

Shannon, Claude E. "A Mathematical Theory of Information." *Bell System Technical Journal* 27 (1948): 379–423, 623–56.

———. "A Symbolic Analysis of Relay and Switching Circuits." *Transactions of the American Institution of Electrical Engineers* 57 (1938): 713–23.

———. "Programming a Digital Computer for Playing Chess." *Philosophy Magazine* 41 (1950): 365–75; 1950(a).

———. "A Chess-Playing Machine." *Scientific American*, February 1950, p. 48, 1950(b); reprinted in *The World of Mathematics*, edited by J. R. Newmann. New York: Simon and Schuster, 1956, pp. 2124–33.

Shortliffe, Edward H. *MYCIN: Computer-based Medical Consultations*. New York: Elsevier Press, 1976.

Simon, Herbert A. *Administrative Behavior*. New York: Macmillan, 1947.

Stockmeyer, Larry J., and Ashok K. Chandra. "Intrinsically Difficult Problems." *Scientific American*, May 1979, pp. 140–59.

Suppes, Patrick. *Introduction to Logic*. New York: Van Nostrand, 1957.

Tambe, Milind, et al. "Intelligent Agents for Interactive Simulation Environments." *AI Magazine*, Spring 1995, pp. 15–39.

Taube, Mortimer. *Computers and Common Sense: The Myth of Thinking Machines*. New York: Columbia University Press, 1961.

Thomas, Lewis. "On Societies as Organisms." In *The Lives of a Cell*. New York: Viking, 1974; reprinted by Bantam in New York in 1975.

Tipler, Frank. *The Physics of Immortality*. New York: Doubleday, 1994.

Tuchman, Barbara. *The Zimmermann Telegram.* New York: Macmillan, 1958.

Turing, Alan M. "On Computable Numbers, With an Application to the Entscheidungs-problem." *Proceedings of the London Mathematical Society,* Series 2, 42 (1936): 230–65.

———. "Computing Machinery & Intelligence." *Mind* 59 (October 1950): 433–60; reprinted in Feigenbaum and Feldman, *Computers and Thought,* p. 22; also in Luger, *Computation and Intelligence,* pp. 23–46.

Turkle, Sherry. *The Second Self: Computers and the Human Spirit.* New York: Simon and Schuster, 1984.

Vinge, Vernor. Presentation at the VISION-21 Symposium sponsored by NASA, Lewis Research Center, at the Ohio Aerospace Institute, March 30–31, 1993(a).

———. "The Coming Technological Singularity: How to Survive in the Post-Human Era." *Whole Earth Review,* pp. 88–95 (Winter 1993[b]).

Waldrop, M. Mitchell. *Man-Made Minds: The Promise of Artificial Intelligence.* Walker, 1987.

Waltz, David L. "Generating semantic descriptions from drawings of scenes with shadows." AI-TR-271, Cambridge, Mass.: MIT AI Lab, 1972.

———. "Artificial Intelligence." *Scientific American,* October 1982, p. 118.

Wang, Hao. "Toward Mechanical Mathematics." *IBM Journal for Research and Development* 4 (1960): 2–22; reprinted in Sayre and Cooson, *The Modeling of Mind.*

Weaver, Warren. "Translation." In *Machine Translation of Languages,* edited by W. N. Locke and A. D. Booth. Cambridge, Mass.: Technology Press of MIT/New York: John Wiley, 1955. (Original paper 1949.)

Weber, Bruce. "Mean Chess-Playing Computer Tears at Meaning of Thought." *New York Times,* February 19, 1996(a).

———. "It's Man Over Machine as Kasparov Beats Chess Computer in Decisive Game." *New York Times,* February 18, 1996(b).

Weizenbaum, Joseph. "ELIZA—A Computer Program for the Study of Natural Language Communication Between Man and Machine." In *Communications of the Association for Computing Machinery* 9, no. 1 (January 1965): 36–45.

———. *Computer Power and Human Reason.* San Francisco: W. H. Freeman & Co., 1976.

West, Nigel. *G.C.H.Q.: The Secret Wireless War 1900–1986.* London: Hodder & Stoughton, 1987.

Wiener, Norbert. *Cybernetics.* Cambridge, Mass.: MIT Press, 1947.

Winograd, T. "A Procedural Model of Language Understanding." (1971), reprinted in Luger, *Computation and Intelligence,* pp. 203–34.

———. *Understanding Natural Language.* New York: Academic Press, 1972.

Winograd, Terry, and Fernando Flores. *Understanding Computers and Cognition.* Reading, Mass.: Addison Wesley, 1986.

Winston, Patrick. "Learning Structural Descriptions from Examples." Report TR-76, Project MAC. Cambridge, Mass.: MIT Press (1970).

Winterbotham, Fred. *The Ultra Secret.* New York: Harper & Row, 1974.

Woods, William A. "Transition Network Grammars for Natural Language Analysis." *Communications of the Association for Computing Machinery* 13, no. 10 (October 1970): 591–606.

INDEX

ABOUT THE AUTHOR

JAMES P. HOGAN was born in London and was educated at the Cardinal Vaughan school, Kensington. He studied general engineering at the Royal Aircraft Establishment, Farnborough, subsequently specializing in electronics and digital systems. After working with ITT, Honeywell, and the Digital Equipment Corporation in England, he moved to the United States in 1977 to become a senior sales training consultant, concentrating on the application of minicomputers in science and research, for DEC. In 1979 he became a full-time writer, and now divides his time between the Republic of Ireland and Florida. Details of his work and background can be obtained from his site on the World Wide Web at http://www.global.org/jphogan.